Gospelspeak

The New Testament

Nelson P. Miller

Gospelspeak—the New Testament.

Miller, Nelson P.

Published by:

Crown Management LLC – June 2018

1527 Pineridge Drive
Grand Haven, MI 49417
USA

ISBN-13: 978-1-7322387-4-9

All Rights Reserved
© 2018 Nelson P. Miller
c/o 111 Commerce Avenue S.W.
Grand Rapids, MI 49503
(616) 560-0632
millern57@gmail.com

For the lakeshore pastors: may you find enjoyable and rewarding your preaching and study of God's word by a beautiful inland sea where Christ's Spirit dwells richly in his people. And thank you, Bob and Chris, while welcome Marshall.

Table of Contents

Introduction — 1

Part I: Light — 4
Father. Son. Spirit. Creation. Resurrection. Return.

Father — 5
God. King. Creator. Word. Father. Spirit. Reconciler. Resurrector. Savior. Giver. Qualities.

Son — 12
God. Son. Messiah. Lord. Priest. Shepherd. Tempting. Preaching. Teaching. Parables. Healing. Raising. Crowds. Feeding. Solitude. Prayer. Rejection. Division. Opposition. Suffering. Plotting. Anointing. Betrayal. Garden. Arrest. Trial. Sentence. Crucifixion. Death. Burial. Resurrection. Appearance. Ascension. Witnesses. Eternal. Savior. Gifts. Return.

Spirit — 45
God. Christ. Coming. Pentecost. Apostles. Gifts. Sanctification. Wisdom. Word. Written. Truth. Savior. Sacrifice. Salvation. Sharing. Covenant. Old. New. Benefits.

Creation — 59
God. Christ. Light. Darkness. People. Genealogy. Incarnation. Presentation. Announcement. Maturation. Divine. Baptism. Baptist. Baptizing. Christ. Effect. Death. Apostles. Transfiguration.

Resurrection — 72
Crucifixion. Death. Cross. Meaning. Result. Resurrection. Confirmation. Life. Meaning. You. Body. Result. Kingdom. Qualities. Worthy. Unworthy. Heaven.

Return — 85
Fulfillment. Christ. End. Timing. Watching. You. Pursuit. Dead. Heaven. Way. You. Throne. Scroll. Seals. Judge. Justice. Rebellion. Condemned. Angels. Judging. Return. Separation. Blasts. Dragon. Beasts. Lamb. Plagues. Wrath. Explanation. Babylon. Warrior. Satan. New. Eternity. Destiny.

Part II: Darkness — 110
Satan. Law. Deceivers. World.

Satan — 111
Enemy. Spirits. Resistance. Christ. Possession. Opposition. Idols. Disobedience. Nature. Cursed. Law. Judgment. You. Freedom. Temptation. Anger. Holiness. Death. Jesus. Resurrection. Teachers. You. Life.

Law — 126
Sin. Death. Shadow. Legalism. Christ. Faith. Obedience. Circumcision. Sacrifices. Tabernacle. Hypocrites. Woes. Priests. Christ. Freedom. Opposition. Others.

Deceivers 136
Deception. Resisting. Truth. Christ. Teaching. Learning. Judgment. Ancestors. Corruption. Godless. Christ. Desertion. Reinstatement. Rejection. Persecution. Martyrs. Believers. Attitude.

World 149
Evil. Overcome. Slavery. Freedom. Disputes. Reconciliation. Greed. Schemes. God. Giving. Flesh. Christ. Spirit. Curse. Woes. Wrath. Belief. Worry. Trials. Perseverance. Strength. Comfort. Christ. Weakness.

Part III: Difference 164
Faith. Redemption. Obedience. Church. Teaching. Families.

Faith 165
Defined. Heroes. Abraham. Moses. Christ. Demonstrations. Pursuit. Opposition. Others. Absence. Conversions. Saul. Confessions. Professions. Disciples. People. You. Christ. Calling. Impartiality. Nations. Children. Christ. Distinction. Discipline. Inheritance.

Redemption 185
Justification. Blood. Evil. Result. Sanctification. Faith. Christ. Pursuit. Sin. Conduct. Freedom. Grace. Source. Mercy. Peace. Rest. Seeking. Glory. Jesus. Shared. Pursuit. Power. Christ. Evil. You. Others.

Obedience 203
Obedience. God. Others. Strive. Authority. Instituted. Rulers. Others. Repentance. Christ. Humility. Boasting. Clearheadedness. Ambition. Forgiveness. Others. Service. Faith. Charity. Others. Gifts. God. Christ. Gospel. Share. Strive. Sowing. Good.

Church 220
Role. Body. Unity. Meeting. Communion. Order. Leaders. Servants. Elders. Administrators. Gifts. Support. Jesus. Fellowship. Greeting. Kindness. Benefit. Christ. Sharing. Comfort. Care. Workers. Love. Expression. God. Christ. Enemies. Cautions. Joy. Others. Demonstrations.

Teaching 239
Teaching. Preaching. Courage. God. Christ. Doctrine. Evangelism. Sinners. Others. Wages. Volunteers. Building. Builder. Temple. Discerning. Obedient. Mature. Listening. Christ. Striving. Wisdom. Speaking. Distinguishing. World.

Families 252
Unmarried. Marriage. Divorce. Husbands. Wives. Intimacy. Children. Body. Church. Parts. You. Rules. Heaven. Giving. Generosity. Measure. Others. Types. Apostles. Prayer. Confident. Intercessory. Sin. Faith. Christ. Apostles. Fasting. Gratitude. Others. Healing. Raising. Apostles.

Conclusion 269

Appendices 270
Abbreviations 271
Authors 272
Audiences 284

Introduction

This second Gospelspeak volume studying the whole of the Bible's New Testament extends the work of the first volume addressed only to the New Testament's twenty-one epistles. The premise of both volumes is that the Bible has a tremendous amount to say to us on all topics of profound spiritual significance. Yet the Bible's spectacularly unprecedented format, as a collection of sixty-six books of various types spanning a millennium and a half, makes difficult the critical task of integrating its teaching on any one of those topics. Some readers, like me, feel a strong need to gather in one place, from each of several New Testament books and letters, what the Bible says on a certain topic, to read and reread the verses until they make greater sense together. That gathering, organizing, and reorganizing is, after all, what good preachers do, thumbing back and forth through the scriptures to weave the coherent, integrated, and wondrous story. And so, this second volume adds a parsing, sorting, and reorganizing of the verses of the four Gospels, Acts, and Revelation, to the first volume's parsing of the twenty-one epistles. You have here a gathering, section by organized section, of all the New Testament's verses on each of dozens of different topics that the New Testament indicates should be important to us.

One way of using the book is to read it cover to cover, as one would any other book. The effect immerses the reader in New Testament study, not through the words of a preacher, theologian, commentator, scholar, or other author, but in the Bible's own words. As with the first volume on the epistles, I have rewritten verses only to separate and accentuate their themes, simplify the sentence construction, and clarify the implied actors. Strict translations tend to use passive language disguising the actors, compound sentences mixing topics and themes, and prepositional phrases, making harder to discern the actors, actions, and objects of their actions. The verses here as I have rewritten them are shorter, more focused to single topics, and more active, to make your study easier integrating and emphasizing common meanings across verses. If you read the whole book, cover to cover in order, then you will have completed a New Testament study unlike any other, digesting the whole New Testament through the lens of its topics. You will, in effect, have had only a silent commentator, the one who reorganized the verses into their topics, nudging you to see how the many verses on each topic together inform the whole of any topic.

Another way to use this volume, though, is to choose any topic of interest and read only that topic, followed by any other topics to which the reading leads you. Used in that way, this Gospelspeak volume supplants and improves upon the work of a concordance or electronic search function. Rather than flipping back and forth from concordance to New Testament, and back and forth through the New Testament locating the concordance-identified verses, you can instead read in one place what the New Testament says on any of the dozens of topics. Not only is this method quicker and more convenient, but you also get to read a lot more verses than when using a concordance or electronic-search function. The Bible routinely uses several different terms to address the same topic. A concordance search or electronic search for a certain term only gets you verses with that term, not verses that use other terms for the same topic. This Gospelspeak volume gathers in one place all verses on each topic, whether the verses use one term or a different term. Concordances and electronic searches don't accomplish the same function, at least not as easily.

Why two volumes? I first conceived of a study of the epistles in this parsing, editing, sorting, organizing, reorganizing, scripture-verses-only form, having little idea of how long that first volume would take me or what it would produce. I wanted to know more about the epistles. And indeed, the epistles study taught me a lot, unpacking and integrating the letters in fresh ways. Yet just as I was finishing the project and thinking about the next one, I realized that not having Jesus's words that the Gospels capture, and his actions that the Gospels describe, in the mix for each of the dozens of topics, was a significant omission. The first volume was a helpful study of the epistles but was not treating comprehensively any of the topics, given the omission of the Lord's own words and actions. The book of Acts, too, has hugely important statements and descriptions that serve as lessons on and elaborations of the included topics. And so, to degrees, does the New Testament's concluding book of Revelation. This second Gospelspeak volume thus seemed a natural extension of the first volume. I hope that it serves you in some way. Studying God's word of course has practical benefits but, like reflecting Jesus's sacrificial love or worshiping in the Holy Spirit, is also one of the few inherently good things that we can do, no matter how the study ultimately affects us and those around us. Read God's word, worshiping and glorifying him as you do. He made us to do so.

> Many have tried to write about the things that happened recently, as foretold long ago, just as accounts have also reached us from the word's eyewitnesses and servants. And so I, who have carefully investigated everything from the beginning, have also decided to write a clear account for you, most excellent Theophilus, so that you accept as certainty the things that others have already taught you. *Luke 1:1-4*

Part I: Light

Father. Son. Spirit. Creation. Resurrection. Return.

The New Testament tells the great story of light coming into the world as the life of humankind. That light is the good-news story, that glorious bit of meaning making every bit of difference to the meaning, purpose, conduct, and outcome of our lives. The story begins with the Father, Son, and Holy Spirit, in loving trinity and unity, pre-existent and glorious. God then created the world, placing humankind in it, knowing that we would reject him to follow our own way. But the good news is that God then sent, baptized, vitalized, sacrificed, and resurrected his glorious Son to show us how much God loves us and wants us back with him. The story unfolds that our faith in God's Son justifies and redeems us as God's children through his rich mercy and grace. His Spirit carries his blessing, calling us apart from the world's slavery to a righteous freedom enjoying God's increasing kingdom, while we eagerly await Jesus's full return, after which we will live with him in paradise forever. See how the New Testament addresses the great light surrounding, guiding, and inviting us. Do you follow the light knowing its spectacularly loving source?

Father

The New Testament shows God revealing himself to us as Father, Son, and Holy Spirit. The New Testament teaches relationship, that God is both Father to our Lord Jesus and our own Father, making us his sons and daughters whom he himself seeks. Yet the New Testament adds that the Father also gave us the exquisite gifts of his Spirit and his word. The New Testament also shows the Father's attributes as divine, unchanging, unknowable but revealed, and judging but patient, forgiving, compassionate, loving, and giving of the unsurpassable gift of our Lord Jesus Christ, along with many other good and perfect gifts. See how the New Testament reveals the Father to us. Do you tremble in awe at the mention of his name?

God. The Lord God says he is the Alpha and Omega, the who is, was, and is to come, the Almighty._{Rev 1:8} The one on the throne told the apostle John that he is the Alpha and Omega, Beginning and End, giving water to the thirsty from the spring of life while giving everything to the victorious who are his children._{Rev 21:6-7} Jesus said not to call anyone on earth father because you have one Father in heaven._{Matt 23:2} The Lord Almighty says that God is a Father to us, and we are his sons and daughters._{2Co 6:18} We kneel before the Father, from whom every family in heaven and on earth derives its name._{Eph 3:14-15} Those who did not seek God found him because he revealed himself to those who did not ask for him._{Ro 10:20} God our Savior wants all people saved and to know the truth._{1Ti 2:3-4} God chose you out of nowhere to be royal and holy, his special possession, calling you out of darkness into his wonderful light._{1Pe 2:9-10} Give joyful thanks to the Father, who has qualified you to share with his holy people in the kingdom of light._{Col 1:12} God continuously held out his hands to a disobedient and obstinate chosen people._{Ro 10:21} We don't give to God in that he must repay us because everything is from him, through him, and for him._{Ro 11:35-36} God called you to eternal life when you confessed before many witnesses.*1Ti 6:12* You cannot please God without faith because you must believe that God exists and rewards those who earnestly seek him.*Heb 11:6* Our common faith as a family of believers is in grace and peace from God the Father and Christ Jesus our Savior.*Tit 1:4*

King. God calls you into his kingdom.*1Th 2:12* God will count you worthy of his kingdom for which you suffer.*2Th 1:5* The Father shares his kingdom of light.*Col 1:12* God brings us into the kingdom of the Son whom he loves.*Col 1:13* Remain in view of God's kingdom.*2Ti 4:1* The Lord will bring us safely to his heavenly kingdom.*2Ti 4:18* God's kingdom is not about eating and drinking but righteousness, peace, and joy in the Holy Spirit.*Ro 14:17* Draw near to God with faith's full assurance.*Heb 10:22* God to you is not like the dark, gloomy, and stormy mountain burning with fire, a harsh trumpet blast, or frightening voice the commands from which you cannot bear, terrifying you so that you tremble with fear.*Heb 12:18-21* You have instead come to the city of the living God, the heavenly Jerusalem, with millions of angels in joyful assembly.*Heb 12:22* You have come to the church of the firstborn whose names God wrote in heaven.*Heb 12:23* Before he created the world, God chose us in him to be holy and blameless in his sight.*Eph 1:4* God prepares a city for those in whom he has no shame, when they call him their God.*Heb 11:16* You have a Master in heaven.*Col 4:1*

Creator. God finished his works when creating the world.*Heb 4:3* God rested from all his works on the seventh day of creation.*Heb 4:4* Creation eagerly waits for God to reveal his children.*Ro 8:19* God delays so he can liberate creation from its decay, bringing it into the freedom and glory of God's children.*Ro 8:21* Creation groans as in childbirth just as we who have the Spirit's firstfruits groan as we wait eagerly for God to adopt us as his children and redeem our bodies.*Ro 8:22-23* Don't you, a mere person, talk back to your creator God, who though all-powerful still leaves you to your own will.*Ro 9:19-20* God has the right to create both the special and common.*Ro 9:21* The Father made us his creation's firstfruits.*Jas 1:18* You have put on the new self that God renews in knowledge in his image as Creator.*Col 3:10* Everything God created is good, not to reject but to receive with thanksgiving.*1Ti 4:4* God calls into being things that were not.*Ro 4:17* God gives life to the dead.*Ro 4:17* The God of peace, through the blood of the eternal covenant, raised from the dead our Lord Jesus, the great Shepherd of the sheep.*Heb 13:20* God sees everything in all creation, uncovered and laid bare before him to whom we must give account.*Heb 4:13*

Word. God's word brings to us mysteries God shared by revelation.*Eph 3:3* In reading God's word, we understand insight into the mystery of Christ that God disclosed to people in prior generations, as his Spirit revealed it through holy apostles and prophets.*Eph 3:4-5* The Father gave us spiritual birth through the word of truth.*Jas 1:17-18* Carry the Spirit's sword, which is the word of God.*Eph 6:17* Accept God's word from one another not as a human word but as it is, the word of God, which works in you who believe.*1Th 2:13* Receive anything consecrated by the word of God.*1Ti 4:5* While someone might chain a gospel witness, no one chains God's word.*2Ti 2:9* God breathed all Scripture for teaching, rebuking, correcting, and training in righteousness.*2Ti 3:16-17* God enriches us in him in every way including all kinds of speech and with all knowledge, confirming testimony about Christ in us.*1Co 1:5-6* The law is still the very words of God.*Ro 2:2* God's word did not originate with you, and you are not the only people it has reached.*1Co 14:36* God's word lives actively, like a sharp blade penetrating to divide soul from spirit, joints from marrow, judging the heart's thoughts and attitudes.*Heb 4:12*

Father. Every family in heaven derives its name from the Father.*Eph 3:14-15* Jesus said to baptize in the name of the Father, Son, and Holy Spirit.*Matt 28:18-20* Jesus said that no one knows the Father except the Son and those to whom the Son chooses to reveal the Father.*Matt 11:27* Jesus said that he was going to the Father, for which the disciples should have been glad because the Father is greater than Jesus.*Jn 14:28* God chose Christ before creating the world but only revealed him recently for your sake.*1Pe 1:20* God's Son Jesus is from heaven.*1Th 1:10* In the Son, God created everything in heaven and on earth, visible and invisible, rulers and authorities, through the Son and for him.*Col 1:16* The Son is before everything, holding everything together.*Col 1:17* God named Jesus his Son and said he was his Father.*Heb 1:5* God appointed Jesus the Son of God through the Spirit of holiness.*Ro 1:4* God called Jesus Son and said he was his Father.*Heb 5:5-6* God did not put angels over the world to come but put the Son of Man, Jesus Christ, leaving nothing over which he will not rule, even though we do not yet see all that he will rule.*Heb 2:5-8* God exalted Jesus over everyone for his glory as the Father.*Php 2:11* At Jesus's baptism, God the Father gave Jesus glory from heaven.*2Pe 1:17* When God did not spare his own Son but gave him up for us, he showed that he graciously gives us everything.*Ro 8:32* God presented Christ as a sacrifice of atonement, through the shedding of his blood._{Ro 2:25-26} God delivered Jesus over to death for our sins._{Ro 4:25} Jesus Christ, the Righteous One, is not only your advocate with the Father._{1Jn 2:1-2} The Father sent his Son as the world's Savior._{1Jn 4:13-14} Anyone who acknowledges Jesus as God's Son lives in God and God in them._{1Jn 4:15} When we are like Jesus, God makes love complete among us so that we may pass his judgment._{1Jn 4:17} Approach God's throne with confidence for mercy and grace when in need._{Heb 4:16} You are a child of God who can cry to your Father._{Ro 8:15} Thank the Father, who has qualified you to share in the inheritance of his holy people._{Col 1:12}

Spirit. God poured his love into our hearts through the Holy Spirit, whom he gave to us._{Ro 5:5} If God's Spirit lives in you, then you pursue the Spirit rather than the flesh. Those whom the Spirit of God leads are the children of God._{Ro 8:14} The Spirit does not make you fearful slaves but makes you a child of God who can cry to your Father._{Ro 8:15} The Spirit testifies with our spirit that we are God's children who, if we suffer with Christ, inherit Christ's glory with him._{Ro 8:16-17} God who searches our hearts knows the Spirit's mind as the Spirit intercedes for God's people in God's will._{Ro 8:27} God gives to each one the Spirit's manifestation for the common good._{1Co 12:7} To one God gives wisdom through the Spirit, to another knowledge by the same Spirit, to another faith by the same Spirit, to another gifts of healing by that one Spirit, to others miraculous powers, prophecy, distinguishing between spirits, speaking in different tongues, or interpretation of tongues._{1Co 12:8-10}

Reconciler. God makes us stand firm in Christ, having anointed us._{2Co 1:21} Grace to you from God our Father and the Lord Jesus Christ._{Php 1:2} We receive grace, mercy and peace from God the Father through Jesus Christ, in truth and love._{2Jn 3} Grace to each of you from God our Father and the Lord Jesus Christ._{Gal 1:3} God brings us to fullness in Christ._{Col 2:10} God the Father loves us, keeping us for Jesus Christ while blessing us with abundant mercy, peace, and love._{Jude 1-2} God made Christ who had no sin to be sin for us, so that in Christ we would show God's righteousness._{2Co 5:21} God our Father asked Jesus to give himself for our sins to rescue us from how evil things are these days._{Gal 1:4} God reconciled us to himself through Christ, giving us the ministry of reconciliation._{2Co 5:18} God reconciled the world to himself in Christ, not counting people's sins against them, as he commits the reconciliation message to us._{2Co 5:19} When Jesus returns, God will punish with permanent destruction those who do not obey the Lord Jesus's gospel._{2Th}

1:8-10 The living God is the Savior of all people, especially those who believe.*1Ti 4:10* Peace to you from God our Father.*Col 1:2* Peace to those in God the Father and the Lord Jesus Christ.*1Th 1:1* Peace from God the Father and the Lord Jesus Christ.*2Th 1:1-2* Peace is from God the Father and Christ Jesus our Lord.*2Ti 1:2*

Resurrector. Because the glory of the Father raised Jesus Christ from the dead, we also live a new life.*Ro 6:3-4* If the Spirit of God who raised Jesus from the dead lives in you, then God who raised Christ from the dead will also give your body life because of his Spirit who lives in you.*Ro 8:11* God the Father raised Jesus Christ from the dead.*Gal 1:1* God raised Jesus from the dead.*Ro 4:22-24* God delivered Jesus over to death for our sins and raised him to life for our justification.*Ro 4:25* God appointed Jesus the Son of God through the Spirit of holiness and resurrected him from the dead as Jesus Christ our Lord.*Ro 1:4* We should thank God the Father of our Lord Jesus Christ for his great mercy giving us new birth into living hope through Jesus's resurrection from the dead.*1Pe 1:3* If the Spirit of God who raised Jesus from the dead lives in you, then God who raised Christ from the dead will also give your body life because of his Spirit who lives in you.*Ro 8:11* God made us alive in Christ when we were dead in our sins.*Col 2:13* God raised you with Christ.*Col 3:1* You died, and your life now hides with Christ in God.*Col 3:3* Wait for God's Son Jesus, whom God raised from the dead.*1Th 1:10* Thank God for victory through our Lord Jesus Christ.*1Co 15:57*

Savior. Jesus said that his Father's will is that he lose none of those whom God gave him but instead is to raise them up at the last day.*Jn 6:39* The Father's will is that everyone who looks to and believes in the Son gains eternal life, Jesus raising them up at the last day.*Jn 6:40* Jesus added that no one can come to him to rise up at the last day unless the Father draws them to him.*Jn 6:44* Jesus repeated that no one can come to him unless the Father enables them.*Jn 6:65* Those who hear and learn from the Father come to Jesus.*Jn 6:45* The apostle Peter said that we find salvation in no one other than Jesus, whose name is the only one under heaven to save us.*Acts 4:12* God's power for believers is the same as the mighty strength he exerted when he raised Christ from the dead and seated him at his right hand in the heavenly realms, over all rule, authority, power, and dominion, and every name not only now but in the future.*Eph 1:19-21* You choose, but whoever believes in the Son of God accepts God's testimony, while whoever does not believe makes God out to be a liar.*1Jn 5:10* The testimony is that God gave us eternal life in his Son and only in his Son.*1Jn 5:11-13* Our Lord Jesus Christ and God our Father by his grace gave us good hope of eternity.*2Th 2:16-17* Praise to the God and Father of our Lord Jesus Christ, the Father of compassion, and the God of all comfort.*2Co 1:3* When God brought his firstborn Son Jesus into the world, God said that the angels would worship Jesus.*Heb 1:6* God's oath appointed the Son, whom God made perfect forever.*Heb 7:28* God loves having all his fullness dwell in the Son.*Col 1:19* Through the Son, God reconciles to himself all things on earth and in heaven.*Col 1:20* God said to the Son to sit at his right hand until God made his enemies a footstool for his feet.*Heb 1:13* God gave Jesus Christ our Lord glory, majesty, power, and authority.*Jude 24-25* God favors us now and saves us now.*2Co 6:2*

Giver. When you believed, God marked you in him with the seal of the promised Holy Spirit, who guarantees our inheritance until God redeems those whom he possesses.*Eph 1:13-14* God saved us through rebirth's washing and renewal by the Holy Spirit whom he poured out on us generously through Jesus Christ our Savior.*Tit 5:6* God gives you his Holy Spirit with instruction.*1Th 4:8* The Spirit God gave us does not leave us timid but gives us power, love, and self-discipline.*2Ti 1:7* When leading others to obey God, you act through the Spirit of God's power.*Ro 15:18-19* God revealed to us by his Spirit things that he prepared for those who love him, that no eye had seen, ear heard, or mind conceived.*1Co 2:9-10* The Spirit searches everything, even God's deep things.*1Co 2:10* No one knows God's thoughts except God's Spirit, just as only one's own spirit knows one's own thoughts.*1Co 2:11* We received God's Spirit, not the world's spirit, so that we can understand what God freely gave us.*1Co 2:12* Your body is a temple of the Holy Spirit, who is in you and whom you received from God.*1Co 6:19* God makes us ministers of the Spirit's new covenant through which the Spirit gives life.*2Co 3:6* God gave us the Spirit as a deposit to guarantee life to come.*2Co 5:5* The Holy Spirit testifies that God put his laws in our hearts and minds, and no longer remembers our sins and lawless acts.*Heb 10:16*

Qualities. We see and understand God's invisible qualities including his eternal power and divine nature from what he made.*Ro 1:20* No one knows the Lord's mind or can give him counsel.*Ro 11:34* Time differs to the Lord to whom a day is like a thousand years and thousand years like a day.*2Pe 3:8* The Father in heaven, who does not change, gives the good and perfect gifts from above.*Jas 1:17* The wisdom and knowledge of God are deeply rich.*Ro 11:33* God makes his angels spirits and his servants flames of fire.*Heb 1:7* God destroys the wise's wisdom and frustrates the intelligent's intelligence, but the cross is God's power to us whom God saves.*1Co 1:18-19* God who calls you is faithful.*1Th 5:24* That the Father calls us his children shows his lavish love for us.*1Jn 3:1-2* You have come to the God who is the Judge of all and to spirits of the righteous he made perfect.*Heb 12:23* God is pure light without any darkness.*1Jn 1:5* The gospel reveal's God's righteousness, which we live out by faith.*Ro 1:17* The gospel declares that God judges people's secrets through Jesus Christ.*Ro 2:16* God is the blessed, honored, mighty, eternal, and only Ruler, the King of kings and Lord of lords, who alone is immortal, living in unapproachable light, whom no one has seen or can see.*1Ti 6:15-16* God gives life to the dead.*Ro 4:17* When God said to let light shine out of darkness, he shined his light into our hearts, lighting our knowledge of God's glory in Christ's face.*2Co 4:6* Worship God with reverence and awe as you would a consuming fire.*Heb 12:28-29* Praise God the Father of our Lord Jesus Christ, who brings us every spiritual blessing in Christ.*Eph 1:3*

Son

The New Testament carries the good news about God's Son Jesus. Whether expressed or implied, every chapter and verse reflect to some degree on Jesus, God's Son and our Savior. Jesus is the authors' reason to write, without whom our faith means nothing but with whom the world takes its ordained course. The authors saw, heard, and knew Jesus, or heard hundreds who did see, hear, and know Jesus and who witnessed his resurrection. The authors knew that history hinged on the Son of God, and their writings said so. The New Testament shows Jesus in each of the roles by which we know him, as God, Lord, High Priest, and Savior, and God's Son. The New Testament captures Jesus's birth, ministry, suffering, crucifixion, and resurrection, declaring him eternal. The New Testament also describes his gifts. See how consistently and richly the New Testament testifies to Jesus. Do you with your whole spirit hail the Son, as you follow, embrace, and become part of his story?

God. In the beginning was the Word, the Word with God, and the Word God himself, he with God in the beginning.*Jn 1:1-2* Jesus said that before Abraham was, Jesus was, literally *I am*.*Jn 8:58* Jesus said that he and the Father are one.*Jn 10:30* Jesus said that whoever looks at him looks at the one who sent him.*Jn 12:45* Jesus told the disciples that if they know him, then they know the Father, and that they did know and see the Father because anyone who has seen Jesus has seen the Father.*Jn 14:7-9* Jesus is in the Father, and the Father is in him.*Jn 14:10* All that belongs to the Father belongs to Jesus.*Jn 16:15* The Messiah Jesus is God over all, forever praised.*Ro 9:5* The Son is the invisible God's image, the firstborn over all creation.*Col 1:15* The Son radiates God's glory, exactly representing his being, while sustaining all things by his powerful word.*Heb 1:3* Christ is the Deity's fullness living in bodily form.*Col 2:9* God loves having all his fullness dwell in the Son.*Col 1:19* Jesus Christ was the same in the past as he is today and will be forever.*Heb 13:8* Jesus Christ our Lord is the one before all ages to whom God gave glory, majesty, power, and authority.*Jude 24-25* Christ is the head over every power and authority.*Col 2:10* Our ancestors all ate the same spiritual food and drank the same spiritual drink from the spiritual rock Christ who accompanied them.*1Co 10:3-4* We know about our Lord Jesus Christ's coming not as a cleverly devised story but from eyewitnesses to his majesty.*2Pe 1:16* God spoke to our ancestors through the prophets, but in these last days he has spoken to us by his Son, who is his heir through whom he made the universe.*Heb 1:2* Everything is garbage next to the surpassing worth of knowing Christ Jesus our Lord, for whose sake we should lose all things.*Php 3:8* The Son of God came as the true God and eternal life that we may know him and be in him who is true.*1Jn 5:20*

Son. The Word became flesh, dwelling among us, so that we saw the glory of the one and only Son from the Father, full of grace and truth.*Jn 1:14* No one but the one and only Son has seen God, because the Son is God in closest relationship with the Father, making God known.*Jn 1:18* No one has seen the Father except the one from God.*Jn 6:46* Jesus is the Son of God who came just as the prophet Isaiah foretold.*Mk 1:1* God so loved the world that he gave his one and only Son that whoever believes in him does not perish but has eternal life.*Jn 3:16* The Father loves the Son, having placed all things in the Son's hands.*Jn 3:35* Jesus said that the reason the Father loves him is because he laid down his life of his own accord, only to take it up again, as his Father commanded.*Jn 10:17-18* Jesus said that he came from the Father and was going back to the Father.*Jn 16:28* Jesus revealed in prayer that although the world does not know the righteous Father, Jesus knows him.*Jn 17:25* Jesus prayed that all he has is the Father's, and all the Father has is his.*Jn 17:10* Jesus said that his Father had committed all things to him, the Son.*Lk 10:22* Jesus added that no one knows who the Son is other than the Father, and no one knows the Father other than the Son and those to whom the Son reveals him.*Lk 10:22* Jesus said that he knows and obeys his Father.*Jn 8:55* Jesus repeated to the Jews in the temple courts who tried to stone him that he was God's Son, the Father was in him, and he was in the Father.*Jn 10:36-38* God named Jesus Son and said he was his Father.*Heb 1:5* God's oath appointed the Son, whom God made perfect forever.*Heb 7:28* When God brought his firstborn Son into the world, he said that the angels would worship him.*Heb 1:6* To the Son God says his throne, as God, will last forever, with a scepter of justice for his kingdom.*Heb 1:8* The Son is the beginning and firstborn from among the dead, supreme in everything.*Col 1:18* As God's Son, Jesus is without father or mother or genealogy, without beginning or end.*Heb 7:1-17* Christ, as God's Son, is far superior to the angels.*Heb 1:4-5* Through the Son, God reconciles to himself all things on earth and in heaven.*Col 1:20* God said his Son loved righteousness and hated wickedness, and so had set the Son above, anointing him with the oil of joy.*Heb 1:9* God said to the Son, not the angels, to sit at his right hand until God made his enemies a footstool for his feet.*Heb 1:13* Jesus is the Son of God and our great high priest who ascended into heaven.*Heb 4:14* As to his earthly life, God's Son Jesus descended from David.*Ro 1:3* God appointed Jesus the Son of God through the Spirit of holiness.*Ro 1:4* At Jesus's baptism, God the Father gave Jesus honor and glory from heaven, saying, with the same voice from heaven that disciples heard on the sacred mountain, that Jesus is his Son whom he loves and with whom he is well pleased.*2Pe 1:17-18* Jesus said that his Father committed all things to him, the Son whom no one knows but the Father.*Matt 11:27* Even demons possessing two violent men called Jesus the Son of God.*Matt 8:28-29*

Messiah. When the Samaritan woman at the well told Jesus that the Messiah was coming to explain everything, Jesus replied that he was the Messiah.*Jn 4:25-26* Jesus is the Messiah bringing the good news, just as the prophet Isaiah foretold.*Mk 1:1* Magi from the east came to Jerusalem asking to see and worship the star-announced one born king of the Jews.*Matt 2:1-2* The Messiah's announcement disturbed King Herod and all Jerusalem.*Matt 2:3* All the chief priests and law teachers said that the Messiah would be born in Bethlehem.*Matt 2:4-6* The star led the Magi to the place where the Messiah was born.*Matt 2:9-10* When the Magi saw the newborn Messiah with his mother Mary, they bowed down and worshiped him, giving him treasures of gold, frankincense, and myrrh.*Matt 2:11* Jesus the Messiah has an earthly genealogy tracing through David to Abraham.*Matt 1:1-17* Jesus the Messiah's mother Mary became pregnant with him through the Holy Spirit.*Matt 1:18* The prophets searched for salvation, the grace that was to come to us, to discover through Christ's Spirit when and how the Messiah would come, suffer, and receive his glory.*1Pe 1:10-11* Some people thought that Jesus was John the Baptist or possibly Elijah or another of the prophets, but Peter said that Jesus was the Messiah.*Mk 7:27-30, Lk 9:18-20* When at Jesus's trial the high priest charged Jesus to say whether Jesus was the Messiah, the Son of God, Jesus replied that the high priest had said so and that they would indeed see the Son of Man sitting at the Mighty One's right hand and coming on heaven's clouds.*Matt 26:63-64* The apostle Peter said that we find salvation in no one other than Jesus, whose name is the only one under heaven to save us.*Acts 4:12* The Messiah Jesus is God over all, forever praised.*Ro 9:5* When Jesus asked the Pharisees whose son the Messiah was, and they answered David's son, he pointed out that even David called the Messiah Lord.*Matt 22:41-46, Mk 12:35-37, Lk 20:41-44* Jesus praised his Father, Lord of heaven, for hiding the gospel from the wise and learned while revealing it to little children.*Matt 11:25-26* Jesus is the one whom God chose as his servant, in whom God delights, and on whom God put his Spirit, in whose name the nations place their hope, as Isaiah prophesied.*Matt 12:18* The Messiah is your one Instructor.*Matt 23:10*

Lord. Jesus said that the disciples rightly called him Lord because that is who he is.*Jn 13:13* Jesus our Lord came from the order of the king of peace and righteousness.*Heb 7:1-17* God exalted Jesus to the highest place, giving him the name above every other name that every knee in heaven, on earth, and under earth should bow and every tongue acknowledge that Jesus Christ is Lord.*Php 2:9-11* Jesus made a triumphal entry into Jerusalem, riding across cloaks and branches spread on the road, on a donkey colt, as the prophesied king, to the shouts of a very large crowd that Jesus was the Son of David and the Lord, stirring the whole city.*Matt 21:1-11, Mk 11:1-11, Lk 19:28-38, Jn 12:12-16* The Pharisees told Jesus to rebuke his disciples for celebrating the Lord's coming, but Jesus replied that if they kept quiet, then the stones would cry out.*Lk 19:39-40* The governor Pilate said that Jesus was a king, to which Jesus replied that the governor had said so.*Jn 18:37* Revere Christ as Lord.*1Pe 3:15* Jesus said that he, the Son of Man, greater than the old temple, is Lord of the Sabbath.*Matt 12:1-8, Lk 6:1-5* We need no longer teach one another to know the Lord because we all, from least to greatest, know him.*Heb 8:11* Jesus Christ became a stumbling stone to those who pursued righteousness by law and works but salvation to those who believed in him.*Ro 9:32-33* We must all appear before Christ's judgment seat.*2Co 5:10* God did not put angels over the world to come but the Son of Man, Jesus Christ, leaving nothing over which he will not rule, even though we do not yet see all that he will rule.*Heb 2:5-8* Learn more of the grace of our Lord and Savior Jesus Christ to whom we give glory now and forever.*2Pe 3:17-18* The Lord waits patiently to return, wanting everyone to repent rather than any to perish.*2Pe 3:9* The Lord is near.*Php 4:5* Christ must reign until all enemies are under his feet.*1Co 15:25* The last enemy Christ destroys is death.*1Co 15:26* God has put everything under Christ's feet other than God himself.*1Co 15:27* When the Son finishes, the Son will subject himself to the Father who put everything under him, so that God is everything in all.*1Co 15:28* Come, Lord.*1Co 16:22* When times reach fulfillment, God will unify everything in heaven and on earth under Christ.*Eph 1:8-10*

Priest. Jesus is the great priest over God's house.*Heb 10:21* Our high priest Jesus empathizes with our weaknesses, like us tempted in every way, but without sin.*Heb 4:15* Christ did not proclaim for himself the glory of a high priest, but God instead called him Son and said he was his Father, making Christ a priest forever.*Heb 5:5-6* God designated Jesus to be high priest in long-established order.*Heb 5:10* Jesus our Lord is an indestructible priest forever rather than from the Levitical priesthood that administered the law.*Heb 7:1-17* Our forerunner Jesus entered the inner sanctuary for us as our high priest forever from long-established order.*Heb 6:19-20* The Lord swore not to change his mind that Jesus is a priest forever.*Heb 7:20-21* Other priests die, ending their office, but Jesus lives forever in permanent priesthood.*Heb 7:23-24* Jesus thus saves completely those who come to God through him, because he lives forever interceding for them.*Heb 7:25* The high priest Jesus thus truly meets our need, as holy, blameless, pure, set apart from sinners, and exalted above the heavens.*Heb 7:26* Jesus needs no daily sacrifices for his own sins or the people's sins because he sacrificed once for all, offering himself.*Heb 7:27* We have a high priest who sat down at the right hand of the Majesty's throne in heaven, who serves in the Lord's own inner sanctuary, and not as a mere human.*Heb 8:2* Every high priest offers gifts and sacrifices, and so Jesus also offered, but not as a priest serving the law would offer.*Heb 8:3-4*

Shepherd. Jesus said that he is the good shepherd who lays down his life for the sheep, having come so that they may have life to the full.*Jn 10:10-11* Jesus's sheep know and follow his voice as he calls them out by name and leads them out, not the voice of the stranger from whom they instead run.*Jn 10:3-5* Jesus is the good shepherd who knows his sheep and whose sheep know him, just as the Father knows him and he knows the Father, as he lays down his life for the sheep, unlike the hired hand who runs when the wolf comes because the hired hand does not own or care for the sheep.*Jn 10:12-15* Jesus also said that he is the gate to the sheep pen, so that he saves whoever enters through him.*Jn 10:7-9* The sheep do not listen to the thieves and robbers who came before Jesus to steal, kill, and destroy, and who climb in the sheep pen rather than coming through Jesus, the gate.*Jn 10:1, 8-10* Jesus said that he has other sheep who will also listen to his voice to make one flock under one shepherd.*Jn 10:16* Jesus repeated that his sheep know his voice and follow him, he gives them eternal life, and no one can snatch them out of his hand or his Father's hand.*Jn 10:27-29* Our Lord Jesus is the great Shepherd of the sheep.*Heb 13:20* When many from all the towns ran after Jesus and the disciples, Jesus had compassion for the crowds because they were harassed and helpless, like sheep without a shepherd.*Matt 9:36, Mk 6:33-34* Jesus said that a man owning a hundred sheep would leave the ninety-nine sheep to find the one lost sheep.*Matt 18:12, Lk 15:3-4* When the sheep owner finds the one lost sheep, the owner is happier for finding it than for the ninety-nine sheep that never wandered.*Matt 18:13, Lk 15:5-6* Jesus said that his heavenly Father treats his own little ones the same way that none would perish.*Matt 18:14* Heaven rejoices more over one sinner who repents than over ninety-nine righteous persons who have no need to repent.*Lk 15:7* On the night of his arrest, Jesus told the disciples that they would all fall away on his account, as the scriptures foretold that with the shepherd struck, the sheep would scatter.*Matt 26:31, Mk 14:27* Shepherd God's flock eagerly as the example that God wants you to be, so that the Chief Shepherd can give you an eternal crown of glory.*1Pe 5:4* When Jesus returns on his glorious throne with all the nations gathered before him, he will separate people like a shepherd sorting sheep from goats, sheep to the right, goats to the left.*Matt 25:32* Jesus said that he knocks at the door saying he is right here and that he will join and eat with anyone who opens the door.*Rev 3:20*

Tempting. Right after Jesus's baptism, the Spirit led Jesus into the wilderness for forty days, for the devil to tempt him.*Matt 4:1, Mk 1:12-13* The Holy Spirit filled Jesus when he left the Jordan River for the wilderness for forty days of the devil's tempting.*Lk 4:1-2* Jesus fasted forty days and nights, leaving him hungry.*Matt 4:2, Lk 4:2* Jesus was with the wild animals, with angels attending him.*Mk 1:13* The devil tempted Jesus, saying that if he was the Son of God, then he should tell stones to become bread, to satisfy his hunger.*Matt 4:3, Lk 4:3* Jesus quoted scripture to the devil that men do not live on bread alone but on every word from God's mouth.*Matt 4:4, Lk 4:4* The devil also had Jesus stand on the Temple's highest point, inviting Jesus, if he was God's Son, to jump, quoting scripture to Jesus that God would command his angels to catch him.*Matt 4:6, Lk 4:9-11* Jesus quoted scripture to the devil, not to put the Lord your God to the test.*Matt 4:7, Lk 4:12* The devil also took Jesus to a mountaintop to show him the splendor of all the world's kingdoms, offering all of it to Jesus if he would bow and worship the devil.*Matt 4:8-9, Lk 4:5-7* Jesus told the devil to leave, quoting scripture to worship and serve only the Lord your God._{Matt 4:10, Lk 4:8} The devil left, while angels appeared to attend to Jesus._{Matt 4:11} The devil left until an opportune time._{Lk 4:13}

Preaching. After his baptism and tempting, Jesus began to preach repentance because the kingdom of heaven had come near._{Matt 4:17} After the king put John the Baptist in prison, Jesus went into Galilee proclaiming God's good news that God's kingdom had come near and to repent and believe the good news._{Mk 1:14-15} Jesus would preach in one place and then take the disciples to another village for him to preach, saying that was why he came._{Mk 1:38} News of Jesus spread quickly throughout Galilee._{Mk 1:28} The people would gather in such large numbers that they had no room, not even outside, and Jesus would preach the word to them._{Mk 2:1-2} Jesus would say that he must proclaim the good news of God's kingdom to other towns, too, because that was why God sent him._{Lk 4:43-44} Jesus traveled from one town and village to another, proclaiming the good news of God's kingdom, with the twelve disciples and several women who helped to support them out of their own means._{Lk 8:1-3} Jesus preached in Galilee's towns._{Matt 11:1} Jesus appointed twelve disciples to send out to preach._{Mk 3:13-14}

Teaching. Martha, whom Jesus loved, called Jesus the Teacher._{Jn 11:28} Jesus said that the disciples rightly called him Teacher because that is who he is._{Jn 13:13} Jesus returned to Galilee in the Spirit's power to teach in the synagogues._{Lk 4:14-15} Jesus traveled throughout Galilee, teaching in synagogues, proclaiming the kingdom's good news._{Matt 4:23, Mk 1:39} Jesus's teaching amazed the people because unlike the law teachers, Jesus taught with authority._{Mk 1:21-22, Mk 6:1-2, Lk 4:31-32} Nicodemus of the Jewish ruling council visited Jesus in the night, saying that he knew Jesus was a teacher from God because of the signs Jesus did that only one from God could do._{Jn 3:1-2} Jesus traveled through all the towns and villages, teaching in synagogues while proclaiming the kingdom's good news._{Matt 9:35} Jesus had compassion for the crowds because they were harassed and helpless, like sheep without a shepherd, and so he taught them many things._{Matt 9:36, Mk 6:34} Jesus taught in Galilee's towns._{Matt 11:1} Jesus taught such large crowds that he once sat in a boat on the lake to teach the people on the shore, because they were crowding him._{Matt 13:1-2, Mk 3:7-9, Mk 4:1, Lk 5:1-2} Jesus amazed people in his hometown synagogue, with his teaching._{Matt 13:53-54} Jesus astonished the crowds with his teaching._{Matt 22:33} Early each morning, Jesus taught at the temple courts, spending each evening out on the Mount of Olives._{Lk 21:37-38} After a while, the religious leaders realized that they could not say a word in reply to Jesus's teaching, and so no one dared to ask him any more questions.*Matt 22:46* When he taught in the temple courts, Jesus amazed the people, who asked where Jesus got his learning without having been taught.*Jn 7:15* Jesus said that his teaching was not his own but instead from God, because he sought not his own glory but God's glory, which proves a teacher true.*Jn 7:16-18* Jesus said not to call one another teacher because you have one Teacher and are all brothers.*Matt 23:8* Don't even call one another instructors because you have one Instructor who is the Messiah.*Matt 23:10* Jesus no longer calls us servants but instead calls us friends because servants don't know their master's business, and Jesus taught us everything that he learned from the Father.*Jn 15:15*

Parables. Jesus taught many things in parables.*Matt 13:3, Mk 4:2* Jesus did not teach anything without using a parable, as much as the crowds could understand, explaining the parables when he was alone with the disciples.*Mk 4:33-34* When the disciples asked him why he taught in parables, Jesus explained that he had given the disciples, but not others, knowledge of heaven's kingdom.*Matt 13:11, Mk 4:10-12, Lk 8:10* Whoever has a heart for truth, Jesus will give more, but whoever does not have that heart will lose the little truth that they have.*Matt 13:12, Lk 8:18* Jesus spoke in parables so that those who lacked a heart for him would hear but not hear and see but not see, fulfilling Isaiah's prophecy about a hard-hearted people who close their eyes and hardly hear, when Jesus was right there to heal them.*Matt 13:14-15, Lk 8:10* Jesus blesses those who hear with their ears and see with their eyes because many prophets and righteous persons longed to see and hear Jesus but were unable to do so.*Matt 13:16-17* Jesus explained that his parable about the sower of seeds meant that those who hear God's word but don't grasp it lose it to the evil one like a seed sown on a path.*Matt 13:19, Mk 4:14-15, Lk 8:4-12* Those who hear and receive the word with joy but fall away at the first trouble or persecution over it are like a seed sown on rocky soil that grows no root and thus dies in the first scorching heat.*Matt 13:20-21, Mk 4:16-17, Lk 8:13* Those who hear and receive the word but lose it to life's worries and wealth's deceitfulness are like seed sown and choked among thorns.*Matt 13:22, Mk 4:18-19, Lk 8:14* Those who hear and pursue the word, producing a crop thirty, sixty, or a hundredfold, are like seed falling on good soil.*Matt 13:23, Mk 4:20, Lk 8:15* Jesus spoke to the crowds in parables, fulfilling the prophecy that he would utter things hidden since creation.*Matt 13:34-35*

Healing. Jesus traveled throughout Galilee, healing the people's every disease and sickness._{Matt 4:23} Jesus instantly healed a man with leprosy who asked if Jesus was willing, to which Jesus said, indignantly, that he was willing._{Matt 8:2-3, Mk 1:40-42, Lk 5:12-13} Jesus healed a centurion's servant from a distance, amazed at the faith of the centurion's request._{Matt 8:5-13, Lk 7:1-10} Jesus also healed a royal official's son from a distance when the official begged him, the son healing at the exact time that Jesus had said the son would live._{Jn 4:46-54} Telling him to pick up his mat and walk, Jesus healed an invalid at a pool near Jerusalem's Sheep Gate after asking the invalid if he wanted to get well._{Jn 5:1-9} Jesus healed Simon Peter's mother-in-law lying in bed with a fever, by touching her hand, after which she got up to wait on him._{Matt 8:14-15, Mk 1:29-31, Lk 4:38-39} People brought to Jesus many demon-possessed persons, for him to drive out the spirits with a word and heal all the sick, fulfilling Isaiah's prophecy that Jesus took up our infirmities and bore our diseases._{Matt 8:16-17} Jesus's healing of the paralyzed man on the mat so awed the crowd that they praised God for giving him such authority._{Matt 9:8, Lk 5:26} Jesus healed a woman who said to herself that a touch to Jesus's cloak would heal her._{Matt 9:20-22, Mk 5:25-34, Lk 8:40-48} Jesus restored sight to two blind men after they confirmed that they believed that he could do so._{Matt 9:27-31} Jesus traveled through all the towns and villages, healing every disease and sickness._{Matt 9:35} Jesus healed a man with a shriveled hand._{Mk 3:1-6} Jesus told a man with a shriveled hand to stretch it out, and Jesus had healed it as good as the other hand._{Matt 12:13, Lk 6:6-10} Jesus healed a blind, mute, demon-possessed man so that the man could talk and see._{Matt 12:22} Jesus healed the demon-possessed daughter of a Canaanite woman who showed Jesus that the woman had great faith._{Matt 15:21-28} Jesus healed a Greek woman's daughter after she showed Jesus that she had great faith._{Mk 7:24-30} Jesus healed a deaf and mute man by putting his fingers in the man's ears, touching the man's tongue, looking to heaven, and saying to open._{Mk 7:31-35} Jesus healed a blind man by spitting on the man's eyes, putting his hands on him, and when the man could only see what looked like trees walking around, putting his hands on the man's eyes again._{Mk 7:22-26, Jn 9:1-12} Jesus restored the sight of two blind men sitting by Jericho's roadside, calling to the Lord, Son of David, to have mercy on them._{Matt 20:29-34} A blind beggar shouted to Jesus, Son of David, to have mercy on him, and when the crowd told him that Jesus was calling for him, he got up and ran to Jesus who told him that the man's faith had restored his sight, and he indeed could then see._{Mk 10:46-52, Lk 18:35-43} Jesus healed the blind and lame who came to him at the temple._{Matt 21:14} The apostle Peter said that Jesus healed all who were under the devil's power because God was with him.*Acts 10:38*

Raising. Jesus said that with his coming, the blind were seeing, lame walking, lepers cleansed, deaf hearing, and dead raised.*Matt 11:4-5* When Jesus saw a procession carrying a widow's dead son on a bier, his heart went out to the widow, and he touched the bier, raising the widow's son to life.*Lk 7:11-15* The people, filled with awe, said that God had come to help his people, and news spread throughout Judea.*Lk 7:16-17* Jesus raised from the dead a synagogue leader's daughter, after the leader told Jesus that Jesus's putting his hand on her would make her live again.*Matt 9:18-26, Mk 5:21-43, Lk 8:40-56* Jesus raised from the dead Lazarus, whose sister Mary poured perfume on Jesus's feet and wiped his feet with her hair, after Lazarus had been dead four days, so that those who saw it would believe.*Jn 11:1-44*

Crowds. When Jesus returned to Galilee in the Spirit's power after his baptism and tempting, to teach in the synagogues, news spread of him throughout the countryside, with everyone praising him.*Lk 4:14-15* Once a crowd gathered and pressed in so hard that Jesus and the disciples could not even eat.*Mk 3:20* In another instance, Jesus taught a large crowd beside a lake.*Mk 2:13* In yet another instance, Jesus sat up on a mountainside, teaching crowds.*Matt 5:1-2* When Jesus came down from the mountainside after teaching, large crowds followed him.*Matt 8:1* Jesus would tell those whom he healed not to say anything, but they would anyway, and the news spread all the more, so that crowds came for his teaching and healing.*Lk 5:15* Jesus's healing attracted large crowds from Galilee, the Decapolis, Jerusalem, Judea, and the region across the Jordan.*Matt 4:25* Jesus attracted a great number of people from all over Judea, Jerusalem, and the coastal region around Tyre and Sidon, to hear his teaching and for his healing.*Lk 6:17-18* People were trying to touch him for the power that was coming from him for their healing.*Lk 6:19* Jesus healed so many that those with diseases would push forward through the crowds to touch him for healing.*Mk 3:10* In one instance, the crowd listening to Jesus teach was so large that men bringing a paralyzed man to Jesus for healing dug through the roof to let him down in front of Jesus, for Jesus to heal him.*Mk 2:3-12, Lk 5:17-25* The amazed people, who had never seen anything like it, praised God for Jesus's healing.*Mk 2:12* Word spread so much that Jesus could not enter a town openly and instead stayed outside in lonely places, but people still came to him from everywhere.*Mk 1:45* News spread all over Syria about Jesus's healing, so that people brought him all with diseases, and Jesus healed even those in severe pain, demon-possessed, having seizures, and paralyzed.*Matt 4:24* The whole town would gather, bringing their sick, and Jesus would heal many diseases.*Mk 1:32-34* When Jesus's disciples returned from proclaiming the good news and healing the sick, Jesus tried to withdraw with them, but the crowds learned and followed them, and so Jesus welcomed them, taught them about God's kingdom, and healed those who needed it.*Lk 9:10-11* Large crowds followed Jesus, and he healed all the ill.*Matt 12:15* Once, a crowd of many thousands gathered, so that people were trampling one another.*Lk 12:1* When Jesus would arrive at a place, word would go out, and people would bring all their sick to him, begging him to let the sick touch the edge of his cloak, and he healed all who did so.*Matt 14:34-36, Mk 6:53-56* Jesus went into the Judean region on the Jordan River's other side, where large crowds followed him, and he healed them.*Matt 19:1-2* Jesus later went up on a mountainside where great crowds brought the lame, blind, mute, and many others to him, laying them at Jesus's feet where he healed them, amazing the crowds.*Matt 15:29-31* Jesus entered a house not wanting anyone to know, but he could not keep his presence secret.*Mk 7:24* The more that Jesus would tell people not to spread news of his healing, the more people kept talking about it, overwhelmed with amazement at how well Jesus did everything.*Mk 7:36-37* Jesus's custom when crowds came to him was to teach them.*Mk 10:1* Jesus's teaching delighted the crowds.*Mk 12:37* Jesus's wonderful things delighted the people while humiliating his opponents.*Lk 13:17*

Feeding. Jesus's disciples told Jesus that he needed to send the crowds away from the remote place where he had been teaching and healing them, so that they could return to villages to buy food to eat.*Matt 14:15, Mk 6:35-36, Lk 9:12* Jesus said that they didn't need to leave to eat.*Matt 14:16* Jesus told the disciples to give them something to eat.*Mk 6:37, Lk 9:13* Jesus had asked the disciple Philip where they would buy bread for the people to eat, as a test for Philip, because Jesus already knew what he was going to do.*Jn 6:5-6* The disciples said that buying bread would take more than a half year's wages.*Mk 6:37, Jn 6:7* But they also said that they had five loaves of bread and two fish.*Lk 9:13* The disciple Andrew brought forward a boy with five small barley loaves and two small fish but wondered how far they would go.*Jn 6:8-9* So Jesus took the five loaves of bread and two fish, thanked God for them, and broke the loaves, out of which the disciples fed five thousand men plus more women and children, leaving twelve basketfuls of bread and fish.*Matt 14:17-21, Mk 6:38-44, Lk 9:16-17, Jn 6:10-13* Jesus later went up on a mountainside where great crowds came to him for healing, for three days without food.*Matt 15:29-32* Jesus didn't want to send them away hungry to collapse, and so he asked his disciples for the seven loaves of bread and few small fish that they had.*Matt 15:33-34, Mk 7:1-5* Jesus thanked God, broke the loaves, and gave the food to the disciples, who fed the people until they were satisfied, with seven basketfuls of food left over.*Matt 15:36-37, Mk 7:6-8* Four thousand men ate, not counting the women and children who ate.*Matt 15:38, Mk 7:9* Jesus later reminded the disciples that he had supplied five thousand men out of five loaves and four thousand men out of seven loaves, with basketfuls left over.*Matt 16:9-10*

Solitude. Jesus would withdraw to a solitary place, but the people would search for him, find him, and try to keep him from leaving.*Lk 4:42* Jesus saw how large crowds followed him when he withdrew to solitary places and so had compassion on them and healed all their sick.*Matt 14:13-14* When the people began saying in response to Jesus feeding five thousand that surely Jesus was the Prophet who was to come, and Jesus knew that they intended to make him king by force, Jesus withdrew to a solitary mountain.*Jn 6:14-15* Jesus would get up very early in the morning to go alone to a solitary place, so that the disciples would have to go looking for him.*Mk 1:35-37* Jesus would withdraw to lonely places.*Lk 5:16* When so many people crowded around Jesus and the disciples that they did not even have a chance to eat, he told them to come away with him to a quiet place to get some rest, and so they sought a solitary place.*Mk 6:30-32* When Jesus could no longer move about publicly, he withdrew with the disciples to a wilderness region.*Jn 11:54* When many went up to Jerusalem for the Passover festival, they kept asking whether Jesus wasn't coming at all because he had withdrawn.*Jn 11:55-56* After speaking to the crowds, Jesus would leave and hide himself from them.*Jn 12:36*

Prayer. Jesus would get up very early in the morning to pray.*Mk 1:35-37* Jesus would withdraw to pray.*Lk 5:16* When the disciples were unable to cast a spirit out of a demon-possessed boy, Jesus told them that this kind of spirit only comes out with prayer.*Mk 9:28-29* When Jesus raised Lazarus from the dead, he looked up to thank the Father for always hearing him, saying so for the benefit of the people present there with him, so that they would believe that the Father sent him.*Jn 11:41-42* Jesus said at the Last Supper that he had prayed for the disciples that Satan would not sift them as wheat but that Peter would instead turn back in faith to strengthen his brothers.*Lk 22:31-32* Jesus looked toward heaven to pray that the Father, in his hour that had come, would glorify his Son and his Son glorify him._Jn 17:1_ Jesus prayed that the Father had granted him authority over all people so that he could give eternal life to all those whom the Father had given him._Jn 17:2_ Jesus prayed that eternal life is to know the Father, the only true God, and his Son Jesus Christ whom the Father sent._Jn 17:3_ Jesus prayed that he had brought the Father glory on earth by finishing his assigned work and that the Father now glorify Jesus in his presence with the glory that Jesus had with the Father before the world began._Jn 17:4-5_ Jesus prayed that he had revealed the Father to those whom the Father had given him, who were the Father's, and who obeyed the Father's word, knowing that everything that the Father had given Jesus comes from the Father who sent Jesus._Jn 17:6-8_ Jesus prayed for the disciples, not for the world, but for those whom the Father had given him who are the Father's, who had brought glory to Jesus._Jn 17:9-10_ Jesus prayed that while he was leaving the world to come to the Father, the Father would protect the disciples who remained in the world, by the power of the Father's name, the name the Father gave Jesus, so that the disciples would be one as the Father and Jesus are one._Jn 17:11_ Jesus prayed that while he was with the disciples, he had protected the disciples by the name that the Father had given him, without losing any other than the doomed one who fulfilled the scriptures._Jn 17:12_ Jesus prayed not only for the disciples but for all those who believe in Jesus through the disciples' message, that all may be one in the Father and Jesus, just as the Father is in Jesus and Jesus in the Father, in complete unity, so that the world believes that the Father sent Jesus and loves all believers even as he loves Jesus._Jn 17:20-23_ Jesus prayed that those whom the Father gave him be with Jesus and see his glory that the Father gave him because the Father loved Jesus before creating the world._Jn 17:24_ Jesus prayed that believers knew that the Father had sent Jesus into the world because Jesus had made the Father known to them and would continue to do so, so that the love the Father has for Jesus will be in them and Jesus himself will be in them._Jn 17:25-26_

Rejection. After he had preached throughout the countryside, with everyone praising him, Jesus went to his hometown Nazareth to preach in the synagogue._Lk 4:16_ He stood up to read the scroll of the prophet Isaiah that someone had handed him, reading the passage saying that the Lord's Spirit was on him to proclaim the good news to the poor and freedom for the prisoner._Lk 4:16-18_ When finished reading, he sat down and, with all eyes on him, said that he had fulfilled this scripture today._Lk 4:21_ All spoke well of him, amazed at his gracious words, and asking whether he wasn't Joseph's son.*Lk 4:22* But Jesus responded that they would demand that he do in his hometown the miracles he had done elsewhere and would give him no honor.*Lk 4:23-24* Jesus told them that God had sent Elijah to feed and heal others, not the people of Israel.*Lk 4:25-27* His words made all the people in the synagogue furious.*Lk 4:28* People in Jesus's hometown synagogue, where they knew his mother, brothers, and sisters, though amazed at his teaching, didn't know where he got his teaching and so took offense at him.*Matt 13:54-57, Mk 6:1-3* Jesus, amazed at their lack of faith, said that a prophet has no honor in his hometown and could do no miracles there for their lack of faith, other than to heal a few sick people.*Mk 6:4-6* The people drove Jesus out of his hometown, taking him to a hill at the edge of town where they prepared to throw him off its cliff, but he walked right through the crowd and on his way.*Lk 4:29-30* Jesus said that the people had seen him and yet still not believed.*Jn 6:36* The disciples grumbled that Jesus's teaching that he was the bread of life and they must eat his flesh and drink his blood was a hard teaching.*Jn 6:60-61* From that time, many of his disciples left him.*Jn 6:66* Even Jesus's brothers, who told him to stop doing things in secret and instead show himself to the world, did not believe in him.*Jn 7:2-5* Jesus told them that his time was not yet here, when for them any time would do, because the world hated only him, not them, for his testifying that its works were evil.*Jn 7:6* When the Pharisees challenged him, saying his testimony was invalid, Jesus pointed to his Father's testimony and told the Pharisees that they did not know him or his Father.*Jn 8:13-19* The Pharisees decided that they would put out of the synagogue anyone who acknowledged Jesus as the Messiah.*Jn 9:22* The Jews in the temple courts said to Jesus to them plainly if he was the Messiah, but Jesus replied that he did tell them and they did not believe because they were not his sheep.*Jn 10:22-26*

Division. Some in the crowds said Jesus was a good man, while others said he deceived the people, but all kept quiet for fear of the leaders.*Jn 7:12-13* When many in the crowd believed in Jesus because the Messiah would not perform more signs than Jesus had, the chief priests and Pharisees sent temple guards to arrest Jesus, but again his time had not yet come.*Jn 7:31-44* Some said that Jesus was the Prophet and the Messiah, while others disputed that the Messiah could come from Galilee rather than Bethlehem, as scriptures said, so that belief in Jesus divided the people.*Jn 7:40-43* When the temple guards, whom the chief priests and Pharisees had sent to arrest Jesus, came back without him, and the chief priests and Pharisees asked why they hadn't arrested him, the guards answered that no one spoke like Jesus.*Jn 7:45-46* The Pharisees retorted that Jesus had deceived them because neither the Pharisees nor the rulers had believed in Jesus, and only the cursed mob that knew nothing of the law had believed.*Jn 7:45-49* The ruling council member Nicodemus pointed out that the law would give Jesus a hearing before his condemnation, but the Pharisees replied that Jesus, coming from Galilee, could not be a prophet.*Jn 7:50-52* When the Jews asked Jesus who he was, and he replied that he was the Son of Man whom they would lift up, that he spoke as the Father taught him, and that the Father who sent him was with him, many believed.*Jn 8:25-30* When Jesus gave sight to a man born blind, and the Pharisees said Jesus was not from God because he had healed the man on the Sabbath, others disagreed because a sinner could not do such things, and so Jesus divided them.*Jn 9:16* When the man told the Pharisees that God does not listen to sinners, they told him that sin steeped him from birth, and they threw him out.*Jn 9:28-34* When the man told Jesus that he believed that Jesus was the Son of Man, Jesus told him that Jesus had come into the world to judge, so that the blind would see and the sighted would not see.*Jn 9:35-39* When Jesus said that he was the shepherd who laid down his life for the sheep, only to take it up again, his words again divided the Jews, some of whom said he was mad and demon-possessed, and others of whom said a demon-possessed man cannot open blind eyes.*Jn 10:19-21* While many in the crowds did not believe, many others even among the leaders did believe, although they would not profess their faith because they feared being put out of the synagogue where they would lose human praise for God's praise.*Jn 12:39-43*

Opposition. Jesus said that when he came eating and drinking, people called him a drunkard and glutton who ate with tax collectors and sinners.*Matt 11:19, Lk 7:34* Teachers of the law called Jesus a blasphemer for forgiving the paralyzed man whom Jesus healed.*Matt 9:3, Lk 5:21* Jews grumbled against Jesus for saying that he was the bread of life from heaven, when to them he was just Joseph's son.*Jn 6:41-43* Jesus's own family came to take charge of him because they thought him out of his mind.*Mk 3:21* A noisy crowd in the house of the synagogue leader whose daughter died and Jesus raised, laughed at Jesus claiming that she would live.*Matt 9:23-24, Mk 5:39-40, Lk 8:53* The Pharisees said that Jesus drove out demons by the prince of demons and was demon possessed.*Matt 9:34, Mk 3:22* The law teachers were saying that Jesus had an impure spirit.*Mk 3:29* Jesus said that he sent his disciples out like sheep among wolves and so to be on guard, taking no purse or bag and greeting no one on the road.*Matt 10:16-*

17, Lk 10:3 Even the Samaritans refused to welcome Jesus when he was heading for Jerusalem.*Lk 9:51-53* James and John asked if Jesus wanted them to call fire down from heaven to destroy them, but Jesus rebuked them and took them to another village.*Lk 9:54-56* When a man said that he would follow Jesus wherever Jesus went, Jesus said that animals have dens and nests, but the Son of Man has no place to rest.*Lk 9:57-58* After all that Jesus did, Pharisees and Sadducees nonetheless came to Jesus testing him, asking for a sign from heaven, to which Jesus replied with a sigh that they would have no sign.*Mk 7:12* Jesus called them a wicked and adulterous generation that would have no sign other than Jonah's sign of a rainbow from heaven.*Matt 16:1-2, Lk 11:16, 11:29-32* The chief priests and law teachers were indignant that children were shouting praises to the Son of David, as scripture prophesied.*Matt 21:15-16* They kept trying to catch Jesus in his words.*Mk 12:13* The Pharisees and law teachers opposed Jesus fiercely, besieging him with questions, trying to catch him in something that he said.*Lk 11:53-54* The Pharisees told Jesus to leave because Herod wanted to kill him, but Jesus said that he would press on driving out demons and healing because no prophet can die outside Jerusalem.*Lk 13:31* The Pharisees, who loved money but heard Jesus criticizing the love of money, sneered at Jesus.*Lk 16:14* When the Jews said Jesus was demon-possessed, Jesus replied that he was not but instead honored his Father.*Jn 8:48-49* Jesus said that others would judge him among the transgressors, just as written, and as he must fulfill.*Lk 22:37*

Suffering. Jesus explained over time to his disciples that he must suffer many things from the elders, chief priests, and law teachers, who would have him killed, but that the third day he would rise to life.*Matt 16:21, Mk 8:31-32, Lk 9:21-22* Peter tried rebuking Jesus, but Jesus said for Satan to get behind him, not to be a stumbling block to him, without the concerns of God but only human concerns.*Matt 16:22-23, Mk 8:32-33* Jesus said again to the disciples in Galilee that one would deliver Jesus into the hands of men who would kill him but that he would rise on the third day.*Matt 17:22-23, Mk 9:30-32* The disciples did not understand Jesus and were afraid to ask him what he meant.*Lk 9:43-45* Jesus predicted his death another time on the way to Jerusalem, when he pulled aside his disciples to tell them someone would hand him over to the chief priests and law teachers for condemnation, mocking, flogging, and crucifixion, but that he would rise to life.*Matt 20:17-19, Mk 10:32-34, Lk 18:31-33* The disciples were astonished and those who followed afraid when Jesus led them to Jerusalem anyway.*Mk 10:32* Jesus did not want to go about in Judea publicly because he knew the Jewish leaders wanted to kill him.*Jn 7:1* When Jesus did speak publicly, people wondered why the authorities would let him do so when the authorities were trying to kill him, and wondered whether the authorities believed that Jesus was the Messiah.*Jn 7:25-27* When Jesus confirmed that they knew that God had sent him, they tried seizing him, but his time had not yet come.*Jn 7:28-30* Jesus said that they were trying to kill him because they had no room for his word.*Jn 8:37* When Jesus said that he and the Father are one, the Jews in the temple courts picked up stones to stone him for claiming to be God.*Jn 10:30-33* Jews in Judea tried to stone Jesus.*Jn 11:7-8* Jesus said that the approaching hour troubled his soul but that he would not ask the Father to save him from the hour because he had come for that hour.*Jn 12:27-28* Jesus said that he had eagerly desired the last Passover supper before he suffered.*Lk 22:15* After Pentecost, Peter told the crowd that they had disowned and killed the Holy and Righteous One in ignorance, so that God could fulfill what he foretold through the prophets that his Messiah would suffer.*Acts 3:12-18* Even though Jesus was God's Son, Jesus learned obedience from what he suffered.*Heb 5:8* Once Jesus's suffering made him perfect, he became eternal salvation's source for all who obey him.*Heb 5:9* Christ is our sacrificed Passover lamb.*1Co 5:6-7* Jesus, who did nothing wrong and never lied, just took it when accusers hurled insults at him because he trusted the just God.*1Pe 2:22-23* The mediator Christ Jesus gave himself as ransom for all.*1Ti 2:5* Non-believers killed the Lord Jesus and the prophets, and so they may also drive you out, even though they displease God and are hostile to all while trying to keep you from saving others.*1Th 2:15-16*

Plotting. Jewish leaders who learned that Jesus had healed an invalid on the Sabbath, causing the invalid to break the law by picking up his mat and walking, persecuted Jesus, who in his defense said that his Father was always at work, causing the leaders to try all the more to kill Jesus for calling God his own Father.*Jn 5:1-18* The Pharisees looked for reasons to bring charges against Jesus, questioning him for that purpose.*Matt 12:10* The Pharisees plotted how they might kill Jesus.*Matt 12:14* When the Pharisees saw Jesus heal a man with a shriveled hand on the Sabbath, the Pharisees began to plot with government officials how to kill Jesus.*Mk 3:1-6* They were furious and began to plot what they could do to Jesus.*Lk 6:11* When the chief priests and law teachers saw how Jesus amazed whole crowds with his teaching, they feared him and looked for a way to kill him.*Mk 11:18* The chief priests, law teachers, and elders wanted to arrest Jesus because they knew that he spoke against them, but they were afraid of the crowds.*Mk 12:12, Lk 20:19* The chief priests, law teachers, and leaders of the people tried to kill Jesus but couldn't because everyone hung on his words.*Lk 19:47-48* The leaders persecuted Jesus, who in his defense said that his Father was always at work, causing the leaders to try all the more to kill Jesus for calling God his own Father.*Jn 5:16-18* When Jesus asked the Jews why they were trying to kill him, they called him demon-possessed and denied that they were trying to kill him.*Jn 7:19-20* When Jesus raised Lazarus from the dead and many Jews who were there believed in him, the Pharisees and chief priests called a Sanhedrin meeting to plot to take his life so that more would not believe and they would not lose the temple and nation to the Romans.*Jn 11:46-53* The chief priests and Pharisees gave orders that anyone who saw Jesus should report it so that they could arrest him.*Jn 11:57* When a large crowd of Jews went to Lazarus's home where Jesus had returned for a dinner in his honor, the chief priests made plans to kill Lazarus, too, because many Jews were believing in Jesus because of Lazarus.*Jn 12:9-11* When the crowd that was with Jesus when Jesus raised Lazarus continued to spread the word, and many people went out to meet Jesus as he entered Jerusalem for the Passover festival, the Pharisees realized that they were getting nowhere because the whole world had gone after him.*Jn 12:17-19* Jesus said repeatedly that others would crucify and kill him, even though he would then rise to life.*Matt 16:21, Matt 17:22-23, Matt 20:17-19, Matt 26:1-2, Lk 18:31-33*

Anointing. When a sinful woman wet Jesus's feet with her tears, wiped them with her hair, and anointed them with expensive perfume, Jesus forgave her sins and said that her faith had saved her.*Lk 7:36-50* Jesus said that he had forgiven her many sins and to go in peace because her faith had saved her and she loved much, while the one like his Pharisee host who sought little forgiveness loved little.*Lk 7:36-50* Shortly before Jesus's arrest and crucifixion, a woman anointed Jesus with an expensive perfume, which the disciples said they should have sold to care for the poor but which Jesus said was a beautiful thing that she had done to prepare Jesus for his burial.*Matt 26:6-13, Mk 14:3-9* Mary, the sister of Lazarus and Martha whom Jesus loved, anointed Jesus's feet with perfume and wiped his feet with her hair, when Jesus attended a dinner at their home given in his honor shortly before the Passover.*Jn 12:1-3* The betrayer Judas asked why they hadn't instead sold the perfume to give to the poor, not because he cared for the poor but because he was a thief who helped himself to the money bag.*Jn 12:4-6* Jesus said to leave Mary alone because the perfume was for his burial, and they would always have the poor among them but not always have him.*Jn 12:7-8* When people preach the gospel throughout the world, they will also tell about the woman who anointed Jesus with an expensive perfume to prepare him for burial.*Matt 26:12-13, Mk 14:3-9*

Betrayal. Jesus said that some of his disciples would not believe him, and he knew from the beginning who would not believe and who would betray him.*Jn 6:64* Jesus added that one of the twelve disciples was a devil, referring to Judas Iscariot who would betray Jesus.*Jn 6:70* After hearing Jesus's parables condemning them, the chief priests and Pharisees looked for a way to arrest him.*Matt 21:45-46* Just before his arrest, Jesus told the disciples again that someone would hand over the Son of Man for crucifixion.*Matt 26:1-2* The chief priests and elders assembled in the high priest's palace, scheming to arrest Jesus secretly and kill him, only not during the festival because they felt that the people might riot.*Matt 26:3-4, Mk 14:1-2* The chief priests and law teachers were looking for a way to get rid of Jesus because they feared the people.*Lk 22:1-2* Satan entered one of the disciples Judas Iscariot, who went to the chief priests and temple-guard officers to discuss how he might betray Jesus.*Lk 22:3-4* Judas went to the chief priests to betray Jesus and hand him over in exchange for thirty pieces of silver.*Matt 26:14-16* That Judas offered to betray Jesus, and watch for an opportunity to hand Jesus over to the chief priests when no crowd was around, delighted the chief priests who in return promised Judas money.*Mk 14:11, Lk 22:5-6* When Jesus gathered with the disciples for his final Passover meal (the Last Supper), Jesus told them that one of them would betray him.*Matt 26:17:21, Mk 14:16-17, Lk 22:21, Jn 13:21* When they asked who, Jesus told them the one who dipped his hand in the bowl with him.*Matt 26:22-23, Mk 14:19-20, Lk 22:21* Jesus said that the betrayer would be the one to whom he gave a piece of bread after dipping the bread in the dish.*Jn 13:25-26* Jesus said that it was so to fulfill scripture that the one who shared his bread would turn against him.*Jn 13:18* Judas Iscariot asked if Jesus meant him, and Jesus said that Judas had said so.*Matt 26:24-25* Satan entered Judas as soon as Jesus gave the dipped bread to Judas.*Jn 13:26-27* The devil prompted Judas to betray Jesus.*Jn 13:2* Jesus told Judas to do quickly what Judas was going to do.*Jn 13:26* Judas left promptly, while dark out.*Jn 13:30* Jesus said that although the other disciples were clean, not every one of them was clean, because he knew that Judas would betray him.*Jn 13:10-11* Jesus also said that the Son of Man would go as written but woe to the one who betrayed him because the betrayer would have been better not to be born.*Matt 26:24, Mk 14:21, Lk 22:22*

Jesus told his disciples before the betrayal happened so that the disciples would believe Jesus was who he was.*Jn 13:19* After the betrayal, remorse seized Judas who tried to return the silver for having betrayed an innocent, but the chief priests and elders said they didn't care and that Judas was responsible.*Matt 27:3-4* So Judas threw the silver into the temple and hanged himself.*Matt 27:5* The chief priests used the blood money to buy the potter's field for foreigner burials, fulfilling Jeremiah's prophecy.*Matt 27:6-10* After Jesus's resurrection, Peter told the disciples and other believers that Judas, the guide for those who arrested Jesus, had to fulfill the Holy Spirit's speaking through the scriptures.*Acts 1:16*

Garden. On the night of his betrayal, Jesus took the disciples to a garden, the place of his betrayal, asking them to sit while he prayed nearby.*Matt 26:36, Mk 14:32, Lk 22:39, Jn 18:1* Jesus first said to pray that they not fall into temptation.*Lk 22:40* He then took Peter, James, and John aside with him, telling them that sorrow overwhelmed his soul to the point of death and asking that they watch with him.*Matt 26:37-38, Mk 14:33-34* He then went about a stone's throw away to kneel and pray.*Lk 22:41* He fell facedown to pray that his Father would take this cup from him, yet not as Jesus willed but as his Father willed.*Matt 26:39, Mk 14:35-36, Lk 22:42* An angel from heaven appeared and strengthened Jesus.*Lk 22:43* Jesus prayed in anguish, even more earnestly, his sweat like drops of blood falling.*Lk 22:44* Jesus returned to his disciples but found them sleeping.*Matt 26:40, Mk 14:37* Sorrow had exhausted them.*Lk 22:45* Jesus asked Peter whether Peter couldn't keep watch for just one hour.*Matt 26:40, Mk 14:37* Jesus said to get up, watch, and pray so as not to fall into temptation.*Matt 26:41, Mk 14:38, Lk 22:46* He added that the spirit is willing but the flesh weak.*Matt 26:41, Mk 14:38* Jesus went aside again, prayed the same again, and came back to find the disciples sleeping again.*Matt 26:42-43, Mk 14:39-40* Jesus went aside a third time, prayed the same again, and came back to again find the disciples sleeping, this time telling them to rise because the hour had come for the betrayer to deliver the Son of Man into sinners' hands.*Matt 26:44-46, Mk 14:41-42*

Arrest. The betrayer Judas knew the garden because Jesus had often met there with his disciples.*Jn 18:2* While Jesus was still speaking to the disciples in the garden after praying, Judas arrived with a large, armed crowd that the chief priests and elders had sent.*Matt 26:47, Mk 14:43, Lk 22:47* Soldiers and officials accompanied them, and they carried torches and lanterns along with their weapons.*Jn 18:3* Jesus knew all that would happen and so went out to ask them whom they wanted.*Jn 18:4* When they said that they wanted Jesus, and Jesus told them that he was the one, they drew back, falling to the ground.*Jn 18:5-6* Jesus asked again whom they wanted, and when they again answered Jesus, he again said that he was the one but added to let the others go, so that he would lose none, as he had foretold.*Jn 18:7-8* Judas, having arranged a signal with the crowd to arrest the one whom he kissed, went straight to Jesus to greet him with a kiss, but Jesus asked Judas if Judas intended to betray the Son of Man with a kiss.*Lk 22:47-48* Jesus also said to do that for which Judas came.*Matt 26:48-50, Mk 14:44-45* Men from the crowd stepped forward to arrest Jesus.*Matt 26:50* One of Jesus's companions drew a sword with which he cut off the high priest's servant's ear.*Matt 26:51, Lk 22:49-50* Peter was the one who drew the sword, and the servant was Malchus.*Jn 18:10* Jesus told Peter to put away the sword because Jesus must drink the cup that the Father had given him.*Jn 18:11* Jesus said to put away the sword because those who live by the sword die by it, and Jesus could have called on his Father to give him legions of angels except that events must fulfill the scriptures.*Matt 26:52-54* After Jesus said to stop, he touched the servant's ear, healing the servant.*Lk 22:51* Jesus then told the crowd that he was not leading a rebellion that they would need swords and clubs but had instead taught openly in the temple courts when they hadn't bothered to arrest him.*Matt 26:55, Mk 14:48, Lk 22:52-53* Jesus added that darkness was their hour.*Lk 22:53* Jesus repeated that these events had happened to fulfill the prophets' writings.*Matt 26:56, Mk 14:49* The soldiers' detachment with its commander, and the Jewish officials, then arrested and bound Jesus.*Jn 18:12* The disciples and others all then fled.*Matt 26:56, Mk 14:50* Indeed, a young man who had followed Jesus, wearing only a linen garment, fled naked when they tried to seize him, leaving his only garment behind.*Mk 14:51-52*

Trial. Those who arrested Jesus first took him to Annas, father in law of the high priest Caiaphas who had advised the Jewish leaders that one man should die for the people.*Jn 18:13-14* The high priest Annas questioned Jesus about his disciples and teaching, to which Jesus replied that he had spoken openly to the world, in synagogues, and at the temple, with nothing in secret, and so to ask those who heard him.*Jn 18:19-21* When an official slapped Jesus for speaking so to the high priest, Jesus replied that the official should testify to what Jesus said wrong or, if Jesus spoke the truth, then justify why the official struck him.*Jn 18:22-23* They then took Jesus to the high priest Caiaphas where the law teachers and elders had assembled.*Matt 26:57, Mk 14:53, Lk 22:54* The disciple John who knew the high priest went with Jesus.*Jn 18:15* Peter, who had followed at a distance, first sat outside until John came back, talked with the servant girl there, and brought Peter into the courtyard.*Jn 18:16* Peter sat with the guards in the courtyard to see what would happen.*Matt 26:58, Mk 14:54, Lk 22:54, Jn 18:16* The chief priests and Sanhedrin looked for false evidence with which to convict Jesus to put him to death.*Matt 26:59, Mk 14:55* Although many false witnesses testified, they found no convicting evidence.*Matt 26:60, Mk 14:56* Two witnesses came forward saying that Jesus had said he could destroy the temple to rebuild it in three days.*Matt 26:60, Mk 14:57* Yet their testimony did not even agree.*Mk 14:58* The high priest Caiaphas demanded that Jesus answer, but Jesus remained silent.*Matt 26:61-63, Mk 14:60-61* The high priest then charged Jesus to say whether Jesus was the Messiah, the Son of God.*Matt 26:63, Mk 14:61* The council of the elders demanded that he tell them whether he was the Messiah.*Lk 22:66-67* Jesus said that they would not believe him if he told them.*Lk 22:67* Jesus also replied that he was the Messiah.*Mk 14:62* Jesus also replied that the high priest had said so.*Matt 26:64* Jesus added that they would indeed see the Son of Man sitting at the Mighty One's right hand and coming on heaven's clouds.*Matt 26:64, Mk 14:62, Lk 22:69* They all asked him whether he was then God's Son, to which Jesus said that they said that he was.*Lk 22:70* The high priest then tore his clothes, saying that they needed no more evidence, having heard Jesus's supposed blasphemy from his own lips.*Matt 26:65, Mk 14:63-64, Lk 22:71* The rest, agreeing that Jesus was worthy of death, spit in his face, struck him with fists, and slapped his face, while mocking him, saying to prophecy as the Messiah.*Matt 26:66-68, Mk 14:64-65* They also blindfolded Jesus, and guards took him, mocked him, and beat him, with many others saying insulting things to him.*Mk 14:65, Lk 22:63-65* The chief priests, law teachers, and elders then planned his execution, leading him away bound, to the governor.*Matt 27:1-2, Mk 15:1*

Sentence. The Jewish leaders stood Jesus before the governor Pontius Pilate in the early morning, outside the palace so that the leaders would not be ceremonially unclean.*Jn 18:28* When the governor came out to ask the charges, the leaders said that they wouldn't have handed over Jesus unless he were a criminal, but the governor told them to judge Jesus by their own law.*Jn 18:29-31* The leaders replied that they could not execute anyone, fulfilling how Jesus would die.*Jn 18:31-32* The governor then brought Jesus into the palace.*Jn 18:33* The governor asked Jesus if he was the Jews' king, to which Jesus replied that the governor had said so.*Matt 27:11, Mk 15:2, Lk 23:3* Jesus asked the governor if that was his own idea or others had told him so.*Jn 18:33* The governor asked why Jesus's own people had handed him over, to which Jesus replied that his kingdom was not of this world but another world.*Jn 18:35-36* The governor said that Jesus was a king then, to which Jesus replied that the governor had said so but that Jesus was born and had come into the world to testify to the truth.*Jn 18:37* The governor retorted asking what truth is and then went out to tell the Jews that he found no basis to charge Jesus.*Jn 18:38* The chief priests and elders made accusations that Jesus claimed to be king and opposed paying taxes.*Matt 27:12, Mk 15:1-2, Lk 23:1-2* Jesus did not respond, even when the amazed governor asked if he didn't hear the charges.*Matt 27:13-14, Mk 15:5* The governor told the chief priests and crowd that he found no basis for charges, but they insisted that he stirs up everyone with his teaching.*Lk 23:4-5* When the governor heard that Jesus was a Galilean, he sent him to Herod, whom the referral greatly pleased, because Herod expected to see signs of some sort from Jesus.*Lk 23:6-8* But Jesus said nothing to Herod's many questions, even with the chief priests and law teachers accusing Jesus vehemently.*Lk 23:9-10* So Herod and his soldiers ridiculed and mocked Jesus before sending him back to the governor in an elegant robe.*Lk 23:11-12* The governor repeated that neither he nor Herod had found any basis for a charge, and so the governor would punish and release him, but the crowd kept shouting to crucify Jesus, until the governor relented.*Lk 23:13-23* The governor typically released a prisoner to honor the crowd at the festival, so he asked the crowd whether he should release the notorious prisoner Barabbas, who had taken part in an uprising, or Jesus, whom the governor knew the chief priests and elders had handed over for their own interests.*Matt 27:15-18, Mk 15:6-10, Jn 18:39* The governor's wife sent him a message saying not to mistreat the innocent Jesus because she had suffered a great deal over a dream for him.*Matt 27:19-20* Yet the chief priests and elders had convinced the crowd to demand Barabbas's release instead and Jesus's crucifixion.*Matt 27:22-23, Mk 15:11-14, Jn 18:40* And so, the governor washed his hands of Jesus's innocent blood, leaving the crowd responsible.*Matt 27:23-24* The people agreed that Jesus's blood was on them and their children.*Matt 27:25* The governor had Jesus flogged and sent for crucifixion.*Matt 27:26, Mk 15:15, Jn 19:1* The soldiers led Jesus into the palace before the whole company.*Mk 15:16* The soldiers first stripped and robed Jesus, put a crown of thorns on his head and staff in his hand, and knelt before him to mock him as the Jews' king, also spitting on him and striking him with the staff before leading him away for crucifixion.*Matt 27:27-31, Mk 15:17-20, Jn 19:2-3* When Jesus came out wearing the crown of thorns and purple robe, the governor repeated to the Jews that he found no basis for a charge, but the chief priests and their officials shouted again to crucify him because he claimed to be God and their law said he must die, making the governor even more afraid.*Jn 19:4-8* The governor questioned Jesus again, but Jesus did not answer.*Jn 19:9-10* When the governor told Jesus that he had the power to crucify him, Jesus said that the governor's only power was what came from above and that the one who had handed him over to the governor was guilty of greater sin.*Jn 19:10-11* The governor kept trying to set Jesus free, but the Jewish leaders said that if the governor did so, then he would not be Caesar's friend because Jesus's claiming to be a king opposed Caesar.*Jn 19:12-13* The governor said that Jesus was their king, but the Jewish leaders said they have no king other than Caesar and to crucify Jesus, at which the governor finally handed Jesus over for crucifixion.*Jn 19:14-16*

Crucifixion. Jesus carried his own cross toward the place of crucifixion known as the Skull.*Jn 19:16-17* As the guards led Jesus to the place of crucifixion, they forced a man from the crowd to carry Jesus's cross.*Matt 27:32-33, Mk 15:21, Lk 23:26* The man was Simon from Cyrene, whose sons were Alexander and Rufus.*Mk 15:21* A large number of people followed them, including women who mourned and wailed for Jesus, to whom Jesus turned to say to weep for themselves and their children.*Lk 23:27-31* At the crucifixion place, they first offered Jesus wine mixed with gall and then, after he refused, they stripped and crucified him, casting lots for his clothes while watching him die on the cross under a sign saying that Jesus was the Jews' king.*Matt 27:34-37, Mk 15:23-26, Jn 19:19-24* The chief priests protested to the governor not to write that Jesus was their king but only that he claimed to be king, but the governor said that he had written what he had written.*Jn 19:21-22* The sign was in three languages so that many Jews read it as they passed by.*Jn 19:19-20* The guards crucified two rebels with Jesus, one on either side.*Matt 27:38, Mk 15:27, Lk 23:32-33, Jn 19:18* Jesus prayed to his Father to forgive them for not knowing what they were doing.*Lk 23:34* The rebels, passersby, and the chief priests, elders, and law teachers mocked and insulted Jesus for saying he was going to destroy and rebuild the temple when he, Israel's king and the Son of God, couldn't even save himself.*Matt 27:39-40, Mk 15:29-32* The people watched and rulers sneered, saying that if he was God's Messiah, the Chosen One, then he should save himself.*Lk 23:35* The soldiers also mocked Jesus, saying that if he was the Jews' king, as the sign above him said, then he should save himself.*Lk 23:36-38* When one of the crucified criminals hurled insults at Jesus to save himself and them, the other criminal rebuked him, saying to fear God for their just punishment because Jesus had done nothing wrong.*Lk 23:39-41* That criminal said to Jesus to remember him when coming into his kingdom, to which Jesus replied that the criminal would that day be with Jesus in paradise.*Lk 23:42-43* Jesus's mother, his mother's sister, and other women who cared for him stood near.*Jn 19:25* When Jesus saw his mother and the disciple John, he told his mother that John was her son and John that his mother was John's mother, following which John took Jesus's mother into his home.*Jn 19:26-27* Rulers indeed crucified the Lord of glory.*1Co 2:8* Men crucified Christ in weakness, but Christ lives by God's power.*2Co 13:4* Christ triumphed over evil powers and authorities by the cross.*Col 2:15* Christ endured the cross for the joy before him, scorning the cross's shame, to sit down at the right hand of God's throne.*Heb 12:2* Christ's purpose on the cross was to reconcile in him one new peaceful humanity out of the divided two sides, putting to death their hostility.*Eph 2:15-16* God reconciles to himself all things on earth and in heaven, by making peace through the Son's blood, shed on the cross.*Col 1:20* Our old self's crucifixion with Christ killed the sinful body, setting us free from sin and making us no longer slaves to sin.*Ro 6:6-7* We submit to crucifixion with Christ so that we no longer live on our own, but by our faith, Christ, who loved us and gave himself for us, lives in us.*Gal 2:20* The cross of our Lord Jesus Christ crucified the world to us and us to the world.*Gal 6:14*

Death. While Jesus was still alive on the cross, darkness fell for three hours, even though the time was from noon to three in the afternoon, because the sun stopped shining.*Matt 27:45, Mk 15:33, Lk 23:44-45* Then, Jesus cried out, asking why God had forsaken him.*Matt 27:46, Mk 15:34* Bystanders said he was calling Elijah.*Matt 27:47, Mk 15:35* Knowing that he had finished everything, Jesus said that he was thirsty.*Jn 19:28* One put vinegar in a sponge on a staff to offer to Jesus as drink.*Matt 27:48, Mk 15:36, Jn 19:29* That one said to leave Jesus alone to see if Elijah came to take him down.*Mk 15:36* The others said to leave him alone to see if Elijah came.*Matt 27:49* After Jesus received the drink, he said that he had finished, bowed his head, and gave up his spirit.*Jn 19:30* Jesus cried out, giving up his spirit and breathing his last.*Matt 27:50, Mk 15:37* Jesus called out that into his Father's hands he committed his spirit, breathing his last.*Lk 23:46* At that moment, the temple's curtain tore in two.*Matt 27:51, Mk 15:38, Lk 23:45* The earth shook, rocks split, tombs broke open, and many holy ones rose to life, who after Jesus's resurrection came out of the tombs into the holy city to appear to many people.*Matt 27:51-53* When the centurion and others with him guarding Jesus saw everything happen at the moment of Jesus's death, they exclaimed that surely Jesus was the Son of God.*Matt 27:54, Mk 15:39* The centurion said that surely Jesus was a righteous man.*Lk 23:47* When all the gathered people saw what happened, they beat their breasts and walked away.*Lk 23:48* Many women who had followed Jesus to care for him were present, watching from a distance.*Matt 27:55, Mk 15:40-41* All those who knew Jesus stood watching from a distance.*Lk 23:49* Not wanting bodies left on crosses during the Sabbath, the Jewish leaders asked the governor to order the legs broken and bodies taken down.*Jn 19:31* Soldiers broke the legs of the other two but not Jesus, who was already dead.*Jn 19:32-33* Instead, a soldier pierced Jesus's side with a spear, letting out a flow of blood and water, fulfilling scripture that no one would break his bones and that they would look on the one whom they pierced.*Jn 19:34, 36-37* The apostle Peter would later proclaim that the Jews killed Jesus by hanging him on a cross.*Acts 10:39*

Burial. Near evening, a rich disciple Joseph of Arimathea, a prominent Council member who was waiting for God's kingdom and had not consented to the Council's decision and action, went boldly to the governor asking for Jesus's body.*Matt 27:57, Mk 15:42-43, Lk 23:50-52, Jn 19:38* Joseph was a secret disciple out of fear of the Jewish leaders.*Jn 19:38* Because the governor was surprised to hear that Jesus had already died, he first confirmed with the centurion before granting Joseph's request for Jesus's body.*Mk 15:44-45* Nicodemus, the Sanhedrin member who had visited Jesus at night, accompanied Joseph to help retrieve, prepare, and entomb Jesus's body according to Jewish burial customs, bringing seventy-five pounds of myrhh and aloes with which to do so.*Jn 19:39-40* Joseph took Jesus's body, wrapped it in linen strips, and placed it in Joseph's new tomb cut out of the rock in a garden, rolling a big stone across the entrance.*Matt 27:58-60, Mk 15:45-46, Lk 23:53, Jn 19:41-42* Two of the women sat opposite the tomb, seeing where they laid Jesus.*Matt 27:61, Mk 15:47, Lk 23:55* Those women went home to prepare spices and perfumes but rested the next day on the Sabbath.*Lk 23:56* The next day, the chief priests and Pharisees went to the governor saying that Jesus had predicted his resurrection in three days and asking that the governor secure the tomb against the disciples stealing the body to perpetrate a resurrection hoax.*Matt 27:62-64* The governor ordered the tomb secured with a seal and guard.*Matt 27:65-66*

Resurrection. Jesus said repeatedly that although others would crucify him, he would then rise to life.*Matt 16:21, Matt 17:22-23, Matt 20:17-19* Two of the women went to the tomb after the Sabbath, where with a violent earthquake they saw the Lord's angel, his appearance like lightning and with clothes white as snow, descend from heaven, roll back the stone, and sit on it.*Matt 28:1-3* The guards shook with fear, becoming like dead men.*Matt 28:4* The angel told the women not to fear as they looked for the crucified Jesus because he had risen just as he said, and they should look where he once lay, before they ran to tell the disciples to meet Jesus in Galilee.*Matt 28:5-8* The women hurried away in joy and fear, but Jesus met and greeted them, and they clasped his feet in worship.*Matt 28:9* Jesus repeated the angel's instruction to tell his brothers to meet him in Galilee.*Matt 28:10* While the women ran to tell the disciples, some of the guards reported the tomb events to the chief priests who paid them a lot of money to say that the disciples had stolen the body while they slept, promising to keep them out of trouble with the governor.*Matt 28:11-15* The women told the eleven disciples, who did not believe them.*Lk 24:9-10* Peter, though, ran to the tomb where he saw the linen strips and wondered what had happened.*Lk 24:12* Three of the women who had cared for Jesus bought spices and went to the tomb to anoint Jesus's body, wondering who would roll the stone away.*Mk 16:1-3, Lk 24:1* But when they got to the tomb, they saw the stone rolled back.*Mk 16:4, Lk 24:2* When they entered the tomb, Jesus's body was not there.*Lk 24:3* Inside the tomb, they saw a young white-robed man who told them not to be afraid because Jesus the Nazarene had risen.*Mk 16:5-6* The white-robed man told them to go tell the disciples and Peter that Jesus was going ahead of them into Galilee where they would see him, just as he had told them.*Mk 16:7* The women saw two men in clothes gleaming like lightning.*Lk 24:4* The women bowed down, but the men asked why they looked for the living among the dead, when the Son of Man had risen just as he said, on the third day after crucifixion.*Lk 24:5-7* Trembling and bewildered, the women fled, saying nothing because they were afraid.*Mk 16:8* Mary Magdalene went to the tomb early, in darkness, and saw that the stone no longer covered the entrance.*Jn 20:1* She ran to tell Peter and the disciple John whom Jesus loved, telling them that someone had removed the Lord from the tomb to an unknown place.*Jn 20:2* Peter and John ran to the tomb, seeing the linen strips and cloth that had been around Jesus's head.*Jn 20:3-8* John saw and believed, but as they left the tomb, they still did not grasp from scriptures that Jesus must rise from the dead.*Jn 20:8-9* Mary Magdalene wept outside the tomb until she saw two angels in white, seated inside the tomb, asking her why she cried.*Jn 20:11-13* Mary told them that someone had taken the Lord away, but she then turned around and saw Jesus standing there, without realizing who it was.*Jn 20:13-14* Jesus asked her why she cried, and Mary, thinking he was the gardener, asked where he might have put Jesus's body.*Jn 20:15* Jesus then called her name, and she recognized him, crying out "Teacher."*Jn 20:16*

Appearance. After Jesus suffered, he presented himself to the disciples, giving many convincing proofs that he was alive, appearing to them over forty days while speaking about God's kingdom.*Acts 1:3* The same day as the women discovered the empty tomb, two disciples were walking to a village Emmaus about seven miles from Jerusalem, discussing everything that had happened, when Jesus came up and walked along with them, even though they didn't recognize him.*Lk 24:13-16* The disciples explained to Jesus what had happened including the empty tomb's discovery.*Lk 24:17-24* Calling them foolish and slow to believe, Jesus explained everything to them from the scriptures about himself.*Lk 24:25-27* As they approached the village, Jesus planned to continue on, but the two disciples urged him strongly to stay with them, which he did until he broke bread over a meal with them, they recognized him, and Jesus disappeared from sight.*Lk 24:28-31* The two disciples returned to Jerusalem to tell the eleven disciples that Christ had indeed risen.*Lk 24:33-35* While they were still talking, Jesus stood among them, saying peace to them.*Lk 24:36, Jn 20:19* The disciples were together behind locked doors.*Jn 20:19* Jesus told the startled and frightened disciples to look at his hands and feet, touch him, and confirm that he was no ghost.*Lk 24:37-40* Jesus showed them his hands and side, and they were overjoyed at seeing the Lord.*Jn 20:20* When they still didn't believe what they were seeing, Jesus asked for something to eat and took and ate the broiled fish that they gave him, reminding them that he had said that he must fulfill everything written about him.*Lk 24:41-44* Then he opened their minds so that they could understand scripture, explaining again how the Messiah would suffer and rise from the dead after three days, so that they could preach repentance for forgiveness of sins.*Lk 24:45-47* Jesus said that the disciples had witnessed these things.*Lk 24:48* Jesus repeated that peace be with them, adding that as the Father had sent him, so he sent them.*Jn 20:21* Jesus then breathed on them, telling them to receive the Holy Spirit.*Jn 20:22* Jesus added that they could now forgive or not forgive anyone's sins.*Jn 20:23* The disciple Thomas, who was not with the others, did not believe the others when they told him that they had seen the Lord, adding that he would not believe unless he put his fingers where the nails were and his hands in Jesus's pierced side.*Jn 20:24-25* A week later, Jesus appeared again to the disciples, again through locked doors, again wishing that peace be with them.*Jn 20:26* When Jesus told Thomas to put his fingers in Jesus's hands and Thomas's hand into Jesus's side, Thomas cried out "my Lord and my God," to which Jesus replied that Thomas had believed because he saw but blessed are those who believe without seeing.*Jn 20:27-29* Later, Jesus appeared to the disciples by the Sea of Galilee, after they had fished all night without catching anything.*Jn 21:1-3* Jesus stood on the shore telling them to throw their net on the boat's right side, which they did, catching so many fish that they couldn't haul in the net.*Jn 21:4-6* Only then did John realize who Jesus was, saying to Peter that the figure on the beach was the Lord, causing Peter to jump in the water to head for shore.*Jn 21:7* When the other disciples landed with the net full of fish, Jesus had a fire with fish and bread for them on the shore, inviting them to come and eat.*Jn 21:9-14*

Ascension. Jesus told Mary Magdalene at the tomb not to hold onto him because he had not yet ascended but to go tell the disciples that he was ascending to his Father and their Father, his God and their God, which Mary did, saying that she had seen the Lord.*Jn 20:17-18* Hearing the news, the disciples went to the mountain in Galilee where they saw and worshiped Jesus.*Matt 28:16-17* Jesus told them that God had given him all authority in heaven and on earth and that they should go making disciples of all nations, baptizing in the name of the Father, Son, and Holy Spirit, teaching obedience in all that Jesus said, as Jesus would be with them to the age's end.*Matt 28:18-20* Jesus led the eleven disciples out near Bethany, lifted his hands, blessed them, and went up into heaven, after which the disciples returned to Jerusalem with great joy, praising God continually at the temple.*Lk 24:50-53* After Jesus told the disciples that they would be his witnesses to the ends of the earth, the Father took Jesus up before their very eyes, hiding him in a cloud.*Acts 1:9* The disciples looked intently up in the sky until two men dressed in white suddenly stood beside them, asking why they looked up when Jesus who went to heaven would come back in the same way that they saw him leave.*Acts 1:10-11*

Witnesses. The apostle Peter said to the crowd at Pentecost that they were all witnesses to God raising Jesus to life.*Acts 2:32* Peter proclaimed that God raised Jesus from the dead on the third day, for God's chosen witnesses to see.*Acts 10:40-41* Christ indeed rose on the third day after burial, as the scriptures also say.*1Co 15:3* God raised our Lord Jesus from the dead.*Heb 13:20* The risen Christ appeared to Peter, then the twelve disciples, then more than five hundred brothers and sisters at the same time, most of whom were still living when authors wrote about it._{1Co 15:5-6} Christ next appeared to his brother James, then to the apostles, and last to the apostle Paul, as one abnormally born._{1Co 15:7-8} The Spirit of God raised Jesus from the dead._{Ro 8:11} God the Father raised Jesus Christ from the dead._{Gal 1:1} God raised Jesus from the dead._{Ro 4:22-24} God raised Jesus to life for our justification._{Ro 4:25} God resurrected Jesus from the dead as Christ our Lord._{Ro 1:4} God the Father of our Lord Jesus Christ gave us new birth through Jesus's resurrection from the dead._{1Pe 1:3} We hope in God for raising Christ from the dead._{1Pe 1:21} Jesus Christ's resurrection saves you because he is in heaven at God's right hand with angels._{1Pe 3:21-22} God exerted mighty strength when he raised Christ from the dead._{Eph 1:19-21} God raised Christ from the dead._{Col 2:12} Wait for God's Son Jesus, whom God raised from the dead._{1Th 1:10} Christ died and returned to life so that he might be the Lord of both the dead and the living._{Ro 14:9} By his power, God raised the Lord from the dead and will also raise us._{1Co 6:14} God has raised Christ from the dead as the first among those who have died._{1Co 15:20} We know that God who raised the Lord Jesus from the dead will also raise us with Jesus, presenting us to himself._{2Co 4:14} Jesus said that the disciples would receive the Holy Spirit's power to be Jesus's witnesses to the ends of the earth._{Acts 1:8} Peter said that the disciples should choose someone from among those who had lived with Jesus and them, to replace the betrayer Judas, to be a witness with them to Christ's resurrection, and so they prayed that the Lord, who knows everyone's heart, would choose the right candidate by lot._{Acts 1:21-22}

Eternal. Because God raised Christ from the dead, he cannot die again, and death no longer has mastery over him._{Ro 6:9} Our Savior Christ Jesus destroyed death and brought immortality._{2Ti 1:10} Those who die with Christ will also live with him._{2Ti 2:11} Those of the earth are as the earthly man was, but those of heaven are as the heavenly man is._{1Co 15:48} Thank God for victory through our Lord Jesus Christ._{1Co 15:57} The covenant under which God raised our Lord Jesus from the dead is eternal._{Heb 13:20} We receive the promised eternal inheritance, now that Christ has died as a ransom to set us free from the sins committed under the first covenant._{Heb 9:15} Christ's one sacrifice made perfect forever, you whom God is making holy._{Heb 10:14} Wait for the mercy of our Lord Jesus Christ to bring you to eternal life._{Jude 20-21} Our Lord Jesus Christ and God our Father gave us good hope of eternity._{2Th 2:16-17} Those who believe in Christ Jesus receive eternal life._{1Ti 1:16} The elect, obtaining salvation in Christ Jesus, receive eternal glory._{2Ti 2:10} Grace brings eternal life through Jesus Christ our Lord.*Ro 5:21* God's gift is eternal life in Christ Jesus our Lord.*Ro 6:21-22* The Son's throne, as God, will last forever.*Heb 1:8* The earth and heavens will perish, wearing out like garments, but the Lord will remain.*Heb 1:11* The Lord will roll up earth and heavens like a robe, changing them like a garment, but the Lord will remain the same, for never-ending years.*Heb 1:12* Jesus said that the Father's will is that everyone who looks to and believes in the Son gains eternal life, Jesus raising them up at the last day.*Jn 6:40* The one who believes has eternal life.*Jn 6:47* While those who ate God's manna died, anyone who eats the bread that comes down from heaven, Jesus's flesh, does not die but lives forever.*Jn 6:50-51* Whoever eats Jesus's flesh and drinks his blood has eternal life, Jesus raising them up at the last day, because his flesh and blood are real food and drink.*Jn 6:52-55* Eating his flesh and drinking his blood keeps one in Jesus, so that the one who feeds on Jesus lives because of him.*Jn 6:56-57* Whoever feeds on Jesus's bread lives forever.*Jn 6:58*

Savior. Adam, the first to sin, was a pattern of the one to come, the sinless Jesus.*Ro 5:14* Jesus came under the sign of water baptism and to give his blood—both water and blood—the Spirit confirming that truth as God's own testimony about his own Son.*1Jn 5:6-9* The Lord's angel told Joseph that Mary would give birth to a son whom Joseph was to name Jesus because he would save his people from their sins.*Matt 1:21* Because of the Samaritan woman's testimony, many people from her town believed, and when they convinced Jesus to stay with them, his words convinced many others to believe that Jesus was the world's Savior.*Jn 4:39-42* The high priest Caiaphas said that better one man Jesus die for the people than the whole nation perish, not realizing that he prophesied that Jesus would die to bring together the scattered children of God, making them one.*Jn 11:49-52* Jesus said to Peter that unless Jesus washed Peter, Peter had no part with Jesus.*Jn 13:6-10* Jesus said that the disciples knew the way to the place where Jesus was going and that he is the way, truth, and life, no one coming to the Father except through Jesus.*Jn 14:4-6* After the Son provided purification for sins, he sat down at the right hand of the Majesty in heaven.*Heb 1:3* When Christ as high priest offered for all time one sacrifice for sins, he sat down at God's right hand, waiting for his enemies to be his footstool.*Heb 10:12-13* Although Christ Jesus is in very nature God in human likeness, Christ did not use equality with God to his own advantage but instead made himself nothing in the very nature of a servant, humbly obedient even to death on a cross.*Php 2:6-8* You choose, but whoever believes in the Son of God accepts God's testimony, while whoever does not believe makes God out to be a liar.*1Jn 5:10* The testimony is that God gave us eternal life in his Son and only in his Son.*1Jn 5:11-13* Jesus said that the Son of Man has authority on earth to forgive sins.*Matt 9:6, Lk 5:24* As you approach the living stone Jesus, whom God chose as precious but humans rejected, God is building you like living stones into a spiritual house and ministry, offering sacrifices God accepts through Jesus.*1Pe 2:4-5* The Bible says that God laid his chosen and precious cornerstone Jesus in Israel so that those who trust in him will never find shame.*1Pe 2:6* We see Jesus, whom God lowered beneath angels for a little while before crowning him with glory and honor, dying by God's grace for everyone.*Heb 2:9* You have come to Jesus, the new covenant's mediator, under the sprinkled blood that speaks a better word than Abel's blood.*Heb 12:24*

Gifts. God the Father loves us, keeping us for Jesus Christ while blessing us with abundant mercy, peace, and love.*Jude 1-2* God hides in Christ all the treasures of wisdom and knowledge.*Col 2:3* Do not lose connection with the head, Christ, from whom the whole body grows as God causes it to grow.*Col 2:19* The promise of life is in Christ Jesus.*2Ti 1:1* Remember Jesus Christ, raised from the dead, descended from David.*2Ti 2:8* Remain in view of Christ's appearing.*2Ti 4:1* For anyone in Christ, the old creation is gone and the new creation here.*2Co 5:17* God reconciled us to himself through Christ, giving us the ministry of reconciliation.*2Co 5:18* God reconciled the world to himself in Christ, not counting people's sins against them, as he commits the reconciliation message to us.*2Co 5:19* Jesus keeps safe from the evil one those born of God who thus do not continue to sin.*1Jn 5:18* We receive grace, mercy and peace from God the Father and from Jesus Christ, in truth and love.*2Jn 3* In Christ and through faith in him we approach God with freedom and confidence.*Eph 3:12* We are Christ's ambassadors, God as if appealing through us, imploring on Christ's behalf to reconcile to God.*2Co 5:20* God made Christ who had no sin to be sin for us, so that in Christ we would show God's righteousness.*2Co 5:21* Through Jesus, continually offer God a sacrifice of praise, openly professing his name.*Heb 13:15*

Return. The Lord will indeed return.*2Pe 3:9* Christ will return in just a little while and will not delay.*Heb 10:37* When the Lord comes down from heaven, with a loud command, with the voice of the archangel and with the trumpet call of God, those who died in Christ will rise first.*1Th 4:16* Then, God will catch up in the clouds together with the rising dead, the living who remain, to meet the Lord in the air to be with him forever.$_{1Th\ 4:17}$ The Lord's return will not surprise believers, who know the truth.$_{1Th\ 5:4}$ God will reveal the Lord Jesus from heaven in blazing fire with his powerful angels.$_{2Th\ 1:7}$ We indeed look forward to the Lord's promised righteous new heaven and new earth after Christ's return.$_{2Pe\ 3:13}$ Christ's second appearance will not be to bear sin but to bring salvation to those awaiting him.$_{Heb\ 9:27-28}$ When he returns in his Father's glory with the holy angels, the Son of Man will be ashamed of anyone who shows shame for him and his words now, in an adulterous and sinful generation.$_{Mk\ 8:38}$ When Christ returns, dear children of God, we do not yet know what we will be, but we know we will be like him, seeing him as he is.$_{1Jn\ 3:2}$ We know that God who began a good work in us will continue until the day Christ Jesus returns.$_{Php\ 1:6}$ When Christ appears, you will appear with him in glory.$_{Col\ 3:4}$ Be blameless and holy in the presence of our God and Father when our Lord Jesus returns with all his holy ones.$_{1Th\ 3:13}$ The Lord Jesus in the splendor of his return will overthrow and destroy the lawless one.$_{2Th\ 2:7-8}$ Christ comes first, then when he comes, those who belong to him.$_{1Co\ 15:23}$

Spirit

The New Testament celebrates God's Holy Spirit as the intimate presence of God, leading his children to salvation and eternal life in the Son of God, Jesus Christ. While the Spirit is ours as God's guarantee of eternal life to come, the Spirit also brings us abundant present gifts in the loving, discerning, and sanctifying character of Christ. See how the New Testament articulates the Spirit's nature, presence, benefits, and role. Do you know the Spirit with the intimacy that he desires?

God. God poured his love into our hearts through the Holy Spirit, whom he gave to us.*Ro 5:5* If God's Spirit lives in you, then you pursue the Spirit rather than the flesh. If the Spirit of God who raised Jesus from the dead lives in you, then God who raised Christ from the dead will also give your body life because of his Spirit who lives in you.*Ro 8:11* Those whom the Spirit of God leads are the children of God.*Ro 8:14* The Spirit does not make you fearful slaves but makes you a child of God who can cry to your Father.*Ro 8:15* When you believed, God marked you in him with the seal of the promised Holy Spirit, who guarantees our inheritance until God redeems those whom he possesses.*Eph 1:13-14* God gives you his Holy Spirit with instruction.*1Th 4:8* God revealed to us by his Spirit things that he prepared for those who love him, that no eye had seen, ear heard, or mind conceived.*1Co 2:9-10* The Spirit searches everything, even God's deep things.*1Co 2:10* No one knows God's thoughts except God's Spirit, just as only one's own spirit knows one's own thoughts.*1Co 2:11* We received God's Spirit, not the world's spirit, so that we can understand what God freely gave us.*1Co 2:12* Do not grieve the Holy Spirit of God.*Eph 4:30* God makes us ministers of the Spirit's new covenant through which the Spirit gives life.*2Co 3:6* God gave us the Spirit as a deposit to guarantee life to come.*2Co 5:5* Jesus said that the Spirit gives life, while the flesh counts for nothing, and that his words were full of the Spirit and life.*Jn 6:63* God gives the Spirit without limit.*Jn 3:34*

Christ. Jesus's mother Mary was to marry Joseph, but before they came together, Mary was pregnant through the Holy Spirit.*Matt 1:18* The Lord's angel appeared to Joseph in a dream saying Mary had conceived from the Holy Spirit.*Matt 1:20* The one who sent John the Baptist to baptize with water had told John that the one on whom he saw the Spirit descend would baptize with the Holy Spirit.*Jn 1:33* At his baptism, Jesus was praying as heaven opened to the Spirit descending on him in bodily form like a dove.*Lk 3:21-22* When John baptized Jesus, Jesus went up out of the water, heaven opened, and God's Spirit descended and alighted on Jesus like a dove.*Matt 3:16, Mk 1:10* John testified that he saw the Spirit come down from heaven as a dove and remain on Jesus.*Jn 1:32* The Spirit led Jesus into the wilderness after his baptism for a time of the devil's tempting.*Matt 4:1* Jesus said that the thirsty should come to him to drink so that, believing in him, living waters would flow from within them, meaning the Spirit whom believers would soon receive when God glorified Jesus.*Jn 7:37-39* Jesus said that the Spirit of truth glorifies Jesus because the Spirit receives from Jesus what he reveals to you.*Jn 16:14* Jesus said so because all that belongs to the Father belongs to Jesus.*Jn 16:15* The apostle Peter said that God anointed Jesus with the Holy Spirit and power.*Acts 10:38* God has given us his Spirit, through whom we see and testify that the Father sent his Son as the world's Savior.*1Jn 4:13-14* Anyone without the Spirit of Christ does not belong to Christ.*Ro 8:9* If Christ is in you, then even though your body dies because of sin, the Spirit gives life because of righteousness.*Ro 8:10* If the Spirit of God who raised Jesus from the dead lives in you, then God who raised Christ from the dead will also give your body life because of his Spirit who lives in you.*Ro 8:11* The Spirit testifies with our spirit that we are God's children who, if we suffer with Christ, inherit Christ's glory with him.*Ro 8:16-17* God who searches our hearts knows the Spirit's mind as the Spirit intercedes for God's people in God's will.*Ro 8:27* Know the Spirit's gifts.*1Co 12:1* No one who speaks by God's Spirit can curse Jesus, just as no one claims Jesus as Lord other than by the Holy Spirit.*1Co 12:3* God saved us through rebirth's washing and renewal by the Holy Spirit, whom he poured out on us generously through Jesus Christ our Savior.*Tit 5:6* The Spirit vindicated Christ.*1Ti 3:16* The Lord is the Spirit, and with the Lord's Spirit comes freedom.*2Co 3:17* The Lord's glory comes from the Lord who is the Spirit.*2Co 3:18*

Coming. Jesus said that if you love him, keeping his commands, then he will ask the Father to give you the Spirit of truth as an advocate to help you forever.*Jn 14:15-16* Jesus said to the disciples that they knew the Spirit who lives with them and in them.*Jn 14:17* Jesus said that the Advocate, the Holy Spirit, whom the Father would send in his name, teaches us all things, reminding us of everything that Jesus said.*Jn 14:25-26* Jesus added that the Advocate, the Spirit of truth who goes out from the Father and whom he would send from the Father, testifies about Jesus.*Jn 15:26* Jesus said that he was going to the Father for the disciples' good because unless he went away, the Advocate would not come to them, but if Jesus went, then he would send the Advocate to them.*Jn 16:7* Jesus said that the Advocate would prove the world wrong about sin because people did not believe, about righteousness because Jesus was going to the Father, and about judgment because the world's prince now stood condemned.*Jn 16:8-11* To the disciples consternation and grief, Jesus told them that in a little while they would see him no more, because he was going to the Father, then after a little while they would see him again.*Jn 16:16-19* Jesus told the disciples that they would rejoice when he returned again, like a woman giving birth forgets her anguish out of joy for the child, and no one would take away the disciples' joy.*Jn 16:21-22* After his resurrection, Jesus told the eleven disciples that he was going send them what his Father had promised and to stay in Jerusalem until power clothed them from on high.*Lk 24:49* Jesus then breathed on the disciples, telling them to receive the Holy Spirit.*Jn 20:22* On one occasion after his resurrection, while he was eating with the disciples, Jesus told them to wait in Jerusalem for the gift that his Father promised about which Jesus spoke, when the Holy Spirit would baptize them.*Acts 1:4-5* Jesus added that the disciples would receive the Holy Spirit's power to be Jesus's witnesses to the ends of the earth.*Acts 1:8*

Pentecost. The disciples were all together in one place when Pentecost came after Jesus's ascension, when from heaven came a sound like a violent wind, filling the whole house where they sat.*Acts 2:1-2* What looked like tongues of fire separated, coming to rest on each of them, filling them with the Holy Spirit so that they began speaking in other languages as the Spirit enabled them.*Acts 2:3-4* A crowd came together in bewilderment, from among the God-fearing Jews who were then visiting Jerusalem from every nation, because each heard the disciples speaking their own language.*Acts 2:5-6* That Galilean disciples could declare God's wonders in so many languages utterly amazed them, making them wonder what the event meant, although some made fun that the disciples had drunk too much.*Acts 2:7-13* Peter stood up with the other disciples, though, explaining that they were not drunk, the time being nine in the morning, but were instead fulfilling Joel's prophecy that in the last days God would pour out his Spirit on all people to save everyone who calls on the Lord's name.*Acts 2:14-21* Peter explained that God accredited Jesus to them through miracles, wonders, and signs, but also handed Jesus over to them and wicked men to put Jesus to death on the cross, only to raise Jesus from the dead because death could not hold him, as David had prophesied.*Acts 2:22-31* Peter added that they were all witnesses to God raising Jesus to life so that, exalted to God's right hand, Jesus could receive the promised Holy Spirit from the Father to pour out what they now saw and heard.*Acts 2:32-33* When Peter said that God had made Jesus, whom they had crucified, both Lord and Messiah, his words cut them to the heart so that they asked what they could do, to which Peter replied that they should repent, get baptized in Jesus's name for forgiveness of sins, and receive the Holy Spirit.*Acts 2:36-38* Peter warned them with many other words, the disciples baptized those who accepted his words, and about three thousand became believers, with the Lord adding to their numbers daily those whom he saved.*Acts 2:39-41, 47*

Apostles. The Holy Spirit filled Peter when the religious leaders seized and jailed him for questioning, so that Peter proclaimed to them that they had crucified Jesus Christ whom God then raised from the dead as humankind's only salvation.*Acts 4:8-12* After the religious leaders jailed and released Peter and John, Peter and John went back to the believers to pray that the Lord enable his servants to speak with great boldness, after which the place shook and the Holy Spirit filled them.*Acts 4:22-31* Peter and the other apostles told the Sanhedrin that God gives the Holy Spirit to those who obey him.*Acts 5:32* God's power filled Stephen, who performed great signs and wonders, and against whom opposition could not stand as he spoke with the Spirit's wisdom.*Acts 6:8-10* After Philip proclaimed Jesus to Samaria and many believed and were baptized, Peter and John visited Samaria, praying that the believers would receive the Holy Spirit, which they did when Peter and John laid hands on them.*Acts 8:14-17* When a sorcerer Simon, whom the apostles had also baptized, offered money to be able to give the Holy Spirit by laying on his hands, Peter admonished him sharply to repent of his wickedness, Simon replying by asking for their prayers.*Acts 8:18-24* When Peter proclaimed the good news of peace through Jesus Christ to the devout centurion Cornelius and other Gentiles with him, the Holy Spirit came on all who heard Peter's message, astonishing the circumcised believers.*Acts 10:36-48* The Holy Spirit set apart Barnabas and Saul for further work before sending them on their way.*Acts 13:2-4* When Paul found some believers in Ephesus who hadn't heard of the Holy Spirit's baptism, Paul baptized them in Jesus's name, and when he placed his hands on them, the Holy Spirit came on them so that they spoke in tongues and prophesied.*Acts 19:1-7* The Spirit compelled Paul to go to Jerusalem, without Paul knowing what would happen there, except that the Holy Spirit warned Paul that he faced prison and hardships.*Acts 20:22* Through the Spirit some believers urged Paul not to go to Jerusalem, a prophet tying his own hands and feet with Paul's belt while telling him that the Holy Spirit said that the Jewish leaders in Jerusalem would bind Paul to hand him over to the Gentiles.*Acts 21:4*

Gifts. The same Spirit distributes different gifts.*1Co 12:4* God gives to each one the Spirit's manifestation for the common good.*1Co 12:7* To one God gives wisdom through the Spirit, to another knowledge by the same Spirit, to another faith by the same Spirit, to another gifts of healing by that one Spirit, to others miraculous powers, prophecy, distinguishing between spirits, speaking in different tongues, or interpretation of tongues.*1Co 12:8-10* The same Spirit distributes each gift to each one, just as he determines.*1Co 12:11* The Spirit helps us in our weakness, interceding for us with groans when we don't know for what we should pray.*Ro 8:26* The Spirit's fruit is love, joy, peace, patience, kindness, goodness, faithfulness, gentleness, and self-control, none of which law prohibits.*Gal 5:22-23* We live by the Spirit, keeping in step with the Spirit.*Gal 5:25* The Spirit does not leave us timid but gives us power, love, and self-discipline.*2Ti 1:7* The Holy Spirit lives in you, helping you hold to sound teaching.*2Ti 1:13-14* May you overflow with hope by the Holy Spirit's power.*Ro 15:13* Do not quench the Spirit.*1Th 5:19* Let the Spirit fill you so that you speak to one another with psalms, hymns, and songs from the Spirit.*Eph 5:18-19* We love in the Spirit.*Col 1:8* Everyone born of the Spirit is like the wind blowing wherever it pleases.*Jn 3:8*

Sanctification. The Spirit's sanctifying work saves believers.*2Th 2:13* The Holy Spirit sanctifies hearers of the proclaimed gospel.*Ro 15:16* The name of our Lord Jesus Christ and Spirit of our God washed, sanctified, and justified you.*1Co 6:11* Your body is a temple of the Holy Spirit, who is in you and whom you received from God.*1Co 6:19* The Spirit's ministry bringing righteousness is far more glorious than the ministry that brought condemnation.*2Co 3:8-9* The Holy Spirit says that if you hear his voice, then do not harden your hearts in rebellion.*Heb 3:7-8* The Holy Spirit testifies that God put his laws in our hearts and minds, and no longer remembers our sins and lawless acts.*Heb 10:16* True godliness springs from the great mystery that Christ received the Spirit's vindication and ascended in glory.*1Ti 3:16* Conduct yourselves appropriately in purity, understanding, patience, and kindness, in the Holy Spirit.*2Co 6:6-7* God's kingdom is not about eating and drinking but righteousness, peace, and joy in the Holy Spirit.*Ro 14:17* Blaspheming the Holy Spirit is an eternal sin.*Mk 3:29*

Wisdom. Jesus said that when the Spirit of truth comes, he will guide you into all truth, not speaking on his own but only what he hears and what is to come.*Jn 16:13* Jesus gave instructions to the disciples through the Holy Spirit.*Acts 1:2* When leading others to obey God, you act through the Spirit of God's power.*Ro 15:18-19* The message we speak is not human wisdom but as the Spirit taught us, explaining spiritual realities with Spirit-taught words.*1Co 2:13* The person without the Spirit rejects things from God's Spirit, considering them foolishness because one discerns them only through the Spirit.*1Co 2:14* The person with the Spirit judges all things with Christ's mind, while not subject to merely human judgments because no one knows the Lord's mind to instruct.*1Co 2:15-16* We pray for the wisdom and understanding that the Spirit gives.*Col 1:9* The Spirit clearly warns against abandoning the faith.*1Ti 4:1* We serve in the Spirit's new way rather than the written code's old way.*Ro 7:6* The Holy Spirit shares with us from heaven, matters into which even angels long to look.*1Pe 1:12* The gospel came not simply with words but also the Holy Spirit and deep conviction.*1Th 1:5* You are a letter from Christ, the result of another's ministry, written not with ink but with the Spirit of the living God, not on stone tablets but on tablets of human hearts.*2Co 3:3*

Word. Through the Word, God made all things, so that without the Word, God made nothing.*Jn 1:3* The Word became flesh, dwelling among us, so that we saw the glory of the one and only Son from the Father, full of grace and truth.*Jn 1:14* The one from heaven testifies truthfully to what he has seen and heard, for the one whom God sent speaks God's words, God giving the Spirit without limit.*Jn 3:32-34* God's word does not fail.*Ro 9:6* God's word brings to us mysteries God shared by revelation.*Eph 3:3* God's word lives actively, like a sharp blade penetrating to divide soul from spirit, joints from marrow, judging the heart's thoughts and attitudes.*Heb 4:12* The Father gave us spiritual birth through the word of truth.*Jas 1:17-18* Carry the Spirit's sword, which is the word of God.*Eph 6:17* Accept God's word from one another not as a human word but as it is, the word of God, which works in you who believe.*1Th 2:13* Receive anything consecrated by the word of God.*1Ti 4:5* God breathed all Scripture for teaching, rebuking, correcting, and training in righteousness.*2Ti 3:16-17* The law is still the very words of God.*Ro 2:2* Everything in the Scriptures is to teach us, so that we draw hope from the endurance the Scriptures depict and encouragement they provide.*Ro 15:4* As written, in faith's same spirit, we believe and so speak.*2Co 4:13* God's word did not originate with you, and you are not the only people it has reached.*1Co 14:36* The events of Jesus's betrayal and death must fulfill the scriptures, Jesus said.*Matt 26:52-54* Jesus repeated that the events of his arrest had happened to fulfill the prophets' writings.*Matt 26:56* Jesus also said that armies will surround Jerusalem when its dreadful desolation nears in the time of punishment that fulfills everything written.*Lk 21:20-22* The apostle Peter said that the apostles should attend to the ministry of God's word rather than wait on tables.*Acts 6:1-6* As the apostles worked, God's word continued to flourish and spread.*Acts 12:24* Paul said that the word of God's grace can build you up for an inheritance among all the sanctified.*Acts 20:32* The one seated on the throne told the apostle John that he is making everything new and to write down the words as trustworthy and true, for it is done.*Rev 21:5-6*

Written. Jesus said that while heaven and earth will pass away, his words will never pass away.*Matt 24:35, Mk 13:31, Lk 21:32-33* Jesus said that his words are full of the Spirit and life.*Jn 6:63* Jesus also said that the words he speaks are the Father doing his work in Jesus.*Jn 14:10* Jesus said that the words that the disciples heard were not his own words but instead the Father's words.*Jn 14:24* Jesus told the disciples that the time was coming when he would no longer use figurative speech but instead speak plainly so that the disciples would understand.*Jn 16:25* The disciples then said that Jesus was speaking clearly without figures of speech, so that they could now understand him, could see that he knew all things, did not need to ask him questions, and believed that he came from God.*Jn 16:29-30* Jesus prayed that he had given the disciples the words that the Father had given him, and that the disciples accepted.*Jn 17:8* The Jewish leaders study the scriptures diligently thinking that they have eternal life, when the scriptures tell about Jesus whose offer of life they refuse.*Jn 5:39-40* Jesus said that because he to whom the word of God came called them gods, and humans cannot set scripture aside, the one whom the Father set apart as his very own to send into the world must be God's Son.*Jn 10:34-36* Jesus also said that the religious leaders who questioned him were in error because they did not know the scriptures or power of God.*Matt 22:29* Jesus said that he would suffer betrayal and death just as written.*Matt 26:23-24, Lk 22:22* Jesus said that others would judge him among the transgressors, just as written, and as he must fulfill.*Lk 22:37* Jesus said that the religious leaders were trying to kill him because they had no room for his word.*Jn 8:37* Jesus said at his arrest that these events had happened to fulfill the prophets' writings.*Matt 26:56, Mk 14:49* On the road to Emmaus after his resurrection, Jesus explained everything to the two disciples from the scriptures about himself.*Lk 24:25-27* When Jesus first appeared to the eleven disciples after his resurrection, he reminded them that he had said that he must fulfill everything written about him.*Lk 24:41-44* Then he opened their minds so that they could understand scripture, explaining again how the Messiah would suffer and rise from the dead after three days, so that they could preach repentance for forgiveness of sins.*Lk 24:45-47* After Jesus's resurrection, the disciples remembered Jesus's words and believed those words and the scriptures.*Jn 2:22* In reading God's word, we gain insight into the mystery of Christ that God had disclosed to people in prior generations, as his Spirit revealed it through holy apostles and prophets.*Eph 3:4-5* Christ said that he had come to do God's will, just as the Scriptures wrote about him.*Heb 10:7* Faith comes from hearing the word about Christ.*Ro 10:17* The word about Christ reaches everyone to the ends of the world.*Ro 10:18* While someone might chain a gospel witness, no one chains God's word.*2Ti 2:9* The Holy Scriptures are the source for what makes us wise for salvation through faith in Christ Jesus.*2Ti 3:14-15* The Scriptures say that Christ died for our sins, just as the Scriptures said that after burial Christ would rise on the third day.*1Co 15:3* If you think the Spirit has gifted you, then acknowledge the Lord's command because if you ignore the command, then others will ignore you.*1Co 14:37-38* Everything written for you, you should be able to read and understand.*2Co 1:13* You are a letter from Christ, the result of another's ministry, written not with ink but with the Spirit of the living God, not on stone tablets but on tablets of human hearts.*2Co 3:3*

Truth. Jesus said that the reason that he was born and came into the world was to testify to the truth.*Jn 18:37* Jesus said that if he testified about himself, then that testimony would not be true, but instead another, John the Baptist, testifies about him truthfully, not as human testimony but for your salvation.*Jn 5:31-32* Jesus also said that his own works would testify that the Father had sent him.*Jn 5:36* Jesus said that his Father had also testified for Jesus, although the Jewish leaders had not seen or heard the

Father and did not have the Father's word in them because they did not believe._{Jn 5:37-38} Jesus said that the Advocate, the Spirit of truth who goes out from the Father and whom he would send from the Father, testifies about Jesus._{Jn 15:26} Jesus said to the disciples that they must also testify because they had been with him from the beginning._{Jn 15:27} When the Pharisees challenged Jesus for testifying as his own witness, Jesus replied that his testimony is true, that the Father also testifies for him, and that their own law holds that the testimony of two witnesses is true._{Jn 8:13-18} The disciple John saw the things that he wrote in his Gospel and testified that they are true, knowing that he tells the truth, so that you may believe._{Jn 19:35} John wrote his Gospel, recording only some of the many signs that Jesus performed, so that you would believe that Jesus is the Messiah, the Son of God, and that in believing you would have life in Jesus's name._{Jn 20:30} John testified to what his Gospel recorded that those things were true, adding that Jesus did many other things, too numerous to write down even if one had the whole world in which to store the books._{Jn 21:24-25} Luke wrote in his Gospel about all that Jesus did and taught until the Father took him up into heaven._{Acts 1:1-2} After Pentecost, God's word spread, the number of disciples increased, and many priests obeyed the faith._{Acts 6:7} Jesus came under the sign of water baptism and to give his blood—both water and blood—the Spirit confirming that truth as God's own testimony about his own Son._{1Jn 5:6-9} You choose, but whoever believes in the Son of God accepts God's testimony, while whoever does not believe makes God out to be a liar._{1Jn 5:10} The testimony is that God gave us eternal life in his Son and only in his Son._{1Jn 5:11-13}

Savior. God so loved the world that he gave his one and only Son that whoever believes in him does not perish but has eternal life._{Jn 3:16} Jesus, the Messiah and Son of God, brought the good news just as the prophet Isaiah foretold._{Mk 1:1} Jesus said that the disciples knew the way to the place where Jesus was going and that he is the way, truth, and life, no one coming to the Father except through Jesus._{Jn 14:4-6} After the king put John the Baptist in prison, Jesus went into Galilee proclaiming God's good news that God's kingdom had come near and to repent and believe that good news._{Mk 1:14-15} Jesus said that the Son of Man came to seek and save the lost._{Lk 19:10} The apostle Peter said that we find salvation in no one other than Jesus, whose name is the only one under heaven to save us._{Acts 4:12} God, our kind and loving Savior, mercifully appeared to save us._{Tit 3:3-5} God kept the gospel's mystery, the glorious riches of Christ in you, hidden for ages and generations before disclosing it to the Lord's people.*Col 1:26-27* The gospel is not of human origin but Christ's revelation.*Gal 1:11-12* God promised the gospel in the Holy Scriptures beforehand through his prophets.*Ro 1:2* The prophets learned that their prophesying was to serve us in receiving the gospel that the Holy Spirit shares with us from heaven, into which even angels long to look.*1Pe 1:12* Salvation is through our Lord Jesus Christ.*1Th 3:9* Do not sin, but if you do, then know that Jesus Christ, the Righteous One, is not only your advocate with the Father but also the atoning sacrifice for the whole world's sins.*1Jn 2:1-2* The living God is the Savior of all people, especially those who believe.*1Ti 4:10* God revealed the gospel so that all might obey through faith.*Ro 16:26* God favors us now and saves us now.*2Co 6:2* Jesus told John the Baptist that with Jesus's coming, the poor were hearing the good news.*Matt 11:4-5* Jesus said that persons will preach the kingdom's gospel throughout the world, to all nations, when all will then end.*Matt 24:14* Jesus has God's power to forgive, as he explained to the law teachers who objected to Jesus's forgiving the paralyzed man before Jesus healed him.*Mk 2:5-12, Lk 5:17-25*

Sacrifice. Christ died for us when we were powerless sinners, demonstrating his extraordinary love for us because no one dies for sinners, even if one might die for the good.*Ro 5:6-8* Christ justified us by his blood, saving us from God's wrath through him.*Ro 5:9* Jesus bore our sins on the cross, so that we who were going astray would die to sin, live for righteousness, and return to him, his wounds healing us.*1Pe 2:24-25* The death of God's Son reconciled us to God while we were still God's enemies, just as Christ now saves us through his life.*Ro 5:10* We boast in God through our Lord Jesus Christ, having this reconciliation.*Ro 5:11* Christ culminates the law so that everyone who believes has God's righteousness.*Ro 10:4* We have one mediator between God and us, the man Christ Jesus, who gave himself as ransom for all.*1Ti 2:5* Suffering is for the gospel, by the power of God.*2Ti 1:8* Christ Jesus destroyed death and brought life and immortality through the gospel.*2Ti 1:10* When people preach the gospel throughout the world, they will also tell about the woman who anointed Jesus with an expensive perfume to prepare him for burial.*Matt 26:12-13, Mk 14:3-9*

Salvation. God sent his Son into the world to save it through him, not to condemn it.*Jn 3:17* Belief in God's one and only Son overcomes condemnation, while non-belief confirms condemnation.*Jn 3:18* The Lord's angel told Joseph that Mary would give birth to a son whom

Joseph was to name Jesus because he would save his people from their sins.$_{Matt\ 1:21}$ When a wealthy chief tax collector climbed a tree to see Jesus, Jesus went to be his guest, and the tax collector called Jesus Lord, gave half his possessions to the poor, and gave back four times the amount of which he had cheated anyone, Jesus said that salvation had that day come to his house.$_{Lk\ 19:1-9}$ Jesus said that the Son of Man came to seek and save the lost.$_{Lk\ 19:10}$ Jesus also said that salvation is from the Jews.$_{Jn\ 3:22}$ For salvation, you need only declare that Jesus is Lord and believe that God raised him from the dead.$_{Ro\ 10:9}$ Your believing heart justifies you, while your professing mouth saves you, just as Scripture says.$_{Ro\ 10:10-11}$ The gospel has been growing and bearing fruit throughout the world and among you since you first learned it from faithful ministers of Christ.$_{Col\ 1:6-7}$ God our Savior wants all people saved and to know the truth.$_{1Ti\ 2:3-4}$ Rely on and fully accept that Christ Jesus came into the world to save sinners, of whom we may be the worst.$_{1Ti\ 1:15}$ Sinners break the law and are lawless, but the sinless Christ came to take away our sins in that anyone living in him stops sinning.$_{1Jn\ 3:4-6}$ In forgiving our sins, God canceled the indebtedness that stood against and condemned us.$_{Col\ 2:14}$ When we walk in the light the way Jesus is in the light, his blood purifies us from sin.$_{1Jn\ 1:7}$ Anyone who acknowledges Jesus as God's Son lives in God and God in them.$_{1Jn\ 4:15}$ Remember the gospel preached to you, which you received and on which you stand.$_{1Co\ 15:1}$ This gospel saved you, if you hold firmly to the preached word, but otherwise, you will have believed in vain.$_{1Co\ 15:2}$ Jesus winnows wheat from chaff, gathering wheat into the barn but throwing the chaff in the fire.$_{Matt\ 3:12}$ Jesus said how hard the rich find getting into heaven's kingdom, God's kingdom, like passing a camel through the eye of a needle.$_{Matt\ 19:22-24}$ When the astonished disciples asked how anyone could then gain salvation, Jesus said that salvation is impossible for man but that all things are possible for God.$_{Matt\ 19:25-26}$ Jesus said to stand firm in persecution for your salvation in the end.$_{Matt\ 24:9-13,\ Mk\ 13:13}$

Sharing. Jesus said that followers must first preach the gospel to all nations before the age's end.$_{Mk\ 13:10}$ Jesus told the violent, demon-possessed man out of whom he had cast a legion of demons to go home to his own people to tell them how much the Lord had done for him and how the Lord had mercy on him, which the man did, to his people's amazement.$_{Mk\ 5:18-20}$ Jesus said that while Israel proclaimed the law and prophets until John, since then people have preached the good news of God's kingdom, and people have been forcing their way into it.$_{Lk\ 16:16}$

We are servants of the gospel.*Col 1:23* Delight to share God's gospel.*1Th 2:7-8* Speak to non-believers so that they may be saved.*1Th 2:16* Be co-workers in God's service of spreading Christ's gospel.*1Th 3:2* We know that we live in him and he in us because he has given us his Spirit, through whom we see and testify that the Father sent his Son as the world's Savior.*1Jn 4:13-14* God calls and sets aparts leaders for his gospel.*Ro 1:1* Have no shame over the gospel because its power of God brings salvation to everyone who believes.*Ro 1:16* Fully proclaim Christ's gospel.*Ro 15:19* Make your ambition to preach Christ's gospel where not known, so that you do not build on someone else's foundation, and those whom no one told about Christ may see, hear, and understand.*Ro 15:20-21* The gospel is the message we proclaim about Jesus Christ, in keeping with the revelation of the mystery hidden for long ages past but revealed in the prophetic writings by the eternal God's command.*Ro 16:25-26* Pass on the most-important gospel message that you receive, that Christ died for our sins as the Scriptures say, but then, after burial, he rose on the third day as the Scriptures also said.*1Co 15:3* The priestly duty is to proclaim God's gospel so that non-believers may become offerings God accepts, sanctified by the Holy Spirit.*Ro 15:16* The apostle John warned that if anyone adds anything to his prophecy from the vision given to him on the island of Patmos, then God will add to them the plagues that John described, and if anyone takes away any of the prophecy's words, God will take from them any share in the tree of life and in the Holy City.*Rev 22:18-19*

Covenant. Hold unswervingly to the hope you profess, for God who promised is faithful.*Heb 10:23* Abraham received the blessing that God promised, God's oath confirming the promise while ending any argument.*Heb 6:13-16* God's oath confirmed to his heirs the unchanging nature of his promise's purpose.*Heb 6:17* God confirmed his unchangeable promise to greatly encourage us who hold to his hope.*Heb 6:18* You were once separate from Christ, excluded from holy citizenship and foreigners to the promise, without hope and without God in the world.*Eph 2:12* The eternal covenant was for God to raise our Lord Jesus from the dead.*Heb 13:20* God's revealed mystery is that through the gospel we are heirs together with his chosen people, members of one body, sharing the promise in Christ Jesus.*Eph 3:6* Christ became a servant of the Jews on behalf of God's truth, so that God could confirm the promises God made to the patriarchs.*Ro 15:8-9* Because of God's promises, we should revere God by keeping ourselves from anything contaminating body or spirit, perfecting holiness.*2Co 7:1* Be careful not to fall short of God's standing promise of entering his rest.*Heb 4:1*

Old. Christ said that God had not desired sacrifices and offerings, which did not please God, even though our ancestors offered according to the law.*Heb 10:8* When Christ said instead that he was here to do God's will, Christ set aside the first covenant to establish the second.*Heb 10:9* Jesus's ministry is superior to the former ministry just as the covenant he mediates is superior to the former covenant, because the new covenant has better promises.*Heb 8:6* If the first covenant had nothing wrong in it, then God would not have established another.*Heb 8:7* But finding fault with the people, God said that he would make a new covenant with the people.*Heb 8:8* The new covenant is not like the old covenant God made with the ancestors whom God led out of Egypt, but who did not remain faithful to the old covenant, so that God turned away from them.*Heb 8:9* God called the covenant new because he made the first covenant obsolete, while the obsolete and outdated will soon disappear.*Heb 8:13*

New. God's new covenant is to put his laws in our hearts and minds, to be our God and for us to be his people.*Heb 8:10* God forgives our wickedness and remembers our sins no more.*Heb 8:12* Jesus is the new covenant's mediator.*Heb 12:24* Jesus became the guarantor of a better covenant.*Heb 7:22* The Holy Spirit testifies that after Christ's sacrifice, God covenanted that he would put his laws in our hearts, writing them on our minds, and then would no longer remember our sins and lawless acts.*Heb 10:16* Christ mediates a new covenant, that those whom God calls may receive the promised eternal inheritance, now that Christ has died as a ransom to set us free from the sins committed under the first covenant.*Heb 9:15* The Son of God, Jesus Christ, preached among you, has always been yes rather than yes and no.*2Co 1:19* No matter how many promises God made, they are yes in Christ, so that we can say amen to God's glory.*2Co 1:20* God set his seal of ownership on us, putting his Spirit in our hearts as a deposit for what he guarantees will come.*2Co 1:22* No one can deny or add to God's promise, which not even the law that God gave hundreds of years later contradicts.*Gal 3:15-17* At Pentecost, Peter told the crowd that the promise of forgiveness in Jesus's name and of the Holy Spirit was for them, their children, and all who are far off, whom God will call.*Acts 2:39*

Benefits. When we are like Jesus, God makes love complete among us so that we may pass his judgment.*1Jn 4:17* Love drives out fear of God's punishment._1Jn 4:18_   You love and believe in Jesus without even seeing him, your faith rewarding you with salvation._1Pe 1:8-9_   You who once were far away have been brought near by the blood of Christ._Eph 2:13_   God brings us to fullness in Christ._Col 2:10_   The gospel reveal's God's righteousness, which we live out by faith._Ro 1:17_   The gospel declares that God judges people's secrets through Jesus Christ._Ro 2:16_   The gospel came not simply with words but also power, the Holy Spirit, and deep conviction._1Th 1:5_   The hope of salvation is our helmet._1Th 3:8_   Jesus gave himself for our sins to rescue us from how evil things are these days, just as God our Father asked of him._Gal 1:4_   When Jesus returns, God will punish with permanent destruction those who do not obey the Lord Jesus's gospel._2Th 1:8-10_   The gospel calls us to share in our Lord Jesus Christ's glory._2Th 2:14_   The gospel concerns the blessed God's glory._1Ti 1:11_

Creation

The New Testament shows God as the universe's creator. The New Testament reveals, though, that God first chose Christ and only then created everything in heaven and on earth. Indeed, God created through Christ and for Christ, also bringing Christ into the world. The New Testament confirms that we, too, are God's creation, in his image. Yet God's creation groans for its restoration, just as we groan, eagerly waiting God to restore. See how magnificently the New Testament treats God's creation. Do you esteem creation and Creator?

God. Through the Word, God made all things, so that without the Word, God made nothing.*Jn 1:3* The true light giving light to everyone was coming and then came, even though the world that he made and which was his own did not recognize or receive him.*Jn 1:9-11* God calls into being things that were not.*Ro 4:17* Everything God created is good, not to reject but to receive with thanksgiving.*1Ti 4:4* God finished his works when creating the world.*Heb 4:3* God rested from all his works on the seventh day of creation.*Heb 4:4* Creation eagerly waits for God to reveal his children.*Ro 8:19* God delays so he can liberate creation from its decay, bringing it into the freedom and glory of God's children.*Ro 8:21* Creation groans as in childbirth just as we who have the Spirit's first fruits groan as we wait eagerly for God to adopt us as his children and redeem our bodies.*Ro 8:22-23* God has the right to create both the special and common.*Ro 9:21* The Father prepared an inheritance for believers since creation of the world.*Matt 25:34* The Lord laid the earth's foundations, and the heavens are his hands' work.*Heb 1:10*

Christ. In prayer, Jesus revealed that Jesus had glory with the Father before the world began.*Jn 17:4-5* In prayer, Jesus also revealed that the Father loved Jesus before creating the world.*Jn 17:24* God chose Christ before creating the world and revealed him only recently for your sake.*1Pe 1:20* In the Son, God created everything in heaven and on earth, visible and invisible, rulers and authorities, through the Son and for him.*Col 1:16* The Son is before everything, holding everything together.*Col 1:17* The Son is the invisible God's image, the firstborn over all creation.*Col 1:15* The Son radiates God's glory, exactly representing his being, while sustaining all things by his powerful word.*Heb 1:3* Christ is the Deity's fullness living in bodily form.*Col 2:9* God's oath appointed the Son, whom God made perfect forever.*Heb 7:28* When God brought his firstborn Son into the world, he said that the angels would worship him.*Heb 1:6* The Son is the beginning and firstborn from among the dead, supreme in everything.*Col 1:18* As God's Son, Jesus is without father or mother or genealogy, without beginning or end.*Heb 7:1-17* God made Christ who had no sin to be sin for us.*2Co 5:21* God made the first man out of the earth's dust but makes the second man of heaven.*1Co 15:47* Jesus demonstrated his control over creation in many ways. In the first sign to reveal his glory, Jesus turned water into fine wine, at his mother's request, when the host had run out of wine at a wedding banquet.*Jn 2:1-11* After the disciples had fished all night without catching anything, Jesus told them to put out into deep water to let down their nets again, and they caught so many fish that their nets began to break and they filled two boats with fish.*Lk 5:4-7* Because they were all astonished at the event, Peter asked Jesus to leave him, a sinful man, but Jesus told him that he would fish for people.*Lk 5:8-10* Another time, when in a boat with his disciples, Jesus rebuked the wind and waves of a furious storm, making the sea completely calm, amazing and even terrifying the disciples that wind and waves obeyed him.*Matt 8:23-27, Mk 4:35-41, Lk 8:22-25* Jesus walked on water out to the disciples' boat a considerable distance out in the lake, after Jesus had dismissed the crowds, sent the disciples on ahead of him in the boat, and prayed up on a mountainside through the night.*Matt 14:22-25, Mk 6:45-51, Jn 6:16-20* Jesus's action terrified the disciples.*Matt 14:26, Mk 49-50, Jn 6:19-21* But after Peter also walked on water at Jesus's invitation, the disciples worshiped Jesus, saying that he was truly the Son of God.*Matt 14:32-33* The wind died down as soon as Jesus stepped into the boat.*Mk 6:51* The boat also immediately reached the shore where the disciples had headed, when the disciples had been rowing in a strong wind and rough seas for three to four miles.*Jn 6:21* Although many people saw the signs Jesus performed, and believed accordingly, Jesus did not entrust himself to them because he knew what was in each person.*Jn 2:23-25* Jesus told the Jews that he did one miracle, and they were all amazed.*Jn 7:21*

Light. Jesus said that he is the light of the world while in the world.$_{Jn\ 9:5}$ Life was in the Word God, and that life was the light of all humankind.$_{Jn\ 1:4}$ Jesus said that he is the life, whoever believed in him would live even though they die, and whoever lived by believing in him would not die.$_{Jn\ 11:25}$ God sent John the Baptist as a witness to the light, not as the light but as a witness to it, so that all might believe.$_{Jn\ 1:6-8}$ The true light giving light to everyone was coming and then came, even though the world that he made and which was his own did not recognize or receive him.$_{Jn\ 1:9-11}$ Whoever lives by the truth comes into the light so that others may see plainly that they acted in God's sight.$_{Jn\ 3:21}$ Jesus said that God's true bread comes down from heaven, giving life.$_{Jn\ 6:32-33}$ Jesus added that he is the bread of life, so that anyone who comes to him does not hunger or thirst.$_{Jn\ 6:34}$ Jesus repeated that he is the bread of life.$_{Jn\ 6:48}$ Jesus also said that because he lives, we also will live, Jesus in his Father, we in Jesus, and Jesus in us.$_{Jn\ 14:19-20}$ Jesus also said that the Spirit gives life, while the flesh counts for nothing.$_{Jn\ 6:63}$ Jesus said that while day is here, we must do God's works.$_{Jn\ 9:4}$ Jesus said that people should believe in the light while they have the light, so that they may become children of light.$_{Jn\ 12:36}$ God is the blessed, honored, mighty, eternal, and only Ruler, the King of kings and Lord of lords, who alone is immortal, living in unapproachable light, whom no one has seen or can see.$_{1Ti\ 6:15-16}$ Witnesses who heard, saw, and touched God's Son, who existed from the start and is the eternal Word of Life, joyfully proclaim their experience so that we can share with them the Father and his Son Jesus Christ.$_{1Jn\ 1:1-4}$ The message that they share is that God is pure light without any darkness.$_{1Jn\ 1:5}$ Christ Jesus brought life and immortality to light.$_{2Ti\ 1:10}$ Everything light exposes becomes visible, and everything illuminated becomes a light.$_{Eph\ 5:13}$

Darkness. Jesus said that he had come into the world as a light so that no one believing in him would remain in darkness.$_{Jn\ 12:46}$ The light shines in darkness, which cannot overcome the light.$_{Jn\ 1:5}$ The verdict is that although light came into the world, people loved darkness instead of loving light because they did evil.$_{Jn\ 3:19}$ Everyone who does evil hates the light for fear that light will expose their evil deeds.$_{Jn\ 3:20}$ When darkness comes, no one can do God's works.$_{Jn\ 9:4}$ As the prophet Isaiah foretold, people living in the dark land of death's shadow, by the Sea of Galilee, saw a great light dawn.$_{Matt\ 4:13-16}$ Jesus said that whoever follows him never walks in darkness.$_{Jn\ 8:12}$ Jesus repeated that whoever walks in the daytime does not stumble, but whoever walks at night stumbles for having no light.*Jn 11:9-10* When Jesus predicted his death by crucifixion, and the crowd asked why the Son of Man and Messiah must die when the Messiah should live forever, Jesus replied that they would have the light just a little longer before darkness overtook them.*Jn 12:34-35* Jesus continued that those who walk in the dark don't know where they are going.*Jn 12:35* The message is both an old one from the beginning and a new one, with darkness passing, that we see and shine truth in Jesus Christ, the true light who already shines.*1Jn 2:7-8* Light and darkness have nothing in common.*2Co 6:14* Jesus said that everything concealed comes to light, while everything hidden becomes known, like a lamp intended for a stand rather than hidden under a bowl.*Matt 10:26, Mk 4:21-22, Lk 8:16-17, Lk 11:33* Everything comes to light, whether said in the dark or whispered in inner rooms.*Lk 12:2-3*

People. The Father made us his creation's first fruits.*Jas 1:18* Even though we praise our Lord and Father, we somehow turn right around and immediately curse others whom God made in his likeness.*Jas 3:9-12* Don't you, a mere person, talk back to your creator God who, though all-powerful, still leaves you to your own will.*Ro 9:19-20* You have put on the new self that God renews in knowledge in his image as Creator.*Col 3:10* Since the world's creation, we have seen and understood God's invisible qualities including his eternal power and divine nature from what he made, so that people are without excuse.*Ro 1:20* God, to whom we must give account, sees everything in all creation, uncovered and laid bare before him.*Heb 4:13* Jesus once called believers people of the light.*Lk 16:8* Jesus said that your eye is your body's lamp, so that if your eye is healthy, your body fills with light, but when your eye is unhealthy, your body fills with darkness.*Lk 11:34* Jesus said to see that your body is full of light, not darkness, just as if a lamp were shining on you.*Lk 11:35-36* Jesus said that the time had come when the dead would hear the Son of God's voice and would live because the Father has life in himself and had also granted the Son life in himself.*Jn 5:25-26* God chose you out of nowhere to be royal and holy, his special possession, calling you out of darkness into his wonderful light.*1Pe 2:9-10* When God said to let light shine out of darkness, he shined his light into our hearts, lighting our knowledge of God's glory in Christ's face.*2Co 4:6* The book of life has the names of those who contend in the gospel's cause.*Php 4:3* You who were once darkness are now light in the Lord and so should live as children of light in all goodness, righteousness, and truth, pleasing the Lord.*Eph 5:8-10* Shine in a corrupt world like stars in the sky as you hold firmly to the word of life.*Php 2:15-16* You who claim light remain in darkness if you hate a fellow follower, and will stumble around in your darkness, while you who love followers are in the light and will not stumble.*1Jn 2:9-11* Wake up, rising from the dead so that Christ shines on you.*Eph 5:14* Christ is your life with whom you will appear in glory.*Col 3:4* The night is nearly over and day almost here, so time to put aside dark deeds to put on light's armor.*Ro 13:12* We are all children of the light and children of the day, not belonging to the night or darkness.*1Th 5:5* We belong to the day.*1Th 3:8* Give joyful thanks to the Father, who has qualified you to share with his holy people in the kingdom of light.*Col 1:12* Jesus calls you the light of the world, not to hide but to shine before others who may see your good deeds and glorify your Father in heaven.*Matt 5:14-16*

Genealogy. As to his earthly life, God's Son Jesus descended from David.*Ro 1:3* The genealogy of Jesus the Messiah, the son of David, the son of Abraham, is fourteen generations from Abraham to David, fourteen from David to the exile to Babylon, and fourteen from the exile to the Messiah.*Matt 1:1-17* Scripture traces Jesus's genealogy back, generation by generation, from Joseph, whose son people thought Jesus was, through Levi, Simeon, Judah, and Joseph, through David, Jesse, Obed, and Boaz, through Perez, Judah, Jacob, Isaac, and Abraham, and through Enosh, Seth, and Adam, to God.*Lk 3:23-38* Jesus the Messiah's mother Mary was to marry Joseph, but before they came together, Mary was pregnant through the Holy Spirit.*Matt 1:18* The Lord's angel appeared to Joseph in a dream saying not to be afraid to take Mary as his wife because she had conceived from the Holy Spirit.*Matt 1:20* The Lord's angel told Joseph that Mary would give birth to a son whom Joseph was to name Jesus because he would save his people from their sins.*Matt 1:21* Caesar issued a decree for a census of the entire Roman world, requiring that everyone return to their hometown.*Lk 2:1-3* Joseph took Mary, who was pregnant, from Nazareth in Galilee to Bethlehem in Judea because Joseph came from David's line.*Lk 2:4-5*

Incarnation. Mary gave birth to her firstborn son in Bethlehem, wrapping him in cloths and putting him in a manger because no guest rooms were available for them.*Lk 2:6-7* The Lord's angel appeared in the night to shepherds who were watching flocks nearby, terrifying them with the Lord's glory shining around them.*Lk 2:8-9* The angel told the shepherds not to be afraid because he brought them good news of great joy for all the people that a Savior, the Messiah, the Lord had been born in Bethlehem, where they would find him wrapped in cloths in a manger.*Lk 2:10-12* A great company of the heavenly host suddenly appeared with the angel, praising God with glory in the highest heaven and peace on earth to those on whom his favor rests.*Lk 2:13-14* When the angel had returned to heaven, the shepherds hurried off for Bethlehem where they found Mary and Joseph with the baby in the manger.*Lk 2:15-16* They then spread their amazing word, glorifying God that they had seen just what the angel had told them, while Mary treasured and pondered everything in her heart.*Lk 2:17-20* When during Jesus's ministry a woman said that God should bless the mother who gave Jesus birth and nursed him, Jesus said that God instead blesses those who hear and obey God's word.*Lk 11:27-28*

Presentation. On the eighth day, the time of circumcision, Mary and Joseph named the baby Jesus, just as the angel had said before Mary conceived.*Lk 2:21* Joseph and Mary then took Jesus to Jerusalem to present him to the Lord at the temple for purification rites and to offer a sacrifice, as the Lord's law required for firstborn males.*Lk 2:22-24* A devout and righteous man Simeon was waiting in Jerusalem for Israel's consolation, with the Holy Spirit on him, the Spirit having shown him that he would not die before seeing the Lord's Messiah.*Lk 2:25-26* The Spirit moved Simeon to enter the temple courts just as Mary and Joseph brought Jesus in for the rites that the law required.*Lk 2:27* Simeon took Jesus in his arms and praised God, saying that he could now die in peace, having seen the Sovereign Lord's salvation prepared before all nations as a light for Gentiles and Israel's glory.*Lk 2:28-32* As Mary and Joseph marveled at Simeon's words, Simeon blessed them, while saying to Mary that the child would cause many to rise and fall, a sign spoken against, revealing many hearts' thoughts, and piercing Mary's own soul.*Lk 2:33-35* An old prophetess Anna was also there, widowed for most of her eighty-four years, dedicated to worshiping, fasting, and praying night and day at the temple.*Lk 2:36-37* She approached Mary and Joseph at that very moment, thanking God while speaking about the child Jesus to all who awaited Jerusalem's redemption.*Lk 2:38*

Announcement. Magi from the east came to Jerusalem asking to see and worship the star-announced one born king of the Jews.*Matt 2:1-2* The Messiah's announcement disturbed King Herod and all Jerusalem.*Matt 2:3* All the chief priests and law teachers said that the Messiah would be born in Bethlehem.*Matt 2:4-6* The star led the Magi to the place where the Messiah was born.*Matt 2:9-10* When the Magi saw the newborn Messiah with his mother Mary, they bowed down and worshiped him, giving him treasures of gold, frankincense, and myrrh.*Matt 2:11* Jesus's birth fulfilled what the Lord said through the prophet that the virgin would conceive, giving birth to a son called Immanuel, meaning God with us.*Matt 1:22-23* Joseph took Mary and the child to Egypt after the Lord's angel told him in a dream that king Herod would try to kill the child, where they stayed until Herod's death, fulfilling the prophecy that the Lord would call his Son out of Egypt.*Matt 2:13-15,19-21* Herod did kill all young boys in Bethlehem's vicinity, fulfilling the prophecy that the vicinity's mothers would weep over their lost sons.*Matt 2:16:18* Joseph took Mary and Jesus to Nazareth to avoid Herod's reigning son, fulfilling the prophecy that the Messiah would be a Nazarene.*Matt 2:22-23*

Maturation. After Joseph and Mary had done everything that the Lord's law required of them in Jerusalem, they returned to Nazareth in Galilee where the child Jesus grew strong.*Lk 2:39-40* God's wisdom filled him, and God's grace was on him.*Lk 2:40* Every year, though, Joseph and Mary returned to Jerusalem for the Passover festival.*Lk 2:41* When Jesus was twelve years old, he stayed behind in Jerusalem as his parents were returning home, thinking that Jesus was with them.*Lk 2:42-44* When they noticed him missing and could not find him among their relatives and friends, Joseph and Mary returned to Jerusalem where they searched three days for Jesus, until they found him sitting listening to the teachers in the temple courts and asking them questions.*Lk 2:45-46* Jesus's understanding and answers amazed everyone.*Lk 2:47* His parents were astonished, Mary asking Jesus why he had left them anxiously searching for him.*Lk 2:48* Jesus asked why they had searched for him when they should have known that he had to be in his Father's house, although they did not understand.*Lk 2:49* Jesus then returned with them to Nazareth where he obeyed his parents while growing in wisdom, stature, and favor with God and men, as Mary treasured all these things in her heart.*Lk 2:51-52* Jesus was about thirty years old when he began his ministry.*Lk 3:23*

Divine. As God's Son, Jesus is without father or mother or genealogy, without beginning or end.*Heb 7:1-17* God named Jesus Son and said he was his Father.*Heb 1:5* When God brought his firstborn Son into the world, he said that the angels would worship him.*Heb 1:6* The Son is the beginning and firstborn from among the dead, supreme in everything.*Col 1:18* Christ, as God's Son, is far superior to the angels.*Heb 1:4-5* Jesus is the Son of God.*Heb 4:14* God appointed Jesus the Son of God through the Spirit of holiness.*Ro 1:4* At Jesus's baptism, God the Father said, with the same voice from heaven that disciples heard on the sacred mountain, that Jesus is his Son whom he loves and with whom he is well pleased.*2Pe 1:17-18* God, our kind and loving Savior, mercifully appeared to save us.*Tit 3:3-5* The Son is the invisible God's image, the firstborn over all creation.*Col 1:15* The Son radiates God's glory, exactly representing his being, while sustaining all things by his powerful word.*Heb 1:3* Christ is the Deity's fullness living in bodily form.*Col 2:9* God loves having all his fullness dwell in the Son.*Col 1:19* The Son of God came as the true God and eternal life that we may know him and be in him who is true.*1Jn 5:20*

Baptism. A righteous priest Zechariah and his righteous wife Elizabeth observed all the Lord's commands blamelessly but were childless and old.*Lk 1:5-7* The priesthood chose Zechariah by lot to go into the Lord's temple to burn incense with all the assembled worshipers praying outside.*Lk 1:8-10* The Lord's angel, standing at the altar's side, startled Zechariah, whom fear gripped.*Lk 1:11-12* The angel told him not to be afraid but, in answer to his prayers, to expect his wife Elizabeth to bear him a son whom they should name John.*Lk 1:13* John would delight them and many others because he would be great in the Lord's sight, never drinking wine but with the Holy Spirit filling him from before his birth.*Lk 1:14-15* John would restore many Israelites to the Lord and, in Elijah's spirit and power, turn parents' hearts to their children and the disobedient to the righteous's wisdom, while preparing the Lord's way.*Lk 1:16-17* When Zechariah asked how he could be so sure, the angel Gabriel said that God had sent him with this good news but that John would be mute until John's birth because he had not believed.*Lk 1:18-20* The people realized from Zechariah's muteness that he had indeed seen a vision.*Lk 1:21* Elizabeth conceived just as foretold.*Lk 1:23-25* Mary, Jesus's mother, visited Elizabeth, in whose womb John lept when he heard Mary's voice.*Lk 1:39-41* Filled with the Holy Spirit, Elizabeth blessed the mother of her coming Lord.*Lk 1:41-45* Mary in turn blessed the Lord in song for his mercy, deeds, and love, and care for Israel.*Lk 1:46-55*

Baptist. God sent John the Baptist as a witness to the light, not as the light but as a witness to it, so that all might believe.*Jn 1:6-8* When Elizabeth bore John, and they were going to name the child after his father Zechariah, Elizabeth told them instead that he would be John.*Lk 1:57-60* Zechariah, still mute, confirmed on a tablet that the child would be John, at which Zechariah could speak again, praising God.*Lk 1:61-64* The Holy Spirit filled Zechariah who prophesied that John would be a prophet of the Most High, going before the Lord to prepare his way, for the Lord to bring salvation.*Lk 1:67-79* The event filled the neighbors with awe, and news of John spread, the people wondering what he would be because the Lord's hand was with him.*Lk 1:65-66* John grew strong in spirit, living in the wilderness until his public appearance.*Lk 1:80* John ate no bread and drank no wine, but people still said that he had a demon.*Lk 7:33* John the Baptist was indeed the messenger calling in the wilderness to prepare straight paths for the coming Lord, as the prophet Isaiah foretold.*Mk 1:2* John preached repentance of sins for the coming kingdom of heaven, as the prophet Isaiah foretold.*Matt 3:1-3, Mk 1:3* John, who wore camel-hair clothing with a leather belt and ate locusts and honey, said that one more powerful than he would come, whose sandals he was not worthy to untie.*Mk 1:6-7* John cried out that Jesus was the one who, though coming after him, would surpass him because he was before him.*Jn 1:15* John confessed freely that he was not the Messiah, Elijah, or the prophet but was instead the voice calling out in the wilderness to make a straight way for the Lord.*Jn 1:19-23* Jesus said about John that no one naturally born, outside heaven's kingdom, is greater than John but that the least in the kingdom is greater than John.*Matt 11:11, Lk 7:28* Jesus told the crowds who had seen John the Baptist that they had not gone into the wilderness to see John dressed in fine clothes but instead to hear a prophet and God's messenger to prepare the way for God's Son Jesus.*Matt 11:7-10, Lk 7:24-27* Jesus said that if he testified about himself, then that testimony would not be true, but instead John the Baptist testified about him truthfully, not as human testimony but for your salvation.*Jn 5:31-32* John was a lamp whose light people enjoyed for a time.*Jn 5:35* Jesus said that the chief priests and elders, although they heard John, refused to repent and believe him.*Matt 21:32* Jesus also said that the law and prophets prophesied until John, and called John the Elijah whom scripture said would come.*Matt 11:14*

Baptizing. God's word came to John the Baptist in the wilderness to go into all the country around the Jordan River, preaching a baptism of repentance for forgiveness of sins.*Lk 3:1-3* John was, as the prophet Isaiah had written, the voice of one calling in the wilderness to make straight paths for the Lord and to see God's salvation.*Lk 3:4-6* John baptized in the wilderness's Jordan River, all those who came confessing their sins.*Matt 3:4-6* All the Judeans in the countryside and all Jerusalem went out to John to confess their sins and for baptism in the Jordan River.*Mk 1:5* John told the crowds who came for baptism that they were broods of vipers fleeing from the coming wrath.*Lk 3:7* He urged them to produce repentance's fruit rather than rely on their heritage as Abraham's children because the ax was ready to cut down every tree that did not produce good fruit.*Lk 3:8-9* When the crowd asked what they should do, John told them to share food and clothing with those who had none, that tax collectors should collect no more than required, and that soldiers should not extort and falsely accuse but instead be content with their pay.*Lk 3:10-14* While John baptized the confessing, John condemned the religious officials who traced their ancestry from Abraham rather than relying on repentance.*Matt 3:7-8* John said that God could raise children for Abraham out of stones.*Matt 3:9* John also warned that God's ax was at the tree root, ready to cut down and throw in the fire ones not producing repentance's fruit.*Matt 3:10* John baptized with water representing repentance, but the more-powerful Jesus, whose sandals John was not worthy to carry, baptizes with the Holy Spirit and fire.*Matt 3:11, Lk 3:16* John said that while he baptized with water, the one to come would baptize with the Holy Spirit.*Mk 1:8* After his resurrection, Jesus told the disciples to wait in Jerusalem, not for John's baptism but for the Holy Spirit's baptism.*Acts 1:4-5* John told the Pharisees who questioned him that he baptized only with water, while he was unworthy to untie the straps of the sandals of the one standing among them whom they did not know.*Jn 1:24-28* John used many other words to exhort the people and proclaim the good news to them.*Lk 3:18* The chief priests and elders much later asked Jesus when he taught in the temple courts who gave him such authority.*Matt 21:23, Mk 11:27-28, Lk 20:1-2* Jesus replied that he would tell them only if they told him the source of John's baptism, whether heaven or human.*Matt 21:24-25, Mk 11:29-30, Lk 20:3-4* They refused to answer Jesus, and so Jesus refused to answer them.*Matt 21:25-27, Mk 11:31-33, Lk 20:5-8*

Christ. Jesus came from Nazareth in Galilee to the Jordan River for John's baptism.*Matt 3:13, Mk 1:9* When John saw Jesus coming, John said to look at the Lamb of God who takes away the world's sin and who, though coming after John, came before John and surpasses John, as John's baptizing came to reveal.*Jn 1:29-31* John at first told Jesus that John needed Jesus's baptism, but Jesus corrected John that John should baptize Jesus to fulfill all righteousness.*Matt 3:14-15* And so John baptized Jesus as he had baptized all the people who came to him.*Lk 3:21* Jesus was praying as heaven opened to the Spirit descending on him in bodily form like a dove.*Lk 3:21-22* When John baptized Jesus, Jesus went up out of the water, heaven opened, and God's Spirit descended and alighted on Jesus like a dove.*Matt 3:16, Mk 1:10* John testified that he saw the Spirit come down from heaven as a dove and remain on Jesus.*Jn 1:32* The one who sent John to baptize with water had told John that the one on whom he saw the Spirit descend would baptize with the Holy Spirit, and so John testified that Jesus was God's Chosen One.*Jn 1:33-34* God's voice then said from heaven that Jesus was his Son whom he loved and who had pleased him.*Matt 3:17, Mk 1:11, Lk 3:22* At once, the Spirit sent Jesus into the wilderness for forty days for Satan's tempting.*Mk 1:12-13* At Jesus's baptism, God the Father gave Jesus glory from heaven.*2Pe 1:17* The next day when he saw Jesus passing by, John said to look at God's Lamb.*Jn 1:35* When later in prison John heard about the Messiah's actions, John sent his disciples to ask Jesus if Jesus was the one to come.*Matt 11:2-3, Lk 7:18-20* Jesus replied that the blind were seeing, lame walking, lepers cleansed, deaf hearing, and dead raised, while the poor heard the good news.*Matt 11:4-5, Lk 7:21-22* Some people thought that Jesus was John the Baptist or possibly Elijah or another of the prophets, but Peter said that Jesus was the Messiah.*Mk 7:27-30* Much later, after John's baptism, Jesus said that he still had a baptism to undergo and was under great constraint until that baptism was done.*Lk 12:50* When late in his ministry, Jesus returned to where John had baptized, many people came to him saying that although John had never performed a sign, everything that John said about Jesus was true, and many believed.*Jn 10:40-42*

Effect. All the people whom John baptized agreed with Jesus that God's way was right, even though the Pharisees and law experts rejected God's purpose for them because John had not baptized them.*Lk 7:29-30* When Jesus's disciples also began to baptize, John repeated that he was not the Messiah but just sent ahead of him, that his joy was now complete, and that Jesus must become greater and John less.*Jn 3:22-30* All those baptized into Christ Jesus were buried with him through baptism into death so that just as the glory of the Father raised Christ from the dead, we also live a new life.*Ro 6:3-4* Baptism buried us with Christ while raising us with him through our faith in God's working.*Col 2:12* All who receive baptism into Christ are clothed with Christ.*Gal 3:27* Baptism in water symbolizes not removing dirt from the body but cleansing one's conscience toward God.*1Pe 3:21* Do not quarrel among you by claiming to follow different teachers whom no one crucified and in whose name no one baptized you, when Christ himself is not so divided.*1Co 1:11-15* You have only one Lord, one faith, and one baptism.*Eph 4:5* One Spirit baptized all, whether insider or outsider, slave or free, to form one body, giving each the same Spirit to drink.*1Co 12:13* Our ancestors were all under the cloud and passed through the sea, baptized into Moses in the cloud and in the sea.*1Co 10:1-2* Without resurrection, baptism means nothing.*1Co 15:29* Jesus said to baptize in the name of the Father, Son, and Holy Spirit.*Matt 28:18-20*

Death. The tetrarch Herod killed John the Baptist, who had opposed Herod's marriage to his brother's wife.*Matt 14:3-12, Mk 6:14-16* Herod had first had John arrested, bound, and imprisoned for opposing Herod's marriage to his brother's wife.*Mk 6:17-18, Lk 3:19-20* Herod's wife had nursed a grudge against John, hoping to kill him, but Herod had protected John out of fear, knowing that John was righteous and holy.*Mk 6:19-20* John's preaching greatly puzzled Herod, who liked to listen to John.*Mk 6:20* But the time soon came when Herodias was able to manipulate Herod into killing John, when on Herod's birthday Herodias's daughter's dancing pleased Herod, Herod offered her anything up to half his kingdom, and at her mother's urging she asked for John the Baptist's head.*Mk 6:21-28* John's disciples came for John's body to lay it in a tomb.*Mk 6:29* Herod later heard of Jesus's miraculous powers and said that he was John the Baptist raised from the dead.*Matt 14:1-2, Mk 6:14* People told Herod that John had risen, Elijah had appeared, or one of the other prophets of old had come back to life, perplexing Herod because he had beheaded John and couldn't determine who Jesus was.*Lk 9:7-9* Jesus told the disciples that John the Baptist was the Elijah whom prophets had foretold would come and that the Son of Man would suffer just as Herod had killed John the Baptist.*Matt 17:10-13, Mk 9:11-13*

Apostles. At Pentecost, Peter warned the crowd with many words, the apostles baptized those who accepted his words, and about three thousand became believers, with the Lord adding to their numbers daily those whom he saved.*Acts 2:39-41, 47* Philip proclaimed to Samaria the Messiah, God's kingdom, and Jesus Christ's name, so that many believed and were baptized, including a sorcerer Simon whom Philip's signs and miracles astonished.*Acts 8:5-13* When Peter proclaimed the good news of peace through Jesus Christ to the devout centurion Cornelius and others with him, and the Holy Spirit came on the Gentiles who heard Peter's message, they baptized the Gentiles in Jesus Christ's name.*Acts 10:44-48* The Lord opened the cloth seller Lydia's heart to respond to Paul's message, after which they baptized her and the members of her household.*Acts 16:13-15* A jailer and his household believed in God and accepted baptism after the imprisoned Paul and Silas prayed and sang, the earth shook, the prison doors flew open, and their chains fell off.*Acts 16:25-34* The Jews in Corinth opposed Paul's message that Jesus was the

Messiah and became abusive, causing Paul to go next door to preach to others who heard, believed, and were baptized.*Acts 18:5-8* When Priscilla and Aquila heard a Jew Apollos teach with great fervor and accurately about Jesus, but only knowing John's baptism, they explained to him God's way more adequately.*Acts 18:24-28* When Paul found some believers in Ephesus who, though they had received John's baptism, hadn't even heard of the Holy Spirit's baptism, Paul baptized them in Jesus's name, and when he placed his hands on them, the Holy Spirit came on them so that they spoke in tongues and prophesied.*Acts 19:1-7*

Transfiguration. Jesus said that he was the light of the world and also the light of life for whoever followed him.*Jn 8:12* Jesus took the disciples Peter, James, and John with him up a high mountain where God transfigured Jesus so that his face shone like the sun and his clothes were as white as the light.*Matt 17:1-2, Mk 9:2-3, Lk 9:28-29* Moses and Elijah appeared, and Jesus spoke with them.*Matt 17:3, Mk 9:4, Lk 9:30* They spoke about Jesus's coming departure at Jerusalem.*Lk 9:31* The event frightened Peter, James, and John, and Peter didn't know what to say.*Mk 9:5-6, Lk 9:33* The disciples were very sleepy but when fully awake saw Jesus and the two others.*Lk 9:32* A bright cloud then covered them, and God's voice from the cloud said that Jesus was his Son whom God loved and who pleased God.*Matt 17:5, Mk 9:7, Lk 9:34-35* Hearing, the disciples fell face down in terror, but Jesus touched them and told them to get up and not be afraid.*Matt 17:6-7* Jesus was suddenly alone again.*Mk 9:8, Lk 9:36* Jesus then told the disciples not to tell anyone what they had seen until God had raised the Son of Man from the dead.*Matt 17:9, Mk 9:9* Peter, James, and John talked about what Jesus meant by rising from the dead.*Mk 9:10* But they kept Jesus's transfiguration to themselves.*Lk 9:36*

Resurrection

Christ's story surely did not end with crucifixion. The New Testament depicts the cross as only a momentary waystation, testifying at length instead to the resurrection's following power. Christ rose from the dead, conquering death and bringing eternal life not only for himself but for those who believe. The New Testament assures that God supplies each of us a resurrected body to enjoy in heaven. See how powerfully the New Testament depicts the resurrection. Are you fully anticipating your own resurrection, in great joy as you should?

Crucifixion. As the guards led Jesus to the place of crucifixion, they forced a man from the crowd to carry Jesus's cross.*Matt 27:32-33, Mk 15:21, Lk 23:26* A large number of people followed them, including women who mourned and wailed for Jesus, to whom Jesus turned to say to weep for themselves and their children.*Lk 23:27-31* At the crucifixion place, they first offered Jesus wine mixed with gall and then, after he refused, they stripped and crucified him, casting lots for his clothes while watching him die on the cross under a sign saying that Jesus was the Jews' king.*Matt 27:34-37, Mk 15:23-26* The guards crucified two rebels with him, one on either side.*Matt 27:38, Mk 15:27, Lk 23:32-33* Jesus prayed to his Father to forgive them for not knowing what they were doing.*Lk 23:34* The rebels, passersby, and the chief priests, elders, and law teachers mocked and insulted Jesus for saying he was going to destroy and rebuild the temple when he, Israel's king and the Son of God, couldn't even save himself.*Matt 27:39-40, Mk 15:29-32* The people watched and rulers sneered, saying that if he was God's Messiah, the Chosen One, then he should save himself.*Lk 23:35* The soldiers also mocked Jesus, saying that if he was the Jews' king, as the sign above him said, then he should save himself.*Lk 23:36-38* When one of the crucified criminals hurled insults at Jesus to save himself and them, the other criminal rebuked him, saying to fear God for their just punishment, when Jesus had done nothing wrong.*Lk 23:39-41* That criminal said to Jesus to remember him when coming into his kingdom, to which Jesus replied that the criminal would that day be with Jesus in paradise.*Lk 23:42-43* Rulers indeed crucified the Lord of glory.*1Co 2:8* Men crucified Christ in weakness, but Christ lives by God's power.*2Co 13:4* Christ triumphed over evil powers and authorities by the cross.*Col 2:15* Christ endured the cross for the joy before him, scorning the cross's shame, to sit down at the right hand of God's throne.*Heb 12:2* Christ's purpose on the cross was to reconcile in him one new peaceful humanity out of the divided two sides, putting to death their hostility.*Eph 2:15-16* God reconciles to himself all things on earth and in heaven, by making peace through the Son's blood, shed on the cross.*Col 1:20* Our old self's crucifixion with Christ killed the sinful body, setting us free from sin and making us no longer slaves to sin.*Ro 6:6-7* We submit to crucifixion with Christ so that we no longer live on our own, but by our faith, Christ, who loved us and gave himself for us, lives in us.*Gal 2:20* The cross of our Lord Jesus Christ crucified the world to us and us to the world.*Gal 6:14*

Death. While Jesus was still alive on the cross, darkness fell for three hours, even though the time was from noon to three in the afternoon, because the sun stopped shining.*Matt 27:45, Mk 15:33, Lk 23:44-45* Then, Jesus cried out, asking why God had forsaken him.*Matt 27:46, Mk 15:34* Bystanders said he was calling Elijah.*Matt 27:47, Mk 15:35* One put vinegar in a sponge on a staff to offer to Jesus as drink.*Matt 27:48, Mk 15:36* That one said to leave Jesus alone to see if Elijah came to take him down.*Mk 15:36* The others said to leave him alone to see if Elijah came.*Matt 27:49* Jesus then cried out again, giving up his spirit and breathing his last.*Matt 27:50, Mk 15:37* Jesus called out that into his Father's hands he committed his spirit, breathing his last.*Lk 23:46* At that moment, the temple's curtain tore in two.*Matt 27:51, Mk 15:38, Lk 23:45* The earth shook, rocks split, tombs broke open, and many holy ones rose to life who after Jesus's resurrection came out of the tombs into the holy city to appear to many people.*Matt 27:51-53* When the centurion and others with him guarding Jesus saw everything happen at the moment of Jesus's death, they exclaimed that surely Jesus was the Son of God.*Matt 27:54, Mk 15:39* The centurion said that surely Jesus was a righteous man.*Lk 23:47* When all the gathered people saw what happened, they beat their breasts and walked away.*Lk 23:48* Many women who had followed Jesus to care for him were present, watching from a distance.*Matt 27:55, Mk 15:40-41* All those who knew Jesus stood watching from a distance.*Lk 23:49* Near evening, a rich disciple

Joseph of Arimathea, a prominent Council member who was waiting for God's kingdom and had not consented to the Council's decision and action, went boldly to the governor asking for Jesus's body.*Matt 27:57, Mk 15:42-43, Lk 23:50-52* The governor was surprised to hear that Jesus had already died, and so the governor first confirmed with the centurion.*Mk 15:44-45* With the governor's order, Joseph took Jesus's body, wrapped it in linen, and placed it in Joseph's new tomb cut out of the rock, rolling a big stone across the entrance.*Matt 27:58-60, Mk 15:45-46, Lk 23:53* Two of the women sat opposite the tomb, seeing where they laid Jesus.*Matt 27:61, Mk 15:47, Lk 23:55* Those women went home to prepare spices and perfumes but rested the next day on the Sabbath.*Lk 23:56* The next day, the chief priests and Pharisees went to the governor saying that Jesus had predicted his resurrection in three days and asking that the governor secure the tomb against the disciples stealing the body to perpetrate a resurrection hoax.*Matt 27:62-64* The governor ordered the tomb secured with a seal and guard.*Matt 27:65-66*

Cross. Jesus said that just as Moses lifted up the snake on a pole to heal Israel in the wilderness, so people must lift up the Son of Man so that everyone who believes in him may have eternal life.*Jn 3:14-15* Jesus said that men would lift him up from the earth, to show the kind of death he would suffer, but that he would then draw all to himself.*Jn 12:32-33* Jesus said that he would spend three days and nights in the earth's heart, like Jonah spent three days and nights inside a whale.*Matt 12:40* Rulers crucified the Lord of glory.*1Co 2:8* Men crucified Christ in weakness, but Christ lives by God's power.*2Co 13:4* God nailed our indebtedness to the cross.*Col 2:14* Christ triumphed over evil powers and authorities by the cross.*Col 2:15* Many live as enemies of Christ's cross.*Php 3:18* The cross of our Lord Jesus Christ crucified the world to us and us to the world.*Gal 6:14* Christ's purpose on the cross was to reconcile in him one new peaceful humanity out of the divided two sides, putting to death their hostility.*Eph 2:15-16* The cross's message is foolishness to those who perish because God destroys the wise's wisdom and frustrates the intelligent's intelligence, but the cross is God's power to us whom God saves.*1Co 1:18-19* Don't be foolish, letting others bewitch you into abandoning the crucifixion's truth.*Gal 3:1* Those who fall away from God's heavenly gift mean to crucify God's Son all over again, subjecting him again to public disgrace.*Heb 6:6* Do not follow other teachers whom no one crucified, when Christ himself is not so divided.*1Co 1:11-15* We who belong to Christ Jesus have crucified the flesh's passions and desires.*Gal 5:24*

Meaning. God presented Christ as a sacrifice of atonement, through the shedding of his blood.*Ro 2:25-26* God delivered Jesus over to death for our sins.*Ro 4:25* Christ's love convinces us that he died for all and thus all died with him.*2Co 5:14* Christ is our sacrificed Passover lamb.*1Co 5:6-7* We submit to crucifixion with Christ so that we no longer live on our own, but by our faith, Christ, who loved us and gave himself for us, lives in us.*Gal 2:20* Wise and eloquent preaching must not empty Christ's cross of its power.*1Co 1:17* The thanksgiving cup for which we give thanks participates in Christ's blood, while the bread we break participates in Christ's body, just as eating the sacrifices participates in the altar.*1Co 10:16,18* God reconciles us by Christ's physical body, through death, to present you holy, without blemish, and free from accusation, in his sight.*Col 1:22* Christ redeems us through his blood, the forgiveness of sins, as God lavished his grace's riches on us.*Eph 1:7-8* The perfect lamb Christ's precious blood, not perishable things like precious metals, redeemed you from the empty life your family handed down to you.*1Pe 1:18-19* Jesus shared in our humanity because we are human, so that by his death he would break the devil's power of death.*Heb 2:14* Christ redeemed us from law's curse when crucifixion cursed Christ who died for us.*Gal 3:13* Proclaim God's testimony not with eloquence or human wisdom but instead knowing only Jesus Christ crucified, and that in weakness with great fear and trembling.*1Co 2:1-3* Jews demand signs and Greeks look for wisdom, but we preach Christ crucified, a stumbling block to Jews and foolishness to other non-believers but God's power and wisdom to those whom God called.*1Co 1:22-24*

Result. God reconciles to himself all things on earth and in heaven, by making peace through the Son's blood, shed on the cross.*Col 1:20* Christ endured the cross for the joy before him, scorning the cross's shame, to sit down at the right hand of God's throne.*Heb 12:2* Christ entered the Most Holy Place not by animal blood but once for all by his own blood, for eternal redemption.*Heb 9:12* When God did not spare his own Son but gave him up for us, he showed that he graciously gives us everything.*Ro 8:32* Our old self's crucifixion with him killed the sinful body, setting us free from sin and making us no longer slaves to sin.*Ro 6:6-7* You died, and your life now hides with Christ in God.*Col 3:3* Christ died for all, so that we should no longer live for ourselves but for him who died for us and rose again.*2Co 5:15* Jesus suffered outside the city gate to make the people holy through his own blood.*Heb 13:12* Go to Jesus outside the camp, bearing the disgrace he bore, because we have no enduring city here, instead looking for the city to come.*Heb 13:14* Christ's one sacrifice made perfect forever those whom God is making holy.*Heb 10:14* Be confident entering the Most Holy Place by Jesus's blood, the new and living way he opened for us through the curtain, that is, his body.*Heb 10:19-20* Jesus frees those held in slavery by their fear of death.*Heb 2:15* Jesus said that to be his disciple, one must deny oneself and take up one's cross to follow him.*Matt 16:24, Mk 8:34, Lk 9:23* Whoever wants to save their life will lose it, but whoever loses their life for Christ will find it.*Matt 16:25, Mk 8:35, Lk 9:24* Anyone who loves their life will lose it, while those who hate their life will have eternal life.*Jn 12:25* Jesus said that we do no good to gain the whole world, yet forfeit our soul, because we have nothing to give for our soul.*Matt 16:26, Mk 8:36-37, Lk 9:25*

Resurrection. Jesus said that he is the resurrection and the life, whoever believed in him would live even though they die, and whoever lived by believing in him would not die.*Jn 11:25* Jesus said repeatedly that although others would crucify him, he would then rise to life.*Matt 16:21, Matt 17:22-23, Matt 20:17-19* When his disciples grumbled over his hard teaching, Jesus asked how they would feel if they saw the Son of Man ascend to where he was before.*Jn 6:60-62* Jesus told the disciples that he was going to the Father.*Jn 14:12* When Jesus repeated that he was going to the Father, he said so in order that when it happened, the disciples would believe.*Jn 14:28-29* Jesus said that he was going to the Father for their good.*Jn 16:5-7* Two of the women went to the tomb after the Sabbath, where with a violent earthquake they saw the Lord's angel, his appearance like lightning and with clothes white as snow, descend from heaven, roll back the stone, and sit on it.*Matt 28:1-3* The guards shook with fear, becoming like dead men.*Matt 28:4* The angel told the women not to fear as they looked for the crucified Jesus because he had risen just as he said, and they should look where he once lay, before they ran to tell the disciples to meet Jesus in Galilee.*Matt 28:5-8* The women hurried away in joy and fear, but Jesus met and greeted them, and they clasped his feet in worship.*Matt 28:9* Jesus repeated the angel's instruction to tell his brothers to meet him in Galilee.*Matt 28:10* While the women ran to tell the disciples, some of the guards reported the tomb events to the chief priests who paid them a lot of money to say that the disciples had stolen the body while they slept, promising to keep them out of trouble with the governor.*Matt 28:11-15* The women told the eleven disciples, who did not believe them.*Lk 24:9-10* Peter, though, ran to the tomb where he saw the linen strips and wondered what had happened.*Lk 24:12* Three of the women who had cared for Jesus bought spices and went to the tomb to anoint Jesus's body, wondering who would roll the stone away.*Mk 16:1-3, Lk 24:1* But when they got to the tomb, they saw the stone rolled back.*Mk 16:4, Lk 24:2* When they entered the tomb, Jesus's body was not there.*Lk 24:3* Inside the tomb, they saw a young white-robed man who told them not to be afraid because Jesus the Nazarene had risen.*Mk 16:5-6* The white-robed man told them to go tell the disciples and Peter that Jesus was going ahead of them into Galilee where they would see him, just as he had told them.*Mk 16:7* The women saw two men in clothes gleaming like lightning.*Lk 24:4* The women bowed down, but the men asked why they looked for the living among the dead, when the Son of Man had risen just as he said, on the third day after crucifixion.*Lk 24:5-7* Trembling and bewildered, the women fled, saying nothing because they were afraid.*Mk 16:8* Mary Magdalene went to the tomb early, in darkness, and saw that the stone no longer covered the entrance.*Jn 20:1* She ran to tell Peter and the disciple John whom Jesus loved, telling them that someone had removed the Lord from the tomb to an unknown place.*Jn 20:2* Peter and John ran to the tomb, seeing the linen strips and cloth that had been around Jesus's head.*Jn 20:3-8* John saw and believed, but as they left the tomb, they still did not grasp from scriptures that Jesus must rise from the dead.*Jn 20:8-9* Mary Magdalene wept outside the tomb until she saw two angels in white, seated inside the tomb, asking her why she cried.*Jn 20:11-13* Mary told them that someone had taken the Lord away, but she then turned around and saw Jesus standing there, without realizing who it was.*Jn 20:13-14* Jesus asked her why she cried, and Mary, thinking he was the gardener, asked where he might have put Jesus's body.*Jn 20:15* Jesus then called her name, and she recognized him, crying out "Teacher."*Jn 20:16* Jesus told Mary Magdalene at the tomb not to hold onto him because he had not yet ascended but to go tell the disciples that he was ascending to his Father and their Father, his God and their God, which Mary did, saying that she had seen the Lord.*Jn 20:17-18*

Confirmation. The same day as the women discovered the empty tomb, two disciples were walking to a village Emmaus about seven miles from Jerusalem, discussing everything that had happened, when Jesus came up and walked along with them, even though they didn't recognize him.*Lk 24:13-16* The disciples explained to Jesus what had happened including the empty tomb's discovery.*Lk 24:17-24* Calling them foolish and slow to believe, Jesus explained everything to them from the scriptures about himself.*Lk 24:25-27* As they approached the village, Jesus planned to continue on, but the two disciples urged him strongly to stay with them, which he did until he broke bread over a meal with them, they recognized him, and Jesus disappeared from sight.*Lk 24:28-31* The two disciples returned to Jerusalem to tell the eleven disciples that Christ had indeed risen.*Lk 24:33-35* While they were still talking, Jesus stood among them, saying peace to them.*Lk 24:36* Jesus told the startled and frightened disciples to look at his hands and feet, touch him, and confirm that he was no ghost.*Lk 24:37-40* When they still didn't believe it, he asked for something to eat and took and ate the broiled fish that they gave him, reminding them that he had said that he must fulfill everything written about him.*Lk 24:41-44* Then he opened their minds so that they could understand scripture, explaining again how the Messiah would suffer and rise from the dead after three days, so that they could preach repentance for forgiveness of sins.*Lk 24:45-47* Jesus said that the disciples had witnessed these things.*Lk 24:48* The disciples also went to the mountain in Galilee where they saw and worshiped Jesus.*Matt 28:16-17* Jesus told them that God had given him all authority in heaven and on earth and that they should go making disciples of all nations, baptizing in the name of the Father, Son, and Holy Spirit, teaching obedience in all that Jesus said, as Jesus would be with them to the age's end.*Matt 28:18-20* While Christ died for our sins as the scriptures say, he indeed rose on the third day after burial, as the scriptures also say.*1Co 15:3* The God of peace, through the blood of the eternal covenant, raised from the dead our Lord Jesus, the great Shepherd of the sheep.*Heb 13:20* The risen Christ appeared to Peter, then the twelve disciples, then more than five hundred brothers and sisters at the same time, most of whom were still living when authors wrote about it.*1Co 15:5-6* Christ next appeared to his brother James, then to the apostles, and last to the apostle Paul, as one abnormally born.*1Co 15:7-8* God the Father raised Jesus Christ from the dead.*Gal 1:1* God raised Jesus from the dead.*Ro 4:22-24* God appointed Jesus the Son of God through the Spirit of holiness and resurrected him from the dead as Jesus Christ our Lord.*Ro 1:4* God raised Christ from the dead.*Col 2:12*

Life. Without resurrection, Christ is still in the grave.*1Co 15:13* And if Christ never rose, then preaching and faith are useless, and we witness falsely about God.*1Co 15:14-15* If no one rises, then Christ hasn't either, your faith is futile, you remain sinful, and those already dead are lost.*1Co 15:16-18* If only for this life we hope in Christ, pity us the most.*1Co 15:19* But God has raised Christ from the dead as the first among those who have died.*1Co 15:20* God gives life to the dead.*Ro 4:17* Because God raised Christ from the dead, he cannot die again, and death no longer has mastery over him.*Ro 6:9* Christ died once for all and so lives to God.*Ro 6:10* The Lord Jesus died for us so that, whether we are alive or dead, we may live together with him.*1Th 3:10* Those who die with Christ will also live with him.*2Ti 2:11* Christ died and returned to life so that he might be the Lord of both the dead and the living.*Ro 14:9* Our Savior Christ Jesus destroyed death and brought immortality.*2Ti 1:10* Jesus explained to the Sadducees, who didn't believe in resurrection, that they were badly mistaken because in Moses's account of the burning bush, God said that God is the God of the living, not the dead.*Mk 12:26-27, Lk 20:37-40* Jesus said that just as the Father raises the dead, giving them life, the Son also gives life to those whom he wishes.*Jn 5:21*

Meaning. Jesus said that he was going to the Father, for which the disciples should have been glad because the Father is greater than Jesus.*Jn 14:28* God delivered Jesus over to death for our sins and raised him to life for our justification.*Ro 4:25* Desire to know the power of Christ's resurrection and participation in his sufferings, becoming like him in his death and so attaining to resurrection from death.*Php 3:10-11* We should thank God the Father of our Lord Jesus Christ for his great mercy, giving us new birth into living hope through Jesus's resurrection from the dead.*1Pe 1:3* Through Christ you believe in God and place your hope in God, for raising Christ from the dead and glorifying him.*1Pe 1:21* Jesus Christ's resurrection saves you because he is in heaven at God's right hand with angels, authorities, and powers submitting to him.*1Pe 3:21-22* We neither live nor die for ourselves alone but live and die for the Lord, either way belonging to the Lord.*Ro 14:7-8* Because death came through a man, resurrection also comes through a man.*1Co 15:21* In Adam all died so that in Christ all could live.*1Co 15:22* Without resurrection, baptism means nothing.*1Co 15:29* Without resurrection, we may as well not endanger ourselves every hour.*1Co 15:30* Without resurrection, one may as well give up fighting for Christ and instead just eat and drink today, to die tomorrow.*1Co 15:32* The Sadducees held that resurrection, angels, and spirits do not exist, while the Pharisees believed in each of those things.*Acts 23:8*

You. Because the glory of the Father raised Jesus Christ from the dead, you also live a new life.*Ro 6:3-4* God made you alive in Christ when you were dead in your sins.*Col 2:13* God raised you with Christ.*Col 3:1* Because you joined him in a death like his, you will certainly also join with him in a resurrection like his.*Ro 6:5* Because you died with Christ, you believe that you will also live with him.~Ro 6:8~ If Christ is in you, then even though your body dies because of sin, the Spirit gives life because of righteousness.~Ro 8:10~ If the Spirit of God who raised Jesus from the dead lives in you, then God who raised Christ from the dead will also give your body life because of his Spirit who lives in you.~Ro 8:11~ You died to the law so that you could belong to Christ raised from the dead, bearing fruit for God.~Ro 7:4~ Jesus said that when you hold a banquet, invite the poor, crippled, lame, and blind who cannot repay you by inviting you back, so that at the righteous's resurrection you receive your repayment.~Lk 14:12-14~ When Jesus raised Lazarus from the dead by calling him to come out, Jesus added to take off his grave clothes to let him go.~Jn 11:43-44~

Body. Jesus told religious leaders who did not believe in resurrection that God is indeed the God of the living rather than the dead, so that resurrected persons will be like angels in heaven.~Matt 22:29-32~ Jesus said that to produce many seeds from one seed, a wheat kernel must first die.~Jn 12:24~ Anyone who loves their life will lose it, while those who hate their life will have eternal life.~Jn 12:25~ Don't worry foolishly about how resurrection happens.~1Co 15:35-36~ The plant must die to sow the seed that comes to life.~1Co 15:36~ Sowing is not planting what will be but instead planting only the seed of what will be.~1Co 15:37~ God gives the seed a body as he determines, giving each seed its own body.~1Co 15:38~ Not all flesh is alike, because people have one kind of flesh, animals another, birds another, and fish another.~1Co 15:39~ Heavenly bodies differ in splendor than earthly bodies.~1Co 15:40~ The sun has one kind of splendor, the moon another, and the stars another, while star differs from star in splendor.~1Co 15:41~ Resurrection is the same way, the body sown perishable but raised imperishable.~1Co 15:42~ God sows the body in dishonor but raises it in glory, sows it in weakness but raises it in power.~1Co 15:43~ God sows a natural body but raises a spiritual body because to have a natural body is to anticipate a spiritual body.~1Co 15:44~ When religious leaders asked Jesus whose wife a woman would be at the resurrection if she married seven times with each marriage ending in her husband's death, Jesus answered that people at the resurrection will not be married because they will be like angels in heaven.~Matt 22:23-30, Lk 20:27-36~

Result. God's power for believers is the same as the mighty strength he exerted when he raised Christ from the dead and seated him at his right hand in the heavenly realms, over all rule, authority, power, and dominion, and every name not only now but in the future.~Eph 1:19-21~ The resurrection of the dead has not yet taken place.*2Ti 2:18* We have yet to obtain resurrection through faith, which is our goal, but we press on to that goal for which Christ Jesus embraced us.*Php 3:12-13* Our Savior the Lord Jesus Christ will by his complete power transform our lowly bodies to be like his glorious body.*Php 3:20-21* Wait for God's Son Jesus, whom God raised from the dead.*1Th 1:10* By his power God raised the Lord from the dead and will also raise us.*1Co 6:14* We know that God who raised the Lord Jesus from the dead will also raise us with Jesus, presenting us to himself.*2Co 4:14* To live is Christ even though in dying we gain.*Php 1:20-21* Whether to live or die tears us because living means fruitful labor while departing means to be with Christ, which is far better.*Php 1:22-23*

Kingdom. Heaven's kingdom is like a king preparing a wedding banquet for his son, inviting those who ignored the invitation and instead went off to their fields and businesses or even killed the servants carrying the invitation.*Matt 22:1-6* The king would destroy those murderers and their city, and instead invite good and bad people off the streets to fill the wedding hall.*Matt 22:7-10* But those attending would still need to wear wedding clothes, or the king would have them thrown outside, because God invites many but chooses few.*Matt 22:11-14* Jesus told a similar parable of a man who prepared a great banquet, inviting many fortunate guests who nonetheless gave excuses for not attending.*Lk 14:16-20* Angered, the man then told his servant to invite the poor, crippled, blind, and lame, and to go out to the country roads and lanes to compel more to come in to fill his house, while none of the first invited guests get to taste the banquet.*Lk 14:21-24* God calls you into his kingdom.*1Th 2:12* Jesus told his disciples to proclaim that the kingdom of heaven has come near.*Matt 10:7* God will count you worthy of his kingdom for which you suffer.*2Th 1:5* The Lord will bring us safely to his heavenly kingdom.*2Ti 4:18* Remain in view of God's kingdom.*2Ti 4:1* You receive God's kingdom that does not shake.*Heb 12:28-29* The Father shares his kingdom of light.*Col 1:12* God brings us into the kingdom of the Son whom he loves.*Col 1:13* Our Lord and Savior Jesus Christ offers us a rich welcome into his eternal kingdom.*2Pe 1:10-11* The kingdom we seek to inherit is of Christ and God.*Eph 5:5* The poor who are rich in faith and love God inherit his promised kingdom.*Jas 2:5* The pure inherit the kingdom of Christ and God.*Eph 5:5* God's kingdom is not about eating and drinking but about righteousness, peace, and joy in the Holy Spirit.*Ro 14:17* God's kingdom is not a matter of talk but of power.*1Co 4:20* Only free children, not slave children, share our inheritance from God.*Gal 4:30-31*

Qualities. Jesus said that his kingdom was not of this world but another world.*Jn 18:35-36* Jesus said that God's kingdom is like scattered seed that sprouts and grows night and day, the sower does not even know how, producing grain for the sower's harvest.*Mk 4:26-29* Jesus also told a parable that heaven's kingdom is like good wheat seed sowed in a field in which the enemy sows weeds, both growing until the harvest when the wheat goes into the barn but the weeds into the fire.*Matt 13:24-30* The Son of Man is the sower, the world the field, the good wheat seed the people of God's kingdom, and the weeds people who follow the evil one, sown by the devil.*Matt 13:36-38* At the age's end, the Son of Man will send his angels to weed out all sin and evil for the blazing furnace so that the righteous shine in their Father's kingdom.*Matt 13:40-43* Heaven's kingdom is like the tiniest mustard seed growing into a tree in which birds shelter.*Matt 13:31-32, Mk 4:30-32, Lk 13:18-19* Heaven's kingdom is also like a little yeast working all through a great quantity of dough.*Matt 13:33, Lk 13:20-21* Heaven's kingdom is also like treasure hidden in a field for which a person would sell everything.*Matt 13:44* Heaven's kingdom is also like a merchant looking for the finest pearl for which he would then sell everything.*Matt 13:45-46* Heaven's kingdom is also like a net full of good and bad fish that the fishermen would sort, throwing away the bad like the angels will separate the wicked for destruction at the age's end.*Matt 13:47-50* Heaven's kingdom is also like the landowner who paid the same wage to his workers whether they worked all day or just part of the day, in that the last will be first and first last, because the landowner may do as he wishes with his money.*Matt 20:1-16* Many who are first will be last and last will be first.*Mk 10:31, Lk 13:30* During the forty days that Jesus appeared to the disciples after his crucifixion and resurrection, he spoke to the disciples about God's kingdom.*Acts 1:3* When the disciples asked Jesus whether he was at that time going to restore God's kingdom, Jesus said that they were not to know the time the Father sets by his own authority.*Acts 1:6-7* When the Pharisees asked when God's kingdom would come, Jesus answered that one cannot observe its coming, as if to say here or there it is, because God's kingdom is in our midst.*Lk 17:20-21* Jesus said that just as when you see the trees sprout leaves, you know summer is near, when you see the desolations that he described, you know that God's kingdom is near, and so to watch, pray, and avoid life's anxieties.*Lk 21:29-36*

Worthy. Jesus said at the Last Supper that his disciples were those who had stood by him in trials, for which Jesus conferred on them a kingdom just like his Father conferred a kingdom on him, so that they would eat and drink with him in his kingdom.*Lk 22:28-30* Jesus said that God blesses those who are poor, granting them his kingdom.*Lk 6:20* People thought that God's kingdom was going to appear at once, but Jesus told them the parable of the servants to whom the king gave ten minas, and while one put the money to work to earn ten more, and another put the money to work to earn five more, each receiving huge rewards, the third servant laid the money away in a cloth believing that the king was a hard man who reaped what he did not sow.*Lk 19:11-23* The king took the ten minas away from that man to give to the others who already had more, saying that whoever has will get more, while whoever does not have will lose the little that they have, and that he would kill the enemies who did not want him as king.*Lk 19:24-27* When one of the crucified criminals said to Jesus to remember him when coming into his kingdom, Jesus replied that the criminal would that day be with Jesus in paradise.*Lk 23:42-43* Those who sin do not inherit God's kingdom.*Gal 5:19-21* Wrongdoers, the sexually immoral, idolaters, adulterers, men who have sex with men, thieves, the greedy, drunkards, slanderers, and swindlers do not inherit God's kingdom.*1Co 6:9-10* Idolaters do not inherit the kingdom of Christ and God.*Eph 5:5* Flesh and blood do not inherit God's kingdom, just as the perishable does not inherit the imperishable.*1Co 15:50* When his disciples asked who is the greatest in heaven's kingdom, Jesus said that you must be like little children even to enter the kingdom, where the greatest is the one who takes a lowly position like a child.*Matt 18:1-4, Lk 9:48* Jesus said that until he came, violent people had raided the kingdom, subjecting it to violence.*Matt 11:12* The Son has a scepter of justice for his kingdom.*Heb 1:8* Do your best to confirm your calling and election so that you receive a rich welcome into our Lord and Savior Jesus Christ's eternal kingdom.*2Pe 1:10-11* Welcome and comfort co-workers for God's kingdom when they visit.*Col 4:10-11* Teachers who are kingdom disciples are like homeowners who bring out both old and new stored treasures.*Matt 13:52* Thank God that you receive his kingdom.*Heb 12:28-29* Give joyful thanks to the Father for sharing in the kingdom of light.*Col 1:12*

Unworthy. Jesus told Nicodemus of the Jewish ruling council that no one can enter God's kingdom unless born again, of both water and Spirit, because flesh bears flesh but Spirit bears spirit, which should surprise no one.*Jn 3:3-7* Jesus said how hard the rich find getting into heaven's kingdom, God's kingdom, like passing a camel through the eye of a needle.*Matt 19:22-24, Mk 10:23-25, Lk 18:24-25* When the astonished disciples asked how anyone could then gain salvation, Jesus said that salvation is impossible for man but that all things are possible for God.*Matt 19:25-26, Mk 10:26-27, Lk 18:26-27* Jesus told the parable of the two sons, one who said he wouldn't do his father's work but changed his mind and did it, and the other who said he would but didn't.*Matt 21:28-30* Doing is what counts, Jesus added, like the prostitutes and tax collectors who repented and entered the kingdom, and not like the chief priests and elders who refused to repent.*Matt 21:31-32* Jesus also told the parable of the tenants who refused to pay the landowner's servants come to collect the rents and who instead beat, stoned, and killed them.*Matt 21:33-36, Mk 12:1-5, Lk 20:9-12* The landowner next sent his son, whom the tenants also killed.*Matt 21:37-39, Mk 12:6-8, Lk 20:13-14* Jesus told the chief priests and law teachers that as the scriptures foretold, they, too, had rejected the cornerstone and in so doing lost God's kingdom to those who produced its fruit.*Matt 21:42-43, Mk 12:9-11, Lk 20:16-19*

Heaven. The Scriptures say that the first man Adam lived, and so Christ, the last Adam, brings a living spirit.*1Co 15:45* The spiritual follows the natural.*1Co 15:46* God made the first man out of the earth's dust but makes the second man of heaven.*1Co 15:47* Those of the earth are as the earthly man was, but those of heaven are as the heavenly man is.*1Co 15:48* We begin as the earthly man's image but end bearing the heavenly man's image.*1Co 15:49* The mystery is that we will not all die, but we will all be changed.*1Co 15:51* Our change will be in a flash, the twinkling of an eye, when the last trumpet sounds for God to raise the dead imperishable.*1Co 15:52* The perishable must clothe itself with the imperishable, the mortal with immortality.*1Co 15:53* When the perishable puts on the imperishable, and the mortal immortality, then the Scriptures' saying that victory swallowed up death will be true.*1Co 15:54* Death has no victory or sting when death's sting is sin and sin's power is the law.*1Co 15:55-56* Thank God for victory through our Lord Jesus Christ.*1Co 15:57* Just stand firm, nothing moving you, while always giving yourselves fully to the Lord's work, because you know that your labor in the Lord is not in vain.*1Co 15:58*

Return

The New Testament addresses at length Christ's anticipated return. Every believer should celebrate Christ's second coming in which God fulfills all. We do not know the timing of Christ's return other than that his return is near, keeping us alert and sober. Yet Christ's return is not simply for eager believers. On his return, Christ will redeem everything, raising the dead and bringing a new heaven and earth. See how the New Testament addresses Christ's return. Are you longing as you should for his glorious coming?

Fulfillment. God gave his word and Jesus Christ's testimony and revelation, as an angel made known to his servant John who so testifies, to show his servants what must take place.*Rev 1:1-2* God blesses those who hear, read aloud, and take to heart John's prophecy about the time that is near.*Rev 1:3* John, companion in Jesus's suffering, kingdom, and patient endurance, was in the Spirit on the Lord's Day, on the island of Patmos because of God's word and Jesus's testimony, when a loud voice like a trumpet told him to write and share what he saw now and will take place later.*Rev 1:9-11, 19* With all wisdom, God made known to us his will's mystery, as was his good pleasure in Christ when times reach fulfillment, to unify everything in heaven and on earth under Christ.*Eph 1:8-10* We indeed look forward to the Lord's promised righteous new heaven and new earth after Christ's return.*2Pe 3:13* God will reveal the Lord Jesus from heaven in blazing fire with his powerful angels.*2Th 1:7* The Lord Jesus in the splendor of his return will overthrow and destroy the lawless one.*2Th 2:7-8* After Christ sacrificed himself once to take away the sins of many, his second appearance will not be to bear sin but to bring salvation to those awaiting him.*Heb 9:27-28* Fellow believers will be your glory when our Lord Jesus returns.*1Th 2:20* Encourage one another with how God treats believers on Christ's return.*1Th 4:18* The Lord will on that day award righteousness's crown to all who have longed for his appearing.*2Ti 4:8*

Jesus said that when persons have preached the kingdom's gospel throughout the world, to all nations, then all will end.*Matt 24:14* When the Son of Man comes in his glory, with all the angels, he will sit on his glorious throne.*Matt 25:31* That day will come for all those who live on earth's face.*Lk 21:35*

Christ. Christ comes first, then when he comes, those who belong to him.*1Co 15:23* Then the end will come when he hands God's kingdom to the Father after destroying all dominion, authority, and power.*1Co 15:24* Christ must reign until all enemies are under his feet.*1Co 15:25* The last enemy Christ destroys is death.*1Co 15:26* God has put everything under Christ's feet other than God himself.*1Co 15:27* When the Son finishes, the Son will subject himself to the Father who put everything under him, so that God is everything in all.*1Co 15:28* Come, Lord.*1Co 16:22* Boast of one another as you will boast in the day of the Lord Jesus.*2Co 1:14* When Christ ascended, he took many captives while giving gifts to his people.*Eph 4:8* Christ, who also descended to the lower, earthly regions, ascended higher than heaven, so high as to fill the whole universe.*Eph 4:9-10* Christ ascended in glory.*1Ti 3:16* Keep meeting together, all the more as the last day approaches.*Heb 10:25* Christ will return in just a little while and will not delay.*Heb 10:37* Jesus said that the Son of Man is going to come in his Father's glory with his angels to reward each person according to what they have done.*Matt 16:27* Jesus said that a judge exists who judges those who reject him rather than accepting his words, because the words he speaks, which the Father commanded him to speak, will condemn them at the last day.*Jn 12:48* In the apostle John's vision from the island of Patmos, Jesus said that he is coming soon, bringing his reward with him, as the Alpha and Omega, First and Last, Beginning and End.*Rev 22:12-13* Jesus says yes, he is coming soon.*Rev 22:20*

End. When the disciples asked Jesus when the age's end would come, he replied not to let others deceive you, claiming that they were Jesus and the end was near.*Matt 24:3-4, Mk 13:3-5, Lk 21:7-8* We should not fear the wars and rumors of war, nations rising against nations, and famines and earthquakes, all birth pains that must happen before the end to come.*Matt 24:6-8, Mk 13:7-8, Lk 21:9-11* Jesus said to flee in the end times, when the prophesied abomination causing desolation stands in the holy place, without going back for anything in one's house because the time will be of dreadful distress, never before or since equaled.*Matt 24:15-21, Mk 13:14-19* Armies will surround Jerusalem when its dreadful desolation is near and when you should flee from the punishment that fulfills everything written.*Lk 21:20-22* If God did not cut short those end times for the elect's sake, as he will do, then no one would survive.*Matt 24:22, Mk 13:20* Don't believe it then, when people point here and there to the supposed Messiah because many false messiahs and prophets will do great signs and wonders trying to fool the elect.*Matt 24:23-26, Mk 13:21-23* Instead, the Son of Man's coming will be obvious, like lightning visible from east to west.*Matt 24:27* Jesus said that the Son of Man's day would be like lightning lighting up the sky from one end to the other.*Lk 17:24* The sun and moon will be dark and stars will fall from the sky, shaking the heavenly bodies.*Matt 24:29, Mk 13:24-25* The sun, moon, and stars will show signs, nations will share anguish over the tossing seas, the heavenly bodies will shake, and people will faint from terror.*Lk 21:25-26* When these things happen, which they surely will, the end is near.*Matt 24:32-34* Then, heaven will reveal the Son of Man's sign, causing all people to mourn when they see the Son of Man coming on heaven's clouds with power and great glory.*Matt 24:30, Mk 13:26* Then the Son will send his angels with a loud trumpet call to call his elect from the four winds and heaven's ends.*Matt 24:31, Mk 13:27* People will see the Son of Man coming in a cloud with power and great glory, when you should stand up and lift up your head toward your nearing redemption.*Lk 21:27* Look, because he is coming with the clouds and every eye will see him, even those who pierced him, all peoples on earth mourning because of him.*Rev 1:7*

Timing. Only the Father knows the day and hour when the end will come, not the angels in heaven nor even the Son.*Matt 24:36, Mk 13:32* The Son of Man will come when you do not expect him.*Lk 12:40* The return of the Son of Man will be like Noah's flood, no one suspecting it.*Matt 24:37-39, Lk 17:27* The Son of Man's return will be like in the days of Lot when he left Sodom, and fire and sulfur from heaven destroyed all those who were going about their business.*Lk 17:28-30* Of two men working together, God will take one but not the other, just as he will take one of two women working, and one of two people in one bed.*Matt 24:40-41, Lk 17:34-35* Time differs to the Lord, to whom a day is like a thousand years and thousand years like a day.*2Pe 3:8* The Lord will indeed return but in waiting is just being patient, wanting everyone to repent rather than any to perish.*2Pe 3:9* The last days will be terrible times.*2Ti 3:1* But the Lord's return will come sneaking up when fire destroys the elements and the Lord lays everything bare.*2Pe 3:10* The Lord is near.*Php 4:5* Wait for God's Son Jesus, who rescues us from the coming wrath.*1Th 1:10* Don't look for times and dates because the Lord's return will come unexpectedly.*1Th 5:1-2* Do not worry as some say that our Lord Jesus Christ's return has already come because it hasn't.*2Th 2:2-3* Jesus will not return until the rebellion occurs and the man of lawlessness appears.*2Th 2:3-6* God will bring about our Lord Jesus Christ's return in his own time, until which you should keep God's commands without spot or blame.*1Ti 6:14-15* The Lord's return will not surprise believers, who know the truth.*1Th 5:4* Judge nothing before the appointed time, but wait until the Lord comes.*1Co 4:5* Then each will receive their praise from God.*1Co 4:5* Jesus said to his disciples that some who were standing there would not taste death before they saw the Son of Man coming in his kingdom.*Matt 16:28, Mk 9:1, Lk 9:27* Jesus also told them that they would long to see one of the Son of Man's days but would not see it and should not go running after him when people say that he is here or there.*Lk 17:22-23* Jesus said you will not know the time he comes, like a thief.*Rev 3:3* Jesus said to look, stay awake, and remain clothed because he comes like a thief and you must not be naked and shamefully exposed.*Rev 16:15*

Watching. Because you won't know until he comes, you must keep watch.*Matt 24:42, Mk 13:33, Lk 21:36* You must be ready, like an owner guarding the house, because the Son of Man and heaven's kingdom will come unexpectedly.*Matt 24:43-44, Mk 13:34-35* Jesus said to the disciples what he said to everyone, which is to watch!*Mk 13:37* Be the faithful and wise servant whom the master puts in charge of the house and who feeds the servants on time.*Matt 24:45, Lk 12:42-43* God will reward that wise servant, putting him in charge of all his possessions.*Matt 24:46-47, Lk 12:44* The master will cut to pieces the wicked servant who notices that the master has been away a long time, beats his fellow servants, and parties with drunkards, until the master comes at a day and hour when the wicked servant does not expect him.*Matt 24:49-51, Lk 12:45-46* The Lord's return will be like ten brides going out to meet him with lamps, but only the five wise brides taking oil for the lamps.*Matt 25:1-4* When the bridegroom delayed, the brides fell asleep until midnight when he arrived and the wise brides woke up to trim their lamps.*Matt 25:5-7* The foolish brides asked the wise brides for oil, but the wise brides sent them away to buy oil.*Matt 25:8-9* The bridegroom arrived and took the wise brides in for the wedding banquet, leaving the foolish brides outside when they returned.*Matt 25:10-12* Be dressed and ready for your master's service, like servants waiting for the master to return from a wedding banquet, whom the master will reward with his own service.*Lk 12:35-37* Do not return to your house or look back like Lot's wife because whoever tries to preserve their life will lose it and whoever loses it will preserve it.*Lk 17:31-33* Keep watch because you don't know the day or hour.*Matt 25:13* Be like the servants who put their journeying master's money to work, earning more money and receiving their master's reward on his return.*Matt 25:14-23* Don't be like the wicked, lazy, and worthless servant who hid his master's money, believing his master hard and unjust, and so lost the little that the master had given to him and ended up thrown out into darkness.*Matt 25:24-30* Be alert and aware, ready to pray because all things are about to end.*1Pe 4:7* Now is the time to wake up from your slumber because salvation is nearer now than when you first believed.*Ro 13:11*

You. Pray that you may escape all that is to happen and may stand before the Son of Man.*Lk 21:36* When Christ appears, you will appear with him in glory.*Col 3:4* The Lord's holy people who believed in Jesus, including you, will glorify Jesus and marvel at him on his return.*2Th 1:10-11* When Christ returns, dear children of God, we do not yet know what we will be, but we know we will be like him, seeing him as he is.*1Jn 3:2* Our expectation of his return keeps us trying to stay pure, just as he is pure.*1Jn 3:3* We should patiently await the Lord's near coming like the farmer waits patiently for rains to bring a valuable crop and like the prophets suffered while speaking in the Lord's name.*Jas 5:7-8,10* God's power shields us in our faith until the salvation comes that he will reveal in the last time.*1Pe 1:5* Keep alert and sober for the grace that Jesus Christ's coming revelation will bring to you.*1Pe 1:13* Be able to boast at Christ's return that you did not run or labor in vain.*Php 2:16* We know that God who began a good work in us will continue until the day Christ Jesus returns.*Php 1:6* We lack no spiritual gift as we eagerly wait for God to reveal our Lord Jesus Christ.*1Co 1:7* God will keep you firm to the end, so that no one blames you on the day of our Lord Jesus Christ.*1Co 1:8*

Pursuit. When he returns in his Father's glory with the holy angels, the Son of Man will be ashamed of anyone who shows shame for him and his words now, in an adulterous and sinful generation.*Mk 8:38, Lk 9:26* Because the end exposes everything, you should live holy and godly, looking forward to the Lord's speedy coming when all ends.*2Pe 3:11-12* When Jesus returns, God will punish with permanent destruction those who do not know God and do not obey the Lord Jesus's gospel, shutting them out from the Lord's presence and glory of his might.*2Th 1:8-10* Make every effort to be spotless, blameless and at peace with the patient God of salvation, as you await the end of all things as scripture accurately foretells but ignorant and unstable people distort to their own destruction.*2Pe 3:14-16* Forewarned, be on guard so that lawlessness's error does not cause you to fall from your secure position, but instead learn more of the grace of our Lord and Savior Jesus Christ to whom we give glory now and forever.*2Pe 3:17-18* May deep insight abound in your growing love, so that you are discerning, pure, and blameless for Christ's return.*Php 1:9-10* Be blameless and holy in the presence of our God and Father when our Lord Jesus returns with all his holy ones.*1Th 3:13* Be blameless at our Lord Jesus Christ's return.*1Th 5:23*

Dead. The resurrection of the dead has not yet taken place.*2Ti 2:18* Know how God treats those who died as Christ followers, so that you do not grieve like non-believers who have no hope.*1Th 4:13* Believe that Jesus died and rose again, so that God brings with Jesus those who died in him.*1Th 4:14* The Lord's word is that we who are alive when the Lord returns will certainly not go with him before believers who have already died go with him.*1Th 4:15* Instead, when the Lord comes down from heaven, with a loud command, with the voice of the archangel and with the trumpet call of God, those who died in Christ will rise first.*1Th 4:16* Then, God will catch up in the clouds together with the rising dead, the living who remain, to meet the Lord in the air to be with him forever.*1Th 4:17* God saves a person's spirit on the Lord's day.*1Co 5:4-5*

Heaven. God's word created the heavens and the earth.*2Pe 3:5* The unchanging Father in heaven gives heaven's good and perfect gifts.*Jas 1:17* God makes his angels spirits, and his servants flames of fire.*Heb 1:7* The Holy Spirit shares matters with us from heaven, into which even angels long to look.*1Pe 1:12* Every family in heaven derives its name from the Father.*Eph 3:14-15* You have a Master in heaven.*Col 4:1* God reveals his wrath from heaven.*Ro 1:18* God warns you from heaven with a warning that you cannot escape.*Heb 12:25* God promises that his voice will shake earth and heaven, leaving only what does not shake.*Heb 12:26-27* God intends that the church make his wisdom known to the rulers and authorities in the heavenly realms.*Eph 3:10-11* Every creature under heaven hears proclamation of the gospel.*Col 1:23* Set your mind on things above, not on earthly things.*Col 3:2* Jesus said not to despise a little child because their heavenly angels always see his Father's face in heaven.*Matt 18:10* Jesus also said to let the little children come to him because heaven's kingdom belongs to such as them, and to enter the kingdom, one must receive it like a little child.*Matt 19:13-15, Lk 18:15-17* Jesus said how hard the rich find getting into heaven's kingdom, God's kingdom, like passing a camel through the eye of a needle.*Matt 19:22-24* When the astonished disciples asked how anyone could then gain salvation, Jesus said that salvation is impossible for man but that all things are possible for God.*Matt 19:25-26* Jesus said at the Last Supper that where he was going, the disciples could not come then but would follow later.*Jn 13:33, 36*

Way. Jesus told Nicodemus of the Jewish ruling council that no one had gone into heaven except the Son of Man who had come from heaven.*Jn 3:13* When Jesus called Nathanael, and Nathanael called Jesus the Son of God for seeing him under a fig tree, Jesus said that Nathanael would see greater things including heaven open for God's angels to descend on and ascend from the Son of Man.*Jn 1:50* Jesus said that he would be on earth only for a short time before returning to the one who sent him, where others could not come, although the Jews did not understand him.*Jn 7:33-36* After Jesus told the disciples that they would be his witnesses to the ends of the earth, the Father took Jesus up before their very eyes, hiding him in a cloud.*Acts 1:9* The disciples looked intently up in the sky until two men dressed in white suddenly stood beside them, asking why they looked up when Jesus who went to heaven would come back in the same way that they saw him leave.*Acts 1:10-11* After Pentecost, Peter told the crowd that heaven must receive Jesus until God restores everything.*Acts 3:21* God's Son Jesus is from heaven.*1Th 1:10* The one from heaven is above all who are from the earth.*Jn 3:31* Christ, as God's Son, is far superior to the angels.*Heb 1:4-5* When God brought his firstborn Son into the world, he said that the angels would worship him.*Heb 1:6* God the Father gave Jesus honor and glory from heaven at Jesus's baptism.*2Pe 1:17-18* Christ did not just enter the human tabernacle but entered heaven itself to appear for us in God's presence.*Heb 9:24* Christ did not enter heaven to offer himself repeatedly, the way a human high priest entered the Most Holy Place every year with animal blood.*Heb 9:25* When God raised Christ from the dead, he seated him at his right hand in the heavenly realms, over all rule, authority, power, and dominion.*Eph 1:19-21* The Son sits at the right hand of the Majesty in heaven.*Heb 1:3* Jesus Christ is in heaven at God's right hand with angels, authorities, and powers submitting to him.*1Pe 3:21-22* When times reach fulfillment, God will unify everything in heaven and on earth under Christ.*Eph 1:8-10* When Christ ascended, he took many captives, while giving gifts to his people.*Eph 4:8* Christ, who also descended to the lower, earthly regions, ascended higher than heaven, so high as to fill the whole universe.*Eph 4:9-10* Christ ascended in glory.*1Ti 3:16* Every knee in heaven will bow with every tongue acknowledging that Jesus Christ is Lord.*Php 2:9-11*

You. God calls us heavenward in Christ Jesus.*Php 3:13-14* Make your citizenship heaven, eagerly awaiting heaven's Savior the Lord Jesus Christ.*Php 3:20-21* God raised us up with Christ and seated us with him in the heavenly realms so that he might soon show us the incomparable riches of his grace.*Eph 2:6-7* God keeps in heaven for us an inheritance that can never perish, spoil or fade.*1Pe 1:4* On his return, the Lord will come down from heaven and, with a loud command in the archangel's voice and with God's trumpet call, will catch up living and dead believers together in the clouds to meet him in the air and be with him in heaven forever.*1Th 4:17* The Lord will bring us safely to his heavenly kingdom.*2Ti 4:18* If the earthly tent in which we live suffers destruction, God gives us an eternal house in heaven, not built by human hands.*2Co 5:1* In our earthly tent, we groan with burden, fearing deadly exposure while wanting heaven's protection from death.*2Co 5:4* You receive God's kingdom that does not shake.*Heb 12:28-29* We long to be in our heavenly dwelling, which will not leave us exposed.*2Co 5:2-3* We look forward to the Lord's promised righteous new heaven and new earth.*2Pe 3:13* Our faith and love spring from the hope stored up for us in heaven, about which we hear in the true gospel message.*Col 1:5* Set your heart on things above where Christ sits at God's right hand.*Col 3:1* Jesus said that whatever you bind on earth, you bind in heaven, and whatever you loose on earth, you loose in heaven, implying to guide and discipline according to God's heavenly plan.*Matt 18:18* When one of the crucified criminals said to Jesus to remember him when coming into his kingdom, Jesus replied that the criminal would that day be with Jesus in paradise.*Lk 23:42-43*

Throne. Standing before a door open in heaven, the apostle John heard a voice like a trumpet telling him to see what would happen next.*Rev 4:1* At once in the Spirit, John saw someone looking like jasper and ruby sitting on a throne encircled by a rainbow shining like emerald and surrounded by twenty-four other thrones with seated elders.*Rev 4:2-4* Flashes of lightning and peals of thunder came from the throne, in front of which blazed seven lamps as the spirits of God on a crystal-clear sea of glass.*Rev 4:5-6* Around the throne were four living creatures covered with eyes, the first like a lion, second like an ox, third with the face of a man, and fourth like a flying eagle, each of them with six eye-covered wings, all of them night and day saying that the Lord God Almighty, who is, was, and is to come, is holy, holy, holy.*Rev 4:6-8* The twenty-four elders fell down each time the creatures gave glory, honor, and thanks to the one on the throne who lives forever, as the elders laid their crowns before the throne saying their Lord and God is worthy of glory, honor, and power for creating all things and giving them their being.*Rev 4:9-11*

Scroll. In his vision of heaven, the apostle John saw a scroll in the right hand of the one on the throne, with writing on both sides and seven seals, and a mighty angel asking in a loud voice who was worthy to break the seals and open the scroll.*Rev 5:1-2* John wept and wept because no one was worthy, but one of the elders told him not to weep because the triumphant Lion of Judah and Root of David was worthy to open the seals and scroll.*Rev 5:3-5* A slain Lamb approached the throne, surrounded by the four creatures and twenty-four elders, the Lamb having seven horns and eyes as the God's seven spirits sent out into all the earth, and took the scroll from the right hand of the one sitting on the throne, at which the creatures and elders fell down before the Lamb.*Rev 5:6-7* With harps and golden incense bowls as the prayers of God's people, the creatures and elders sang a new song saying the Lamb was worthy to open the seals and scroll because slain to purchase for God with his blood, persons from every nation as a kingdom and as priests, to serve God and reign on earth.*Rev 5:8-10* One-hundred-million angels around the throne sang that the slain Lamb is worthy to receive power, wealth, wisdom, strength, honor, glory, and praise.*Rev 5:11-12* Then every creature everywhere said praise, honor, glory, and power forever to the Lamb, with which the four creatures and elders fell down and worshiped.*Rev 5:13-14*

Seals. As the Lamb opened the first seal and the apostle John heard one of the four creatures say to come, a white horse appeared with a rider holding a bow and receiving a crown, at which the rider rode out as a conqueror.*Rev 6:1-2* As the Lamb opened the second seal and the second creature said to come, a fiery red horse came out, its rider given a large sword and power to take peace from the earth so that people killed each other.*Rev 6:3-4* As the Lamb opened the third seal and the third creature said to come, a black horse emerged, its rider holding a pair of scales, and a voice said to measure wheat and barley for a day's wages, and not to damage the oil and wine.*Rev 6:5-6* As the Lamb opened the fourth seal and the fourth living creature said to come, a pale horse emerged, its rider named Death, with Hades following close behind, and they received power to kill a fourth of the earth by sword, famine, plague, and wild beasts.*Rev 6:7-8* When the Lamb opened the fifth seal, the apostle John saw under the altar the souls of those slain because they testified for God's word, who called out asking how long before the holy and true Sovereign

Lord would judge the earth, avenging their blood, to which each received a white robe to wait a little longer until the full number of their fellow servants joined them as slain.$_{Rev\ 6:9-11}$ As the Lamb opened the sixth seal, the earth quaked, the sun turned black, the moon turned blood red, the stars fell to earth, figs dropped from a tree shaken by strong wind, and the heavens receded like a rolled-up scroll, removing every mountain and island.$_{Rev\ 6:12-14}$ Everyone on earth hid in caves and mountain rocks, calling to the mountains to fall on them to hide them from the one on the throne and the Lamb's wrath, for wrath's great day had come, which no one can withstand.$_{Rev\ 6:15-17}$ Four angels stood at the earth's corners, holding back the four winds, while another angel coming from the east with the living God's seal called out in a loud voice to the four powerful angels not to harm land or sea until they put a seal on the foreheads of God's servants.$_{Rev\ 7:1-3}$ The number of those sealed was 144,000, an equal 12,000 number from each of Israel's twelve tribes.$_{Rev\ 7:4-8}$ Then the apostle John saw a great uncountable multitude from every nation, standing before the throne and Lamb, wearing white robes, holding palm branches, and crying out that salvation belongs to God on the throne and the Lamb.$_{Rev\ 7:9-10}$ All the angels fell facedown before the throne, worshiping God while saying praise, glory, wisdom, thanks, honor, power, and strength to God forever.$_{Rev\ 7:11-12}$ One of the elders told John that the multitude had come out of the great tribulation, having washed their robes and made them white in the Lamb's blood.$_{Rev\ 7:13-14}$ The multitude was before the thone to serve God and for God to shelter with his presence so that never again would they hunger or thirst, or have sun or heat scorch them, because the Lamb will shepherd them to springs of living water, and God will wipe away their every tear.$_{Rev\ 7:15-17}$ When the Lamb opened the seventh seal, silence fell for about half an hour, until seven angels standing before God took seven trumpets, another angel with a golden censer offered on the golden altar much incense prayer of all God's people, and the angel then filled the censer with the altar's fire, hurling it to earth, from which came pealing thunder, lightning flashes, and quakes.$_{Rev\ 8:1-2}$

Judge. Jesus said that the one who seeks glory is the judge.$_{Jn\ 8:50}$ Fear with dread to fall into the living God's hands.$_{Heb\ 10:31}$ God has wrath and anger for those who are self-seeking, reject the truth, and follow evil.$_{Ro\ 2:8}$ The Lord will sentence earth with speed and finality.$_{Ro\ 9:28}$ God is both kind and stern, kind to you while you remain in his kindness but stern to those who fall, which could be you if you are not careful.$_{Ro}$

11:22 The word says that every knee will bow before the Lord and every tongue will acknowledge God.*Ro 14:11* Each of us must account to God.*Ro 14:12* Keep the attitude of a foreigner, living here in reverent fear, because your Father judges each person's work impartially.*1Pe 1:17* Judgment begins with God's people but will be far harder for the ungodly sinners.*1Pe 4:17-18* God judges anyone who does wrong.*Col 3:25* God will especially judge those who follow the corrupt desire of the flesh and despise authority.*1Pe 2:10* God reveals his wrath against all godlessness and wickedness of people suppressing the truth.*Ro 1:18* The Lord punishes all who commit sins, as others have warned you.*1Th 4:6* Judgment will come suddenly even while people assume that they are safe, but they will not escape.*1Th 5:3* Jesus said that he came to bring fire on the earth and wished that it was already kindled.*Lk 12:49* Jesus said that the Father judges no one, instead entrusting all judgment to the Son so that all honor the Son like the Father, because whoever does not honor the Son does not honor the Father.*Jn 5:22-23* Jesus said that the Father had given him authority to judge because he is the Son of Man.*Jn 5:27* As his crucifixion approached, Jesus said that judgment was then on the world, when he would drive out the world's prince to draw all people to himself.*Jn 12:30-32* Peter said that God commanded the apostles to preach and testify that Jesus is the one whom God appointed to judge the living and dead.*Acts 10:42-43*

Justice. God is just in bringing his wrath on us and judging the world.*Ro 2:5-6* God sees everything in all creation, uncovered and laid bare before him to whom we must give account.*Heb 4:13* God judges people's secrets.*Ro 2:16* God's judgments one cannot search or trace out.*Ro 11:33* We have plenty of evidence that God's judgment is right.*2Th 1:5* God repays each person for what they do.*Ro 2:6* God said he avenges and repays, judging his people.*Heb 10:30* God pays back for the harm sinners do, as they feast, carouse, and revel in pleasures in broad daylight.*1Pe 2:13* The person with the Spirit judges all things with Christ's mind, while not subject to merely human judgments because no one knows the Lord's mind to instruct.*1Co 2:15-16* Care little if a person or human court judges you, indeed as you do not even judge yourself.*1Co 4:3* Even if your conscience is clear, you may not be innocent, because the Lord judges you.*1Co 4:4* The Lord brings to light what one hides in darkness, and exposes the heart's motives, after which each will receive their praise from God.*1Co 4:5* Jesus said that on judgment day, everyone must account for every empty word they've spoken because words either acquit or condemn.*Matt 12:36-37*

Rebellion. Whoever rejects the Son will not see life because God's wrath remains on them.*Jn 3:36* If we deliberately keep on sinning after learning the truth, then no sacrifice for sins remains and instead only fearful judgment and raging fire that consumes God's enemies.*Heb 10:27* Those who rejected Moses's law died without mercy on two or three witnesses' testimony.*Heb 10:28* Those who trample on the Son of God, treating as unholy the covenant's blood that sanctified them, and insulting the Spirit of grace, deserve much more severe punishment.*Heb 10:29* Be humble rather than arrogant, and be careful, because if God rejected his chosen people, then he can reject you, too.*Ro 11:21* Everyone who does evil faces trouble and distress.*Ro 2:9* God judges adulterers and the sexually immoral.*Heb 13:4*

Condemned. Jesus said that a judge exists who judges those who reject him rather than accepting his words, because the words he speaks, which the Father commanded him to speak, will condemn them at the last day.*Jn 12:48* God did not spare the ancient world when he brought the flood on its ungodly people while protecting Noah, a preacher of righteousness, and seven others.*1Pe 2:5* God condemned the cities of Sodom and Gomorrah by burning them to ashes and made them an example of what is going to happen to the ungodly.*1Pe 2:6* God has doomed to destruction the lawless man who opposes and exalts himself over everything connected with God, trying to take God's place and make himself God.*2Th 2:3-4* Non-believers blaspheme in matters they don't even understand, like unreasoning creatures of instinct whom God catches and destroys.*1Pe 2:12* Jesus pronounced woes on towns where he did most of his miracles, when they did not repent, saying that even Sodom would have it better on judgment day.*Matt 11:20-24* Jesus said that on judgment day, Nineveh's men who repented at Jonah's preaching, and the South's Queen who listened to Solomon's wisdom, would condemn the generation that rejected Jesus, who is so much greater than Jonah and Solomon.*Matt 12:41-42* Jesus said that the Advocate would prove the world wrong about sin because people did not believe, about righteousness because Jesus was going to the Father, and about judgment because the world's prince now stood condemned.*Jn 16:8-11*

Angels. The Lord who delivers also destroys in eternal fire those who do not believe and instead give themselves up to sexual immorality and perversion, even binding for judgment day angels who refuse his authority.*Jude 5-7* God did not spare angels when they sinned, but sent them to hell, putting them in chains of darkness to be held for judgment.*1Pe 2:4* Dreams and animal instincts lead ungodly people to pollute their bodies, reject authority, heap abuse on angels, and slander whatever they do not understand, when even the archangel Michael did not dare condemn the devil's slander but said instead that the Lord would rebuke him.*Jude 8-10* Bold and arrogant non-believers heap abuse even on angels who, although stronger and more powerful, do not heap abuse on non-believers when bringing the Lord's judgment on them.*1Pe 2:10-11* Believers will not only judge angels but how much more the things of this life.*1Co 6:3* At the age's end, the Son of Man will send his angels to weed out all sin and evil for the blazing furnace so that the righteous shine in their Father's kingdom.*Matt 13:40-43* Angels will separate the wicked for destruction at the age's end.*Matt 13:47-50*

Judging. Jesus said that if anyone hears but does not keep his words, he does not judge them, because he did not come to judge the world but to save it.*Jn 12:47* Jesus said not to judge, or you, too, face judgment.*Matt 7:1* If you do not judge or condemn, then you will not face judgment or condemnation.*Lk 6:37* You face judgment just as you judge others and measurement just as you measure others.*Matt 7:2* Don't hypocritically see and try to correct the little defect another one has, while ignoring the big defect that you have.*Matt 7:2-4, Lk 6:41-42* First fix your own big problems so that you can help fix others' small problems.*Matt 7:5* Jesus also said to stop judging by mere appearances and instead judge correctly.*Jn 7:24* Jesus said to let the one who is without sin (which is no one) cast the first stone to condemn another of sin.*Jn 8:7* You have no excuse when you judge someone else because wherever you judge another, you condemn yourself because you do the same things.*Ro 2:1* God judges based on truth, so when mere humans judge others for doing the same things, they do not escape God's judgment.*Ro 2:2-3* Just because your faith is strong, don't judge the one who has weak faith, because God accepts them.*Ro 14:2-3* You are no one to judge another's servant, when each servant depends on their own master's judgment, and the Lord will help the one of weak faith stand.*Ro 14:4* Neither judge your brother or sister nor treat them with contempt because we will all stand before God's judgment seat.*Ro 14:10* Stop passing judgment on one another.*Ro 14:13* No more slandering others because speaking against another judges the law rather than keeps the law.*Jas 4:11* We have no grounds to judge another because only God, who is both Lawgiver and Judge, can save or destroy.*Jas 4:12* God is just in paying back trouble to those who trouble you, while relieving you from trouble.*2Th 1:6-7* Nonbelievers who oppose you heap up their sins to the limit, facing God's wrath.*1Th 2:16* Do not repay anyone evil for evil.*Ro 12:17* Do not take revenge, but leave it to God's wrath as the Lord says.*Ro 12:19* If your enemy is hungry, then feed him and if thirsty, then give him something to drink, having the effect of heaping coals on his head.*Ro 12:20* Do not be overcome by evil, but overcome evil with good.*Ro 12:21* Let no one pay back wrong for wrong.*1Th 5:15* Put up with one another, forgiving any against whom you have a grievance, just like the Lord forgave you.*Col 3:13* Forgive those who fail to come to your defense and instead desert you.*2Ti 4:16*

Return. In the last days, scoffers will follow their evil desires while questioning Jesus's return and any influence of God in the world.*2Pe 3:3-4* Those scoffers deliberately ignore that God's word created the heavens and the earth, God then deluged the earth with water, and God reserves the earth for fire and the ungodly for destruction on judgment day.*2Pe 3:5-7* God will judge all when the Lord Jesus returns.*2Th 1:7* When Jesus returns, God will punish with permanent destruction those who do not know God and do not obey the Lord Jesus's gospel, shutting them out from the Lord's presence.*2Th 1:8-10* God and Christ Jesus will judge the living and the dead.*2Ti 4:1* Jesus winnows wheat from chaff, gathering wheat into the barn but throwing the chaff in the fire.*Matt 3:12* The Lord is the righteous Judge who rewards all who long for his appearing.*2Ti 4:8* The Lord rescues the godly while holding the unrighteous for punishment on judgment day, just as God rescued Lot, a righteous man, whom the depraved conduct of the lawless distressed.*1Pe 2:7-9* Stubborn and unrepentant hearts store up God's wrath for judgment day.*Ro 2:5* Judge nothing before the appointed time, but wait until the Lord comes.*1Co 4:5* We must all appear before Christ's judgment seat to receive our due for things we did in the body, whether good or bad.*2Co 5:10* No one condemns those who are in Christ Jesus.*Ro 8:1* Jesus said that he does nothing by himself but judges justly because he seeks only to please the one who sent him.*Jn 5:30*

Separation. Jesus said that a time is coming when all in their graves would come out at his voice, those who have done good to rise to live but those who have done evil to face condemnation.*Jn 5:28-29* Jesus said that he had much to say in judgment of those who did not believe in him.*Jn 8:26*

When a man born blind to whom Jesus had given sight told Jesus that he believed that Jesus was the Son of Man, Jesus told him that Jesus had come into the world to judge, so that the blind would see and the sighted would not see.*Jn 9:35-39* Jesus said not to think that he brings peace to earth but instead division, dividing even family members against one another.*Lk 12:51-53* When Jesus returns on his glorious throne with all the nations gathered before him, he will separate people like a shepherd sorting sheep from goats, sheep to the right, goats to the left.*Matt 25:32* To those righteous sheep on his right, the King will say that his Father has blessed them to take their inheritance prepared for them since creation.*Matt 25:34* The King will say that he was hungry and the righteous gave him food, thirsty and they gave him drink, a stranger and they invited him in, without clothes and they clothed him, sick and they cared for him, and a prisoner and they visited him.*Matt 25:35-36* The righteous will ask when they did these things for him, and the King will answer that they did these things for him every time that they did them for his least brothers and sisters.*Matt 25:37-40* To the unrighteous goats on his left, the King will say to depart from him, as cursed for the eternal fire prepared for the devil and his angels.*Matt 25:41* The King will say that he was hungry but the unrighteous gave him nothing to eat, thirsty but they gave him no drink, a stranger but they did not invite him in, without clothes but they did not clothe him, and sick and in prison but they did not care for him.*Matt 25:42-43* The unrighteous will ask when they failed to do those things for him, and the King will reply that whatever they did not do for his least brothers and sisters, they did not do for him.*Matt 25:44-45* The righteous will then enjoy eternal life but the unrighteous face eternal punishment.*Matt 25:46* When evildoers see Abraham, Isaac, Jacob, and all God's prophets in God's kingdom, they will weep for God throwing them out, as others come from all directions to take their place at the kingdom's feast.*Lk 13:28-29*

Blasts. The apostle John in his vision from the island of Patmos saw the seven angels with the seven trumpets preparing to sound them.*Rev 8:6* When the first angel sounded his trumpet, hail and fire mixed with blood fell, burning up one third of earth, a third of its trees, and the grass.*Rev 8:7* When the second angel sounded his trumpet, a huge blazing mountain fell in the sea, a third of which turned to blood, killing a third of the sea creatures and destroying a third of the ships.*Rev 8:8-9* When the third angel sounded his trumpet, a great blazing star named Wormwood fell on a third of the rivers and springs, turning a third of the waters bitter and killing many people.*Rev 8:10-11* When the fourth angel sounded his trumpet, a third of the sun, moon, and stars turned dark, and a third of the day and night were without light.*Rev 8:12* The apostle John then heard a flying eagle call out woes on earth's inhabitants because of the coming trumpet blasts of the three remaining angels.*Rev 8:13* When the fifth angel sounded his trumpet, a star fallen to earth opened the shaft to the Abyss, emitting smoke as from a gigantic furnace, darkening the sky and bringing locusts with scorpion power.*Rev 9:1-3* The locusts tortured only those who didn't have God's seal on their forehead, with agony like a scorpion's sting, so that they sought death but could not find it.*Rev 9:4-6* The locusts were like horses ready for battle, wearing gold-like crowns, with human faces, women's hair, lions' teeth, iron breastplates, thundering wings, stingers that torment their victims for five months, and the Abyss's Destroyer angel as their king.*Rev 9:9-11* A first woe ended here with two more to come.*Rev 9:12* When the sixth angel sounded his trumpet, a loud voice from the golden altar's four horns said to release the four angels kept at the Euphrates River, to kill a third of humankind, with two-hundred-million mounted troops.*Rev 9:13-16* The riders wore fiery red, blue, and yellow breastplates, and their mounts had powerful lion heads with fire, smoke, and sulfur coming out of their mouths, and powerful tails like snakes with heads that injured.*Rev 9:17-19* Yet the rest of humankind that survived did not repent from worshiping demons and idols that could not see, hear, or walk, or from murder, magic arts, and sexual immorality.*Rev 9:20-21* Another angel came down from heaven robed in a cloud with a rainbow above his head, face like the sun, and legs like fiery pillars, holding a little scroll, while planting his feet on the sea and land, and giving a lion's roar emitting the voices of seven thunders, but a voice told the apostle John not to write down what the voices said.*Rev 10:1-4* Then the angel swore by the one who lives forever that without delay, the seventh trumpet should accomplish God's mystery.*Rev 10:5-7* The voice from heaven told John to take the scroll from the angel's hand, and the angel told John to eat the scroll, which was sweet in John's mouth but sour in his stomach, and to prophecy about many nations.*Rev 10:9-11* John received a measuring rod with which to measure the temple, while the angel told of two witnesses who will prophesy until the beast comes up from the Abyss to overpower and kill them, but God would give the witnesses breath again and bring them up to heaven, ending the second woe.*Rev 11:1-14* Then the seventh angel will sound the last trumpet so that the world's kingdom becomes the Messiah's kingdom for his reign forever, while the twenty-four elders fall on their faces worshiping God, giving thanks to the Lord God Almighty for beginning to reign, judging the dead, destroying those who destroy the earth, and revealing the ark of his covenant in heaven with lightning, thunder, quakes, and storms.*Rev 11:15-19*

Dragon. A pregnant woman crying out in birth pains, clothed with the sun, the moon under her feet, and twelve stars crowning her head, appeared as a great sign, followed by an enormous red dragon with seven heads, ten horns, and seven crowns on its head.*Rev 12:1-3* The dragon's tail swept a third of the stars to the earth, while standing in front of the woman waiting to devour her children as soon as born.*Rev 12:4* But as soon as the woman bore a son who would rule all nations with an iron scepter, God snatched the son up to heaven, and the woman fled to a wilderness place God prepared for her to wait.*Rev 12:5-6* War then broke out in heaven between the dragon and Michael and his angels, who hurled the dragon, that ancient serpent called the devil or Satan, and his angels to earth.*Rev 12:7-9* A loud voice in heaven confirmed that now had come God's salvation, power, and kingdom, and the Messiah's authority, with the defeat of the one who accuses the brothers and sisters who triumphed over him with the Lamb's blood and word of their testimony.*Rev 12:10-11* Heaven rejoiced while the devil filled the woeful earth with his fury, knowing his time was short.*Rev 12:12* On earth, the dragon pursued the woman who received a great eagle's wings to fly to her wilderness place, the dragon spewing water to overtake her but the earth swallowing the river and enraging the dragon who warred against the woman's children, those who keep God's commands while holding fast to their testimony to Jesus.*Rev 12:13-17*

Beasts. As the dragon stood on the sea's shore, from the sea emerged a beast with ten horns, seven heads, ten crowns on its horns, and a blasphemous name on each head, the beast looking like a leopard but with bear's feet and lion's mouth, to which the dragon gave its power, throne, and authority.*Rev 13:1-2* Although one of the beast's heads had a fatal-looking wound that had healed, the beast nonetheless filled with wonder the whole world, which followed the beast, people worshiping both the beast and the dragon that had given power to the beast, thinking that none could war against it.*Rev 13:3-4* The beast had authority to utter proud words and blasphemies for forty-two months, blaspheming God and slandering his name, heaven, and those who live in heaven.*Rev 13:5-6* The beast received power and authority to conquer God's holy people, so that all earth's inhabitants worshiped the beast, other than those whose names were in the Lamb's book of life, who were instead taken into captivity or killed, requiring God's people to endure patiently in faithfulness._{Rev 13:7-8} Then out of the earth came a second beast with two horns like a lamb but speaking like a dragon, with the first beast's authority, to make the earth's inhabitants worship the first beast with the healed wound._{Rev 13:11-12} The second beast performed great signs, such as fire coming down from heaven, deceiving the earth's inhabitants so that the inhabitants set up an image to honor the first beast, and the second beast then gave breath to the image, which then spoke and killed all who refused to worship the image._{Rev 13:13-15} The image also forced all people to receive a mark of the name or number of the beast, which is 666 and the number of man, on their hand or forehead, without which they could not buy or sell._{Rev 13:16-18}

Lamb. Yet the Lamb then stood on Mount Zion with 144,000 who had his name and his Father's name on their foreheads, singing a new song like roaring waters, loud thunder, and harps, that only the redeemed 144,000 could learn._{Rev 14:1-3} Male virgins purchased from among humankind and offered as firstfruits to God and the Lamb followed the Lamb, the virgins blameless and without lies in their mouths._{Rev 14:4-5} A first angel flew with the eternal gospel to every nation, saying to fear God, give him glory, and worship him who made everything, because his judgment's hour had come._{Rev 14:6-7} A second angel followed, saying that Babylon, which made the nations drink her adulteries, had fallen._{Rev 14:8} A third angel followed, saying that those who took the beast's mark would face God's full-strength fury, tormented continuously with burning sulfur in the presence of the Lamb and holy angels forever._{Rev 14:9-10} The people of God who keep his commands while remaining faithful to Jesus must endure patiently, while God blesses those who die in the Lord, the Spirit saying that they will rest from their labors with their deeds following them._{Rev 14:12-13} One like a son of man, with a gold crown, seated on a white cloud, and with a sharp sickle in his hand, heeded another angel's call that the time to reap had come, swinging his sickle over the earth to harvest it._{Rev 14:14-16} Another angel came out of heaven's temple with a sharp sickle, heeding still another angel's call to gather the grape clusters from the earth's ripe vines, the first angel swinging his sickle on the earth to gather its grapes for the great winepress of God's wrath, trampling blood out of the press rising as high as a horse's bridle for 180 miles._{Rev 14:17-20}

Plagues. Then the apostle John saw in heaven another great and marvelous sign, seven angels with the seven last plagues with which God completes his wrath.*Rev 15:1* Those who had been victorious over the beast and its image stood beside a sea glowing with fire, holding God's harps.*Rev 15:2* They sang the song of Moses and the Lamb that God's great and marvelous deeds and just and true ways bring glory to his name and reveal his righteous acts, causing all nations to worship him.*Rev 15:2-4* In heaven, the covenant law's tabernacle within the temple was open, and out with the seven plagues came the seven angels dressed in shining linen and golden sashes.*Rev 15:5-6* One of the four creatures gave to the seven angels seven golden bowls filled with God's wrath, filling the temple with smoke from God's glory and power, so that no one could enter the temple until the seven plagues were complete.*Rev 15:7-8*

Wrath. A loud voice from the temple told the seven angels to pour out the seven golden bowls of God's wrath on the earth, the first angel pouring out festering sores on the people who had the beast's mark and worshiped its image, the second angel pouring out blood like that of a dead person killing everything in the sea, and the third angel pouring out just judgments on the waters until they became blood.*Rev 16:2-7* The fourth angel poured out his bowl on the sun so that it scorched and seared the people with intense heat until they cursed God, but they still would not repent and glorify him.*Rev 16:8-9* The fifth angel poured out his bowl on the beast's throne, plunging its kingdom into darkness so that the people were in agony and cursed God, but they still refused to repent of what they had done.*Rev 16:10-11* The sixth angel poured out his bowl on the Euphrates River, drying it up.*Rev 16:12* But impure spirits like frogs came out of the mouths of the dragon, beast, and false prophet, demonic spirits that performed signs to gather the world's kings at Armageddon for the battle on God Almighty's great day.*Rev 16:13-16* Finally, the seventh angel poured out his bowl, a loud voice from the temple saying it was done.*Rev 16:17* Then came lightning flashes, rumblings, and thunder, until a tremendous earthquake like no other split the great city into thirds, while the earth's cities collapsed, as God gave Babylonian the cup filled with the fury of his wrath.*Rev 16:18-19* Every island fled, mountains disappeared, and huge hailstones weighing one hundred pounds each fell on the people, who cursed God for the terrible hail.*Rev 16:18-21*

Explanation. One of the seven angels with the seven bowls told the apostle John to let the angel show John the punishment of the great prostitute with whom the earth's kings committed adultery, the wine from which intoxicated earth's inhabitants.$_{Rev\ 17:1-2}$ The angel carried John in the Spirit away into the wilderness to show him a woman sitting on a scarlet beast having seven heads and ten horns, and covered with blasphemous names, the woman dressed in purple and scarlet, glittering with precious stones, and holding in her hand a golden cup filled with the abominable filth of her adulteries.$_{Rev\ 17:3-4}$ The woman's name written on her forehead was Babylon the great, mother of prostitutes and the earth's abominations, and she was drunk with the blood of God's holy people who testified to Jesus.$_{Rev\ 17:5-6}$ When the angel saw John greatly astonished, the angel explained that the beast would return, the beast astonishing the earth's people whose names were not in the book of life.$_{Rev\ 17:7-8}$ The beast's seven heads are seven hills and seven kings, five of whom have fallen, and the beast, an eighth king, will also fall.$_{Rev\ 17:9-11}$ The ten horns are ten kings not yet come but who will gain one hour's authority with the beast, giving their power and authority to the beast to war against the Lamb, but the Lamb will triumph as Lord of lords and King of kings, with his called, chosen, and faithful followers.$_{Rev\ 17:12-14}$ The waters are peoples, multitudes, nations, and languages.$_{Rev\ 17:15}$ The beast and ten horns will hate and ruin the prostitute, burning her with fire and eating her flesh, because God put into their hearts to accomplish his purpose, to give the beast their royal authority until God fulfills his words.$_{Rev\ 17:16-17}$ The woman is the great city that rules over the earth's kings.$_{Rev\ 17:18}$

Babylon. Another angel with great authority came down from heaven, illuminating the earth with his splendor while saying with a might voice that Babylon had fallen, becoming a dwelling and haunt for demons and every impure spirit.$_{Rev\ 18:1-2}$ The nations had drunk the maddening wine of her adulteries, the earth's kings had committed adultery with her, and the earth's merchants had grown rich from her excessive luxuries.$_{Rev\ 18:3}$ Another voice from heaven warned heaven's people to come out of Babylon so as not to share in her sins piled up to heaven or receive her plagues for her crimes.$_{Rev\ 18:4-5}$ The voice asked God to give her back a double portion from her own cup for what she has done, as much torment and grief as glory and luxury she had given herself, after she had boasted at her enthronement as queen.$_{Rev\ 18:6-7}$ Plagues, death, mourning, and famine will overtake her, and fire will consume her, for the mighty Lord God will judge her.$_{Rev\ 18:8}$ The earth's kings will stand far off, terrified at Babylon's judgment, her luxury and splendor vanished forever, while they weep and mourn because no one buys their luxury cargoes anymore, including slaves, to make them rich._{Rev 18:9-19} The heavens, people of God, apostles, and prophets will rejoice because God judged her with the judgment that she imposed on others._{Rev 18:20} Then a mighty angel threw a boulder into the sea, saying that with such violence Babylon will fall and disappear forever, never to be heard from again, for her magic spells led all nations astray and she slaughtered the prophets and God's holy people._{Rev 18:21-24} A great multitude roared in heaven over the smoke of Babylon going up forever, saying salvation, glory, and power belong to God for his true and just judgments condemning the great prostitute and avenging the blood of God's servants._{Rev 19:1-3} The twenty-four elders and four creatures echoed amen and hallelujah._{Rev 19:4} Then a great multitude shouted for the Lord God Almighty's reign, rejoicing that the Lamb's wedding had come, his bride ready in fine linen, representing the righteous acts of God's holy people._{Rev 19:6-8} The angel told John to write the true words of God that God blesses those whom he invites to the Lamb's wedding supper._{Rev 19:9} John fell at the angel's feet to worship him, but the angel told John not to do so because he was a fellow servant with John and the other brothers and sisters who testify to Jesus, and instead to worship God for the Spirit of prophecy testifying to Jesus._{Rev 19:10}

Warrior. The apostle John next saw heaven standing open to a white horse the rider of which was Faithful and True._{Rev 19:11} The rider's eyes blazed like fire, his head bore many crowns, he bore a name no one but he knows, he wore a robe dipped in blood, and his name is the Word of God._{Rev 19:12-13} Heaven's armies followed him, also riding white horses and dressed in fine white linen._{Rev 19:14} A sharp sword to strike down the nations came from the rider's mouth, as an iron scepter with which to rule the nations, while he tread the winepress of the fury of God's wrath._{Rev 19:15} The rider's robe and thigh bore the words King of kings and Lord of lords._{Rev 19:16} An angel called out to the birds to gather for God's great supper to eat the flesh of kings, generals, and all people._{Rev 19:17-18} The rider and his army then captured the beast and false prophet, throwing them alive into the fiery lake of burning sulphur, and killing the rest of the beast's army with the sword coming from his mouth, so that the birds gorged themselves on the army's dead flesh._{Rev 19:19-21}

Satan. An angel then came down from heaven with the key to the Abyss and a great chain with which the angel bound the dragon, referring to the devil or Satan, for a thousand years._{Rev 20:1-2} The angel threw Satan into the Abyss and locked the Abyss to keep Satan from deceiving the nations for the thousand years, after which Satan would be free for a short time.*Rev 20:3* Those with authority to judge sat on thrones, while the blessed and holy souls of those beheaded for testifying to Jesus and God's word came to life to reign with Christ as priests of God and Christ for the thousand years, as the first resurrection (the rest of the dead not coming to life until after the thousand years).*Rev 20:4-6* When the thousand years end, Satan will once again go out to deceive the nations and to gather them for battle, surrounding God's people in the city God loves, with an army numbered like sand on the seashore.*Rev 20:7-9* But fire came down from heaven to devour them, throwing Satan into the fiery lake with the beast and false prophet where they will suffer torment continuously forever.*Rev 20:10* Then the earth and heavens fled from one seated on a great white throne before whom stood the dead, and books opened, one of them the book of life, and the one on the throne judged the dead according to what the books recorded.*Rev 20:11-12* The sea, death, and Hades all gave up their dead so that each dead faced judgment according to the books.*Rev 20:13* Then death and Hades were thrown into the fiery lake as the second death and, with them, anyone whose name was not in the book of life.*Rev 20:14-15*

New. The apostle John then saw a new heaven and earth, the old having passed away.*Rev 21:1* The Holy City, the new Jerusalem, descended out of heaven from God, as a bride beautifully dressed for her husband.*Rev 21:2* A loud voice from the throne said to look at God's dwelling place now among his people, where he will be with them and be their God, wiping every tear from their eyes.*Rev 21:3-4* Death, mourning, crying, and pain will be no more, the old order having passed away.*Rev 21:4* The one seated on the throne said he is making everything new and to write down the words as trustworthy and true, for it is done.*Rev 21:5-6* He said that he is the Alpha and Omega, Beginning and End, giving water to the thirsty from the spring of life and everything to the victorious who are his children.*Rev 21:6-7* He will consign to the fiery lake the cowardly, unbelieving, vile, murderers, sexually immoral, idolaters, liars, and those who practice magic arts, in the second death.*Rev 21:8* One of the seven angels told the apostle John to come see the Lamb's bride, the angel carrying John in the Spirit to a great and high mountain to see the Holy City, Jerusalem, coming down out of heaven from God.*Rev 21:9-10* Jesus had said that the new Jerusalem will come down from heaven from God.*Rev 3:12* The city shone with God's glory, like a very precious jewel, jasper, clear as crystal, having a great high wall with twelve gates and an angel at each gate, and twelve foundations with each apostle's name on a foundation._{Rev 21:11-14} The angel had a gold measuring rod to show the city 1,400 miles long, wide, and high, with a wall 200 feet thick made of jasper, and the city made of glass-pure gold._{Rev 21:15-18} The foundations were each of a different precious stone, the gates each a single pearl, and the streets of pure, transparent gold._{Rev 21:19-21} The city had no temple because the Lord God Almighty and Lamb are its temple._{Rev 21:22} The city needed no light from sun or moon because God's glory lights the city and the Lamb is its lamp, the nations walking by that light._{Rev 21:23-24} The city's gates never shut because no night exists._{Rev 21:25} The nation's glory and kings' splendor enter the city._{Rev 21:24, 26} Nothing impure and no one who is shameful or deceitful enters the city but only those whose names are in the Lamb's book of life._{Rev 21:27} The water of life flows from the throne of God and the Lamb down the city's great street, with the tree of life on the river's each side, bearing twelve crops of fruit, one each month, the leaves healing the nations._{Rev 22:1-2} The throne will be in the city, his servants serving God and the Lamb, whose face they will see._{Rev 22:3}

Eternity. Jesus said that whoever believes in the Son has eternal life, while whoever rejects the Son will not see life because of God's wrath._{Jn 3:36} Jesus also said that whoever obeys his word will never see death._{Jn 8:51} When a law expert questioned Jesus about what the expert must do to inherit eternal life, Jesus pointed him to the law's commands to love the Lord your God with all your heart, soul, strength, and mind, and to love your neighbor like yourself._{Lk 10:25-28} Jesus said that the Father's commands, those that he said just as the Father told him to say, lead to eternal life._{Jn 12:50} Our Savior Christ Jesus brought immortality to light._{2Ti 1:10} The King eternal, immortal, invisible, the only God, has honor and glory forever._{1Ti 1:17} Everyone is like grass withering or flowers falling, but the Lord's word endures forever, just as you have heard._{1Pe 1:24-25} The covenant under which God raised our Lord Jesus from the dead is eternal._{Heb 13:20} While sin reigned in death, grace reigns through righteousness, bringing eternal life through Jesus Christ our Lord._{Ro 5:21} Fix your eyes on the unseen rather than what you see because what you see is temporary, while the unseen is eternal._{2Co 4:18} The Son's throne, as God, will last forever._{Heb 1:8} The earth and heavens will perish, wearing out like garments, but the Lord will remain._{Heb 1:11} The Lord will roll up earth and heavens like a robe, changing them like a garment, but the Lord will remain the same, for never-ending years._{Heb 1:12} When a rich young man asked Jesus how to get eternal life, Jesus first pointed to the commandments, but when the man said he'd kept the commandments, Jesus told him that to be perfect, he should sell his possessions, give to the poor, have treasure in heaven, and follow Jesus.$_{Matt\ 19:16-22,\ Mk\ 10:17-21,\ Lk\ 18:18-22}$ The man's face fell, and he went away sad, because he had great wealth.$_{Mk\ 10:22,\ Lk\ 18:23}$ At his coming, Jesus will separate the righteous from the unrighteous so that the righteous enjoy eternal life but the unrighteous face eternal punishment.$_{Matt\ 25:46}$ Jesus said that just as Moses lifted up the snake on a pole to heal Israel in the wilderness, so people must lift up the Son of Man so that everyone who believes in him may have eternal life.$_{Jn\ 3:14-15}$ For God so loved the world that he gave his one and only Son that whoever believes in him does not perish but has eternal life.$_{Jn\ 3:16}$ Jesus said that whoever hears his word, and whoever believes him who sent Jesus, receives eternal life, crossing over from death to life.$_{Jn\ 5:24}$ Jesus said that the Jewish leaders studied the scriptures diligently thinking that they have eternal life, when the scriptures tell about Jesus whose offer of life they refuse.$_{Jn\ 5:39-40}$ Peter said that the disciples had no one else to whom to go because Jesus, the Son of God, had eternal life's words.$_{Jn\ 6:67-69}$ Jesus repeated that his sheep know his voice and follow him, and he gives them eternal life.$_{Jn\ 10:27-29}$ Jesus prayed that the Father had granted him authority over all people so that he could give eternal life to all those whom the Father had given him.$_{Jn\ 17:2}$ Jesus also prayed that eternal life is to know the Father, the only true God, and Jesus Christ whom the Father sent.$_{Jn\ 17:3}$

Destiny. The Father's will is that everyone who looks to and believes in the Son gains eternal life, Jesus raising them up at the last day.$_{Jn\ 6:40}$ The one who believes has eternal life.$_{Jn\ 6:47}$ While those who ate God's manna died, anyone who eats the bread that comes down from heaven, Jesus's flesh, does not die but lives forever.$_{Jn\ 6:50-51}$ Anyone who loves their life will lose it, while those who hate their life will have eternal life.$_{Jn\ 12:25}$ Justified by God's grace, we are heirs to eternal life.$_{Tit\ 3:7}$ We receive the promised eternal inheritance, now that Christ has died as a ransom to set us free from the sins committed under the first covenant.$_{Heb\ 9:15}$ Our Lord Jesus Christ and God our Father gave us good hope of eternity.$_{2Th\ 2:16-17}$ Those who believe in Christ Jesus receive eternal life.$_{1Ti\ 1:16}$ The living and enduring word of God has given you rebirth, not perishable but imperishable.$_{1Pe\ 1:23}$ Christ's one sacrifice made you, whom God is making holy, perfect forever.$_{Heb\ 10:14}$ When you build yourself up in your most holy faith and pray in the Holy Spirit, you keep yourself in God's love, waiting for the mercy of our Lord Jesus Christ to bring you to eternal life.*Jude 20-21* Fight faith's good fight to take hold of eternal life.*1Ti 6:12* The elect obtaining salvation in Christ Jesus receive eternal glory.*2Ti 2:10* God gives eternal life to those who by persistence in doing good seek glory, honor, and immortality.*Ro 2:7* One reaps no benefit from sin, only shame and death, but one reaps holiness and eternal life as a slave to God, because sin's wage is death, but God's gift is eternal life in Christ Jesus our Lord.*Ro 6:21-22* Everyone in competition has strict training to get a temporary crown, but you train to get a crown that lasts forever.*1Co 9:25* Our eternal glory far outweighs the light and momentary troubles achieving that glory for us.*2Co 4:17* When Jesus asked a Samaritan woman for a drink from a well, and she asked why he, a Jew, asked her, a Samaritan, Jesus said that she should have known God's gift and asked him for living water.*Jn 4:4-10* She said that he had no way to give her water, but Jesus replied that the water he gives satisfies all thirst welling up to eternal life.*Jn 4:11-14* When Peter and the disciples asked what reward they would receive for following Jesus, Jesus replied that anyone who has left houses, family, or fields for him receives one-hundred times as much, plus eternal life.*Matt 19:27-29, Mk 10:28-30, Lk 18:28-30* Jesus said not to work for food that spoils but for food that endures to eternal life, which the Son of Man, on whom God the Father placed his seal of approval, gives you.*Jn 6:26-27* Jesus said that whoever is victorious will eat from the tree of life in God's paradise, the second death will not hurt, will have a white stone with a new name on it known only to its recipient, will rule over nations, and will get the morning star.*Rev 2:7, 11, 17, 26-28* Those who have not soiled their clothes will walk with Jesus, dressed in white as worthy, and he will never blot out their name from the book of life but will acknowledge them before his Father and angels in heaven.*Rev 3:4-5* Jesus will make them a pillar of God's temple so that they never again leave it, and he will write on them God's name and the name of God's city.*Rev 3:12* Jesus will give them the right to sit with him on his throne, just as he sat down with his Father.*Rev 3:21*

Part II: Darkness

Satan. Law. Deceivers. World. Doubt. Trials.

While the New Testament tells the great story of light coming into the world as the life of humankind, giving us ultimate victory over death through Christ's resurrection, the New Testament also tells that spiritual warfare will continue until Christ's return. Darkness retreats but God has not yet banished. Legalism still tempts us to give up our freedom for law's custody. We seek outward adornment, deserting the faith in favor of idols, confused over faith's meaning. Opponents still persecute us, while we also fall prey to our own traditions, temptation, and pride. We unwisely accept a slavery of the flesh, falling under the curse of evil spirits that we should know better to resist. See how the New Testament addresses the darkness around us. Do you see and resist the darkness?

Satan

The New Testament addresses the adversary Satan, the devil and his demons, and all corruption and its effects. We must know the opponent in order that we can resist him, keeping our minds focused on Christ. We must also know our own sin-leaning nature, the bondage into which temptation so readily leads us. Christ triumphed over Satan, for us to share in that triumph. See how the New Testament addresses our formidable adversary, made weak and subject in Christ. Can you identify the devil and his bondage, so that you may resist in the name and power of Christ?

Enemy. Just before his arrest and crucifixion, Jesus said that the prince of the world was coming but had no hold over him and instead would come so that the world learned that Jesus would do exactly what his Father, whom he loved, commanded.$_{Jn\ 14:30\text{-}31}$ Jesus said that the devil was a murderer from the beginning who could not hold to the truth because he had no truth in him.$_{Jn\ 8:44}$ Jesus said that when the devil lies, he speaks his native language because he is a liar and the father of lies.$_{Jn\ 8:44}$ When after Pentecost a man sold a piece of property and with his wife's knowledge kept back some of the money for himself before putting the rest at the apostles' feet, Peter told him that Satan had caused him to lie not just to humans but to the Holy Spirit and God, so that the man promptly died.$_{Acts\ 5:1\text{-}6}$ Watch out because your enemy the devil prowls like a roaring lion looking to devour someone.$_{1Pe\ 5:8}$ Simply believing in God is not enough because even shuddering demons know he exists.$_{Jas\ 2:19}$ The devil traps gospel opponents who don't know truth, so that they are captive to do the devil's will.$_{2Ti\ 2:25\text{-}26}$ Those who hear God's word but don't grasp it, lose it to the evil one like a seed sown along a path.$_{Matt\ 13:19}$ The tempter does his tempting work to destroy your faith.$_{1Th\ 3:5}$ Satan blocks your way from seeing fellow believers.$_{1Th\ 2:17}$ The lawless one will come in the wicked way that Satan works, using all sorts of powerfully deceiving displays, signs, and wonders serving the deadly lie.*2Th 2:9* The difference between God's children and children of the devil is that God's children love one another and stop sinning, while the devil's children do not.*1Jn 3:9* Satan masquerades as an angel of light.*2Co 11:14* No surprise, then, that Satan's servants masquerade as if serving righteousness, but they will end as they deserve.*2Co 11:15* Bitter envy and selfish ambition are earthly and demonic, sowing disorder and evil.*Jas 3:14-16* Satan can send a thorn in the flesh to torment.*2Co 12:7* The Spirit warns against following deceiving spirits and demons.*1Ti 4:1* Do not in sensual desire turn away to follow Satan.*1Ti 5:14-15* The faithful may hand over to Satan those who reject faith and a good conscience, to learn not to blaspheme.*1Ti 1:20* An overseer must not become conceited and fall under the same judgment as the devil.*1Ti 3:6* An overseer must also have a good reputation with outsiders, so that he will not fall into disgrace and into the devil's trap.*1Ti 3:7* Non-believers offer sacrifices to demons, not to God, so do not participate with demons.*1Co 10:20* Satan is the prince of demons.*Matt 9:34* When Peter tried rebuking Jesus for saying that Jesus would die and rise to life, Jesus said for Satan to get behind him, not to be a stumbling block to him over the concerns of God.*Matt 16:22-23* Jesus said that one of the twelve disciples was a devil, referring to Judas Iscariot who would betray Jesus.*Jn 6:70* The devil prompted Judas to betray Jesus.*Jn 13:2* Satan entered Judas as soon as Jesus gave the dipped bread to Judas.*Jn 13:26-27* Jesus said to Peter at the Last Supper that Satan had asked to sift the disciples as wheat but that Jesus had prayed for Peter so that his faith would not fail and Peter would instead turn back to strengthen his brothers.*Lk 22:31-32* Jesus said that the world's prince now stood condemned.*Jn 16:8-11*

Spirits. Rather than trust spirits from the many false prophets, test them to see if God sent them.*1Jn 4:1* Spirits that acknowledge Jesus Christ are from God, while spirits that do not acknowledge Jesus are not from God but from the antichrist about whom you have heard and who is now already here.*1Jn 4:2-3* Followers of Jesus are from God and have overcome false spirits, because God in his followers is greater than the world's antichrist.*1Jn 4:4* False spirits from the world speak from the world's viewpoint, to which those who don't know Jesus readily listen.*1Jn 4:5* God gives to some the gift of distinguishing between spirits.*1Co 12:8-10* Those who know God listen to those of us who are from God, while those who are not from God do not listen to us, which is how we distinguish the Spirit of truth from false spirits.*1Jn 4:6* God makes his angels spirits and his servants flames of fire._{Heb 1:7} Angels are ministering spirits sent to serve those who inherit salvation._{Heb 1:14} The Spirit warns against following deceiving spirits and demons._{1Ti 4:1} We should submit only to the Father of spirits to truly live._{Heb 12:9} You have come to the God who is the Judge of all and to spirits of the righteous he made perfect._{Heb 12:23}

Resistance. Jesus prayed that the Father would protect the disciples from the evil one._{Jn 17:15} We struggle not against flesh and blood but against rulers, authorities, and powers of this dark world and spiritual forces of evil in the heavenly realms._{Eph 6:12} Jesus said that to keep your eyes, which are the body's lamp, healthy so that your whole body fills with light, because if your eyes are unhealthy, then your whole body fills with great darkness, extinguishing the light._{Matt 6:22-23} The devil flees us when we resist him._{Jas 4:7-8} God rescues us from the dominion of darkness._{Col 1:13} The archangel Michael did not dare condemn the devil's slander but said instead that the Lord would rebuke him._{Jude 8-10} Wear God's full armor so that you withstand the devil's schemes._{Eph 6:11} Resist him, standing firm in the faith, because you know that followers everywhere face the same sufferings._{1Pe 5:9} Wear God's full armor so that when evil's day comes, you can stand your ground and remain standing._{Eph 6:13} Do not give the devil a foothold by remaining angry._{Eph 4:27} Be very careful that you live wisely, making the most of every opportunity, because the days are evil._{Eph 5:15-16} Use the shield of faith to extinguish the evil one's flaming arrows._{Eph 6:16} The Lord delivers from the lion's mouth._{2Ti 4:17} The God of peace will soon crush Satan under your feet._{Ro 16:20} Jesus told the parable that the devil sows in the world's field the weeds who are people who follow his evil._{Matt 13:36-38} At the age's end, the Son of Man will send his angels to weed out all sin and evil for the blazing furnace so that the righteous shine in their Father's kingdom._{Matt 13:40-43} God has prepared an eternal fire for the devil and his angels._{Matt 25:41} To the church in Smyrna, Jesus said that he knows the slander of Satan's synagogue but not to fear, and to be faithful to the point of death when the devil puts some of them in prison and persecutes them._{Rev 2:9-10} To the church in Pergamum, Jesus said that he knows that it lives where Satan has his throne but that it remains true to his name and did not renounce its faith in him._{Rev 2:13-16} To the church in Thyatira, Jesus said that some have learned Satan's so-called deep secrets, but that they should repent, or he would repay each of them according to their deeds._{Rev 2:19-24}

Christ. The Spirit led Jesus into the wilderness after his baptism, for the devil to tempt him.*Matt 4:1, Lk 4:1-2* Jesus answered each of the devil's temptings with scripture.*Matt 4:3-11, Lk 4:3-12* Whenever impure spirits saw Christ, they fell down before him, crying out that he was the Son of God, but Jesus would tell them not to tell others.*Mk 3:11-12, Lk 4:41* Jesus told the disciples that he saw Satan fall like lightning from heaven.*Lk 10:18* As his crucifixion approached, Jesus said that judgment was then on the world, when he would drive out the world's prince to draw all people to himself.*Jn 12:30-32* Christ disarmed and triumphed over evil powers and authorities, making a public spectacle of them.*Col 2:15* No harmony exists between Christ and Satan.*2Co 6:15* You cannot drink the Lord's cup and the demons' cup, too, taking part in both the Lord's table and demons' table.*1Co 10:21* Don't let the serpent's cunning lead your minds astray from Christ.*2Co 11:3* Jesus shared in our humanity because we are human, so that by his death he would break the devil's power of death.*Heb 2:14* The Lord protects you from the evil one.*2Th 3:3* Assemble with the Lord Jesus's power present, to hand wrongdoers among you, who practice sexual immorality that not even non-believers practice, over to Satan to destroy the flesh, so that God may save the disobedient one's spirit on the Lord's day.*1Co 5:4-5* If you forgive, then others will also forgive, all in Christ's sight for your sake, so that Satan, of whose schemes we know, does not outwit us.*2Co 2:10-11* To be righteous is to do the right things that Christ does, while to be sinful is to do the opposite as the devil does, that which Christ came to destroy.*1Jn 3:7-8* Neither death nor life, angels nor demons, nor any powers, nor anything else in all creation, can separate us from God's love in Christ Jesus our Lord.*Ro 8:38-39*

Possession. The people would bring all the demon-possessed to Jesus for healing, and Jesus would drive out the demons, not letting them speak because they knew who he was.*Mk 1:32-34* Jesus traveled throughout Galilee, driving out demons.*Mk 1:39* In Capernaum's synagogue, a man whom an impure spirit possessed cried out to Jesus asking whether Jesus had come as God's Holy One to destroy them.*Mk 1:23-24* Jesus told the impure spirit to be quiet and come out of the man, which the spirit did with a violent shake and shriek, amazing the people.*Mk 1:25-27, Lk 4:33-36* Jesus cured those whom impure spirits troubled.*Lk 6:18* Jesus also cast demons out of two violent, demon-possessed men, at the demons' request sending them into a herd of pigs, with the herd rushing into a lake to drown.*Matt 8:28-34* Another gospel records Jesus casting an impure spirit, who said his name was Legion for they were many, out of a violent man living among the tombs.*Mk 5:1-10, Lk 8:26-31* The spirit called Jesus the Son of the Most High God and asked in God's name that Jesus not torture him.*Mk 5:7, Lk 8:28* At their request, Jesus sent the demons into a herd of about two-thousand pigs that then rushed drowning into the lake.*Mk 5:11-13, Lk 8:32-33* Jesus drove a demon out of a man who could not talk, after which the man spoke, amazing the crowd the members of which had never seen anything like it.*Matt 9:32-34* Jesus told his disciples to drive out demons.*Matt 10:8* Jesus gave them authority to do so.*Lk 9:1* The seventy two whom Jesus sent out returned rejoicing that even the demons submitted to them.*Lk 10:17* Jesus replied that they should not rejoice that the spirits submit to them but that heaven had written their names.*Lk 10:20* When some said that Jesus drove out demons by the prince of demons Beelzebub, Jesus said that if the house's head is like Beelzebub, then the members of that house would also be demons.*Matt 10:25* Jesus healed a blind, mute, and demon-possessed man.*Matt 12:22* Jesus healed the demon-possessed daughter of a Canaanite woman who showed Jesus that the woman had great faith.*Matt 15:21-28* Jesus rebuked a demon out of a possessed boy whose father had brought him to Jesus for healing because the boy had seizures that often cast him into fire or water.*Matt 17:14-18, Mk 9:17-27, Lk 9:37-43* Jesus told the disciples, who were unable to cast out the spirit, that this kind of spirit only comes out with prayer.*Mk 9:28-29* He also asked how long he would put up with an unbelieving and perverse generation.*Lk 9:41* The Pharisees told Jesus to leave because Herod wanted to kill him, but Jesus said that he would press on driving out demons and healing because no prophet can die outside Jerusalem.*Lk 13:31* The apostles healed all whom the crowds brought to them, whom impure spirits tormented.*Acts 5:16* Philip proclaimed the Messiah in Samaria, where impure spirits came out of many with a shriek.*Acts 8:5-8* A female slave who had a spirit by which she predicted the future followed the apostle Paul and others around, annoying them by shouting that they were the Most High God's servants, until Paul turned around and rebuked the spirit out of her.*Acts 16:16-18* God did extraordinary miracles through Paul, so that handkerchiefs and aprons that touched him cast evil spirits out of the sick.*Acts 19:11-12*

Opposition. The Pharisees said that Jesus drove out demons by the prince of demons Beelzebub and was himself demon-possessed, but Jesus told them that a kingdom divided against itself, like Satan driving out Satan, cannot stand.*Matt 12:25-26, Mk 3:22-26, Lk 11:17-18* Jesus said that if he drives out demons by Beelzebub, then the Pharisees must also do so, making demons their judge, but that Jesus drove out demons by God's Spirit, meaning God's kingdom had come.*Matt 12:27-28, Lk 11:19-20* Jesus said that no one can plunder a strong man's house unless they first tie up or take away the armor of the strong man.*Matt 12:29, Mk 3:27, Lk 11:21-22* Jesus said that an impure spirit coming out of a person seeks but does not find rest and so returns to the person it left, taking seven other more-wicked spirits, making the person worse than ever.*Matt 12:43-44, Lk 11:24-26* The disciples told someone who was driving out demons in Jesus's name to stop doing so because the person was not one of them, but Jesus said not to stop him because anyone doing a miracle in his name could not say anything against him and whoever is not against them is for them.*Mk 9:38-40, Lk 9:49-50* Jesus noted that people said that John the Baptist had a demon.*Matt 11:18* Jesus said that the Jewish leaders who rejected him were the devil's children, not Abraham's children as they claimed, because they wanted to carry out the devil's murderous lies rather than do as Abraham would have done.*Jn 8:39-44* When Jesus asked the Jews why they were trying to kill him, they called him demon-possessed and denied that they were trying to kill him.*Jn 7:19-20* Seven sons of a Jewish priest tried to invoke Jesus's name to drive evil spirits out of the possessed, but one of the spirits said he knew Jesus and knew about Paul but not them, so that the man with the spirit gave the sons a severe beating.*Acts 19:13-16*

Idols. Non-believers exchange the immortal God's glory for images made to look like a mortal human, birds, animals, and reptiles.*Ro 1:23* They exchange the truth about God for a lie, worshiping and serving created things rather than the Creator whom we forever praise.*Ro 1:25* They destine themselves for destruction when they make their god their stomach and their glory their shame, setting their desire on earthly things.*Php 3:19* Some with weak consciences don't know God but are instead so accustomed to idols that they think the defiled sacrificial food they eat was for a god.*1Co 8:7* But food does not bring us near to God, when to the contrary we are no worse if we do not eat or better if we do eat.*1Co 8:8* Weep that many live as enemies of Christ's cross.*Php 3:18* That Athens was full of idols greatly distressed the apostle Paul, who thus reasoned in the synagogue and marketplace, preaching the good news about Jesus's resurrection.*Acts 17:16-20* Turn from idols to serve the living and true God.*1Th 1:9* An idol is nothing at all in the world because we have only one God.*1Co 8:4* Others claim many so-called gods in heaven and on earth, and many lords.*1Co 8:5* We have only one God, the Father, from whom all things came and for whom we live, and we have only one

Lord, Jesus Christ, through whom all things came and through whom we live._{1Co 8:6} Flee from idolatry._{1Co 10:14} Keep yourselves from idols, from putting other things above God._{1Jn 5:20} Do not partner with the idolater._{Eph 5:7} Put to death idolatrous things belonging to your earthly nature._{Col 3:5} An idol, or food sacrificed to an idol, are nothing._{1Co 10:19-20} The temple of God and idols do not agree._{2Co 6:16} The Jerusalem apostles and elders sent a letter not to make things hard for the new Gentile believers, only requiring that they abstain from sexual immorality, blood, meat of strangled animals, and food idols polluted._{Acts 15:12-21} Before you believed, others influenced and led you astray to mute idols._{1Co 12:2} Be careful to exercise your rights without being a stumbling block to the weak._{1Co 8:9} You embolden a person with weak conscience, to eat food sacrificed to idols, when they see you eat in an idol's temple, even though you know better._{1Co 8:10} Your knowing better can destroy a weak brother or sister for whom Christ died._{1Co 8:11} You sin against Christ when you sin against another by wounding their weak conscience._{1Co 8:12} Better not to eat that food again if what you eat causes your brother or sister to fall into sin._{1Co 8:13} Do not arouse the Lord's jealousy because you are not stronger than he._{1Co 10:22} No idolater inherits the kingdom of Christ and God._{Eph 5:5} Idolatry brings God's wrath._{Eph 5:6}

Disobedience. Jesus said that if he had not come and spoken, then those who now reject him would not be guilty of sin._{Jn 15:22} Jesus added that if he had not done the works that he did, then those who reject him would not be guilty of sin, but they have seen the works and still hated both Jesus and his Father, fulfilling the scripture that they would hate him without reason._{Jn 15:24-25} Sin entered the world through one man, death following for all because all sinned._{Ro 5:12} All turn away from God to become worthless, without any doing good, not even one._{Ro 2:12} All sin, falling short of God's glory._{Ro 2:23} Adam, the first to sin, was a pattern of the one to come, the sinless Jesus._{Ro 5:14} Jesus, though, is different from Adam, in that many died from Adam's trespass, but many lived from the gift of God's grace in Jesus Christ_{Ro 5:15} The penalty of Adam's sin differs from God's gift of grace, in that judgment's condemnation followed sin, but grace's justification followed many sins._{Ro 5:16} Death reigned by one man's sin, but God's abundant grace and righteousness reign in life through one man Jesus Christ's gift._{Ro 5:17} One sin resulted in condemnation for all, while one righteous act resulted in justification and life for all._{Ro 5:18} One man's disobedience made many sinners, yet another man's obedience made many righteous._{Ro 5:19} All wrongdoing is sin.$_{1Jn\ 5:17}$ All are under sin's power.$_{Ro\ 2:8-11}$ Jesus said to the invalid whom Jesus healed at the pool by Jerusalem's Sheep Gate that the man should stop sinning or something worse might happen to him.$_{Jn\ 5:14}$

Nature. Although many people saw the signs Jesus performed and believed accordingly, Jesus did not entrust himself to them because he knew what was in each person.$_{Jn\ 2:23-25}$ We are unspiritual, slaves to sin.$_{Ro\ 7:14}$ We don't understand the bad that we do or why we do it, when we want instead to do good, except that we know sin lives in our sinful nature.$_{Ro\ 7:15-20}$ Whenever we want to do good, evil is right there with us.$_{Ro\ 7:21}$ Sin wages war against our minds, imprisoning us in sin.$_{Ro\ 7:23}$ We are wretched indeed, with minds devoted to God while trapped in bodies with sinful natures subject to death, but we thank God for delivering us through Jesus Christ our Lord.$_{Ro\ 7:24-25}$ Before our salvation, we were foolish, disobedient, deceived and enslaved by passions and pleasures, living in malice and envy, hated and hating others.$_{Tit\ 3:3-4}$ We were once dead in our transgressions and sins, in which we used to live when we followed the world's ways and ways of the evil spirit still at work in the disobedient.$_{Eph\ 2:1-2}$ You once lived debauched as pagans live in lust, drunkenness, and detestable idolatry, and so now they heap abuse on you for not joining them in their reckless living.$_{1Pe\ 4:3-4}$

Cursed. The apostle Paul cursed as the devil's child a sorcerer who opposed their word, immediately blinding him for a time.$_{Acts\ 13:6-12}$ Whoever does not have godly qualities is nearsighted and blind, forgetting that they have been cleansed from their past sins.$_{2Pe\ 1:9}$ Those accursed experts in greed whose eyes fill with adultery, they never stop sinning, seducing the unstable while wandering after the wages of wickedness, so stupid as to suffer rebuke and restraint by an ordinarily speechless animal.$_{1Pe\ 2:14-16}$ Sinners are springs without water and mists driven by a storm, for whom God reserves blackest darkness.$_{1Pe\ 2:17}$ Allow among God's holy people not even a hint of sexual immorality, any impurity, or greed.$_{Eph\ 5:3}$ Banish obscenity, foolish talk, and coarse joking, in favor of thanksgiving.$_{Eph\ 5:4}$ No immoral, impure, or greedy person inherits the kingdom of Christ and God.$_{Eph\ 5:5}$ Immorality is disobedience bringing God's wrath.$_{Eph\ 5:6}$ Do not partner with the immoral.$_{Eph\ 5:7}$ One reaps no benefit from sin, only shame and death, because sin's wage is death.$_{Ro\ 6:21-22}$

Law. Sin and death were in the world before God gave the law, although God charges sin against no one without breaking a command of the law.*Ro 5:13-14* God gave the law to increase sin so that grace would increase even more.*Ro 5:20* The law defines sin for us, such as when the law says not to covet, showing us that coveting is sin.*Ro 7:7* The law makes us conscious of our sin.*Ro 2:20* Yet commands make us want to break them.*Ro 7:8* Apart from the law, sin was dead, and we were alive, but with the commandment, sin sprang to life and we died.*Ro 7:8-9* The commandment that should bring life instead brought death because sin deceived, through the commandment putting us to death.*Ro 7:10-11* The good law did not become death, but sin used the good law to bring death, showing sin's utter sinfulness.*Ro 7:13* Before Jesus returns, the lawless man's rebellion will occur, in which the lawless man, doomed to destruction, will oppose and exalt himself over everything connected with God trying to take God's place and proclaim himself God.*2Th 2:3-4* Lawlessness's secret power already works, even though the Lord Jesus will overthrow and destroy the lawless one.*2Th 2:7-8*

Judgment. All who sin apart from the law perish, while all who sin under the law face law's judgment.*Ro 2:12* God's wrath is coming for sin.*Col 3:6* God got angry with our ancestors who sinned, leaving them to perish in the wilderness, while swearing that those who disobeyed in unbelief would never enter his rest.*Heb 3:17-19* The Lord punishes all who commit sins, as others have warned you.*1Th 4:6* Anyone who does wrong will be repaid for their wrongs.*Col 3:25* Your evil behavior once alienated you from God, making you enemies in your minds.*Col 1:21* Don't worry about those with whom you once sinned and who now persecute you for abandoning them to their sin because they must account to God who judges both the living and dead.*1Pe 4:5* The sins of some are obvious, reaching the place of judgment ahead of them, while the sins of others trail behind them.*1Ti 5:24* Establish accusations by the testimony of two or three witnesses, but do not spare those who sin because Christ is not weak but powerful in dealing with you.*2Co 13:1-3* Jesus said that if a brother or sister sins, then point out their fault to them privately.*Matt 18:15* If they continue sinning, then confront them again with two or three other witnesses.*Matt 18:16* If they refuse to listen, then tell the church, and if they still refuse to listen, then treat them as a pagan or tax collector.*Matt 18:17* After giving sight to a blind man, Jesus said to the Pharisees who claimed that they could see, that the guilt of those who claim they can see remains, while the blind are not guilty of sin.*Jn 9:40-41*

You. You have died to sin and can no longer live in it, so don't sin simply expecting more grace.*Ro 6:1-2* Our old self's crucifixion with Jesus killed the sinful body, setting us free from sin and making us no longer slaves to sin.*Ro 6:6-7* Christ died to sin once for all.*Ro 6:10* Like Christ, count yourselves dead to sin but alive to God in Christ Jesus.*Ro 6:11* Do not let sin reign in your body, obeying its evil desires.*Ro 6:12* Do not offer any part of yourself as an instrument of wickedness.*Ro 6:13* Sin is not your master because you are under grace, not law.*Ro 6:14* Do not sin simply because you are under grace rather than law.*Ro 6:15* You are slaves of the one you obey, if of sin, then leading to death.*Ro 6:16* You may have the right to do anything, but not everything is beneficial, and you should not let anything master you.*1Co 6:12* Come back to your senses as you should, stop sinning, and don't be ignorant of God, otherwise shame on you.*1Co 15:34* Men crucified Christ in weakness, but Christ lives by God's power, just as you are weak in him but live by God's power in dealing with the sin of one another.*2Co 13:4*

Freedom. Thank God that although you were once slave to sin, you now obey the teaching from your heart.*Ro 6:17* God set you free from sin.*Ro 6:18* While sin reigned in death, grace reigns through righteousness, bringing eternal life through Jesus Christ our Lord.*Ro 5:21* Because a great cloud of witnesses surrounds you, throw off anything hindering you, especially the sin that so easily entangles, so that you can run the right race with perseverance.*Heb 12:1* Resist to the point of bleeding, if you must, when struggling against sin.*Heb 12:4* Do not be overcome by evil, but overcome evil with good.*Ro 12:21* You once offered yourselves as slaves to increasing wickedness, and so now offer yourselves as slaves to righteousness.*Ro 6:19* Righteousness cannot influence a slave to sin.*Ro 6:20* Do not yoke yourself to unbelievers, because righteousness and wickedness, and light and darkness, have nothing in common.*2Co 6:14* The Lord says to separate ourselves, staying clean, so that he may receive us.*2Co 6:17* Jesus said that eating food forbidden by human rules does not defile a person, but instead the bad things that come out of a person's mouth, in speaking, defiles the person.*Matt 15:10-11*

Temptation. Jesus said that even looking lustfully at another is to commit adultery in one's heart.*Matt 5:27-28* Never indulge but instead reject absolutely temptations of the eyes and hands so that your whole body doesn't go to hell.*Matt 5:29-30* Jesus said that you'd be better cutting off your hand or foot, or gouging out your eyes, to avoid temptation that leads to hell's eternal fire.*Matt 18:8-9* Better to cut off your hand or foot if it causes you to stumble, and go through life maimed, than with two hands or feet to go to hell.$_{Mk\ 9:43\text{-}44}$ Better to gouge out an eye that causes you to stumble and then to enter God's kingdom with one eye than to go to hell with two eyes, where the fire never dies.$_{Mk\ 9:47\text{-}48}$ Jesus told the woman caught in adultery that although he did not condemn her, she should leave her life of sin.$_{Jn\ 8:11}$ Restore gently the one whom you catch in a sin, while guarding yourself against temptation.$_{Gal\ 6:1}$ Just as evil cannot tempt God, so, too, God does not tempt with evil, which instead comes from our own evil desire inducing sin that leads to death.$_{Jas\ 1:13\text{-}15}$ Rather than think you stand firm, be careful that you don't fall.$_{1Co\ 10:12}$ Only common temptations overtake you, but when they do, God is faithful in not letting them tempt you beyond what you can bear, instead providing a way out so that you endure.$_{1Co\ 10:13}$ Believers in God should flee from sin.$_{1Ti\ 6:11}$ Never unite your body, which is a member of Christ, with a prostitute because the two then become one flesh.$_{1Co\ 6:15\text{-}16}$ Flee sexual immorality because while all other sins are outside the body, sexual sin is against one's own body.$_{1Co\ 6:18}$ Do not sin, and repent of impurity, sexual sin, and debauchery in which others indulge.$_{2Co\ 12:21}$ Let no one be sexually immoral.$_{Heb\ 12:17}$ God did not mean the body for sexual immorality but for the Lord, and the Lord for the body.$_{1Co\ 6:13}$ Foolish and harmful desires for riches tempt, trap, and plunge people into ruin and destruction.$_{1Ti\ 6:9}$ Loving money is an evil root, causing some to wander from the faith while piercing themselves with many griefs.$_{1Ti\ 6:10}$

Anger. Jesus said that anyone who is angry with a brother or sister faces judgment, and anyone showing contempt for a brother or sister is in danger of hell's fire.$_{Matt\ 5:21\text{-}22}$ Don't get angry quickly because anger does not produce God's desired righteousness.$_{Jas\ 1:20}$ Evil hates and murders a righteous one.$_{1Jn\ 3:12}$ You either love or hate, and those who hate die, while those who love in Christ gain eternal life.$_{1Jn\ 3:14\text{-}15}$ Get rid of all malice, deceit, hypocrisy, envy, and slander of every kind.$_{1Pe\ 2:1}$ In your anger do not sin, nor let the sun go down while you are still angry.$_{Eph\ 4:26}$ Get rid of all bitterness, rage, anger, brawling, slander, and other form of malice.$_{Eph\ 4:31}$ While you used to be sinful in your former life, you must now rid yourself of all sin including anger, rage, malice, slander, and bad language.$_{Col\ 3:7\text{-}8}$ Men should pray and lift holy hands without anger.$_{1Ti\ 2:8}$ Love does not easily anger.$_{1Co\ 13:5}$

Holiness. God's will is that he sanctify you, that you avoid sexual immorality, control your own body to be holy and honorable, avoid passionate lust like those who do not know God, and not wrong or take advantage of a brother or sister.*1Th 4:3-6* God called us not to impurity but to holy life.*1Th 4:7* Do not lie to each other, because you have taken off your old self with its practices.*Col 3:9* Do not slumber and get drunk like non-believers but instead be awake and sober.*1Th 5:6-7* Hold on to what is good while rejecting every kind of evil.*1Th 5:19-22* Ask God to deliver you from wicked and evil people.*2Th 3:2* Do not in idleness go from house to house as a busybody talking nonsense you should not say.*1Ti 5:13* Do not share in the sins of others, but keep yourself pure.*1Ti 5:22* Behave decently, as in daytime, not in carousing and drunkenness, sexual immorality and debauchery, or in dissension and jealousy.*Ro 13:13* Celebrate not with malice and wickedness but with sincerity and truth.*1Co 5:8* Our Savior the Lord Jesus Christ will by his complete power transform our lowly bodies to be like his glorious body.*Php 3:20-21*

Death. Jesus told the Jews who did not believe him that they would die in their sin.*Jn 8:21* Jesus repeated that if they did not believe that he was from above, then they would die in their sin.*Jn 8:24* When we were in the flesh's realm, law aroused sinful passions that led to death.*Ro 7:5* Apart from the law, sin was dead, and we were alive, but with the commandment, sin sprang to life, and we died.*Ro 7:8-9* The good did not become death, but sin used the good to bring death, showing its utter sinfulness.*Ro 7:13* The commandment that should bring life instead brought death because sin deceived, through the commandment putting us to death.*Ro 7:10-11* All who sin apart from the law perish, while all who sin under the law face law's judgment.*Ro 2:12* Law just helped us die to the law so that we could live for God.*Gal 2:19* The law has authority over someone only as long as that person lives.*Ro 7:1* For example, a husband's death releases a married woman from the law binding her to him, so that she may marry another man without committing adultery.*Ro 7:2-3* Likewise, you died to the law through the body of Christ so that you could belong to Christ raised from the dead, bearing fruit for God.*Ro 7:4* Death to the flesh released us from the law so that we serve in the Spirit's new way rather than the written code's old way.*Ro 7:6* The godless know God's righteous decree that those who do wrong things deserve death, but they continue to do those things.*Ro 1:32* One reaps no benefit from sin, only shame and death, because sin's only wage is death.*Ro 6:21-22* We must put to death the body's misdeeds to live, rather than live for the flesh, in which case we die.*Ro 8:12-13* Jesus said to follow him, letting the spiritually dead follow their dead traditions for burying the dead.*Matt 8:21-22, Lk 9:59-60* When after Pentecost a man sold a piece of property and with his wife's knowledge kept back some of the money for himself before putting the rest at the apostles' feet, Peter told him that Satan had caused him to lie not just to humans but to the Holy Spirit and God, so that the man promptly died._Acts 5:1-6_ King Herod executed the guards who had attended Peter when the angel led him out of prison._Acts 12:19_ When King Herod then gave a public address, and the people shouted that his voice was that of a god rather than a man, an angel of the Lord promptly struck him dead when he didn't praise God._Acts 12:19-23_

Jesus. God delivered Jesus over to death for our sins and raised him to life for our justification._Ro 4:25_ When living on earth, Jesus prayed and petitioned fervently to God who could save him from death, and God heard Jesus because of his reverent submission._Heb 5:7_ Christ Jesus made himself nothing in the very nature of a servant, humbly obedient even to death on a cross._Php 2:6-8_ The last enemy Christ destroys is death._1Co 15:26_ While Christ died for our sins as the Scriptures say, he rose on the third day after burial, as the Scriptures also say._1Co 15:3_ The God of peace, through the blood of the eternal covenant, raised from the dead our Lord Jesus, the great Shepherd of the sheep._Heb 13:20_ Christ's purpose on the cross was to reconcile in him one new peaceful humanity out of the divided two sides, putting to death their hostility._Eph 2:15-16_ Jesus shared in our humanity because we are human, so that by his death he would break the devil's power of death._Heb 2:14_ Christ redeemed us from law's curse when crucifixion cursed Christ who died for us._Gal 3:13_ All those baptized into Christ Jesus were buried with him through baptism into death so that just as the glory of the Father raised Christ from the dead, we also live a new life._Ro 6:3-4_ Through Christ Jesus, the law of the Spirit who gives life freed us from the law of sin and death._Ro 8:2_ Godly sorrow brings repentance leading to salvation without regret, while worldly sorrow brings only death._2Co 7:10_ Foundational teaching in Christ includes repenting from acts leading to death._Heb 6:1-2_ Jesus said not to fear those who kill the body only but instead fear the One who can destroy both body and soul in hell._Matt 10:28, Lk 12:4-5_ Jesus also said that the vultures gather around a dead body._Lk 17:37_ Jesus said that the time had come when the dead heard the Son of God's voice and would live because the Father has life in himself and had also granted the Son life in himself._Jn 5:25-26_ Jesus said that a time is coming when all in their graves would come out at his voice, those who have done good will rise to live, but those who have done evil will rise to face condemnation._Jn 5:28-29_

Resurrection. Desire to know the power of Christ's resurrection and participation in his sufferings, becoming like him in his death and so attaining to resurrection from death.*Php 3:10-11* We should thank God the Father of our Lord Jesus Christ for his great mercy, giving us new birth into living hope through Jesus's resurrection from the dead.*1Pe 1:3* Through Christ you believe in God and place your hope in God, for raising Christ from the dead and glorifying him.*1Pe 1:21* Jesus Christ's resurrection saves you because he is in heaven at God's right hand with angels, authorities, and powers submitting to him.*1Pe 3:21-22* We neither live nor die for ourselves alone but live and die for the Lord, either way belonging to the Lord.*Ro 14:7-8* Because death came through a man, resurrection also comes through a man.*1Co 15:21* In Adam all died so that in Christ all could live.*1Co 15:22*

Teachers. Some are exposed to death repeatedly for sharing the gospel.*2Co 11:24-26* Some face death daily for Christ Jesus our Lord.*1Co 15:31* Some feel they have received a death sentence, making them rely on God, who raises the dead.*2Co 1:9* Death works against our teachers so that life works in us. *2Co 4:12* To sinners, gospel teachers are an aroma bringing death, while to believers an aroma bringing life.*2Co 2:16* Persecuted preachers always carry around in their body Jesus's death, so that their body may also reveal Jesus's life.*2Co 4:10* They face death for Jesus's sake, so that their mortal body may reveal his life.*2Co 4:11* Jesus said that his faithful witness Antipas was put to death in Pergamum where Satan lives.*Rev 2:13*

You. Those who die with Christ will also live with him.*2Ti 2:11* The death of God's Son reconciled us to God while we were still God's enemies, just as Christ now saves us through his life.*Ro 5:10* God reconciles us by Christ's physical body through death to present you holy, without blemish, and free from accusation, in his sight.*Col 1:22* Jesus frees those held in slavery by their fear of death.*Heb 2:15* Because you joined him in a death like his, you will certainly also join with him in a resurrection like his.*Ro 6:5* Because you died with Christ, you believe that you will also live with him.*Ro 6:8* If Christ is in you, then even though your body dies because of sin, the Spirit gives life because of righteousness.*Ro 8:10* If the Spirit of God who raised Jesus from the dead lives in you, then God who raised Christ from the dead will also give your body life because of his Spirit who lives in you.*Ro 8:11* You died to the law so that you could belong to Christ raised from the dead, bearing fruit for God.*Ro 7:4* Everything is yours, whether that of the world, life or death, or present or future, because you are of Christ, and Christ is of God.*1Co 3:21-23* You've heard from the start: love one another, and you will go from death to life.*1Jn 3:11-14* In our earthly tent, we groan with burden, fearing deadly exposure while wanting heaven's protection from death.*2Co 5:4* Know with confidence that to be at home in the body is to be away from the Lord.*2Co 5:6* Prefer to be away from the body and at home with the Lord.*2Co 5:8* Do not fear death, because God numbers your head's hairs and values you much more than the sparrows for which he also cares.*Matt 10:29-31, Lk 12:6-7*

Life. God gives life to the dead.*Ro 4:17* Because God raised Christ from the dead, he cannot die again, and death no longer has mastery over him.*Ro 6:9* Christ died once for all and so lives to God.*Ro 6:10* The Lord Jesus died for us so that, whether we are alive or dead, we may live together with him.*1Th 3:10* Those who die with Christ will also live with him.*2Ti 2:11* Christ died and returned to life so that he might be the Lord of both the dead and the living.*Ro 14:9* Our Savior Christ Jesus destroyed death and brought immortality.*2Ti 1:10* When the perishable puts on the imperishable, and the mortal immortality, then the Scriptures' saying that victory swallowed up death will be true.*1Co 15:54* Death has no victory or sting when death's sting is sin and sin's power is the law.*1Co 15:55-56* Enoch's faith pleased God so much that God took him away before death.*Heb 11:5* Abraham had faith that God could raise the dead, as in a way God brought Isaac back from death.*Heb 11:19* Faith enabled others to face death by sword, stoning, or sawing in two, and others to go about in sheepskins and goatskins, destitute, persecuted, and mistreated.*Heb 11:37*

Law

The New Testament addresses the law and commandments, under which all lived and died, before God sent his Son with a new commandment. The law is for lawbreakers, highlighting our sin. The law thus brings not life but death. The law's zealous pursuit leads only to deadly legalism. The law was a shadow of Christ's coming righteousness, which freed us from law's judgment of death. The Spirit of Christ keeps the law on our hearts so that we obey the law as our conscience guides us. See how the New Testament addresses law and the customs that grow out of law. Has the Spirit written the law on your heart, even as you avoid legalism's perils?

Sin. The law is for lawbreakers and rebels, the ungodly and sinful, the unholy and irreligious, those who kill their fathers or mothers, murderers, the sexually immoral, those practicing homosexuality, slave traders, and liars and perjurers.*1Ti 1:8-10* The law makes us conscious of our sin.*Ro 2:20* The law, while not in itself sinful, defines sin for us, such as when the law says not to covet, showing us that coveting is sin.*Ro 7:7* When we were in the flesh's realm, law aroused sinful passions that led to death.*Ro 7:5* Commands make us want to break them.*Ro 7:8* The law brings wrath because the law brings transgression. *Ro 4:14-15* The law and commandment are nonetheless holy, righteous, and good.*Ro 7:12* The law is spiritual, but we are unspiritual, slaves to sin.*Ro 7:14* Inside, we delight in God's law, but sin wages war against our minds, imprisoning us in sin.*Ro 7:23* Jesus said that he did not come to abolish the law and prophets but to fulfill them.*Matt 5:17* Jesus said that until heaven and earth disappear, not the smallest letter or penstroke of the law will disappear, until God accomplishes everything.*Matt 5:18, Lk 16:17* Jesus warned not to set aside God's commands or teach others to do so but instead to practice and teach God's commands to have God call you great in the kingdom of heaven.*Matt 5:19*

Death. Apart from the law, sin was dead, and we were alive, but with the commandment, sin sprang to life and we died.$_{Ro\ 7:8-9}$ The good did not become death, but sin used the good to bring death, showing its utter sinfulness.$_{Ro\ 7:13}$ The commandment that should bring life instead brought death because sin deceived, through the commandment putting us to death.$_{Ro\ 7:10-11}$ All who sin apart from the law perish, while all who sin under the law face law's judgment.$_{Ro\ 2:12}$ The law, addressing those under the law, silences every mouth holding the whole world accountable to God.$_{Ro\ 2:19}$ Law just helped us die to the law so that we could live for God.$_{Gal\ 2:19}$ The law has authority over someone only as long as that person lives.$_{Ro\ 7:1}$ For example, a husband's death releases a married woman from the law binding her to him, so that she may marry another man without committing adultery.$_{Ro\ 7:2-3}$ Likewise, you died to the law through the body of Christ so that you could belong to Christ raised from the dead, bearing fruit for God.$_{Ro\ 7:4}$ Death to the flesh released us from the law so that we serve in the Spirit's new way rather than the written code's old way.$_{Ro\ 7:6}$ The one on the throne told the apostle John that he will consign to the fiery lake the cowardly, unbelieving, vile, murderers, sexually immoral, idolaters, liars, and those who practice magic arts, in the second death.$_{Rev\ 21:8}$

Shadow. The law is only a shadow of good things coming, not the reality, and so can never by endless sacrifices make perfect those who draw near to worship.$_{Heb\ 10:1}$ Those of you who want to be under the law had better beware of what the law says.$_{Gal\ 4:21}$ The law contradicts faith, saying that we live by doing certain things.$_{Gal\ 3:12}$ God set aside the former regulation as weak and useless, the law making nothing perfect, to offer us a better hope to draw near to God.$_{Heb\ 7:18-19}$ The law's priests serve at a copy and shadow sanctuary of heaven's sanctuary, which is why God mandated the shadow sanctuary's pattern.$_{Heb\ 8:5}$ Christ said that God had not desired sacrifices and offerings, which did not please God, even though our ancestors offered according to the law.$_{Heb\ 10:8}$ Jesus said that although Moses gave Jews the law, no one kept the law.$_{Jn\ 7:19}$ Jesus said that because the law of Moses permits circumcision on the Sabbath, the Jews should not be upset at Jesus for healing the whole body on the Sabbath.$_{Jn\ 7:22-23}$ The Pharisees said that Jesus was not from God because Jesus did not keep the Sabbath.$_{Jn\ 9:16}$

Legalism. Works of the law declare no one righteous in God's sight.$_{Ro\ 2:20}$ For example, some will forbid people to marry and order them to abstain from certain foods that God created for believers who know the truth to receive with thanksgiving.*1Ti 4:3* God elects us before we do anything good or bad, and not by right but by grace, to show that his call, not our works, makes the difference.*Ro 9:10-12* Salvation depends on God's mercy, not human desire or effort.*Ro 9:16* Legalistic works never justify a person, but faith in Jesus Christ justifies.*Gal 2:16* Christ in no way promotes sin by justifying us outside of the old legalism.*Gal 2:17* We would become lawbreakers all over again if we resumed the legalism that Christ's justification helped us destroy.*Gal 2:18* We first received the Spirit by believing the gospel message, not by works under law, and so we must continue under the Spirit rather than foolishly trying to finish with legalistic works of the flesh, which would only make our belief in vain.*Gal 3:2-4* Jesus said that unless your righteousness surpasses that of the Pharisees and law teachers, you will not enter the kingdom of heaven.*Matt 5:20* When Jesus healed the invalid at the pool near Jerusalem's Sheep Gate, the Jewish leaders objected that he had done so on the Sabbath, causing the man to pick up his mat and walk, violating the law.*Jn 5:9-15*

Christ. God gives us his Spirit and works miracles among us not by works of the law but by our believing what we heard of the gospel.*Gal 3:5* Through Christ Jesus, the law of the Spirit, who gives life, freed us from the law of sin and death.*Ro 8:2* Christ culminates the law so that everyone who believes has God's righteousness.*Ro 10:4* God gave the law because of transgressions but only until Christ had come.*Gal 3:19* The law, which does not impart righteousness and life, in no way opposes God's promises but instead shows everything under the control of sin aside from the righteousness and life that comes through faith in Jesus Christ.*Gal 3:21-22* The law held us in custody like a guardian, until God revealed faith in Christ as our justification, after which we no longer needed law's guardianship.*Gal 3:23-23* The law had no power to free us from sin because the flesh weakened us, but God sent his own Son in the likeness of sinful flesh to condemn sin in the flesh, to meet the law's righteous requirement in those of us who live by the Spirit rather than the flesh.*Ro 8:3-4*

Faith. Our righteousness is not our own from the law but that which is through faith in Christ.*Php 3:9* One must not boast about keeping the law because of the law that requires faith.*Ro 2:27* Faith justifies a person apart from works of the law.*Ro 2:28* Faith upholds the law.*Ro 2:31* While wages are due for working, when we instead fail to keep the law, God still credits our faith as righteousness when we, the ungodly, trust him.*Ro 4:4-5*

God forgives our sins and blesses us with righteousness apart from works of the law.*Ro 4:6-7* The law and prophets testify to God's righteousness.*Ro 2:21* When the Spirit leads us, we are not under the law.*Gal 5:18*

Obedience. Obeying the law, not just hearing the law, makes one righteous in God's sight.*Ro 2:13* When those who do not have the law do what law requires, they are a law for themselves, because even though they do not have the law, they show the law is on their hearts, their consciences guiding them.*Ro 2:14-15* When you rely on the law, you know his will and approve the better, but then when you convince yourself that you guide the blind, light the dark, instruct the foolish, and teach children because law embodies knowledge and truth, you fail to teach yourself because you still steal, commit adultery, rob temples, and, though boasting in the law, dishonor God by breaking the law.*Ro 2:17-24* The law still provides an advantage in having the very words of God.*Ro 2:2*

Circumcision. In sharp dispute with Paul and Barnabas, some people initially taught the new believers that they had no salvation unless they accepted circumcision according to the custom of Moses.*Acts 15:1* The church sent Paul and Barnabas to the apostles and elders in Jerusalem to address the circumcision question.*Acts 15:2* When they got to Jerusalem, some Pharisees there repeated that the Gentiles had to accept circumcision to keep the law of Moses.*Acts 15:5* Peter said that God had given the Gentiles the Holy Spirit without discriminating between Jews and Gentiles because faith had purified the Gentiles' hearts, Jesus had saved them, and they should not test God by putting on the Gentiles a yoke that Jews could not even bear.*Acts 15:7-11* After Paul and Barnabas told them how God had done signs and wonders among the Gentiles, James quoted scripture that even the Gentiles would bear God's name, so that they should not make things hard for the Gentiles, only requiring that they abstain from sexual immorality, blood, meat of strangled animals, and food that idols polluted.*Acts 15:12-21* Watch out for evildoers who would mutilate the flesh with circumcision.*Php 3:2* While some could claim reason for confidence in the flesh, out of zeal for the law, better to consider any gains from such things to be loss for the sake of Christ.*Php 3:4-7* You were once called uncircumcised by those who call themselves the circumcision, which is only done in the body by human hands.*Eph 2:11* Now listen, if you let yourself be circumcised, Christ has no value to you, none, because then you must obey the whole law, alienating you from Christ and his grace.*Gal 5:2-5* Those who agitate against the cross, and for circumcision, should just go ahead and emasculate themselves.*Gal*

5:11-12 People who impress others in the flesh, trying to compel your circumcision, do so to avoid being associated with the cross of Christ.*Gal 6:12* The circumcised do not even keep the law but only want you circumcised to boast about your circumcision.*Gal 6:13* Circumcision has value only if you observe the law, but when you break the law, you are as if uncircumcised.*Ro 2:25* Rather than let yourself be circumcised by others, you should instead through the Spirit eagerly await your hoped-for righteousness from faith.*Gal 5:2-5* Genuine circumcision is to serve God by his Spirit and boast in Christ Jesus while putting no confidence in the flesh.*Php 3:3* God is the God of both the circumcised and uncircumcised because only one God exists, who justifies all through the same faith.*Ro 2:29-30* Christ circumcised us with a circumcision not performed by human hands, putting off our whole self ruled by the flesh.*Col 2:11-12* Uncircumcision of our flesh makes us dead in sin.*Col 2:13* Whether you are circumcised means nothing in Christ Jesus, in whom only faith expressing itself through love counts.*Gal 5:6* Circumcision and uncircumcision mean nothing, while new creation means everything.*Gal 6:15* Among believers, we do not distinguish between circumcised or uncircumcised because Christ is everything.*Col 3:11* When those who are not circumcised keep the law, one may as well regard them as circumcised.*Ro 2:26* The uncircumcised who keep the law condemn the circumcised who break the law.*Ro 2:27* Circumcision is not merely outward and physical but is instead of the heart, by the Spirit rather than the written code, the Spirit whom God rather than people praise.*Ro 2:28-29* God's blessing is for the circumcised and uncircumcised, a righteousness credited to us by faith.*Ro 4:9-10* Abraham's circumcision was a seal of the righteousness that he already had by faith while he was still uncircumcised, just as will be so for all who believe.*Ro 4:11-12* Don't circumcise or uncircumcise yourself, because both are nothing, when keeping God's commands is what counts.*1Co 7:18-19*

Sacrifices. Endless sacrifices can never make perfect those who draw near to worship.*Heb 10:1* The sacrifices would have stopped if they had cleansed the worshipers once for all.*Heb 10:2* Repeated sacrifices only remind of sin.*Heb 10:3* Animal blood cannot take away sins.*Heb 10:4* Priests perform religious duties daily, repeatedly offering the same sacrifices that can never take away sins.*Heb 10:11* Christ did not enter heaven to offer himself repeatedly, the way a human high priest entered the Most Holy Place every year with animal blood.*Heb 9:25* Otherwise, Christ would have had to suffer many times since the world's creation, but he appeared once for all, at the ages' culmination, to do away with sin by his own sacrifice._{Heb 9:26} When Christ as high priest offered for all time one sacrifice for sins, his one sacrifice made perfect forever those whom God is making holy._{Heb 10:12-14} Sacrifice for sin is no longer necessary, where God has forgiven._{Heb 10:18}

Tabernacle. The first covenant had regulations for worship and also an earthly sanctuary with a tabernacle and Holy Place._{Heb 9:1-2} The tabernacle also had a Most Holy Place with a golden altar of incense and gold-covered ark of the covenant containing a gold jar of manna, Aaron's staff that had budded, and the stone tablets of the covenant._{Heb 9:3-4} Above the ark were the cherubim of the Glory, overshadowing the atonement cover, with other detail._{Heb 9:5} The priests entered regularly into the outer room to carry on their ministry._{Heb 9:6} But only the high priest entered the inner room, and that only once a year, and never without blood, which he offered for himself and for the people's sins committed in ignorance._{Heb 9:7} The Holy Spirit was showing that God had not yet disclosed the way into the Most Holy Place while the first tabernacle still functioned._{Heb 9:8} The gifts and sacrifices did not clear the worshiper's conscience but were only external regulations applying until the new order._{Heb 9:10} Those who minister at the old tabernacle have no right to eat at our new altar._{Heb 13:10}

Hypocrites. Pharisees and law teachers came out from Jerusalem to ask Jesus why his disciples broke the elders' tradition of ceremonial hand-washing before eating._{Matt 15:1-2, Mk 7:1-5} The Pharisees and other Jews observed many of the elders' traditions having to do with ceremonial washing of hands, cups, pitchers, and kettles._{Mk 7:4} Jesus said that the Jewish leaders break God's command for traditions' sake when, though God says to honor and not curse parents, they devote things to God instead of helping their parents, nullifying God's word for human traditions._{Matt 15:3-4, Mk 7:9-13} Jesus called them hypocrites who nullify God's word for traditions' sake, honor God only with lips rather than hearts, worship him in vain, and teach only human rules._{Matt 15:6-9, Mk 7:6-8} Things that enter the body pass out, and eating with unwashed hands does nothing, but evil things like slander, false testimony, theft, murder, and adultery, that come from the heart, defile a person._{Matt 15:17-20, Mk 7:20-23} Jesus told the crowd that nothing outside going into a person defiles them but what comes out of a person defiles._{Mk 7:14-15} Jesus repeated to the disciples, who did not understand, that food goes into the stomach, not the heart, thus declaring all foods clean, while out of the heart come the evil things that defile a person.*Mk 7:17-23* Jesus told the crowds and disciples to do what the law teachers and Pharisees say but not to do what they do because they do not practice what they preach but instead burden their hearers with heavy loads that they themselves will not lift.*Matt 23:1-4, Lk 11:46* They are hypocrites who do everything to be seen and honored.*Matt 23:5-7* When Jesus healed a crippled woman while he taught in the synagogue on the Sabbath, and the synagogue leader said to come for healing only on other days, Jesus said that they were hypocrites for caring for their animals on the Sabbath but not healing on the Sabbath.*Lk 13:10-16* Jesus also healed a swollen man, when Jesus ate in a prominent Pharisee's house on the Sabbath, telling the Pharisees and law experts that healing on the Sabbath would be just as lawful as pulling a child or an ox out of a well on the Sabbath.*Lk 14:1-6* The apostle Paul called the high priest a whitewashed wall for purporting to judge Paul according to the law while himself violating the law.*Acts 23:1-3*

Woes. Jesus said woe to the hypocrite law teachers and Pharisees for shutting the door of heaven's kingdom in people's faces while not entering themselves.*Matt 23:13* Jesus said woe to them for traveling far for a convert only to make them hell's child.*Matt 23:15* Jesus said woe to those blind guides for having persons swear by the temple's gold or altar's gift rather than the temple or altar, which are greater, and swearing by God's throne is even greater.*Matt 23:16-21* Jesus said woe to the law teachers and Pharisees for tithing a tenth of their spices while neglecting the more-important law matters justice, mercy, and faithfulness.*Matt 23:23, Lk 11:42* Jesus said that they strain out a gnat while swallowing a camel.*Matt 23:24* Jesus said woe to the law teachers and Pharisees for cleaning the outside of the cup and dish while being full of greed and self-indulgence inside, when they should have cleaned the inside first so that the outside would be clean.*Matt 23:25-26, Lk 11:39-40* Jesus said woe to the Pharisees for loving the important seats and marketplace greetings.*Lk 11:43* Jesus said woe to the hypocrite law teachers and Pharisees for building tombs for prophets whom their ancestors murdered, when they may as well complete the murders that their ancestors started.*Matt 23:29-32, Lk 11:47-48* Jesus called them snakes and broods of vipers who would not escape hell's condemnation.*Matt 23:33* Jesus prophesied that he would send them prophets and teachers whom they would pursue, flog, crucify, and kill, leaving the blood of the righteous on them.*Matt 23:34-36, Lk 11:49-51* Jesus longed to gather Jerusalem's children together as a hen gathers chicks, but they were unwilling, instead stoning and killing the prophets and teachers Jesus sent them, leaving their house desolate.*Matt 23:37-38, Lk 13:34-35*

Priests. God calls high priests, as he did Aaron.*Heb 5:4* The people select a high priest to represent them before God, to offer gifts and sacrifices for their sins.*Heb 5:1* High priests should deal gently with the ignorant and straying because the high priest is likewise weak and must also sacrifice for his own sins.*Heb 5:2-3* Priests die, ending their office.*Heb 7:23* The law appoints weak men as high priests, but God's oath, which came after the law, appointed the Son, whom God made perfect forever.*Heb 7:28* Every high priest offers gifts and sacrifices, and so Jesus also offered, but not as a priest serving the law would offer.*Heb 8:3-4* Unlike the other high priests, Jesus needs no daily sacrifices for his own sins or the people's sins because he sacrificed once for all, offering himself.*Heb 7:27* We have a high priest who sat down at the right hand of the Majesty's throne in heaven, who serves in the Lord's own inner sanctuary, and not as a mere human.*Heb 8:2*

Christ. Jesus our Lord is an indestructible priest forever rather than from the Levitical priesthood that administered the law.*Heb 7:1-17* Jesus lives forever in permanent priesthood.*Heb 7:24* The high priest Jesus truly meets our need, as holy, blameless, pure, set apart from sinners, and exalted above the heavens.*Heb 7:26* Do not compel anyone who wishes to follow the gospel to first give in to tradition.*Gal 2:3* Christ came as high priest of the good things that are now here, the greater and more perfect divine tabernacle, not part of creation.*Heb 9:11* Christ entered the Most Holy Place not by animal blood but once for all by his own blood, for eternal redemption.*Heb 9:12* Animal blood and ashes on the ceremonially unclean sanctify only outwardly.*Heb 9:13* The blood of Christ, who through the eternal Spirit offered himself unblemished to God, cleanse inwardly, clearing our consciences from acts leading to death, so that we serve the living God.*Heb 9:14*

Freedom. False believers who see how free we are in Christ Jesus will infiltrate us, trying to use tradition to make us slaves again.*Gal 2:4* Some will forbid people to marry and will order them to abstain from certain foods that God created for believers, who know the truth to receive with thanksgiving.*1Ti 4:3* Don't give in to them for a moment, but instead preserve the gospel's truth.*Gal 2:5* Useless rules like those not to handle, taste, or touch certain things are merely human commands and teachings having only a false appearance of wisdom based on self-imposed worship, false humility, and the body's harsh treatment._{Col 2:21-23} When Pharisees asked Jesus why his disciples picked grain on the Sabbath, Jesus referred to David and his companions eating consecrated bread out of the house of God and then said that God made the Sabbath for man, not man for the Sabbath, and that the Son of Man is Lord of the Sabbath._{Mk 2:23-28, Lk 6:1-5} Do not let anyone judge you by what you eat or drink, or by a religious festival, celebration, or Sabbath day, which are only shadows of things to come, when we find the reality of those things in Christ._{Col 2:16} Whether you consider one day more sacred than another or not doesn't matter, if you convince your mind and do so for the Lord._{Ro 14:5-6} Whether you eat meat or abstain doesn't matter if you thank God and do so for the Lord._{Ro 14:6} Eat anything sold in the meat market without raising questions of conscience because the earth and everything in it belong to the Lord._{1Co 10:25-26} God's kingdom is not about eating and drinking._{Ro 14:17}

Opposition. Some show extreme zeal for their own traditions, advancing them among their own kind._{Gal 1:14} When the Pharisees saw Jesus heal a man with a shriveled hand on the Sabbath, the Pharisees began to plot with government officials how to kill Jesus._{Mk 3:1-6} The Pharisees were furious and began to plot what they might do to Jesus._{Lk 6:11} The Pharisees would not answer Jesus when he questioned them whether the Sabbath permitted one to do good or evil._{Mk 3:4} The Pharisees and law teachers opposed Jesus fiercely, besieging him with questions, trying to catch him in something he said._{Lk 11:53-54} Oppose to the face those who condemn themselves by drawing apart, in fear that others would exclude them from religious traditions._{Gal 2:11-12} Abandoning the gospel for tradition is hypocrisy that will lead others astray._{Gal 2:13} You should silence the many rebellious people who are full of meaningless talk and deception, and would have believers return to the old traditions, because they disrupt households and teach falsely for dishonest gain._{Tit 1:10-11} False teachers are liars, evil brutes, and lazy gluttons whom you must rebuke sharply, until they become sound in faith and give up their old myths and useless traditions._{Tit 1:12-14}

Others. Do not cause anyone to stumble, whether insiders, outsiders, or God's church._{1Co 10:32} Put no stumbling block or obstacle in the way of a brother or sister._{Ro 14:13} The Lord Jesus persuades us that nothing is unclean in itself, but if someone regards something as unclean, then for that person it is unclean._{Ro 14:14} Do not distress your brother or sister because of what you eat, because doing so is not love and instead destroys someone for whom Christ died.*Ro 14:15* If a non-believer offers you a meal you like, then eat it without raising questions of conscience.*1Co 10:27* But don't eat food offered in sacrifice, for the conscience of the one who offered it.*1Co 10:28-30* Do not destroy God's work for the sake of food because while all food is clean, a person is wrong to eat anything that causes someone else to stumble.*Ro 14:20* Better not to eat meat or drink wine or to do anything else that will cause your brother or sister to fall.*Ro 14:21* Whatever you believe about these things, keep them between yourself and God because God blesses the one who does not condemn himself by what he approves.*Ro 14:22* When Paul returned to Jerusalem telling all that God had done among the Gentiles, the elders told Paul that many thousands of Jews zealous for the laws and their customs had believed and so to purify himself so as not to divide the believers.*Acts 21:20-26*

Deceivers

The New Testament addresses deceivers at length. Unfortunately, we face deceivers, making critical that we resist deception and not let others deceive. We must know and adhere to the truth, especially the gospel about our Lord and Savior Jesus Christ. We must also avoid, ignore, and oppose false teachers, while ensuring that we learn God's truth. God brings judgment on false teachers. See how frequently, consistently, and strongly the New Testament condemns deceivers. Are you identifying, resisting, and opposing those who deceive?

Deception. Jesus said to watch out that no one deceives you, especially those many who will come in his name claiming to be the Messiah.*Matt 24:4-5, Mk 13:5-6* Jesus said that if anyone causes a child who believes in him to stumble, they'd be better having a large millstone hung around their neck for drowning in the sea.*Matt 18:6, Mk 9:42, Lk 17:1-2* Jesus said woe to those through whom come things that cause people to stumble.*Matt 18:7, Lk 17:1* God blesses those who do not stumble on Jesus's account.*Lk 7:23* Jesus said to watch out for the law teachers who like to walk around in flowing robes to receive greetings in the marketplace, sit at places of honor in the synagogue and at banquets, and make showy prayers while devouring widows' houses, and whom God will punish most severely.*Mk 12:38-40, Lk 20:38-40* Jesus said woe to the law experts who take away knowledge's key, hinder those who were entering, and don't enter themselves.*Lk 11:52* The Spirit warns against following deceiving spirits and things taught by demons.*1Ti 4:1* Some people will confuse you with a perverted gospel.*Gal 1:7* False teachers among you will secretly introduce destructive heresies, denying the Lord's salvation while destroying themselves.*1Pe 2:1* Greedy teachers will exploit you with stories they make up, leaving sure condemnation hanging over them.*1Pe 2:3* Some have an unhealthy interest in controversies and quarrels about words that result in envy, strife, malicious talk, and evil suspicions, producing constant friction between people of corrupt mind, robbed of the truth, thinking that godliness means financial gain.*1Ti 6:4-5* Those whom sin loads down and evil desires sway worm their way into homes and gain control over the gullible.*2Ti 3:6* Evildoers and impostors go from bad to worse, deceiving and being deceived.*2Ti 3:13* Those who turn from God are open graves swift to shed blood, speaking deceit, poison, curses, and bitterness, with ruin and misery marking their way.*Ro 2:13-16* If you want to enjoy life with good days, then don't speak evil or lies because the Lord watches and responds.*1Pe 3:10-11*

Resisting. Don't let others deceive you, friends.*Jas 1:16* Do not let another speak evil about what you know is good.*Ro 14:16* Don't be foolish, letting others bewitch you into abandoning the crucifixion's truth.*Gal 3:1* They may be zealous to win you over, but for no good, to alienate you from those who know the truth, so that you have zeal instead for them.*Gal 4:17* Mature believers should no longer be infants, tossed by the cunning and craftiness of deceitful schemers.*Eph 4:14* Let no one deceive you with empty words, especially when saying that disobedience does anything other than bring God's wrath.*Eph 5:6* Let no one deceive you by fine-sounding arguments.*Col 2:4* Let no one capture you through hollow and deceptive philosophy that depends on tradition and this world's elemental spiritual forces rather than on Christ.*Col 2:8* Do not listen to anyone who, unspiritual mind puffed up with idle notions, delights in false humility and goes into great detail about seeing worshiping angels.*Col 2:18* Do not appeal to others in error, from impure motives, or with tricks.*1Th 2:3* Never use flattery, nor a mask to cover up greed.*1Th 2:5* Have nothing to do with godless myths and old wives' tales.*1Ti 4:7* Don't listen to godless chatter and false so-called knowledge that those who have departed from the faith profess.*1Ti 6:20* Don't let anyone deceive because, in fact, bad company corrupts good character.*1Co 15:33*

Truth. Be zealous only for the good, and be so always, not just when around those who know the truth, and make no enemy among those who tell you the truth.*Gal 4:16* Do not perplex those who labor strenuously to see Christ formed in you.*Gal 4:19-20* Act in line with the truth of the gospel, lest someone who does live out that truth calls out your hypocrisy.*Gal 2:14* Many who follow their depraved doctrine will bring disrepute on the way of truth.*1Pe 2:2* A little confusion destroys the whole truth.*Gal 5:9* We renounce secret and shameful ways, not using deception nor distorting God's word.*2Co 4:2* Keep working to cut the ground from under false apostles and deceitful workers masquerading as Christ's apostles.*2Co 11:12-13* The God and Father of the Lord Jesus, praised forever, knows whether we lie.*2Co 11:31* Jesus said not just not to break one's oath but not to swear any oath at all, instead letting your yes be yes and your no be no because anything else comes from the evil one.*Matt 5:33-37*

Christ. The disciples told Jesus that his speaking against the Pharisees' traditions offended them, but Jesus said to leave them because they were blind guides who would just lead them into a pit.*Matt 15:14* The blind cannot lead the blind without them both falling into a pit.*Lk 6:39* Jesus said that many false prophets and deceivers will appear before the age's end.*Matt 24:11* The world has many deceivers, antichrists really, who do not acknowledge Jesus Christ as having come from God.*2Jn 7* Certain individuals, long-condemned ungodly people who deny Jesus Christ our only Sovereign Lord and pervert God's grace as a license for immorality, may secretly slip in among us.*Jude 4* Some will try to deceive you into believing that our Lord Jesus Christ has already returned.*2Th 2:2-3* Those who say that the resurrection of the dead has already taken place, depart from the truth and destroy the faith of some.*2Ti 2:18* Those who teach other than the sound and godly instruction of our Lord Jesus Christ are conceited and understand nothing.*1Ti 6:3-4* Guard against those who strongly oppose the message.*2Ti 4:15* Don't let the serpent's cunning lead your minds astray from sincere and pure devotion to Christ.*2Co 11:3* Stop putting up so easily with those who preach to you a Jesus other than the Jesus you learned, a different spirit from the Spirit you received, or a different gospel from the one you accepted.*2Co 11:4*

Teaching. Jesus said that the mouth speaks that of which the heart is full.*Lk 6:45* Jesus warned the disciples to be on guard against the yeast of the Pharisees and Sadducees, referring to their false teaching.*Matt 16:5-12, Lk 12:1* In their little faith, the disciples thought instead that Jesus was referring to bread.*Matt 16:5-12* Jesus, who knows one's thoughts, asked the law teachers why they entertain evil thoughts in their hearts.*Matt 9:4* Paul warned to be on your guard against men who will arise among you, distorting the truth to draw away disciples after them.*Acts 20:30* When appointed to lead, command others not to teach false doctrines or to devote themselves to myths and long genealogies that promote divisive speculation rather than advancing God's faithful work.*1Ti 1:3-5* Those who want to teach but don't know what they talk about and confidently affirm, turn away from purity, sincerity, and conscience, to meaningless talk.~1Ti 1:6-7~ Avoid deceiving teachings from hypocritical liars whose consciences a hot iron has seared.~1Ti 4:2~ Ignore strange teachings, such as about eating ceremonial foods, which helps no one, but instead let grace strengthen your heart.~Heb 13:9~ The faith rejects teachers who oppose the truth with depraved minds.~2Ti 3:8~ People who teach contrarily are not serving our Lord Christ but their own appetites, deceiving naïve people's minds by smooth talk and flattery.~Ro 16:18~ The chief priests, law teachers, and elders, who tried to catch Jesus in his words, began by using flattery, saying that Jesus had integrity, wouldn't let others sway him, wasn't impressed by reputations, and instead taught God's way of truth.~Mk 12:13-14~

Learning. Some are always learning but never able to come to a knowledge of the truth.~2Ti 3:7~ Watch out for and keep away from those who put obstacles in your way that are contrary to the teaching that you learned.~Ro 16:17~ Do not deceive yourselves, but instead, if anyone claims to be wise by this age's standards, then you should become fools for God so that you may become wise.~1Co 3:18~ The world's wisdom is foolishness in God's sight because he catches the wise in their craftiness.~1Co 3:19~ The Lord knows that the thoughts of the wise are futile.~1Co 3:20~ Come back to your senses as you should, stop sinning, and don't be ignorant of God, otherwise shame on you.~1Co 15:34~ Don't gladly put up with fools or those who enslave or exploit you, take advantage of you, put on airs, or slap you in the face.~2Co 11:19-20~ Encourage one another so that sin's deceitfulness hardens none of you.~Heb 3:13~

Judgment. Jesus said to watch out for false prophets who, though ferocious wolves, come to you in sheep's clothing.~Matt 7:15~ He says that you can tell them from their thornbush-and-thistle fruit because good trees bear good fruit but bad trees bad fruit, with the bad trees cut for the fire.~Matt 7:16-20~ Good trees bear good fruit while bad trees bear bad fruit, a good man bringing good things out of a good heart but an evil man bringing evil things out of an evil heart.~Lk 6:43-45~ Those who accept deception will perish because they refused to love the saving truth.~2Th 2:10~ God permits those who reject the truth and instead delight in wickedness, to suffer the powerful delusion that condemns them as they believe the lie.~2Th 2:11-12~ Those who indulge in godless chatter become more and more ungodly, their teaching spreading like gangrene.~2Ti 2:17~ Opponents of the truth do not get very far because their folly is clear to everyone.~2Ti 3:9~ The Lord repays those who do teachers a great deal of harm.~2Ti 4:14~ The one who confuses you will pay.~Gal 5:9-10~ Don't be deceived because we know that wrongdoers do not inherit God's kingdom.~1Co 6:9-10~ Satan's servants masquerade as if serving righteousness, but they will end as they deserve.*2Co 11:15*

Ancestors. God was displeased with most of our ancestors and scattered their bodies in the wilderness as examples to keep us from setting our hearts on evil things as they did.*1Co 10:5-6* Do not be idolaters, as some of our ancestors were when they ate, drank, and indulged in revelry.*1Co 10:7* We should not commit sexual immorality, as some of our ancestors did, so that in one day twenty-three thousand of them died.*1Co 10:8* We should not test Christ, as some of our ancestors did, and were killed by snakes.*1Co 10:9* We should not grumble, as some of our ancestors did, and were killed by the destroying angel.*1Co 10:10* These things happened to them as examples, recorded as warnings for us, on whom the culmination of the ages has come.*1Co 10:11* God was angry with your ancestors whose hearts were always going astray, while not knowing God's ways, so that God declared in anger that they would never enter his rest.*Heb 3:10-11*

Corruption. All things are pure to the holy, but nothing is pure to the non-believer who is corrupt in mind and conscience.*Tit 1:15* Those who claim to know God but by their actions deny him are detestable, disobedient, and unfit for anything good.*Tit 1:16* The Lord insists that you must no longer live as non-believers do in their futile thinking.*Eph 4:17* Their misunderstanding and ignorance darken them and separate them from God's life because they harden their hearts.*Eph 4:18* No longer sensitive, they pursue sensuality, indulging in every impurity, full of greed.*Eph 4:19* Some people do not put up with sound doctrine but to suit their own desires gather many teachers to say what their itching ears want to hear.*2Ti 4:3* They turn away from the truth to myths.*2Ti 4:4* Land that drinks rain, producing a useful crop for the farmer, receives God's blessing, not cursed and burned land that produces only worthless thorns and thistles.*Heb 6:8* Those who love the world desert their teachers.*2Ti 4:10* The one on the throne told the apostle John that he will consign to the fiery lake the cowardly, unbelieving, vile, murderers, sexually immoral, idolaters, liars, and those who practice magic arts, in the second death.*Rev 21:8*

Godless. Some are yet to enter God's rest, while others who heard the good news rejected God's rest out of disobedience.*Heb 4:6* No one repents again whom the Holy Spirit has already enlightened and has tasted the heavenly gift, goodness of God's word, and coming age's power, but has nonetheless fallen away.*Heb 6:4-6* God gives those who turn away from him a spirit of stupor, eyes that cannot see, and ears that cannot hear.*Ro 11:8* The godless are full of envy, murder, strife, deceit and malice.*Ro 1:29* The godless are gossips, slanderers, God-haters, insolent, arrogant, and boastful, inventing ways of doing evil, and disobeying their parents.*Ro 1:30* The godless have no understanding, fidelity, love, or mercy.*Ro 1:31* The godless know God's righteous decree that those who do wrong things deserve death, but they not only continue to do those things but also approve of those who practice them.*Ro 1:32* All turn away from God to become worthless, without any doing good, not even one.*Ro 2:12* Do not have a sinful, unbelieving heart that turns away from the living God.*Heb 3:12* When you hear God, do not rebel.*Heb 3:15* God takes no pleasure in those who shrink back.*Heb 10:38* Do not belong to those who shrink back to their destruction.*Heb 10:39* Jesus said that whoever hates him, hates his Father as well.*Jn 15:23*

Christ. The whole town's folk who heard that Jesus had cast demons out of violent men and into a herd of pigs pleaded with Jesus to leave their region.*Matt 8:33-34, Mk 5:14-17, Lk 8:34-37* One of the disciples Judas Iscariot went to the chief priests to betray Jesus and hand him over in exchange for thirty pieces of silver.*Matt 26:14-16* Those who disown Christ, he will also disown.*Lk 12:9, 2Ti 2:12* Jesus said that whoever is not with him, gathering, is against him, scattering.*Matt 12:30, Lk 11:23* If we claim to follow Jesus but instead walk in the darkness, we lie and do not live out the truth.*1Jn 1:6* Why would you so quickly desert the one who called you to live in the grace of Christ and turn to a different gospel, which is really no gospel at all?*Gal 1:6-7* If we say we are without sin, then we lie and deceive, while suggesting Christ lies and while rejecting his word, but if we admit sin, the faithful and just Christ forgives and purifies us.*1Jn 1:8-10* Some who should accept the good news do not do so.*Ro 10:16* Insiders who should accept Christ but do not will envy and be angry about those who do accept Christ.*Ro 10:19* They mean to crucify God's Son all over again, subjecting him to public disgrace.*Heb 6:6* Those who reject the precious stone Jesus find that he is nonetheless the cornerstone over which they stumble and fall in disobeying his message, as is their destiny.*1Pe 2:7-8* Keep running the good race rather than letting someone cut you off, someone who persuades apart from God who calls you.*Gal 5:7-8* Jesus said that whoever acknowledges him before others, he acknowledges before his Father in heaven, while whoever disowns him before others, he disowns before his Father in heaven.*Matt 10:32-33, Lk 12:8-9*

Desertion. Many disciples left Jesus because of his hard teaching.$_{Jn\ 6:60-66}$ When many other disciples left Jesus, Jesus asked the twelve if they wanted to leave, too, but Peter answered that they had no one to whom to go, because Jesus, the Son of God, had eternal life's words.$_{Jn\ 6:67-69}$ On the night of his arrest, Jesus told the disciples that they would all fall away on his account, as the scriptures foretold that with the shepherd struck, the sheep would scatter.$_{Matt\ 26:31,\ Mk\ 14:27}$ Jesus said that the time had come when the disciples would scatter, each to his own home, leaving Jesus alone, except that his Father was with him.$_{Jn\ 16:31-32}$ Jesus said that Satan had asked to sift the disciples as wheat but that Jesus had prayed that Peter would instead turn back in faith to strengthen his brothers.$_{Lk\ 22:31-32}$ Peter replied that he would not fall away even if everyone else did so, even to prison or death.$_{Matt\ 26:33,\ Mk\ 14:29,\ Lk\ 22:33}$ Peter said that he would lay down his life for Jesus.$_{Jn\ 13:37}$ Jesus replied that Peter would indeed disown Jesus three times that very night before the rooster crowed.$_{Matt\ 26:34,\ Mk\ 14:30,\ Lk\ 22:34,\ Jn\ 13:38}$ Peter and the other disciples said that they would not disown Jesus even if they had to die.$_{Matt\ 26:35,\ Mk\ 14:31}$ Yet after a large crowd led by the betrayer Judas Iscariot arrested Jesus, the disciples all fled.$_{Matt\ 26:56}$ And when Peter followed the crowd into the high priest's courtyard outside where they tried Jesus, and people in the crowd three times identified Peter as Jesus's follower, Peter all three times denied that he was a follower of Jesus, even calling down curses and saying that he didn't know the man.$_{Matt\ 26:69-74,\ Mk\ 14:66-71,\ Lk\ 22:56-60,\ Jn\ 18:17,\ 25-27}$ Immediately, a rooster crowed just as Jesus had said.$_{Matt\ 26:74-75,\ Mk\ 14:72,\ Lk\ 22:60,\ Jn\ 18:27}$ The Lord then turned and looked out into the courtyard, straight at Peter.$_{Lk\ 22:61}$ Remembering what Jesus had said, Peter went outside and wept bitterly.$_{Matt\ 26:74-75,\ Mk\ 14:72,\ Lk\ 22:62}$

Reinstatement. When the disciples had finished eating with the resurrected Jesus on the Sea of Galilee's shore, Jesus asked Peter if he loved Jesus more than these, to which Peter replied that Jesus knew that he loved him.$_{Jn\ 21:15}$ Jesus told Peter to feed his lambs.$_{Jn\ 21:15}$ Jesus then repeated his question to Peter whether Peter loved him, to which Peter again replied that Jesus knew that Peter loved him.$_{Jn\ 21:16}$ Jesus told Peter to feed his sheep.$_{Jn\ 21:16}$ Jesus then repeated his question to Peter a third time, asking whether Peter loved him, hurting Peter, who answered that the Lord knew that he loved him.$_{Jn\ 21:17}$ Jesus said again to feed his sheep, adding that although Peter dressed himself and went where he wished when he was young, when Peter was old, others would dress him, stretch out his hands, and lead him where he would not want to go, indicating the kind of death by which Peter would glorify God.*Jn 21:17-19* Jesus then said to follow him.*Jn 21:19* When Peter asked what about John, who was walking behind, Jesus said that if John remained until Jesus returned, his doing so made no difference to Peter.*Jn 21:20-22*

Rejection. In Pisidian Antioch, Paul with Barnabas exhorted the Jews in their synagogue with a brief history up to John the Baptist and Jesus, before explaining that God had brought the salvation message to Jews and Gentiles.*Acts 13:13-26* Paul then proclaimed that Jerusalem and its rulers rejected and condemned Jesus, fulfilling scripture, but God raised him from the dead, to which many were now witnesses, as the good news of forgiveness from sins.*Acts 13:27-41* Although many of the Jews wanted to hear more, when Paul and Barnabas returned to speak a week later, and the whole city gathered, the Jews in their jealousy contradicted Paul, heaping abuse on him.*Acts 13:44-45* Paul said that since they now rejected the message, as unworthy of eternal life, Paul would now turn to the Gentiles, as scriptures foretold, and the glad Gentiles honored the Lord's word, all appointed for eternal life believing.*Acts 13:46-48* While the Lord's word spread throughout the region, the Jewish leaders stirred up persecution, expelling Paul and Barnabas from the region, while filling them with the Holy Spirit.*Acts 13:49-52* When Paul and Barnabas preached in Iconium, a great number of Jews and Greeks believed, but the Jews who refused to believe poisoned others' minds against them, dividing the city so that they had to flee from stoning.*Acts 14:1-6* In Thessalonica, Paul reasoned and proved from the scriptures that Jesus was the Messiah who would suffer, die, and rise, causing some Jews and many God-fearing Greeks to believe, but other Jews were jealous, started a riot, and forced the believers to send Paul and Silas away at night, even agitating the crowds in the city to which Paul and Silas went.*Acts 17:1-14* The Jews in Corinth opposed Paul's message that Jesus was the Messiah and became abusive, causing Paul to go next door to preach to others who heard, believed, and were baptized.*Acts 18:5-8* Paul spoke boldly and argued persuasively about God's kingdom in Ephesus's synagogue for three months, but they became obstinate and refused to believe, so Paul left the synagogue for a lecture hall so that all Jews and Greeks heard the Lord's word.*Acts 19:8-10* Silversmiths and related trades in Ephesus created a great disturbance about the Way, seizing Paul's traveling companions, to try to save their income from making shrines of Artemis.*Acts 19:23-41* When large numbers of Rome's Jews came to hear Paul, Paul witnessed to them from morning until evening, explaining about God's kingdom, and trying from the law and prophets to persuade them about Jesus, causing some to believe but not others.*Acts 28:22-23* Paul made a final statement that the Holy Spirit spoke the truth when saying through the prophet Isaiah that the Jews would hear but not understand because of their hard hearts, and that God's salvation thus went to the Gentiles, who would listen.*Acts 28:25-28*

Persecution. Jesus said that everyone would hate and persecute his disciples, who should flee from town to town.*Matt 10:22-23* Persecutors would hand over Jesus's disciples, hated by all nations, to be put to death.*Matt 24:9* Jesus also said not to worry what to say or how to say it when arrested because the Father's Spirit would speak through his disciples.*Matt 10:19-20, Mk 13:11, Lk 12:11-12* The religious leaders seized the apostles Peter and John for proclaiming in Jesus the resurrection of the dead, putting them in jail, questioning them, and warning and commanding them not to speak, before their release.*Acts 4:1-21* The high priest and his associates jailed the apostles again, but an angel of the Lord opened the jail doors, letting them out and telling them to stand in the temple courts telling the people about the new life.*Acts 5:17-20* The captain and his officers brought the apostles in again for the high priest to repeat strict orders not to teach in Jesus's name, but Peter and the other apostles refused, and only the law teacher Gamaliel's intercession for them kept the leaders from putting the apostles to death, flogging them instead.*Acts 5:25-40* After Saul's conversion, the Jews conspired to kill him, but Saul learned and escaped in a basket through an opening in a wall.*Acts 9:23-25* When Saul debated with the Hellenistic Jews, they tried to kill him.*Acts 9:29* King Herod arrested Peter and put him in prison, but with the church earnestly praying to God for Peter, an angel of the Lord rescued him from his chains, led him out of the prison, and then disappeared, leaving Peter to go to the house where believers prayed for him.*Acts 12:3-17* A crowd in Lystra, stirred up by some Jews from Antioch and Iconium, stoned Paul and dragged him outside the city, thinking he was dead, but Paul got up and returned to the city before leaving the next day.*Acts 14:19-20* When Paul rebuked a future-predicting spirit out of a female slave, her owners, realizing that they had lost their way of making money with the slave, had Paul and Silas severely flogged and thrown into prison.*Acts 16:19-24* The Jews of Corinth opposed Paul, became abusive toward him, and made a united attack on him, bringing him before the proconsul, who drove them off because it had to do with their own law.*Acts 18:12-17* Some Jews in Macedonia plotted against Paul.*Acts 20:3* Jews at the temple stirred up the crowd to seize Paul and try to kill him, putting the whole city into an uproar and requiring the Roman commander to save Paul by arresting him.*Acts 21:27-36* The commander nearly had Paul flogged until Paul showed himself a Roman citizen, at which the commander arranged for Paul to have a trial before the Sanhedrin.*Acts 22:22-30* Some Jews then formed a conspiracy, binding themselves with an oath to kill Paul, and so the Roman commander transferred Paul to the governor Felix in Caesarea, before whom Paul stood trial.*Acts 23:12-31, Acts 24* When Paul also stood trial before Felix's successor Festus, and the Jews who had come from Jerusalem made false charges against him, Paul appealed to Caesar.*Acts 25:1-12* Festus brought Paul before King Agrippa to determine the charges on which to send Paul to Rome.*Acts 25:13-27* Paul said that he stood trial before Festus and King Agrippa because of his hope in the resurrection of the dead that God had promised their ancestors.*Acts 26:1-8* Paul told the local Jewish leaders in Rome that chains bound him because of his hope of Israel.*Acts 28:17-20* Apostles become earth's scum, the world's garbage.*1Co 4:13* God puts apostles on display at the end of the procession, like those condemned to die in the arena.*1Co 4:9* God makes apostles a spectacle to the whole universe, to angels as well as to humans.*1Co 4:9* Apostles are weak, dishonored, fools for Christ, while others who are not apostles appear so wise, strong, and honored in Christ.*1Co 4:10* Apostles go hungry and thirsty, in rags, brutally treated, and homeless, while working hard with their own hands.*1Co 4:11-12* Some apostles work harder and are imprisoned more frequently, flogged more severely, and exposed to death repeatedly, while facing many other hardships.*2Co 11:24-26*

Martyrs. God's power filled Stephen, who performed great signs and wonders, and against whom opposition could not stand as he spoke with the Spirit's wisdom, but some stirred up people, elders, and law teachers against him with false witnesses that he spoke blasphemous words against God and Moses.*Acts 6:8-12* False witnesses told the Sanhedrin, before whom they brought Stephen, that he had spoken against the holy place and law, saying that Jesus would destroy the place and change the customs, but Stephen kept the face of an angel.*Acts 6:12-15* When asked if the charges were true, Stephen gave the Sanhedrin Israel's history, condemning them as stiff-necked people whose uncircumcised hearts and ears resisted the Holy Spirit, people who betrayed and murdered the Righteous One and who disobeyed the law they received through angels.*Acts 7:1-53* When the Sanhedrin members showed their fury at Stephen's words, the Holy Spirit filled Stephen, who looked up, saying that he saw heaven open with the Son of Man standing at God's right hand.*Acts 7:54-56* The Sanhedrin members covered their ears, yelled at him, rushed at him, and dragged him out and stoned him, while Stephen prayed that the Lord Jesus receive his spirit and not hold this sin against them, and Saul looked on approvingly.*Acts 7:57-60, Acts 8:1* A great persecution broke out against the church, scattering all except the apostles, with Saul dragging men and women off to prison to destroy the church.*Acts 8:1-3* Saul got from the high priest letters to the synagogues for help in taking prisoner believers in the Way.*Acts 9:1-2* Saul, then the apostle Paul, later wrote that he was the least of the apostles and did not deserve to be called one because he persecuted God's church.*1Co 15:9* King Herod had John's brother James put to death, to persecute the church.*Acts 12:1-2* Jesus said that his faithful witness Antipas was put to death in Pergamum where Satan lives.*Rev 2:13*

Believers. Jesus said that everyone will hate you because of him.*Mk 13:13* Jesus said that if the world hates you, then keep in mind that the world hated him first.*Jn 15:18* If you belonged to the world, then the world would not hate you, but because Jesus chose you out of the world, the world hates you.*Jn 15:19* Jesus said that because they persecuted him, not knowing the one who sent him, they will persecute you, too.*Jn 15:20-21* Jesus taught that God blesses and grants the kingdom of heaven to those whom others persecute because of righteousness.*Matt 5:10* Jesus taught that God blesses you when people insult you, persecute you, and falsely say all kinds of evil against you because of Jesus.*Matt 5:11, Lk 6:22* Jesus says to rejoice and be glad for persecution because of him, because your reward in heaven will be great, just as others persecuted the prophets.*Matt 5:12, Lk 6:23* Some face death daily, even those who boast about you in Christ Jesus our Lord.*1Co 15:31* Know that persecution of a leading believer may serve to advance the gospel.*Php 1:12* Those who participate in and witness persecution will know that the believer wears chains for Christ.*Php 1:13* The chains of a leading believer make brothers and sisters so confident in the Lord as to proclaim the gospel without fear.*Php 1:14* God's provision of Jesus Christ's Spirit, together with prayer, deliver believers who face persecution.*Php 1:19* Know the troubles fellow believers experience under great pressure, beyond their ability to endure, despairing of life.*2Co 1:8* Some will feel they have received a death sentence, but this happens that we rely not on ourselves but on God, who raises the dead.*2Co 1:9* Some will intensely persecute the church, trying to destroy it.*Gal 1:13* Yet those who persecute the church initially, may soon preach the faith that they formerly tried to destroy.*Gal 1:23* Turnabouts of that kind will cause believers to praise God.*Gal 1:24* God will show mercy to a violent persecutor who acts in ignorance and unbelief.*1Ti 1:13* Remember one another's chains.*Col 4:18*

Attitude. Jesus said not to fear persecutors.*Matt 10:26* Jesus said to stand firm in persecution for your salvation in the end, even when many turn away from the faith, betraying and hating one another.*Matt 24:9-13, Lk 21:12-19* Jesus said that those who hear and receive the word with joy but fall away at the first trouble or persecution over it are like a seed sown on rocky soil that grows no root and thus dies in the first scorching heat.*Matt 13:20-21* Paul and Barnabas said that they must go through many hardships to enter God's kingdom.*Acts 14:22* In Corinth, the Lord spoke to Paul in a vision, telling Paul not to be afraid but to keep on speaking because the Lord was with him, and so Paul stayed for a year and a half, teaching God's word.*Acts 18:9-11* Paul said that he served the Lord with great humility and with tears in the midst of severe testing by his Jewish opponents.*Acts 20:19* The Holy Spirit warned Paul that he faced prison and hardships, but he considered his life worth nothing, his only aim to finish the race and task that the Lord Jesus had given him to testify to the good news of God's grace.*Acts 20:23-24* Paul warned to be on your guard against savage wolves who will come among you and not spare the flock.*Acts 20:29-31* Paul said that he was ready not only to be bound but to die for the Lord Jesus's name.*Acts 21:13* After Paul's trial in Jerusalem, when Roman guards held Paul in their barracks, the Lord appeared to Paul to tell him to take courage because Paul would testify about him in Rome.*Acts 23:9-11* Whatever happens, act worthy of Christ's gospel.*Php 1:27* Delight in persecutions for Christ's sake.*2Co 12:10* When others curse you, you should bless, while when others persecute you, you should endure it.*1Co 4:12* Bless rather than curse those who persecute you.*Ro 12:14* When others slander, you should answer kindly.*1Co 4:13* When those who oppose you fail to frighten you, you should show them a sign that God will save you but destroy them.*Php 1:28* You may at times find no rest, harassed at every turn, conflicts on the outside, fears within.*2Co 7:5* God grants for Christ that you not only believe in him but also suffer for him, struggling as other believers struggle.*Php 1:29-30* Wear salvation's helmet against spiritual attack.*Eph 6:17* Non-believers killed the Lord Jesus and the prophets, and so they may also drive you out, even though they displease God and are hostile to all while trying to keep you from saving others.*1Th*

2:15-16 Persevere in faith through persecutions.*2Th 1:4* Warn one another of persecution.*1Co 4:14* God repeatedly delivers us from deadly peril and, we trust, will continue to deliver us.*2Co 1:10* Prayers for one another help defeat persecution, a gracious favor for which many give thanks.*2Co 1:11* Jesus said to stand firm to the end for your salvation.*Mk 13:13*

World

The New Testament addresses the nature of the world into which we come and out of which we must come, as we comprehend and then hold onto our faith. The world is evil, while the Spirit is divine. See how the New Testament addresses the world. Are you of this world, or are you pursuing the kingdom through Christ?

Evil. Jesus said that the Jews who did not believe in him were of this world and would die in their sin.*Jn 8:21-24* Jesus said that the prince of this world was coming but had no hold over him and instead would come so that the world learned that Jesus would do exactly what his Father, whom he loved, commanded.*Jn 14:30-31* Jesus prayed that he had given the disciples the Father's word but the world had hated the disciples because they are not of the world any more than Jesus is of the world.*Jn 17:14-16* Jesus prayed not to take the disciples out of the world but to protect them from the evil one.*Jn 17:15* Jesus prayed that he had sent the disciples into the world as the Father had sent him into the world.*Jn 17:18* The whole world is under the control of the evil one.*1Jn 5:19* The world hates you.*1Jn 3:13* Jesus said that if the world hates you, then keep in mind that the world hated him first.*Jn 15:18* If you belonged to the world, then the world would not hate you, but because Jesus chose you out of the world, the world hates you.*Jn 15:19* The world does not know us because it did not know God.*1Jn 3:1* You cheat on God when you pursue the world as friend because worldly pursuits mean hatred toward God, making you his enemy.*Jas 4:4* Live in the world as a foreigner and exile, abstaining from its sinful desires that destroy your soul.*1Pe 2:11* One's earthly nature is idolatrous, immoral, impure, lustful, evil, and greedy.*Col 3:5* Resist the world's elemental spiritual forces.*Col 2:8* Having died with Christ to the world's elemental spiritual forces, do not act any longer as if you still belong to the world, and do not submit to the world's rules.*Col 2:20* Do not look for praise from people, even when in Christ you could claim reason to do so.*1Th 2:6* To love the world is to desert the teaching.*2Ti 4:10* If jealousy and quarreling are among you, then you are acting worldly like mere humans.*1Co 3:3* The world's people are immoral and greedy, swindlers and idolaters.*1Co 5:10* Jesus said that the world cannot accept the Spirit because the world does not see the Spirit or know the Spirit.*Jn 14:17* Jesus also said that the world would not see him anymore but that we will see him.*Jn 14:19*

Overcome. Jesus said that in this world we will have trouble but to take heart because he had overcome the world.*Jn 16:33* Jesus said that he is not of this world but from above.*Jn 8:23* Do not follow the world's patterns but instead let your renewed mind transform you so that you can discern God's good, pleasing, and perfect will.*Ro 12:2* God longs jealously for the spirit he placed within us, giving us ever more grace.*Jas 4:5-6* God comes near to us when we submit and come near to him, just as the devil flees us when we resist him.*Jas 4:7-8* To overcome the world, one must love God, which means keeping his commands while believing that Jesus is God's son.*1Jn 5:4-5* Be blameless and pure children of God without fault in this warped and crooked generation.*Php 2:15* God judges the world.*Ro 2:5-6* We received God's Spirit, not the world's spirit.*1Co 2:12* Be people who live by the Spirit rather than who are still worldly—mere infants in Christ.*1Co 3:1* Time is so short that the married should live as if not married, mourners as if they do not mourn, the happy as if they were not happy, owners as if their property was not theirs to keep, and those who use the world's things as if not engrossed in them, because this world in its present form is passing away.*1Co 7:29-31* If you can, then avoid the world's affairs, and focus instead on pleasing the Lord, involved in the Lord's affairs.*1Co 7:32-34* Live in the world but not waging war as the world does.*2Co 10:3* Fight instead with weapons not of the world but having divine power to demolish strongholds.*2Co 10:4* Jesus said that the Advocate would prove the world wrong about sin because people did not believe, about righteousness because Jesus was going to the Father, and about judgment because the world's prince now stood condemned.*Jn 16:8-11*

Slavery. Jesus said that everyone who sins is a slave to sin.*Jn 8:34* A slave has no permanent place in the family.*Jn 8:35* Remember that Abraham had a son with a slave woman, born out of flesh, and a son with a free woman, born out of a divine promise.*Gal 4:22-23* Each woman represented a different covenant, one bearing slave children under law and the other bearing free children out of God's promise.*Gal 4:24-28* Slave children persecuted free children then as they do now.*Gal 4:29* Only free children, not slave children, share our inheritance from God.*Gal 4:30-31* Before we knew God, ungodly principles enslaved us.*Gal 4:8* Anyone who, after knowing God and having God know them, turns back to those weak and miserable principles, like observing special days, seasons, and years, is just wishing enslavement all over again.*Gal 4:9-10* Sinners promise others freedom, while they themselves are slaves to sin, which has mastered them.*1Pe 2:19* Strike a blow to your body to make it your slave so that after you preach to others, God will not disqualify you for the prize.*1Co 9:27* One reaps no benefit from sin, only shame and death, because sin's only wage is death.*Ro 6:21-22*

Freedom. Christ freed us for freedom, and so we should stand firm rather than let slavery's yoke burden us again.*Gal 5:1* Jesus frees those held in slavery by their fear of death.*Heb 2:15* We are all together in Christ Jesus, not the insider or outsider, slave or free, or male or female.*Gal 3:28* Though free and belonging to no one, make yourself a slave to everyone to win as many as possible.*1Co 9:19* When we do separate from one another for a little while, we do so that we may have one another back forever, no longer as slaves but as dear brothers and sisters in the Lord.*Phm 15-16* Among believers we see no insider or outside, sinner or saint, slave or free, but Christ is everything and in everyone.*Col 3:11* One reaps holiness and eternal life as a slave to God because God's gift is eternal life in Christ Jesus our Lord.*Ro 6:21-22* Our old self's crucifixion with him killed the sinful body, setting us free from sin and making us no longer slaves to sin.*Ro 6:6-7* One Spirit baptized all, whether insider or outsider, slave or free, to form one body, giving each the same Spirit to drink.*1Co 12:13* The Spirit does not make you fearful slaves but makes you God's child who can cry to your Father.*Ro 8:15*

Disputes. Men should pray and lift holy hands without disputing.*1Ti 2:8* Remind and warn God's people against quarreling about words, which is of no value and only ruins those who listen.*2Ti 2:14* Avoid foolish, unprofitable, indeed useless controversies and arguments about the law.*Tit 3:9* Your desires battling within you, for things that you do not have, cause fights and quarrels among you.*Jas 4:1-2* You do not have things that you desire because you either do not ask God or, when you ask, you ask with wrong motives to spend what you get on your pleasures.*Jas 4:2-3* Do everything without grumbling or arguing.*Php 2:14* Have nothing to do with foolish and stupid arguments that only produce quarrels.*2Ti 2:23* If jealousy and quarreling are among you, then you are acting worldly like mere humans.~1Co 3:3~ When you argue over whom you follow, one teacher or another through whom you came to believe, you are mere humans.~1Co 3:4-5~ The Lord's servant must not be quarrelsome or resentful.~2Ti 2:24~ Take your disputes with other believers before the Lord's people for judgment, not before non-believers.~1Co 6:1-2~ The Lord's people will judge the world and so can competently judge trivial cases.~1Co 6:2~ If you have disputes, then don't seek a ruling from those whose way of life church members scorn.~1Co 6:4~ You should have someone among you wise enough to judge a dispute between believers.~1Co 6:5~ Do not let one brother take another to court in front of unbelievers.~1Co 6:6~ Lawsuits among you have already completely defeated you, when you should instead have preferred that others wrong and cheat you.~1Co 6:7~ Rather than judge by appearances, know that one belongs to Christ just as much as another does.~2Co 10:7~ We must avoid provoking and envying others in our conceit.~Gal 5:26~ Don't grumble against one another, or God, who stands at the door, will judge you.~Jas 5:9~ Accept the one with weak faith, without quarreling over disputable matters.~Ro 14:1~ If instead we bite and devour each other, then we will destroy each other.~Gal 5:15~ Warn a divisive person once and then a second time, but then have nothing to do with them because they are warped, sinful, and self-condemned.~Tit 3:10-11~ Take a mature view, but if you think differently, then let God make truth clear to you.~Php 3:15~ Warn the disruptive.~1Th 5:14~ Keep away from disruptive believers.~2Th 3:6~ Watch out for and keep away from those who cause divisions.~Ro 16:17~

Reconciliation. Christ has made the two groups one and has destroyed the barrier, the dividing wall of hostility, setting aside in his flesh the law with its commands and regulations.~Eph 2:14-15~ Christ's purpose was to create in him one new peaceful humanity, in one body reconciling both sides to God through the cross, by which he put to death their hostility.~Eph 2:15-16~ Christ came preaching peace both to those far away and those near.~Eph 2:17~ Through Christ, both sides have access to the Father by one Spirit.~Eph 2:18~ Do not quarrel among you by claiming to follow different teachers whom no one crucified and in whose name no one baptized you, when Christ himself is not so divided.~1Co 1:11-15~ Jesus said that anyone who is angry with a brother or sister faces judgment, and anyone showing contempt for a brother or sister is in danger of hell's fire.~Matt 5:21-22~ Jesus says instead to reconcile with your brother or sister who has something against you, before you offer gifts in church.~Matt 5:23-24~

Jesus says to settle quickly with a court adversary before the judge rules, throwing you in prison to pay your last penny.*Matt 5:25-26, Lk 12:58-59*

Greed. Jesus said woe to the rich who have already received their comfort, to the well fed who will later go hungry, to those who laugh who will mourn later, and to those about whom everyone speaks well now, like the old false prophets.*Lk 6:24-26* Jesus also said that those who hear and receive the word but lose it to wealth's deceitfulness are like seed sown and choked among thorns.*Matt 13:22* Jesus said to guard against all kinds of greed because life is not abundant possessions.*Lk 12:13-15* Jesus told the parable of the rich man who planned to build bigger barns to store an abundant harvest, but God instead that very night demanded his life, and so it would be for whoever stores up for themselves without being rich toward God.*Lk 12:16-21* Foolish and harmful desires for riches tempt, trap, and plunge people into ruin and destruction.*1Ti 6:9* Don't love money, but instead let what you have be enough, because God never leaves or forsakes you.*Heb 13:5* Do not let loving money tempt you to wander from the faith.*1Ti 6:10* Have nothing to do with people who love money.*2Ti 3:2-5* The rich who hoard wealth should cry because of their coming misery, the corrosion of their wealth testifying against them and eating their flesh.*Jas 5:5* They should have paid their workers fair wages so that the workers' complaints would not reach the Lord Almighty's ears.*Jas 5:4* Hoarding wealth and cheating workers to live in luxurious self-indulgence just fattens the rich for due slaughter for having condemned and murdered innocents.*Jas 5:5-6* You must inevitably associate with the world's greedy people because otherwise you would have to leave this world.*1Co 5:10* The world's people are greedy swindlers.*1Co 5:10* Those accursed experts in greed never stop sinning.*1Pe 2:14-16* Jesus said not to store up destructible treasure on earth but instead indestructible treasures in heaven.*Matt 6:19-20* Your heart is wherever you keep your treasure.*Matt 6:21* The Pharisees, who loved money but heard Jesus criticizing the love of money, sneered at Jesus.*Lk 16:14* The apostle Paul said that he had not coveted anyone's silver, gold, or clothing.*Acts 20:33*

Schemes. Because we disappear so quickly and have no real idea of tomorrow, we should avoid arrogant and evil money-making schemes and instead simply pursue the Lord's will.*Jas 4:13-16* No swearing that you will do this or that but instead just say one way or the other and then go do likewise, or God will condemn.*Jas 5:12* Woe to those who hate other followers, rush for profit to undermine the fellowship, and rebel against

God's appointed leaders.*Jude 11* They are blemishes among you, feeding only themselves without the slightest qualm, producing nothing, blown here and there like wild waves foaming up their shame, wandering and uprooted, and thus twice dead, reserved for blackest darkness forever.*Jude 12-13* When Jesus found people selling animals and exchanging money in the temple courts, he drove the animals out with a whip of cords, scattered the money changers' coins, and turned over their tables, saying to stop turning his Father's house into a market and showing as written that zeal for his house would consume him.*Jn 2:13-17* A second time, Jesus entered the temple courts to drive out all who bought and sold there, turning over the money changers' tables, saying that they had turned his house of prayer into a den of robbers.*Matt 21:12-13, Mk 11:15-17, Lk 19:45-46* The Lord will come with countless holy ones to judge and convict for the ungodly acts and defiant words of the grumblers and faultfinders who follow their own evil desires, boasting about themselves while flattering others for their own advantage.*Jude 14-15* Telling a parable of a shrewd manager who used his master's wealth to win friends for himself, Jesus said to use worldly wealth to make friends so that when the wealth is gone, you gain welcome to eternal dwellings.*Lk 16:1-9*

God. Some of you were greedy swindlers, but the name of the Lord Jesus Christ and Spirit of our God sanctified you.*1Co 6:9-11* Everything is yours, whether that of the world, life or death, or present or future, because you are of Christ, and Christ is of God.*1Co 3:21-23* Those who are rich materially should not be arrogant nor hope in uncertain wealth but instead in God who richly provides everything for enjoyment.*1Ti 6:17* The rich should be rich in good deeds, generous, and willing to share, laying up treasure for themselves as a firm foundation for the coming age for true life.*1Ti 6:18-19* Avoid arrogant and evil money-making schemes and instead simply pursue the Lord's will.*Jas 4:13-16* God gives a depraved mind to those who do not think knowing him worthwhile, so that they fill with greed.*Ro 1:28-29* Overseers are not to be lovers of money.*1Ti 3:2-3* The greedy do not inherit God's kingdom.*1Co 6:9-10* Allow among God's holy people not even a hint of greed.*Eph 5:3* Jesus said you can only serve one master, not two masters, because with two masters, you would hate one while loving the other, and thus you must serve only God, not money.*Matt 6:24, Lk 16:13* Jesus said that whomever God can trust with little, God can trust with much, but whoever is dishonest with little will be dishonest with much.*Lk 16:10* You must be trustworthy with worldly wealth for God to trust you with true riches and trustworthy with others' property to have property of your own.*Lk 16:11-12* Jesus said that what people value highly, God detests.*Lk 16:15* Jesus told the parable of a rich man living in luxury with a beggar by his gate.*Lk 16:19-21* Both the rich man and beggar died, the beggar going to heaven but the rich man tormented in hell.*Lk 16:22-23* The rich man asked Abraham for relief or to send a warning to his family, but Abraham said that if they didn't listen to the law and prophets, then they wouldn't listen even if someone rose from the dead.*Lk 16:24-31*

Giving. When Jesus watched rich people throw large amounts into the temple treasury, while a poor widow gave two small copper coins, he told the disciples that the widow had given more out of her poverty, everything on which she had to live, than the rich gave out of their riches.*Mk 12:41-43, Lk 20:41-44, 21:1-4* Jesus said to sell your possessions to give to the poor, and in doing so you will store indestructible treasure in heaven where your heart will then be.*Lk 12:33* We don't give to God in that he must repay us because everything is from him, through him, and for him.*Ro 11:35-36* Give the poor person just as good a seat and just as much attention in meetings as the rich person, or you will have let evil judge among you.*Jas 2:2-4* God chose the world's poor to be rich in faith.*Jas 2:5* Why should you dishonor the poor when the rich are the ones exploiting you?*Jas 2:6-7* Let your overflowing joy and extreme poverty well up in rich generosity.*2Co 8:2* Conduct yourselves appropriately, poor yet making many rich, and having nothing and yet possessing everything.*2Co 6:8-10* When a rich young man asked Jesus how to get eternal life, Jesus told him that to be perfect, he should sell his possessions, give to the poor, have treasure in heaven, and follow Jesus.*Matt 19:16-22* When the young man went away sad, Jesus said how hard the rich find getting into heaven's kingdom, God's kingdom, like passing a camel through the eye of a needle.*Matt 19:22-24* When the astonished disciples asked how anyone could then gain salvation, Jesus said that salvation is impossible for man but that all things are possible for God.*Matt 19:25-26*

Flesh. Jesus said to be careful or drunkenness and carousing will weigh down your heart, and the last day will close on you like a trap.*Lk 21:34* We all at one time gratified the flesh's cravings, following its desires and thoughts, while deserving of God's wrath.*Eph 2:3* When we were in the flesh's realm, law aroused sinful passions that led to death.*Ro 7:5* The flesh desires sexual immorality and orgies, idolatry and witchcraft, hatred and discord, jealousy and fits of rage, selfish ambition and envy, dissensions and factions, drunkenness, and like things that keep one from inheriting God's kingdom.*Gal 5:19-21* Sinners mouth empty, boastful words appealing to the flesh's lustful desires, enticing people who are just escaping from those who live in error.$_{1Pe\ 2:18}$ They promise them freedom, while they themselves are slaves to sin, which has mastered them.$_{1Pe\ 2:19}$ The flesh makes the mind hostile to God, rejecting God's law and causing disobedience.$_{Ro\ 8:7}$ Uncircumcision of our flesh makes us dead in sin.$_{Col\ 2:13}$ Those who pursue the flesh cannot please God.$_{Ro\ 8:8}$ God gives non-believers over in their hearts' sinful desires to sexual impurity to degrade their bodies with one another.$_{Ro\ 1:24}$ God gives non-believers over to shameful lusts so that, inflamed by lust, both men and women exchange natural sexual relations for unnatural ones, committing shameful acts with the same sex and receiving the due penalty.$_{Ro\ 1:26-27}$ The widow who lives for pleasure is dead even while she lives.$_{1Ti\ 5:6}$ Human rules lack any value in restraining sensual indulgence.$_{Col\ 2:23}$

Christ. The Word became flesh, dwelling among us, so that we saw the glory of the one and only Son from the Father, full of grace and truth.$_{Jn\ 1:14}$ The disciples grumbled that Jesus's teaching that he was the bread of life and they must eat his flesh and drink his blood was a hard teaching.$_{Jn\ 6:60-61}$ While those who ate God's manna died, anyone who eats the bread that comes down from heaven, Jesus's flesh, does not die but lives forever.$_{Jn\ 6:50-51}$ Whoever eats Jesus's flesh and drinks his blood has eternal life, Jesus raising them up at the last day, because his flesh and blood are real food and drink.$_{Jn\ 6:52-55}$ Eating his flesh and drinking his blood keeps one in Jesus, so that the one who feeds on Jesus lives because of him.$_{Jn\ 6:56-57}$ The flesh weakened us, but God sent his own Son in the likeness of sinful flesh to condemn sin in the flesh, to meet the law's righteous requirement in those of us who live by the Spirit rather than the flesh.$_{Ro\ 8:3-4}$ Clothe yourselves with the Lord Jesus Christ rather than thinking about how to gratify the desires of the flesh.$_{Ro\ 13:14}$ The flesh ruled our whole self until Christ circumcised us.$_{Col\ 2:11-12}$ We who belong to Christ Jesus have crucified the flesh's passions and desires.$_{Gal\ 5:24}$ If knowing our Lord and Savior Jesus Christ helps one escape worldly corruption but that person succumbs again, then that person is worse off than ever.$_{1Pe\ 2:20}$ Better not to know righteousness than to have known but turned one's back on its sacred command.$_{1Pe\ 2:21}$ Those who know righteousness but then turn back to sin are like a dog returning to its vomit or a washed sow wallowing again in the mud.$_{1Pe\ 2:22}$ Watch that sensual desires do not overcome dedication to Christ, bringing judgment.$_{1Ti\ 5:11-12}$

Spirit. Death to the flesh released us from the law so that we serve in the Spirit's new way rather than the written code's old way.{Ro 7:6} Those who live for the flesh set their minds on what the flesh desires, while those who live for the Spirit set their minds on what the Spirit desires.{Ro 8:5} Flee the evil desires of youth.{2Ti 2:22} Do not get drunk on wine, which leads to debauchery.{Eph 5:18} The flesh kills the mind, but the Spirit gives the mind life and peace.{Ro 8:6} When we walk by the Spirit, no longer doing whatever we want, we no longer gratify the flesh's contrary desires, with which the Spirit's desires conflict.{Gal 5:16-17} We must put to death the body's misdeeds to live, rather than live for the flesh, in which case we die.{Ro 8:12-13} In the last times, scoffers without the Spirit will follow their natural instincts into their own ungodly desires, while dividing you.{Jude 17-18} Shun and expose the fruitless deeds of darkness that the disobedient do in secret.{Eph 5:11-12} Fear judgment, hating even the clothing stained by corrupted flesh.{Jude 23}

Curse. Let a curse be on anyone who does not love the Lord.{1Co 16:22} Let God curse anyone, even an angel, who preaches a false gospel.{Gal 1:8} Again, let God curse those who preach a false gospel different from the true gospel that you accepted.{Gal 1:9} Those who rely on the works of the law are under a curse because they do not do everything that the law requires.{Gal 3:10} Christ redeemed us from law's curse when crucifixion cursed Christ, who died for us.{Gal 3:13} God gives a depraved mind to those who do not think knowing him worthwhile, so that they do what they should not do, filling with every wickedness, evil, greed, and depravity.{Ro 1:28-29} Have great sorrow and unceasing anguish for the cursed and cut off from Christ, who are of your own people.{Ro 9:2-5} Whoever does not have godly qualities is nearsighted and blind, forgetting that they have been cleansed from their past sins.{2Pe 1:9} Those accursed experts in greed, whose eyes fill with adultery, never stop sinning and seducing.{1Pe 2:14-16} When hungry, Jesus cursed a fig tree that did not bear fruit, causing it immediately to wither.{Matt 21:18-19} Jesus said that those who do not remain in him are branches that others pick up to throw into the fire for burning.{Jn 15:6} The apostle Paul cursed, as the devil's child, a sorcerer who opposed the apostles' preaching, immediately blinding the sorcerer for a time.{Acts 13:6-12}

Woes. Jesus said woe to the hypocrite law teachers and Pharisees for shutting the door of heaven's kingdom in people's faces while not entering themselves.{Matt 23:13} Jesus said woe to them for traveling far for a convert only to make them hell's child.{Matt 23:15} Jesus said woe to those blind guides for having persons swear by the temple's gold or altar's gift rather than the temple or altar, which are greater, when swearing by God's throne is even greater.$_{Matt\ 23:16-21}$ Jesus said woe to the law teachers and Pharisees for tithing a tenth of their spices while neglecting the more-important law matters, justice, mercy, and faithfulness.$_{Matt\ 23:23,\ Lk\ 11:42}$ Jesus said that they strain out a gnat while swallowing a camel.$_{Matt\ 23:24}$ Jesus said woe to the law teachers and Pharisees for cleaning the outside of the cup and dish while being full of greed and self-indulgence inside, when they should have cleaned the inside first so that the outside would be clean.$_{Matt\ 23:25-26,\ Lk\ 11:39-40}$ Jesus said woe to the Pharisees for loving the important seats and loving marketplace greetings.$_{Lk\ 11:43}$ Jesus said woe to the hypocrite law teachers and Pharisees for building tombs for prophets whom their ancestors murdered, when they may as well complete the murders that their ancestors started.$_{Matt\ 23:29-32,\ Lk\ 11:47-48}$ Jesus called them snakes and broods of vipers who would not escape hell's condemnation.$_{Matt\ 23:33}$ Jesus prophesied that he would send them prophets and teachers whom they would pursue, flog, crucify, and kill, leaving the blood of the righteous on them.$_{Matt\ 23:34-36,\ Lk\ 11:49-51}$ Jesus longed to gather Jerusalem's children together as a hen gathers chicks, but they were unwilling, instead stoning and killing the prophets and teachers Jesus sent them, leaving their house desolate.$_{Matt\ 23:37-38,\ Lk\ 13:34-35}$ Jesus said woe to the one who betrayed him because the betrayer would have been better not to be born.$_{Matt\ 26:24,\ Mk\ 14:21,\ Lk\ 22:22}$

Wrath. God hardens whom he wants to harden, to display his power and see his name proclaimed in all the earth.$_{Ro\ 9:17-18}$ Non-believers who oppose you heap up their sins to the limit, facing God's wrath.$_{1Th\ 2:16}$ Sinners are springs without water and mists driven by a storm, for whom God reserves blackest darkness.$_{1Pe\ 2:17}$ Immorality is disobedience, bringing God's wrath.$_{Eph\ 5:6}$ One reaps no benefit from sin, only shame and death, because sin's wage is death.$_{Ro\ 6:21-22}$ God did not spare angels when they sinned, but sent them to hell, putting them in chains of darkness to be held for judgment.$_{1Pe\ 2:4}$ God reveals his wrath against all godlessness and wickedness of people suppressing the truth.$_{Ro\ 1:18}$ Stubbornness and unrepentant hearts store up God's wrath for judgment day.$_{Ro\ 2:5}$ God has wrath and anger for those who are self-seeking, reject the truth, and follow evil.$_{Ro\ 2:8}$ Everyone who does evil faces trouble and distress.$_{Ro\ 2:9}$ God judges people's secrets.$_{Ro\ 2:16}$ God is just in bringing his wrath on us and judging the world.$_{Ro\ 2:5-6}$ God's wrath is coming for sin.$_{Col\ 3:6}$ Idolatry brings God's wrath.$_{Eph\ 5:6}$ God reveals his wrath from heaven._Ro 1:18_ Jesus pronounced harsh woes on towns where he did most of his miracles, when they did not repent, saying that even Sodom would have it better on judgment day._Matt 11:20-24, Lk 10:13-15_ Jesus also wept over Jerusalem, saying that because it did not recognize God's coming to it, enemies would dash the city and the people within its walls to the ground._Lk 19:41-44_

Belief. When you ask God, believe rather than doubt, because the one who doubts tosses about like a wave that the wind blows on the sea._Jas 1:6_ Those who doubt should not expect to receive anything from the Lord. _Jas 1:7_ Doubters are double-minded and unstable in all they do._Jas 1:8_ God makes plain to non-believers what they should know of him._Ro 1:19_ All have seen and understood God's invisible qualities including his eternal power and divine nature from what he made, so that all are without excuse._Ro 1:20_ Let God handle your anxiety because he cares for you._1Pe 5:7_ Non-believers know God, but their thinking is futile and their foolish hearts darkened, and so they neither glorify him as God nor give him thanks._Ro 1:21_ They claim wisdom but are fools_Ro 1:22_ Whoever has doubts is condemned if they eat because their eating is not from faith, and everything that does not come from faith is sin._Ro 14:23_ Be merciful to those who doubt, saving them by snatching them from the fire._Jude 22_ Jesus cursed a fruitless fig tree, which immediately withered, and when the disciples questioned it, he explained that if they also had faith and did not doubt, that they could not only wither the fig tree but have a mountain thrown into the sea._Matt 21:20-21_ The doubting disciple Thomas, who was not with the others, did not believe the others when they told him that they had seen the Lord, adding that he would not believe unless he put his fingers where the nails were and his hands in Jesus's pierced side._Jn 20:24-25_ A week later, Jesus appeared again to the disciples, again through locked doors, again wishing that peace be with them._Jn 20:26_ When Jesus told Thomas to put his fingers in Jesus's hands and Thomas's hand into Jesus's side, Thomas cried out "my Lord and my God," to which Jesus replied that Thomas had believed because he saw but blessed are those who believe without seeing._Jn 20:27-29_

Worry. Jesus said that those who hear and receive the word but lose it to life's worries are like seed sown and choked among thorns._Matt 13:22_ Jesus said not to worry about your lifestyle, like what you eat, drink, or wear, because life involves more than food, and the body more than clothes._Matt 6:25, Lk 12:22-23_ After all, your heavenly Father feeds the birds, who do not even sow, reap, or store up food, and you mean much more to your Father than birds mean.*Matt 6:26, Lk 12:24* And your heavenly Father clothes the field's flowers in finest splendor, even though the flowers do not labor to make clothing, and they're gone in a day, so God will much more clothe you, even when you have little faith.*Matt 6:28-30, Lk 12:27-28* Worrying doesn't add a single hour to your life.*Matt 6:27, Lk 12:25-26* Jesus repeats not to worry about what you eat, drink, or wear, because non-believers run after those things, whereas your heavenly Father knows you need them.*Matt 6:31-32, Lk 12:29--30* Just seek God's kingdom and righteousness, and he will give you what you need.*Matt 6:33, Lk 12:31* Jesus said not to be afraid because God's giving you his kingdom pleases him.*Lk 12:32* Jesus said not to worry about tomorrow because tomorrow worries about itself.*Matt 6:34* Each day brings enough of its own trouble.*Matt 6:34* Jesus said to be careful or life's anxieties will weigh down your heart, and the last day will close on you like a trap.*Lk 21:34*

Trials. Jesus said that those who follow him should know that the cost may be poverty and privation because even the Son of Man had nowhere to lay his head.*Matt 8:19-20* Jesus said that opponents would hand his disciples over to local councils for flogging.*Matt 10:17, Mk 13:9* Jesus added that opponents would arrest his disciples to bring them before governors and kings, to whom his disciples would witness.*Matt 10:18, Mk 13:9, Lk 21:12-13* Jesus said that everyone will hate his disciples because of Jesus, brothers killing brothers, parents killing children, and children killing parents.*Matt 10:21-22, Lk 21:16-17* Jesus said to the large crowds following him that anyone coming to him must be ready to hate family members and even their own life, to be his disciple.*Lk 14:25-26* Jesus said that family members would betray one another over him, having one another put to death.*Mk 13:12* Jesus said that we must take up our cross, follow him, and lose our life for him to be worthy of him and to find true life in him.*Matt 10:38-39, Lk 14:26* Jesus said to sit down and count the cost, like one planning to build a tower to be sure that one can finish, or like a king going off to war to see if the king should instead ask for peace.*Lk 14:28-33* Jesus said that one must give up everything one has to be his disciple.*Lk 14:33* Jesus said that because others persecuted him, not knowing the one who sent him, they will persecute you, too.*Jn 15:20-21* Jesus told his disciples that leaders would put them out of the synagogue and think that by killing them they were doing a service to God because they have not known the Father or Jesus.*Jn 16:2-3*

Perseverance. Trials and challenges that test your faith should make you happy over the perseverance that they produce because perseverance makes you mature and complete.*Jas 1:2-4* When you persevere through test and trial, still loving the Lord, you receive life's crown that the Lord promised.*Jas 1:12* The Lord blesses those who persevere, as the Lord blessed Job, because the Lord is full of compassion and mercy.*Jas 5:11* The grief you suffer now in many trials, lasting only a little while, must not keep you from rejoicing over salvation.*1Pe 1:6* Trials prove your faith genuine, worth more than gold, resulting in praise, glory, and honor on Christ's return.*1Pe 1:7* We forget the past to strain toward the prize for which God called us heavenward in Christ Jesus.*Php 3:13-14* We should persevere in what we have already attained.*Php 3:16* Let the faith of others encourage you when distressed and persecuted.*1Th 3:7-8* Boast among God's churches about others' perseverance in faith through persecutions and trials.*2Th 1:4* The Lord directs the heart into Christ's perseverance.*2Th 3:5* Believers in God should pursue endurance.*1Ti 6:11* Endure hardship.*2Ti 4:5* Suffering produces perseverance, perseverance produces character, and character sustains hope.*Ro 5:3-4* Be patient in affliction.*Ro 12:12* We draw hope from the endurance the Scriptures depict.*Ro 15:4* God gives endurance.*Ro 15:6* The Holy Spirit says that if you hear his voice, then do not harden your hearts in rebellion, even under testing in the wilderness.*Heb 3:7-8* Fix your eyes on the unseen rather than what you see because what you see is temporary, while the unseen is eternal.*2Co 4:18* We share in Christ when we hold our original conviction firmly to the very end.*Heb 3:14* Remember your earlier days after receiving the light, when you endured despite great conflict full of suffering.*Heb 10:32* Others may publicly expose you to insult and persecution, or you may stand side by side with those whom others so treat.*Heb 10:33* Suffer along with the imprisoned, and joyfully accept your property's confiscation, because you know that you have better and lasting possessions.*Heb 10:34* Do not throw away your confidence, but instead expect rich reward.*Heb 10:35* Persevere so that when you have done God's will, you receive what he promised.*Heb 10:36* Be confident that with the Lord helping you, you need not fear, because mere mortals cannot oppose God.*Heb 13:6*

Strength. Jesus said not to worry what to say when arrested and brought to trial because of him, because the Holy Spirit would give you what to say and speak for you.*Mk 13:11* Jesus said that he will give you words and wisdom to say that your adversaries will not be able to resist or contradict.*Lk 21:14-15* God's power filled Stephen, who performed great signs and wonders, and against whom opposition could not stand as he spoke with the Spirit's wisdom.*Acts 6:8-10* Jesus also said at the Last

Supper for the disciples to sell their cloak to buy a sword, but when the disciples said that they had a sword, Jesus said that sword was enough.*Lk 22:35-38* Be strong in the Lord in his mighty power.*Eph 6:10* Stand firm with the belt of truth buckled around your waist, with the breastplate of righteousness in place, and with your feet fitted with the readiness that comes from the gospel of peace.*Eph 6:14-15* In prayer, receive God's strength with all power according to his glorious might so that you endure with great patience.*Col 1:10-11* Do not let trials unsettle you, for you know quite well that your destiny is in them, as others keep telling you and has already occurred.*1Th 3:3-4* Recall prophecies others made about you to help you fight the battle well.*1Ti 1:18* Persecutions and sufferings come to sound teachers, but the Lord rescues from all of them.*2Ti 3:10-11* The Lord stands at our side and gives us strength, so that through us the message might reach all.*2Ti 4:17* Be on guard, standing firm in faith, strong and courageous.*1Co 16:13* The Lord rescues from every evil attack.*2Ti 4:18*

Comfort. Jesus told the disciples at the Last Supper not to let things trouble their hearts because his Father's house with many rooms has a place that Jesus was preparing for them, and that he would come back to take them there so that they could be where he is.*Jn 14:1-3* Jesus also said that the disciples knew the way to that place where Jesus was going and that he is the way, truth, and life.*Jn 14:4-6* Jesus said that he leaves peace with us and gives his peace to us, not as the world gives, and so not to let trouble disturb our hearts or to be afraid.*Jn 14:27* Jesus said that God blesses those who weep now, for later they will laugh.*Lk 6:21* God comforts us in all our troubles, so that we can comfort those in any trouble with the comfort we ourselves receive from God.*2Co 1:4* Just as we share abundantly in the sufferings of Christ, so also our comfort abounds through Christ.*2Co 1:5* Suffer distress for the comfort and salvation of one another, so that comfort in distress produces patient endurance of suffering.*2Co 1:6* Hope firmly for one another, knowing that just as you share in one another's suffering, you also share in comfort.*2Co 1:7* Jesus taught that God blesses the mourner, whom God comforts.*Matt 5:4*

Christ. No one and nothing separates us from the love of Christ, even though we face death all day long.*Ro 8:35-36* In everything we are more than conquerors through him who loved us.*Ro 8:37* Neither death nor life, angels nor demons, present nor future, nor any powers, neither height nor depth, nor anything else in all creation, can separate us from God's love in Christ Jesus our Lord.*Ro 8:38-39* Our suffering does not compare with the glory that God will reveal in us.*Ro 8:18* Don't treat your fiery ordeals as something strange, but instead rejoice for suffering with Christ.*1Pe 4:12* Insults because of Christ bless you, showing that God's glorious Spirit is on you.*1Pe 4:14* Don't murder, steal, or meddle, and suffer, but instead suffer gladly as a Christian, praising God that others know you follow Christ.*1Pe 4:15-16* After you suffer a little while, God who is all grace and who called you to eternal glory in Christ will restore you, making you strong and steadfast.*1Pe 5:10* Join with others in suffering for the gospel, by the power of God.*2Ti 1:8* Join with others in suffering, like a good soldier of Christ Jesus.*2Ti 2:3* Others will persecute everyone living a godly life in Christ Jesus.*2Ti 3:12* Endure everything so that the elect may also obtain salvation in Christ Jesus, with eternal glory.*2Ti 2:10* Those who endure with Christ will also reign with him.*2Ti 2:12* Jesus said at the Last Supper that his disciples were those who had stood by him in trials, for which Jesus conferred on them a kingdom just like his Father conferred a kingdom on him, so that they would eat and drink with him in his kingdom.*Lk 22:28-30*

Weakness. We have the gospel treasure in jars of clay to show that all-surpassing power is from God and not us.*2Co 4:7* Opposition presses us hard on every side without crushing us, perplexing us but not despairing us, persecuting us but not abandoning us, striking us down but not destroying us.*2Co 4:8-9* We always carry around in our body Jesus's death, so that our body may also reveal Jesus's life.*2Co 4:10* We face death for Jesus' sake, so that our mortal body may reveal his life.*2Co 4:11* Do not lose heart because, while you may waste away outwardly, inwardly God renews you daily.*2Co 4:16* Our eternal glory far outweighs the light and momentary troubles achieving that glory for us.*2Co 4:17* As God's servants, conduct yourself appropriately whether in great endurance, troubles, hardships, distresses, beatings, imprisonments, riots, hard work, sleepless nights, and hunger.*2Co 6:4-5* Some apostles will labor and toil without sleep, know hunger and thirst, often go without food, and be cold and naked.*2Co 11:27* Delight in weaknesses, insults, hardships, and difficulties for Christ's sake because when you are weak, you are strong.*2Co 12:10* Be glad whenever you are weak but strong, while praying that God fully restores you.*2Co 13:9*

Part III: Difference

Faith. Redemption. Obedience. Church. Teaching. Families.

While the New Testament tells the great story of light overcoming the continuing threat of darkness, the New Testament also gives us abundant direction for following the light. We must obey those directions, remaining unified in their active pursuit. We need one another's fellowship to do so, in which we must not show favoritism. Above all, we must love, sowing generously the good seed of Christ. We should accept sound teaching and listen to wise counsel, especially in trials to forestall doubt. We should resist judging others and pursuing elaborate schemes for worldly riches but instead encourage one another while persisting in prayer. We should give, accept and exercise our gifts, and show gratitude for all that God does and is. See what sound and life-giving direction the New Testament gives us.

Faith

The New Testament treats the topic of faith more extensively than nearly any other topic, confirming its central role in the gospel message. The New Testament defines faith, gives many faith examples, lists faith heroes, and especially addresses the faith of Moses and of Abraham, whom we know as the father of faith. Yet the New Testament also emphasizes Christ's faith on which we wholly rely. We should pursue faith in the company of fellow believers, against all opposition, but our faith is not in our strength, rather in the victory of Jesus Christ. See how richly the New Testament treats the topic of faith. Where do you stand in your faith?

Defined. Faith is to confidently hope for what you do not see, to the point of assurance.$_{Heb\ 11:1}$ Our faith explains how the observed universe came out of nothing by God's command.$_{Heb\ 11:3}$ You cannot please God without faith because you must believe that God exists and rewards those who earnestly seek him.$_{Heb\ 11:6}$ God tests our heart.$_{1Th\ 2:4}$ God is our witness.$_{1Th\ 2:5}$ God who calls you is faithful.$_{1Th\ 5:24}$ Sincere faith promotes love.$_{1Ti\ 1:5}$ Your hoped-for righteousness is from faith.$_{Gal\ 5:2-5}$ Your good deeds should prove your faith.$_{Jas\ 2:18}$ The Lord is faithful to strengthen and protect you.$_{2Th\ 3:3}$ The Lord directs our heart into God's love and Christ's perseverance.$_{2Th\ 3:5}$ Let the faith's truths nourish you.$_{1Ti\ 4:6}$ Fan into flame the gift of God, in you through the laying on of hands.$_{2Ti\ 1:6}$ We live out the gospel of righteousness by faith.$_{Ro\ 1:17}$ To hope is not to see and have but instead to wait patiently for something we don't yet have.$_{Ro\ 8:24-25}$ Draw near to God with faith's full assurance.$_{Heb\ 10:22}$ Jesus said that with faith as small as a mustard seed, nothing is impossible for you.$_{Matt\ 17:20-21}$ With faith as small as a mustard seed, you can say to a tree to uproot and plant itself in the sea.$_{Lk\ 17:5-6}$ A man who asked Jesus to cast the spirit out of a demon-possessed boy told Jesus that he believed that everything was possible with belief but asked Jesus to help him overcome his unbelief.*Mk 9:23-24* When asked what works God required, Jesus said God's work is to believe in the one whom God sent.*Jn 6:28-29* Jesus also said that whoever believes in him believes also in the one who sent him because the one who looks at him looks at the one who sent him.*Jn 12:44-45* Jesus said to believe him when he says that he is in the Father and the Father in him, or believe on the evidence of the works, because whoever believes will do even greater works.*Jn 14:11-12* Jesus said that the doubting disciple Thomas finally believed because he saw the resurrected Jesus but blessed are those who believe without seeing.*Jn 20:27-29*

Heroes. The Bible's faith heroes were still living by faith when they died without receiving the promised things that they only saw and welcomed from a distance, while they accepted that earth was foreign and strange to them.*Heb 11:13* The world has not been worthy of our faith heroes who wandered in deserts and mountains, living in caves and holes in the ground.*Heb 11:38* God commended all for their faith, yet none received what God promised, because God planned something better for us, so that only together with us would God make them perfect.*Heb 11:39-40* Faith led Abel to offer God a better sacrifice than Cain offered, so that God commended Abel as righteous, Abel's life still speaking to us even though he is dead.*Heb 11:4* Enoch's faith pleased God so much that God took him away before death.*Heb 11:5* God commended the ancients for this faith.*Heb 11:2* Noah's faith led him to build an ark to save his family when warned about the coming flood, condemning the world and inheriting the righteousness that comes from faith.*Heb 11:7* Isaac's faith led him to bless Jacob and Esau for their future.*Heb 11:20* Jacob's faith led him, when dying, to bless Joseph's sons and to worship leaning on his staff.*Heb 11:21* Joseph's faith, when he was dying, led him to foretell the Israelites' exodus from Egypt and to instruct concerning the burial of his bones.*Heb 11:22* Jericho's walls fell by faith, after the army marched around them for seven days.*Heb 11:30* The prostitute Rahab's faith led her to welcome the spies, saving her life when the Israelites killed the disobedient.*Heb 11:31* Gideon, Barak, Samson, Jephthah, David, Samuel, and the prophets were other heroes whose faith conquered kingdoms, administered justice, gained the promise, shut the lions' mouths, quenched the flames, and escaped the sword, whose weakness became strength and who became powerful in battle and routed foreign armies.*Heb 11:32-34* Adopt the faith of your leaders who spoke God's word to you.*Heb 13:7*

Abraham. Abraham's faith led him to obey the call to go to the place he would later inherit, even though he had no idea where he was going.*Heb 11:8* Abraham's faith also led him to live in the promised land like a stranger in a foreign country, in tents, as did Isaac and Jacob who inherited the same promise.*Heb 11:9* Sarah's faith in the faithful God who promised, enabled her to bear children when it was too late, so that countless descendants could come from Abraham, who was also already as good as dead.*Heb 11:11-12* Abraham's faith led him to offer his only son Isaac as a sacrifice when God tested him, even though God had said that Isaac would have the reckoned offspring.*Heb 11:17-18* Abraham had faith that God could raise the dead, as in a way God brought Isaac back from death.*Heb 11:19* God justifies us through our faith and blesses us when we rely on faith, just as God justified and blessed Abraham, the man of faith, through Abraham's faith.*Gal 3:8-9* Abraham himself, our ancestor, had nothing to boast before God from his works but instead got God's credit for righteousness, because Abraham believed God.*Ro 4:1-3* Abraham and his offspring received God's promise through righteousness from faith.*Ro 4:13* Faith invokes the promise of inheritance. *Ro 4:14-15* The promise comes by faith, so that grace guarantees inheritance to all those who have faith like Abraham, who is our father in the sight of God in whom he believed.*Ro 4:16-17* Against all hope, when he was as good as dead, Abraham never wavered but instead had stronger faith, believed God's power and promise, and so became the father of many nations, just as God said.*Ro 4:18-21*

Moses. The faith of Moses' parents led them to hide Moses for three months after his birth, because they saw he was no ordinary child, and they did not fear the king's edict.*Heb 11:23* Moses's faith, when he had grown, led him to refuse to be the son of Pharaoh's daughter and instead to be mistreated along with God's people, rather than to enjoy sin's fleeting pleasures.*Heb 11:24-25* Moses regarded disgrace for Christ's sake as more valuable than Egypt's treasures because he looked ahead to his reward.*Heb 11:26* By faith Moses left Egypt, not fearing the king's anger, because he saw the invisible God.*Heb 11:27* Moses's faith led him to keep the Passover, applying blood so that the destroyer would not touch Israel's firstborn.*Heb 11:28* The people's faith led them to pass through the Red Sea as on dry land, when the Egyptians drowned.*Heb 11:29* Moses was a faithful servant in God's house, witnessing what God would say in the future.*Heb 3:5* Jesus said that Moses, not Jesus, accused the Jewish leaders who rejected Jesus, because Moses wrote about Jesus, and yet they did not believe Moses just as they would not believe Jesus.*Jn 5:45-47*

Christ. Jesus was faithful to God who appointed him, just as Moses was faithful in God's house.*Heb 3:2* Christ is the faithful Son over God's house, where we are God's house, if we hold firmly to our confidence and the hope in which we glory.*Heb 3:6* Our common faith as a family of believers is in grace and peace from God the Father and Christ Jesus our Savior.*Tit 1:4* If we are faithless, Christ remains faithful, for he cannot disown himself.*2Ti 2:13* Faith is for his name's sake.*Ro 1:5* Christ dwells in your heart through faith.*Eph 3:16-17* Jesus Christ establishes you in the gospel.*Ro 16:25-26* Keep living in Christ Jesus after having received him.*Col 2:6* Remain rooted and built up in Christ, strengthened in faith and overflowing with thankfulness.*Col 2:7* Faith justified us, giving us peace with God through our Lord Jesus Christ.*Ro 5:2* God is faithful for having called you into fellowship with his Son, Jesus Christ our Lord.*1Co 1:9* God makes us stand firm in Christ, having anointed us.*2Co 1:21* Have one husband, Christ, and be faithful to him.*2Co 11:2* Examine and test yourself to see if you are in the faith, confirming that Christ Jesus is in you unless you fail the test.*2Co 13:5* Don't fail the test.*2Co 13:6* Hold firmly to the faith that we have in Jesus, Son of God and great high priest who has ascended into heaven.*Heb 4:14* Our hope anchors our soul, firm and secure in the inner sanctuary behind the curtain our forerunner Jesus opened for us.*Heb 6:19-20*

Demonstrations. Jesus said do not believe him unless he does the work of the Father, but if he does the Father's work, then believe the works even though you do not believe him, that you may know that the Father is in him and he in the Father.*Jn 10:37-38* Jesus healed a paralyzed man whom four men had let down in front of him through a hole that the men dug in the roof, because of the faith that the men had exhibited in Jesus.*Mk 2:3-12, Lk 5:17-25* A centurion's faith that Jesus could instantly heal the centurion's servant from a distance amazed Jesus, who promptly healed the servant as the centurion asked.*Matt 8:5-13, Lk 7:1-10* Jesus had not found anyone in Israel with such great faith.*Matt 8:10, Lk 7:9* When Jesus saw the faith of some men who brought a paralyzed man on a mat to Jesus for healing, Jesus forgave and healed the man, telling him to pick up his mat and go home.*Matt 9:1-8* When Jesus healed a woman who said to herself that a touch to Jesus's cloak would heal her, he told her that her faith had healed her.*Matt 9:20-22, Mk 5:25-34* When Jesus restored sight to two blind men after they confirmed that they believed that he could do so, he said that their healing was according to their faith.~Matt 9:27-31~ When a sinful woman wet Jesus's feet with her tears, wiped them with her hair, and anointed them with expensive perfume, Jesus forgave her sins and said that her faith had saved her.~Lk 7:36-50~ After his hometown rejected him, Jesus did no miracles there because they lacked faith.~Matt 13:57-58~ Jesus invited Peter to step out of the boat to walk on water to Jesus, which Peter did until the wind made him afraid and he began to sink.~Matt 14:28-30~ Jesus took Peter's hand to catch him up, saying that Peter had little faith, and asking Peter why he had doubted.~Matt 14:31~ When a Canaanite woman asked Jesus to heal her demon-possessed daughter, and Jesus asked her why children's bread should go to dogs, and she said that even dogs eat crumbs from the table, Jesus said she had great faith and so instantly healed her daughter.~Matt 15:21-28, Mk 7:24-30~ A blind man shouting for Jesus, Son of David, to restore his sight, ran to Jesus, who told him that his faith had restored his sight, and he indeed could then see.~Mk 10:46-52~ Jesus cursed a fruitless fig tree, which immediately withered, and when the disciples questioned it, he explained that if they also had faith and did not doubt, that they could not only wither the fig tree but have a mountain thrown into the sea.~Matt 21:20-21, Mk 11:12-14, 20-23~ Martha told Jesus that her brother Lazarus would have lived if Jesus had been there when Lazarus was dying but that Jesus, the Messiah and Son of God, could even then raise Lazarus from the dead.~Jn 11:21-27~ Mary also told Jesus that her brother Lazarus would have lived if Jesus had been there when Lazarus was dying.~Jn 11:32~ When Jesus raised Lazarus from the dead, many Jews who were there believed in Jesus.~Jn 11:45~ When Jesus told the doubting disciple Thomas to put his fingers in Jesus's hands and Thomas's hand into Jesus's side, Thomas cried out "my Lord and my God," to which Jesus replied that Thomas had believed because he saw but blessed are those who believe without seeing.~Jn 20:27-29~

Pursuit. The disciples asked Jesus to increase their faith.~Lk 17:5~ Look for a country of your own, like these faith heroes who instead of thinking of what they were leaving, longed for a better heavenly country.~Heb 11:14-16~ Faith gave women back their dead, raised to life again.~Heb 11:35~ Faith enabled others to endure torture, face jeers and flogging, and suffer chains and imprisonment, refusing release to gain an even better resurrection.~Heb 11:35-36~ Faith enabled others to face death by sword, stoning, or sawing in two, and others to go about in sheepskins and goatskins, destitute, persecuted, and mistreated.~Heb 11:37~ Look to Jesus, who pioneered and perfected our faith.~Heb 12:2~ God's righteous live by faith.*Heb 10:38* We live by faith, not by sight.*2Co 5:7* Those with faith obey the good news proclaimed to us, while those who do not share the faith do not obey.*Heb 4:2* Faith comes from hearing the message through the word about Christ.*Ro 10:17* Hold unswervingly to the hope you profess, for God is faithful.*Heb 10:23* While we share salvation, we must still contend for the faith that God once for all entrusted to his holy people.*Jude 3* Continue in your faith, established and firm in the hope that the gospel holds out.*Col 1:23* Wear faith as a breastplate.*1Th 3:8* Persevere in faith through persecutions and trials.*2Th 1:4* Rest your faith not on human wisdom but on God's power.*1Co 2:5* Those given a trust must prove faithful.*1Co 4:2* In faith's same spirit, we believe and so speak.*2Co 4:13*

Opposition. Jesus said at the Last Supper that Satan had asked to sift the disciples as wheat but that Jesus had prayed that Peter's faith would not fail and that he would instead turn back to strengthen his brothers.*Lk 22:31-32* The tempter tempts you to destroy your faith.*1Th 3:5* Do not let loving money tempt you to wander from the faith.*1Ti 6:10* Wicked and evil people have no faith.*2Th 3:2* Faith's righteousness rejects the law's constant calculation of who gets to heaven or goes to hell, which attempts to take Christ's place.*Ro 10:6-7* Faith's righteousness instead says that the necessary word you need about faith is right in your mouth and heart.*Ro 10:8* Faith justifies a person apart from works of the law.*Ro 2:28* Faith does not nullify the law but instead upholds it.*Ro 2:31* Jesus said that one need not have been born into traditions to enter and enjoy God's kingdom, while being born into traditions while remaining outside Christ's church is not enough to enjoy the kingdom.*Matt 8:11-12* Hold on to faith and a good conscience, which some reject and so suffer shipwreck with regard to the faith.*1Ti 1:19* The Spirit warns against abandoning the faith.*1Ti 4:1* The unfaithfulness of some does not nullify God's faithfulness because God remains true when every person is a liar.*Ro 2:3-4*

Others. Supply what is lacking in others' faith.*1Th 3:10* Strive together as one for gospel faith.*Php 1:27* Let co-workers in God's service encourage you in your faith.*1Th 3:2* Love one another in the faith.*Tit 3:15* Take joy in others' faith.*1Th 3:9* Pray that you may supply what others lack in faith.*1Th 3:10* Always thank God for brothers and sisters whose faith grows more and more.*2Th 1:3* We are a family in the faith.*1Ti 1:2* God saves women who continue in faith, love, and holiness with propriety.*1Ti 2:15* Be an example in faith for believers.*1Ti 4:11* To not provide for one's own household is to deny the faith.*1Ti 5:8* Believers in God should pursue faith.*1Ti 6:11* Fight faith's good fight.*1Ti 6:12* Recall the sincere faith of others.*2Ti 1:5* Pursue faith with those who call on the Lord out of a pure heart.₂Ti 2:22 The faith of some, others will report all over the world.Ro 1:8 God justifies all through the same faith.Ro 2:29-30 Accept the one with weak faith, without quarreling over disputable matters.Ro 14:1 Just because your faith is strong, don't treat with contempt the one who has weak faith, indeed don't judge them at all, because God accepts them.Ro 14:2-3 You are no one to judge another's servant, when each servant depends on their own master's judgment, and the Lord will help the one of weak faith stand.Ro 14:4 Don't lord it over another's faith, but work with others for their joy, because by faith you stand firm.2Co 1:24 Imitate those who through faith and patience inherit the promised reward.Heb 6:12

Absence. Wicked and evil people have no faith.2Th 3:2 The disciples feared drowning in a furious storm, when in a boat with Jesus, who with a rebuke completely calmed the threatening wind and waves, and then asked why the disciples had so little faith.Matt 8:23-27, Mk 4:35-40, Lk 8:22-25 Your heavenly Father clothes the field's flowers in finest splendor, even though the flowers do not labor to make clothing, and they're gone in a day, so God will much more clothe you, even when you have little faith.Matt 6:28-30 The lack of faith that his hometown showed in him amazed Jesus, who said that a prophet has no honor in his hometown and could do no miracles there for their lack of faith, other than to heal a few sick people.Mk 6:4-6 Jesus said that a prophet has no honor in his own country.Jn 4:44 Jesus said that the disciples were of little faith and had no understanding when they misconstrued his warning to be on guard against the religious leaders' yeast, referring to false teaching, but they thought that he meant bread.Matt 16:5-12, Mk 7:14-16 Jesus reminded the disciples that he had fed five-thousand men and later four-thousand men with but a few loaves of bread, with basketfuls left over.Mk 7:17-21 The disciples were unable to heal a demon-possessed boy whom Jesus healed, saying that the disciples were unable because they had so little faith.Matt 17:14-20, Mk 17-27 Jesus said that many will turn away from the faith, betraying and hating one another, even though God will save you if you stand firm to the end.Matt 24:9-13 Whoever has receives more, while whoever does not have loses the little they had.Matt 25:29 Jesus asked if, when the Son of Man comes, he would find faith on the earth.Lk 18:8 When Jesus wept at Lazarus's tomb just before bringing Lazarus back to life, some Jews wondered why the one who opened blind eyes could not bring the dead back to life.Jn 11:35-37 When Jesus said to take the stone away from Lazarus's tomb, Martha objected that doing so would spread a bad odor from Lazarus having been dead four days, to which Jesus replied that those who believed would see God's glory.*Jn 11:38-40* Even after Jesus performed so many signs in their presence, many Jews still did not believe, fulfilling Isaiah's prophecies that they would have blind eyes and hard hearts.*Jn 12:37-40* The disciple Thomas, who was not with the other disciples when Jesus first appeared after his resurrection, did not believe the others when they told him that they had seen the Lord, adding that he would not believe unless he put his fingers where the nails were and his hands in Jesus's pierced side.*Jn 20:24-25*

Conversions. Many people saw the signs Jesus performed and believed accordingly.*Jn 2:23-25* Because of the Samaritan woman's testimony about how Jesus had told her everything about herself at the well, many people from her town believed, and when they convinced Jesus to stay with them, his words convinced many others to believe that Jesus was the world's Savior.*Jn 4:39-42* Many believed in Jesus because the Messiah would not perform more signs than Jesus had.*Jn 7:31-44* When approaching the Passover, the Jews asked Jesus who he was, and he replied that he was the Son of Man whom they would lift up, that he spoke as the Father taught him, and that the Father who sent him was with him, after which many believed.*Jn 8:25-30* When Jesus healed a blind man, the man told Jesus that he believed that Jesus was the Son of Man.*Jn 9:35-39* When late in his ministry, Jesus returned to where John had baptized, many people came to him saying that although John had never performed a sign, everything that John said about Jesus was true, and many believed.*Jn 10:40-42* When Jesus raised Lazarus from the dead, many Jews who were there believed in him.*Jn 11:46-53* When Jesus told Thomas to put his fingers in Jesus's hands and Thomas's hand into Jesus's side, Thomas cried out "my Lord and my God," to which Jesus replied that Thomas had believed because he saw but blessed are those who believe without seeing.*Jn 20:27-29* When Cyprus's proconsul saw Saul curse, as the devil's child, a sorcerer who opposed their word, and immediately blind him for a time, the proconsul believed, amazed at the teaching about the Lord.*Acts 13:6-12* Paul and Barnabas made all the believers along their way to Jerusalem glad with their news of how their message had converted the Gentiles.*Acts 15:3* The Lord opened the cloth-seller Lydia's heart to respond to Paul's message, after which they baptized her and the members of her household.*Acts 16:13-15* A jailer and his household believed in God and accepted baptism after the imprisoned Paul and Silas prayed and sang, the earth shook, the prison doors flew open, and their chains fell off.*Acts 16:25-34* The Berean Jews received Paul's message with great eagerness, examining the scriptures to see if it was true, and many of them believed, as did a number of Greek men and women.*Acts 17:10-12* When in a meeting of the Areopagus, Paul pointed to an inscription to an unknown God, to explain that God had made the nations to seek him as his offspring, giving proof that he will judge the world with justice by raising Jesus from the dead, some became followers and believed.*Acts 17:22-31* The Jews in Corinth opposed Paul's message that Jesus was the Messiah and became abusive, causing Paul to go next door to preach to others who heard, believed, and were baptized.*Acts 18:5-8* When a man with an evil spirit severely beat seven sons of a Jewish priest who had tried to cast out the spirit, after the spirit said it knew Jesus and knew about Paul but didn't know them, fear seized all the Jews and Greeks living in Ephesus, who then held Jesus's name in high honor, and many believed and confessed, while burning their valuable sorcery scrolls.*Acts 19:13-18*

Saul. As Saul neared Damascus with the high priest's letters to the synagogues to help him take prisoner believers in the Way, a light from heaven flashed, he fell, and Jesus's voice asked why Saul persecuted him.*Acts 9:1-5* Jesus sent Saul into Damascus, led by the speechless men who accompanied Saul, because for three days Saul could not see.*Acts 9:6-9* In Damascus, the Lord in a vision called a disciple Ananias to visit Saul who was praying, to restore Saul's sight, even though Saul had the chief priests' authority to arrest all who called on Jesus's name.*Acts 9:10-14* The Lord said that Saul was his chosen instrument to proclaim his name to the Gentiles, their kings, and Israel, suffering much in the Lord's name.*Acts 9:15-16* Ananias went to Saul, placed his hands on him, and told him that the Lord Jesus who had appeared to Saul had sent Ananias so that Saul could see again and receive the Holy Spirit.*Acts 9:17* Something like scales immediately fell from Saul's eyes, he could see again, and he got up and was baptized.*Acts 9:18-19* After spending several days with the disciples, Saul began preaching in the synagogues that Jesus is God's Son, astonishing all while growing more and more powerful.*Acts 9:20-22* Saul preached fearlessly in Jesus's name, speaking boldly in the Lord's name.*Acts 9:27-28* Some believers whom persecution had scattered began to speak to Greeks about the good news of the Lord Jesus, and because the Lord's hand was with them, a great number turned to the Lord to believe.*Acts 11:19-21* Saul and a good man Barnabas, full of the Holy Spirit and faith, went and stayed with the church there, teaching great numbers of people who came to the Lord.*Acts 11:22-26* In Pisidian Antioch, Saul, then also called Paul, turned to the Gentiles after the Jews rejected and contradicted him, as scriptures foretold, and all Gentiles whom God appointed for eternal life believed.*Acts 13:46-48* Paul and Barnabas then went on to Iconium to preach in the synagogue, where a great number believed.*Acts 14:1* Paul repeated to the crowd the story of his conversion when arrested in Jerusalem, saying that he had persecuted followers of the Way to their death, including the martyr Stephen, but that Jesus had appeared to him and converted him on the road to Damascus, to send him as an apostle to the Gentiles.*Acts 22:1-21* At his trial before the governor Felix, Paul testified that he worships his ancestors' God as a follower of the Way, according to the law and prophets, in expectation of the resurrection.*Acts 24:14-15* Paul spoke again before the governor Felix and his wife about faith in Jesus and righteousness, self-control, and the coming judgment.*Acts 24:24-25* Paul also stood trial before Felix's successor Festus and King Agrippa, when Paul admitted again that he had persecuted the Lord's people including casting his vote against them when the Jews put them to death.*Acts 26:2-11* Paul repeated his story again of his conversion on the road to Damascus.*Acts 26:12-27*

Confessions. At Pentecost, Peter warned the crowd with many other words, the apostles baptized those who accepted his words, and about three thousand became believers, with the Lord adding to their numbers daily those whom he saved.*Acts 2:39-41, 47* Peter, John, and the other apostles proclaimed in Jesus the resurrection of the dead, greatly disturbing the religious leaders but causing many to believe, so that their numbers grew to about five thousand.*Acts 4:1-2* When seized and jailed for questioning, Peter proclaimed to the religious leaders that they had crucified Jesus Christ whom God then raised from the dead as humankind's only salvation.*Acts 4:8-12* Peter told them that they could not help speaking about what they had seen and heard.*Acts 4:20* After the religious leaders jailed and released Peter and John, Peter and John went back to the believers to pray that the Lord enable his servants to speak with great boldness, after which the place shook, the Holy Spirit filled them, and they spoke God's word boldly.*Acts 4:22-31* The apostles continued testifying with great power to the Lord's resurrection.*Acts 4:33* When the high priest and his associates jailed the apostles again, an angel of the Lord opened the jail doors, letting them out while telling them to stand in the temple courts telling the people about the new life, which the apostles did.*Acts 5:17-21,25* The high priest brought the apostles in again, admonishing them not to teach in Jesus's name, but the apostles refused and instead repeated that God raised Jesus from the dead and exalted Jesus to his right hand as Israel's Prince and Savior for forgiveness of sins.*Acts 5:25-31* Philip proclaimed to Samaria the Messiah, God's kingdom, and Jesus Christ's name, so that many believed and were baptized, including a sorcerer Simon whom Philip's signs and miracles astonished.*Acts 8:5-13* An angel of the Lord directed Philip south, where the Spirit showed Philip an Ethiopian eunuch reading the prophet Isaiah.*Acts 8:26-33* Philip told him Jesus's good news beginning with that very passage of Isaiah, and Philip baptized the eunuch before the Spirit carried Philip away to preach in other towns.*Acts 8:34-40* When Peter healed a paralyzed and bedridden man Aeneas, all those who saw the healing turned to the Lord.*Acts 9:32-35* Many people believed when Peter raised the dead believer Tabitha, also known as Dorcas.*Acts 9:42* Peter said that God commanded the apostles to preach and testify that Jesus is the one whom God appointed to judge the living and dead.*Acts 10:42-43* Barnabas, Saul, and John proclaimed God's word in the Jewish synagogues of Cyprus.*Acts 13:2-5* In Corinth, Paul stayed and worked with fellow tentmakers Aquila and Priscilla, while reasoning in the synagogue, trying to persuade Jews and Greeks.*Acts 18:1-4* Paul repeated to the governor Festus and the Jew King Agrippa Paul's story of his conversion on the road to Damascus, ending by asking King Agrippa if he, too, believed the prophets about the suffering and resurrected Messiah who would bring light's message to both Jews and Gentiles, but the king said that Paul would not persuade him in such a short time.*Acts 26:12-27* When large numbers of Rome's Jews came to hear Paul, Paul witnessed to them from morning until evening, explaining about God's kingdom, and trying from the law and prophets to persuade them about Jesus, causing some to believe but not others.*Acts 28:22-24* Paul spent two years in Rome proclaiming God's kingdom and teaching about the Lord Jesus Christ with all boldness and no hindrance.*Acts 28:30-31*

Professions. The Samaritan woman at the well went back to town to tell the people to come see the man who told her everything that she did and who could be the Messiah.*Jn 4:28-30* Because of her testimony, many believed, and when they convinced Jesus to stay with them, his words convinced many others to believe that Jesus was the world's Savior.*Jn 4:39-42* Jesus told the violent, demon-possessed man out of whom he cast legions of demons to return home and tell how much God had done for him.*Lk 8:38-39* While many Jews even among the leaders believed in Jesus, they would not profess their faith because they feared being put out of the synagogue where they would lose human praise for God's praise.*Jn*

12:39-43 Christ Jesus while testifying before Pontius Pilate made the good confession.*1Ti 6:13* God called you to eternal life when you confessed before many witnesses.*1Ti 6:12* Do not be ashamed of the testimony about our Lord or of fellow believers.*2Ti 1:8* The gifts by which you prove yourself lead others to praise God for your obedience in confessing Christ's gospel and generosity in sharing with them and everyone else.*2Co 9:13* Your believing heart justifies you, while your professing mouth saves you, just as Scripture says.*Ro 10:10-11* Through Jesus, continually offer God a sacrifice of praise, openly professing his name.*Heb 13:15* Hold unswervingly to the hope you profess, for God is faithful.*Heb 10:23* God has given us his Spirit, through whom we see and testify that the Father sent his Son as the world's Savior.*1Jn 4:13-14* Celebrate when followers testify about one another's faithfulness to the truth.*3Jn 3-4* Proclaim God's testimony not with eloquence or human wisdom but instead knowing only Jesus Christ crucified, and that in weakness with great fear and trembling.*1Co 2:1-3* Be bold for having hope.*2Co 3:12* We believe and so speak.*2Co 4:13* God prepares a city for those in whom he has no shame when others call him their God.*Heb 11:16* We don't want non-believers to shame us but instead to have enough courage to always exalt Christ whether in living or dying.*Php 1:20*

Disciples. When John the Baptist saw Jesus pass by, the day after Jesus's baptism, and John said to look at God's Lamb, two of John's disciples (one of them Andrew) heard John and followed Jesus.*Jn 1:35-37* Jesus asked them what they wanted, and when they asked Jesus where he was staying, Jesus said to come with him.*Jn 1:38-39* Andrew went and found his brother Simon, telling him that they had found the Messiah and bringing him to Jesus, who said that he would call Simon *Cephas*, which translated is Peter.*Jn 1:40-42* Jesus saw the fishermen Simon Peter and his brother Andrew casting a net into the Sea of Galilee, telling them to follow Jesus to fish for people instead.*Matt 4:18-19, Mk 1:16-18* They immediately left their nets to follow Jesus.*Matt 4:20, Mk 1:16-18* Jesus had sent them out again into the deep to fish after they hadn't caught anything all night, and they caught so many fish that Peter was astonished and wanted Jesus to leave, but Jesus called him to fish for people.*Lk 5:4-11* Going a little farther, Jesus next promptly called James and John, who were in a boat with their father and hired men, preparing fishing nets, and they also immediately left to follow Jesus.*Matt 4:21-22, Mk 1:19-20* Jesus also called Philip, who brought his brother Nathanael to Jesus, whom Nathanael called the Son of God and king of Israel after Jesus had said that he saw

Nathanael under a fig tree with no deceit in him._{Jn 1:43-49} Walking along, Jesus called Levi, also known as Matthew, out of a tax collector's booth, saying to follow him, and Matthew got up and did, after which Jesus had dinner at Matthew's house._{Matt 9:9, Mk 2:14-15, Lk 5:27-32} Jesus went up a mountainside to call to him those whom he wanted as disciples, appointing twelve to be with him and for him to send out to preach._{Mk 3:13-14} Jesus told his disciples that the harvest is plentiful but workers few and so to ask the harvest's Lord to send workers into his harvest field._{Matt 9:37-38, Lk 10:2} When Jesus called his twelve disciples, first Simon Peter and his brother Andrew, then James son of Zebedee and his brother John, Philip, Bartholomew, Thomas, Matthew the tax collector, James son of Alphaeus, Thaddaeus, Simon the Zealot, and the betrayer Judas Iscariot, Jesus gave them authority to drive out impure spirits and heal every disease and sickness._{Matt 10:1-2, Mk 3:16-19, Mk 6:7, Lk 6:12-16, 9:1} When many other disciples left Jesus, Jesus asked the twelve if they wanted to leave, too, but Peter answered that they had no one to whom to go, because Jesus, the Son of God, had eternal life's words._{Jn 6:67-69} The disciple Thomas said that the disciples should return with Jesus to Judea, where they had tried to stone Jesus, so that the disciples could die with Jesus._{Jn 11:15-16} The disciples went out preaching that people should repent, while they drove out demons and healed many sick people, anointing them with oil._{Mk 6:7-13} Jesus told his disciples to heal the sick and cleanse those with leprosy._{Matt 10:8} Jesus sent the disciples out to proclaim God's kingdom and heal the sick._{Lk 9:2} The disciples went from village to village, proclaiming the good news and healing people everywhere._{Lk 9:6} Jesus sent out seventy two to go out two by two to every town and place to which he was on his way._{Lk 10:1} Jesus told his disciples to raise the dead._{Matt 10:8} Jesus said to the disciples that they did not choose him but he chose them and appointed them to go bear fruit that will last, so that whatever they ask in his name the Father will give them._{Jn 15:16} Jesus said to the disciples that they must testify about Jesus because they had been with him from the beginning._{Jn 15:27} Jesus gave instructions to the disciples through the Holy Spirit._{Acts 1:2}

People. Jesus said that whoever accepts anyone he sends accepts him, and whoever accepts him accepts the one who sent him._{Jn 13:20} Jesus said that all those whom the Father gives to him, come to him, and that whoever comes to him he does not drive away._{Jn 6:37} When some Greeks who accompanied those who went up to worship at the Passover festival asked to see Jesus, Jesus said that his hour had come._{Jn 12:20-22} God chooses those whom he loves.*1Th 1:4* God foreknew his chosen people and, despite an appeal to reject them, preserved a remnant who had remained faithful to him.*Ro 11:1-3* Only the elect among God's chosen people obtained what they all so earnestly sought, because God hardened the others.*Ro 11:7* Likewise, God today chooses a remnant by grace.*Ro 11:5* God's chosen people did not stumble beyond recovery but just enough to open rich salvation to all.*Ro 11:11* God's holy chosen people made the believing remnant holy, which made later believers holy.*Ro 11:16* Believers should not consider themselves superior to God's chosen people, who were the supporting holy root for the believers' own salvation.*Ro 11:18* God will take in again his chosen people if they believe, because, unlike you, they were his holy root, the original tree.*Ro 11:23-24* God hardened his chosen people in part until all others who would be saved were saved, after which God will save his chosen people.*Ro 11:25-26* God's chosen people are enemies of the gospel for your sake but are still God's elect, loved on the patriarchs' account.*Ro 11:28* God brought reconciliation to the world when he rejected his chosen people, whose acceptance now means life from the dead.*Ro 11:15* God's full inclusion of his chosen people will bring much greater riches.*Ro 11:12*

You. Jesus said if you hold to his teaching, then you really are his disciple.*Jn 8:31* God called you into fellowship with his Son, Jesus Christ our Lord.*1Co 1:9* God chose the world's foolish things.*1Co 1:27* God chose the world's lowly things, despised things, and even things that are not.*1Co 1:28-29* You were once disobedient to God but received his mercy because of the disobedience of his chosen people.*Ro 11:30* God's chosen people are now disobedient so that they too may now receive God's mercy out of God's mercy to you.*Ro 11:31* God calls for his own purpose those who love him, for whom he now works in all things for their good.*Ro 8:28* God elects us before we do anything good or bad, and not by right but by grace, to show that his call, not our works, makes the difference.*Ro 9:10-12* God is still just, favoring those whom he favors.*Ro 9:14-15* God calls both insiders and outsiders, choosing and loving those whom one would not expect and calling them his children.*Ro 9:24-26* Many descend from the chosen, but few receive salvation.*Ro 9:27* Before he created the world, God chose us in him to be holy and blameless in his sight.*Eph 1:4* When God calls, we must not consult others about whether to follow his call.*Gal 1:16* God chose believers as first fruits.*2Th 2:13* You are God's chosen people, holy and dearly loved.*Col 3:12* God called you to eternal life when you confessed before many witnesses.*1Ti 6:12*

Christ. God calls persons to belong to Jesus Christ._{Ro 1:6} Those whom God knew in advance he also predestined to conform to his Son's image so that the Son would be the firstborn among many brothers and sisters._{Ro 8:29} Those whom God predestined he also called, and those he called he also justified, while those he justified he also glorified._{Ro 8:30} In Christ God chose us, predestined as he planned, God working out everything to conform to his will._{Eph 1:11-12} God sets us apart from our mother's womb, calling us by his grace, pleased to reveal his Son in us so that we might share him among those who don't know him._{Gal 1:15-16} God the Father chose his elect with foreknowledge, to obey Jesus Christ through the Spirit's sanctifying work and under his sprinkled blood._{1Pe 1:2} Do you best to confirm your calling and election so that you never stumble and instead receive a rich welcome into our Lord and Savior Jesus Christ's eternal kingdom._{2Pe 1:10-11} As the Lord's prisoners, we urge one another to live worthy of the calling we have received._{Eph 4:1} God appointed us not to suffer wrath but to receive salvation through our Lord Jesus Christ._{1Th 3:9}

Calling. God called us to holy life._{1Th 4:7} God's gifts and call are irrevocable._{Ro 11:29} God makes us worthy of his calling, by his power granting our every desire for goodness and every deed prompted by faith._{2Th 1:11} God called us through the gospel to share in our Lord Jesus Christ's glory._{2Th 2:14} God our Savior and Christ Jesus choose leaders in the faith._{1Ti 1:1} Christ Jesus our Lord appoints teachers to his service._{1Ti 1:12} God appoints some as heralds and apostles, as true and faithful teachers._{1Ti 2:7} God called us to a holy life out of his own purpose and grace._{2Ti 1:9} Endure everything so that the elect may also obtain salvation in Christ Jesus._{2Ti 2:10} God's solid foundation stands firm because the Lord knows who are his._{2Ti 2:19} God calls apostles from among Christ Jesus's servants._{Ro 1:1} Christ appointed apostles to call non-believers._{Ro 1:5} God calls his holy people._{Ro 1:7} God's will calls apostles of Christ Jesus._{1Co 1:1} Remember what you were like when God first called you, neither wise nor influential, and not many of noble birth._{1Co 1:26} Remain in the situation you were in when God called you._{1Co 7:20} Remain in the same situation you were in when God called you, as responsible to God._{1Co 7:24} Live as the Lord assigns and God calls you, as a rule in all the churches._{1Co 7:17}

Impartiality. God does not show favoritism._{Ro 2:11} God shows no favoritism when paying back for wrongs._{Col 3:25} God treats each alike because all are under sin's power._{Ro 2:8-11} God has no insiders and outsiders because the same Lord is Lord of all, saving and richly blessing all who call on his name.*Ro 10:12-13* Followers of our glorious Lord Jesus Christ must not show favoritism.*Jas 2:1* Give the poor person just as good a seat and just as much attention in meetings as the rich person, or you will have let evil judge among you.*Jas 2:2-4* God chose the world's poor to be rich in faith, loving him, and to inherit his promised kingdom.*Jas 2:5* Why should you dishonor the poor when the rich are the ones exploiting you, dragging you into court while blaspheming God?*Jas 2:6-7* You do right by keeping God's royal law to love your neighbor as yourself rather than by showing favoritism, which convicts you as a lawbreaker.*Jas 2:8-9* Remember that if you break one law you break them all.*Jas 2:10-11* We must not seek approval of others but of God because people pleasers do not serve Christ.*Gal 1:10* That some gain high esteem without encouraging you in carrying the gospel message should make no difference to you because God does not show favoritism.*Gal 2:6* Instruct without partiality or favoritism, as in the sight of God and Christ Jesus, and the elect angels.*1Ti 5:21*

Nations. A devout centurion Cornelius had a vision from an angel of God who told him to send for the apostle Peter, which he did.*Acts 10:1-8* The next day, Peter, while praying, fell into a trance, during which the Lord told him that he could kill and eat things that Peter previously thought unclean.*Acts 10:9-16* When Cornelius's men arrived, the Spirit told Peter to go with them, which he did, Cornelius falling to his knees in reverence when Peter arrived.*Acts 10:19-25* After telling Cornelius to get up because Peter was only a man, Peter explained that God had shown Peter that although Jews do not visit Gentiles, Peter should no longer call anyone unclean.*Acts 10:26-28* Peter continued that God shows no favoritism but accepts every nation who fears him and does right.*Acts 10:34-35* Peter proclaimed the good news of peace through Jesus Christ, Lord of all, killed by the Jews, but raised from the dead.*Acts 10:36-43* The Holy Spirit came on all who heard Peter's message, including the Gentiles, astonishing the circumcised believers, and so they baptized them in Jesus Christ's name.*Acts 10:44-48* When the apostles and other believers throughout Judea heard that the Gentiles had received God's word, the circumcised believers at first criticized Peter but, after he explained what had happened, relented and even praised God for granting Gentiles repentance that leads to life.*Acts 11:1-18* Some believers whom persecution had scattered began to speak to Greeks about the good news of the Lord Jesus, and because the Lord's hand was with them, a great number turned to the Lord to believe.*Acts 11:19-21* Saul and a good man Barnabas, full of the Holy Spirit and faith, went and stayed with the church there, teaching great numbers of people who came to the Lord.*Acts 11:22-26*

Children. To all who received Christ, believing in his name, Christ gave the right to become God's children, not born naturally, by human decision or husband's will, but born of God.*Jn 1:12-13* Those whom the Spirit of God leads are the children of God.*Ro 8:14* The Spirit does not make you fearful slaves but makes you a child of God who can cry to your Father.*Ro 8:15* Creation groans as in childbirth just as we who have the Spirit's first fruits groan as we wait eagerly for God to adopt us as his children.*Ro 8:22-23* That the Father calls us his children shows his lavish love for us.*1Jn 3:1-2* God chooses and loves those whom one would not expect, calling them his children.*Ro 9:24-26* The children of God's promise, not the children of physical descent, receive the promised benefit.*Ro 9:7-9* Our inheritance is as free children of God rather than slave children who do not inherit.*Gal 4:30-31* Because you are God's child rather than his slave any longer, God makes you an heir to his promise.*Gal 4:7* Once we were his children, God could then send the Spirit of his Son into our hearts, the Spirit who calls God Father.*Gal 4:6* We know that we are children of God.*1Jn 5:19* We appeal for those who join us as children in the family of faith, who were formerly useless to us but have become useful to all.*Phm 9-11* The one on the throne told the apostle John that the one on the throne is the Alpha and Omega, Beginning and End, giving water to the thirsty from the spring of life and everything to the victorious who are his children.*Rev 21:6-7*

Christ. Jesus said that a slave to sin has no permanent place in the family but that a son belongs to the family forever.*Jn 8:34-35* Jesus said not to despise a little child because their heavenly angels always see his Father's face in heaven.*Matt 18:10* Jesus also said that his heavenly Father is not willing that any of his little children would perish.*Matt 18:14* Those whom God knew in advance he also predestined to conform to his Son's image so that the Son would be the firstborn among many brothers and sisters.*Ro 8:29* Jesus presents himself to God with the children God gave him.*Heb 2:13* When people told Jesus that his mother and brothers were waiting outside for him, Jesus replied that his disciples were his mother and brothers because whoever does his heavenly Father's will is Jesus's brother, sister, and mother.*Matt 12:46-50, Mk 3:31-35, Lk 8:19-21* Jesus bears no shame calling us brothers and sisters because the one making holy and ones made holy are the same family.*Heb 2:12* Jesus declares your name to his brothers and sisters, singing your praises in the assembly.$_{Heb\ 2:12}$ The Spirit testifies with our spirit that we are God's children who, if we suffer with Christ, inherit Christ's glory with him.$_{Ro\ 8:16-17}$ Through our faith in Christ Jesus we are all children of God.$_{Gal\ 3:26}$ Belonging to Christ makes us Abraham's seed and heirs to God's promise.$_{Gal\ 3:29}$ Before Christ came, we were underage heirs, awaiting the promise's fulfillment while still subject to the world's elemental spiritual forces.$_{Gal\ 4:1-3}$ But the time God set finally came for a woman to bear his Son under the law, to redeem us from under the law, so that God could adopt us as children.$_{Gal\ 4:4-5}$ Jesus taught that God blesses peacemakers, whom God calls his children.$_{Matt\ 5:9}$ Jesus said that he would not leave us as orphans but would come to us.$_{Jn\ 14:18}$

Distinction. The difference between God's children and children of the devil is easy: God's children love one another and stop sinning, while the devil's children do not.$_{1Jn\ 3:9}$ Just because your ancestors were holy doesn't make you holy.$_{Ro\ 9:6}$ Be blameless and pure children of God without fault in this warped and crooked generation.$_{Php\ 2:15}$ Follow God's example as dearly loved children by walking in love's way, like Christ loved and gave himself up for us as a fragrant offering and sacrifice to God.$_{Eph\ 5:1}$ We are all children of the light and children of the day, not belonging to the night or darkness.$_{1Th\ 5:5}$ As obedient children of God, reject the evil desires you had when you didn't know God, and instead be holy in all you do, like God is holy.$_{1Pe\ 1:14-16}$ Be people who live by the Spirit rather than who are still worldly—mere infants in Christ.$_{1Co\ 3:1}$ When Christ returns, dear children of God, we do not yet know what we will be, but we know we will be like him, seeing him as he is.$_{1Jn\ 3:2}$

Discipline. The Lord disciplines those whom he loves and chastens those whom he accepts as his child.$_{Heb\ 12:6}$ Endure hardship as discipline because God is treating you as his child, as any good father disciplines a child.$_{Heb\ 12:7}$ If God did not discipline you, as he does every believer, then you would be illegitimate rather than a true son or daughter.$_{Heb\ 12:8}$ Because we respect our human father for disciplining us, we should submit all the more to the Father of spirits, to truly live.$_{Heb\ 12:9}$ Our human fathers disciplined us briefly as they thought best, but God disciplines us for our good so that we share in his holiness.$_{Heb\ 12:10}$ Discipline is not pleasant but painful when it happens yet later produces a harvest of righteousness and peace for those who accept it.$_{Heb\ 12:11}$ So strengthen your weak arms and knees.$_{Heb\ 12:12}$ Walk level paths so that the paths do not disable you but rather heal you.$_{Heb\ 12:13}$ God's Spirit gives us self-discipline.₂ₜᵢ ₁:₇ Avoid arrogance, or the teacher will bring a rod of discipline rather than love and a gentle spirit.₁Cₒ ₄:₂₁ Delight at how disciplined are your fellow believers.Cₒₗ ₂:₅ An elder must be self-disciplined.ₜᵢₜ ₁:₈ If you lack discernment, then the Lord will judge and discipline you so that God will not finally condemn you with the world.₁Cₒ ₁₁:₃₂ Listen to this encouragement like a child listening to its father, not to make light of the Lord's discipline and not to lose heart when he rebukes you.Hₑᵦ ₁₂:₅ Jesus said that those whom he loves, he rebukes and disciplines.Rₑᵥ ₃:₁₉

Inheritance. God has a glorious inheritance in his holy people.Eₚₕ ₁:₁₈₋₁₉ God keeps in heaven for us an inheritance that can never perish, spoil or fade.₁Pₑ ₁:₄ Abraham and his offspring received God's promise that they would inherit the world through righteousness from faith.Rₒ ₄:₁₃ Faith invokes the promise of inheritance. Rₒ ₄:₁₄₋₁₅ The poor who are rich in faith and love God inherit his promised kingdom.Jₐₛ ₂:₅ Our inheritance is as free children of God rather than slave children who do not inherit.Gₐₗ ₄:₃₀₋₃₁ Only free children, not slave children, share our inheritance from God.Gₐₗ ₄:₃₀₋₃₁ Sin keeps one from inheriting God's kingdom.Gₐₗ ₅:₁₉₋₂₁ Wrongdoers, the sexually immoral, idolaters, adulterers, men who have sex with men, thieves, the greedy, drunkards, slanderers, and swindlers do not inherit God's kingdom.₁Cₒ ₆:₉₋₁₀ Inherit blessing by repaying evil with good.₁Pₑ ₃:₉ Imitate those who through faith and patience inherit the promised reward.Hₑᵦ ₆:₁₂ Do not relinquish your inheritance like the godless Esau who for a single meal sold his right to a blessing, wanted it back, but despite tears could not change what he had done.Hₑᵦ ₁₂:₁₇ Thank the Father, who has qualified you to share in the inheritance of his holy people.Cₒₗ ₁:₁₂ Jesus said that anyone who gives a cup of water to a believer because they belong to the Messiah will certainly receive a reward.Mₖ ₉:₄₁ Paul said that the word of God's grace can build you up for an inheritance among all the sanctified.Aₖₜₛ ₂₀:₃₂ A beneficiary must prove the death of the one who makes a will because a will takes effect only when the testator dies, not while the testator still lives.Hₑᵦ ₉:₁₆₋₁₇ Even the first covenant required animal blood for the covenant that God commanded them to keep.Hₑᵦ ₉:₁₈₋₂₁ The law required that nearly everything be cleansed with blood, without which God would not forgive.Hₑᵦ ₉:₂₂ If the copies of the heavenly things required animal blood, then the heavenly things would require better sacrifices.Hₑᵦ ₉:₂₃ The Spirit testifies with our spirit that we are God's children who, if we suffer with Christ, inherit Christ's glory with him.Rₒ ₈:₁₆₋₁₇ Christ mediates a new covenant, that those whom God calls may receive the promised eternal inheritance, now that Christ has died as a ransom to set us free from the sins committed under the first covenant.*Heb 9:15* Angels are ministering spirits sent to serve those who inherit salvation.*Heb 1:14* The pure inherit the kingdom of Christ and God.*Eph 5:5* Idolaters do not inherit the kingdom of Christ and God.*Eph 5:5* As a hardworking farmer, expect to be first to receive a share of the crops.*2Ti 2:6* You receive an inheritance from the Lord to reward you for sound earthly work, as working for the Lord Christ.*Col 3:24* When Jesus returns on his throne and separates the sheep from the goats, the King will say to the sheep that his Father has blessed them to take their inheritance prepared for them since creation.*Matt 25:34*

Redemption

The New Testament makes clear the extraordinary result of our accepting God's loving sacrifice of his own Son, which is our redemption from all that corrupts and burdens us. Astonishingly, God restores us to his presence and favor. The New Testament confirms that no less than Jesus's blood, his frightening yet ultimately loving sacrifice, suffices to reconcile and redeem, so great was the extent of our appalling wickedness. The New Testament also reminds us of the fabulous result of our redemption, that we are Christ's own brothers and sisters in his glory. See how the New Testament describes God redeeming us out of our sinful nature and sin-filled world. Do you know the power of your redemption?

Justification. God justifies, and no one else.$_{Ro\ 8:33}$ God justifies all freely through the redemption that came by Christ Jesus.$_{Ro\ 2:24}$ God presented Christ as a sacrifice of atonement, for us to receive by faith in Jesus, God justifying us.$_{Ro\ 2:25-26}$ God delivered Jesus over to death for our sins and raised him to life for our justification.$_{Ro\ 4:25}$ Creation groans as in childbirth just as we who have the Spirit's first fruits groan, as we wait eagerly for God to adopt us as his children and redeem our bodies.$_{Ro\ 8:22-23}$ God reconciles us by Christ's physical body through death to present you holy, without blemish, and free from accusation, in his sight.$_{Col\ 1:22}$ Jesus Christ our Lord keeps us from stumbling, to present us before his glorious presence without fault.$_{Jude\ 24-25}$ God will redeem those whom he possesses, marked and guaranteed by his Holy Spirit.$_{Eph\ 1:13-14}$ Christ redeemed us to bless those of us who through faith receive the promise of the Spirit.$_{Gal\ 3:14}$ God sealed you with the Holy Spirit for the day of redemption.$_{Eph\ 4:30}$

Blood. Christ redeems us through his blood, the forgiveness of sins, as God lavished his grace's riches on us.$_{Eph\ 1:7-8}$ The perfect lamb Christ's precious blood, not perishable things like precious metals, redeemed you from the empty life your family handed down to you.*1Pe 1:18-19* Christ entered the Most Holy Place not by animal blood but once for all by his own blood, for eternal redemption.*Heb 9:12* The high priest carried animal blood into the Most Holy Place as a sin offering but burned the bodies outside the camp.*Heb 13:11* And so Jesus also suffered outside the city gate to make the people holy through his own blood.*Heb 13:12* Go to Jesus outside the camp, bearing the disgrace he bore, because we have no enduring city here and instead look for the city to come.*Heb 13:14* Christ's one sacrifice made perfect forever those whom God is making holy.*Heb 10:14* Be confident entering the Most Holy Place by Jesus's blood, the new and living way he opened for us through the curtain, that is, his body.*Heb 10:19-20* Christ Jesus is our redemption.*1Co 1:30*

Evil. Some of you were wrongdoers, sexually immoral, idolaters, adulterers, thieves, greedy, drunkards, slanderers, and swindlers, but the name of the Lord Jesus Christ and Spirit of our God washed and justified you.*1Co 6:9-11* We wait for our blessed hope, which is that we would see our great God and Savior Jesus Christ, who gave himself to redeem us from all wickedness and purify for himself a people that are his own, eager to do good.*Tit 2:13-14* Our redemption and forgiveness of sins is in Jesus Christ.*Col 1:14* Jesus shared in our humanity because we are human, so that by his death he would break the devil's power of death.*Heb 2:14* Jesus frees those held in slavery by their fear of death.*Heb 2:15* Jesus doesn't help angels but us, Abraham's descendants.*Heb 2:16* Jesus had to become like us, fully human in every way, to become a merciful and faithful high priest in service to God, atoning for our sins.*Heb 2:17* Jesus suffered when tempted, making him able to help us when facing temptation.*Heb 2:18*

Result. God enriches us in him in every way including all kinds of speech and with all knowledge, confirming testimony about Christ in us.*1Co 1:5-6* Draw near to God with sincere heart, faith's full assurance, hearts sprinkled to cleanse our guilty conscience, and our bodies washed with pure water.*Heb 10:22* To bring many sons and daughters to glory through salvation, God, for and through whom everything exists, fittingly made salvation's pioneer Jesus Christ perfect through his suffering.*Heb 2:10* Jesus declares your name to his brothers and sisters, singing your praises in the assembly.*Heb 2:12* Jesus presents himself to God with the children God gave him.*Heb 2:13* Better things having to do with salvation convince us.*Heb 6:9* Jesus bears no shame calling us brothers and sisters because the one making holy and ones made holy are the same family.*Heb 2:12* God is just, remembering your work and the love you show him as you help his people.*Heb 6:10* Show the same diligence to the very end, so that you realize that for which you hope.*Heb 6:11* Do not be lazy, but instead imitate those who through faith and patience inherit the promised reward.*Heb 6:12* Jesus said that people will see the Son of Man coming in a cloud with power and great glory, when you should stand and lift up your head toward your nearing redemption.*Lk 21:27*

Sanctification. God's will is that he sanctify you.*1Th 4:3* The law and prophets testify to God's righteousness.*Ro 2:21* God called us to holy life.*1Th 4:7* May the God of peace sanctify you through and through.*1Th 5:23* God is faithful and will sanctify you.*1Th 5:24* The Spirit's sanctifying work saved believing brothers and sisters.*2Th 2:13* True godliness springs from the great mystery that Christ appeared in the flesh, received the Spirit's vindication, had angels see him, had persons preach him among the nations, had people believe in him, and ascended in glory.*1Ti 3:16* Godliness with contentment in food and clothing is great gain because we brought nothing into the world and take nothing out of it.*1Ti 6:6-8* Believers in God should pursue righteousness and godliness.*1Ti 6:11* God called us to a holy life out of his own purpose and grace.*2Ti 1:9* Jesus taught that God blesses the pure in heart, who will see God.*Matt 5:8* Jesus taught that God blesses those whom others persecute because of righteousness but who receive the kingdom of heaven.*Matt 5:10* Jesus prayed that the Father sanctify the disciples by the Father's word, which is truth.*Jn 17:17* Paul said that the word of God's grace can build you up for an inheritance among all the sanctified.*Acts 20:32*

Faith. Abraham, our ancestor, got God's credit for righteousness because Abraham believed God.*Ro 4:1-3* Abraham and his offspring received God's promise through righteousness from faith.*Ro 4:13* Because of what Abraham did, God credited Abraham with righteousness and called him his friend, proving that righteousness comes from faith and action together.*Jas 2:23-24* God even treated the prostitute Rahab as righteous for hiding and saving the Israelite spies.*Jas 2:25* God credits our faith as righteousness when we, the ungodly, trust him.*Ro 4:4-5* God credits to us as righteouness our belief that he raised Jesus from the dead.*Ro 4:22-24* God forgives our sins and blesses us with righteousness apart from our works.*Ro 4:6-7* When we believe God, he credits our belief to us as righteousness.*Gal 3:6* Eagerly await your hoped-for righteousness from faith.*Gal 5:2-5* Jesus said to enter through the narrow gate because wide is the gate and broad the road leading to destruction of many, but small the gate and narrow the road leading to life for few.*Matt 7:13-14* When someone asked Jesus if God would save only a few, Jesus repeated to enter through the narrow door because many will try to enter, but the house's owner will close the door, leaving many knocking and pleading outside, to whom the owner will say that he doesn't know those evildoers.*Lk 13:22-27* Those who did not pursue righteousness by law obtained it by faith, while those who pursued righteousness by law did not obtain it because they pursued it by works.*Ro 9:30-32* For God to judge us righteous, we must live by faith rather than under law, which justifies no one.*Gal 3:11* Our righteousness is not our own from the law but comes from God based on faith in Christ.*Php 3:9* Zealousness for God is not enough when one pursues one's own righteousness rather than submitting to God's righteousness.*Ro 10:2-3* Animal blood and ashes on the ceremonially unclean sanctify only outwardly.*Heb 9:13*

Christ. Jesus prayed that he sanctifies himself so that the disciples, too, may be truly sanctified.*Jn 17:19* Jesus said to be perfect, as your heavenly Father is perfect.*Matt 5:48* Jesus taught that God blesses those who hunger and thirst for righteousness, whom God fills.*Matt 5:6, Lk 6:21* God gives righteousness to all who believe through faith in Jesus Christ.*Ro 2:22* God sanctifies those who call on the Lord Jesus Christ as his holy people in Christ Jesus.*1Co 1:2* Christ Jesus is our righteousness.*1Co 1:30* By sacrificing Christ, God demonstrated his righteousness after having left unpunished prior sins.*Ro 2:25-26* The blood of Christ, who through the eternal Spirit offered himself unblemished to God, cleanses inwardly, clearing our consciences from acts leading to death, so that we serve the living God.*Heb 9:14* The covenant's blood sanctified us.*Heb 10:29* God's righteousness reigns in life through one man Jesus Christ, whose one righteous act resulted in justification and life for all.*Ro 5:17-18* One man's obedience made many righteous.*Ro 5:19* Grace reigns through righteousness, bringing eternal life through Jesus Christ our Lord.*Ro 5:21* We received so precious of a faith through our God and Savior Jesus Christ's righteousness.*2Pe 1:1-2* May God fill you with righteousness's fruit that comes through Jesus Christ, to God's glory and praise.*Php 1:11* May your whole spirit, soul, and body be blameless at our Lord Jesus Christ's return.*1Th 5:23*

Pursuit. Pursue righteousness with those who call on the Lord out of a pure heart.*2Ti 2:22* Be an example in purity for believers.*1Ti 4:11* Offer yourselves to God as those whom he brought from death to life, making every part of yourself an instrument of righteousness.*Ro 6:13* You are slaves of the one you obey, if to obedience, then leading to righteousness.*Ro 6:16* God made you a slave of righteousness.*Ro 6:18* Because we know his glory and goodness, God by his great and precious promises and power gives us everything for a godly life, to participate in his divine nature and escape the world's corruption that evil desires cause.*2Pe 1:3-4* Because God so favors us, we should be good, knowledgeable, self-controlled, persevering, godly, affectionate, and loving, one after another.*2Pe 1:5-7* Have in store for you the crown of righteousness, which the Lord will on that day award to all who have longed for his appearing.*2Ti 4:8* My believing brothers and sisters are full of goodness.*Ro 15:14* Jesus says to be the salt of the earth, rather than lose your saltiness and be good for nothing other than to be walked over or thrown on the manure pile.*Matt 5:13, Lk 14:34-35*

Sin. Rid yourself of all moral filth and the prevalent evil, instead humbly accepting the word that God planted in you that saves you.*Jas 1:21* Have nothing to do with people who love themselves, money, and pleasure rather than God, and are boastful, proud, abusive, disobedient to parents, ungrateful, unholy, without love, unforgiving, slanderous, without self-control, brutal, not lovers of the good but instead treacherous, rash, and conceited, and while having a form of godliness yet denying its power.*2Ti 3:2-5* Some of you were sexually immoral, idolaters, adulterers, thieves, greedy, drunkards, slanderers, and swindlers, but the name of the Lord Jesus Christ and Spirit of our God sanctified you.*1Co 6:9-11* Our unrighteousness brings out God's righteousness more clearly.*Ro 2:5* To be righteous is to do the right things that Christ does, while to be sinful is to do the opposite as the devil does, that which Christ came to destroy.*1Jn 3:7-8* Imitate only what is good, not what is evil, because those who do good are from God, while those who do evil have not seen God.*3Jn 11* Be ready to suffer bodily as Christ suffered, because you do not pursue evil desires in sin when suffering, but instead seek God's will.*1Pe 4:1-2* Offer yourself as a slave to righteousness leading to holiness, as you once offered yourself to wickedness.*Ro 6:19*

Conduct. Jesus said not to practice your righteousness in front of others to be seen by them because then you would have no reward from your Father in heaven.*Matt 6:1* Conduct yourselves appropriately in purity, understanding, patience, and kindness, in the Holy Spirit and sincere love, in truthful speech and God's power, and with weapons of righteousness in both hands.*2Co 6:6-7* Conduct yourselves appropriately through glory and dishonor, bad and good report, while genuine but regarded as impostors, known but regarded as unknown, dying and yet living on, beaten but not killed, sorrowful yet always rejoicing, poor yet making many rich, and having nothing and yet possessing everything.$_{2Co\ 6:8\text{-}10}$ Keep yourself from anything contaminating body or spirit, perfecting holiness.$_{2Co\ 7:1}$ Scripture teaches, rebukes, corrects, and trains in righteousness.$_{2Ti\ 3:16\text{-}17}$ The Holy Spirit sanctifies hearers of the proclaimed gospel.$_{Ro\ 15:16}$ Pray to God not to do anything wrong, not so people see your faith but so you do right even though others believe you failed.$_{2Co\ 13:7}$ Make every effort to be holy because without holiness no one will see the Lord.$_{Heb\ 12:14}$

Freedom. Jesus said that if you hold to his teaching, then you really are his disciple, you will know the truth, and the truth will set you free.$_{Jn\ 8:31\text{-}32}$ Jesus added that if the Son sets you free, then you will be free indeed.$_{Jn\ 8:36}$ God called us to freedom, not to indulge ourselves but instead to serve one another humbly in love.$_{Gal\ 5:13}$ For we fulfill the entire law by loving our neighbor as we love ourselves.$_{Gal\ 5:14}$ Live as God's slaves, which is to live free of evil.$_{1Pe\ 2:16}$ No one condemns because Christ Jesus, who died and God raised to life, is at God's right hand interceding for us.$_{Ro\ 8:34}$ Be anxious about nothing.$_{Php\ 4:6}$ Have no needs, but instead learn contentment whatever your circumstances.$_{Php\ 4:11}$ While you have known both need and plenty, learn contentment's secret for every situation, whether you are fed or hungry, or living in plenty or in want.$_{Php\ 4:12}$ You can do all things through Christ who strengthens you.$_{Php\ 4:13}$ God meets all your needs with the riches of his glory in Christ Jesus.$_{Php\ 4:19}$ If you were bound when God called, then don't let it trouble you, although gain your freedom if you can.$_{1Co\ 7:21}$ The slave called to faith in the Lord is free in the Lord, while the person free when called is Christ's slave.$_{1Co\ 7:22}$ Do not make yourself a slave to another person, recognizing instead that God bought you at a price.$_{1Co\ 7:23}$ King Herod arrested Peter and put him in prison, but with the church earnestly praying to God for Peter, an angel of the Lord rescued him from his chains, led him out of the prison, and then disappeared, leaving Peter to go to the house where believers prayed for him.$_{Acts\ 12:3\text{-}17}$

Grace. Grace to you from God our Father.$_{Col\ 1:2}$ Grace to those in God the Father and the Lord Jesus Christ.$_{1Th\ 1:1}$ Grace to you from God our Father and the Lord Jesus Christ.$_{Php\ 1:2}$ Grace from God the Father and the Lord Jesus Christ.$_{2Th\ 1:1\text{-}2}$ Grace to you from God our Father and the Lord Jesus Christ.$_{1Co\ 1:3}$ Grace to you from God our Father and the

Lord Jesus Christ.*Ro 1:7* Grace to each of you from God our Father and the Lord Jesus Christ.*Gal 1:3* God the Father and Christ Jesus our Lord bring grace and mercy.*1Ti 1:2* The grace of the Lord Jesus be with you.*1Co 16:23* The grace of our Lord Jesus be with you.*Ro 16:20* May the grace of the Lord Jesus Christ be with you.*2Co 13:14* Grace to you from God our Father and the Lord Jesus Christ.*2Co 1:2* The grace of our Lord Jesus Christ be with you.*1Th 5:28* The grace of our Lord Jesus Christ be with you all.*2Th 3:18* The grace of the Lord Jesus be with God's people.*Rev 22:21* Grace be with you.*Col 4:18* Grace be with you.*Heb 13:25* Grace be with you all.*1Ti 6:21* The Spirit is a Spirit of grace.*Heb 10:29* God saved us out of his grace, not because of anything we have done.*2Ti 1:9* God cannot base his grace on your works, or it would no longer be grace.*Ro 11:6* Grace be with you all.*2Ti 4:22* God justifies all freely by his grace.*Ro 2:24* God gives grace to the churches.*2Co 8:1* Sin is not your master because you are under grace, not law.*Ro 6:14* Do not sin, because you are under grace rather than law.*Ro 6:15* God gave the law to increase sin so that grace would increase even more.*Ro 5:20* Jesus is different from Adam in that many died from Adam's sin while many live from the gift of God's grace in Jesus Christ.*Ro 5:15* The penalty of Adam's sin differs from God's gift of grace in that judgment's condemnation followed sin, but grace's justification followed many sins.*Ro 5:16* Grace reigns through righteousness.*Ro 5:21* Stand steady in God's true grace.*1Pe 5:12* God's grace teaches us to reject ungodliness and worldly passions, while living self-controlled, upright, and godly lives.*Tit 2:12* God gives everyone to disobedience so that he can show them all mercy.*Ro 11:32* Plead for relief from the Lord, but the Lord may answer that his grace is sufficient for you, his power made perfect in your weakness.*2Co 12:8* Let no one fall short of God's grace.*Heb 12:15* Let grace strengthen your heart.*Heb 13:9*

Source. The one and only Son from the Father is full of grace and truth.*Jn 1:14* We all receive grace out of the Son's fullness, in place of grace already given, law having come through Moses but grace and truth through Jesus Christ.*Jn 1:16-17* Jesus ate with tax collectors and sinners at Matthew's house, saying to law teachers who objected that the sick, not the healthy, need a doctor and that he had come to call sinners, not the righteous.*Matt 9:11-13, Mk 2:15-17, Lk 5:29-32* God's grace offers salvation to all.*Tit 2:11* We understand the gospel to be God's grace.*Col 1:6* God gave us grace in Christ Jesus before the beginning of time.*2Ti 1:9* Through our Lord Jesus Christ we gained access to the grace in which we now stand.*Ro 5:2* God's abundant grace reigns in life through Jesus Christ's gift.*Ro 5:17*

Because of his great love for us, our merciful God brought us alive with Christ, grace saving us when we were still dead in transgressions.*Eph 2:4-5* God raised us up with Christ and seated us with him in the heavenly realms so that he might soon show us the incomparable riches of his grace, expressed in his kindness to us in Christ Jesus.*Eph 2:6-7* Through Christ we received grace.*Ro 1:5* For grace saved us, through faith, not from ourselves, and not by our works so that we can boast, but by God's gift.*Eph 2:8-9* Do not set aside God's grace because if righteousness came through law, then Christ would have died for nothing.*Gal 2:21* God has given each one of us grace just as Christ apportioned it.*Eph 4:7* Grace to all who have undying love for our Lord Jesus Christ.*Eph 6:24* Let the Lord Jesus Christ's grace be with your spirit.*Php 4:23* Our Lord Jesus Christ and God our Father by his grace gave us good hope of eternity.*2Th 2:16-17* Our Lord pours out his grace abundantly, along with the faith and love that are in Christ Jesus.*1Ti 1:14* Be strong in the grace that is in Christ Jesus.*2Ti 2:1* Grace to you from him who is, was, and is to come, and from Jesus Christ, the faithful witness, firstborn from the dead, and ruler of earth's kings.*Rev 1:4-5*

Mercy. Jesus said to be merciful because your Father is merciful.*Lk 6:36* Jesus said to learn what God meant by saying that he desires mercy rather than sacrifice.*Matt 9:13* Jesus told the demon-possessed man out of whom he had cast a legion of demons to go tell his own people how the Lord had mercy on him.*Mk 5:18-20* Jesus said that if the Pharisees had known what God's words meant, that God desired mercy, not sacrifice, then the Pharisees would not have condemned the innocent.*Matt 12:7* Christ became a servant of the Jews on behalf of God's truth, so that the Gentiles could glorify God for his mercy.*Ro 15:8-11* God has mercy on whom he has mercy, and compassion for whom he has compassion.*Ro 9:14-15* Salvation depends on God's mercy, not human desire or effort.*Ro 9:16* God has mercy on whom he wants to have mercy.*Ro 9:18* Be merciful, as the law that gives freedom and has mercy triumph over judgment requires, because God will judge without mercy those who are unmerciful.*Jas 2:12-13* God has mercy on the believing ill and their believing family and friends, saving the ill from death to spare sorrow upon sorrow.*Php 2:27* God will show mercy to a blasphemer, persecutor, and violent person who acts in ignorance and unbelief.*1Ti 1:13* God has shown mercy to the worst of sinners so that Christ Jesus might display his immense patience, as an example for those who would believe in him and receive eternal life.*1Ti 1:16* Grace and mercy are from God the Father and Christ Jesus our Lord.*2Ti 1:2* The Lord shows mercy to households that seek and refresh, rather than turn away from, suffering believers.*2Ti 1:16-18* Because God is merciful, offer your body as a living sacrifice, holy and pleasing to God, as your true and proper worship.*Ro 12:1* God's mercy grants us a teaching ministry.*2Co 4:1* Approach God's throne with confidence for mercy and grace when in need.*Heb 4:16* Jesus taught that God blesses the merciful, whom God shows mercy.*Matt 5:7* Jesus restored the sight of two blind men sitting by the Jericho roadside, calling to the Lord, Son of David, to have mercy on them.*Matt 20:29-34*

Peace. Jesus said that he leaves peace with us and gives his peace to us, not as the world gives, and so not letting trouble disturb our hearts or letting us be afraid.*Jn 14:27* Jesus told his disciples that he had told them what would happen so that in him they may have peace.*Jn 16:33* God the Father blesses us with abundant peace.*Jude 1-2* God the Father chose his elect to receive peace in abundance.*1Pe 1:2* Peace to you from God our Father.*Col 1:2* The God of peace sanctifies.*1Th 5:23* We receive peace from God the Father and from Jesus Christ.*2Jn 3* Peace to each of you from God our Father and the Lord Jesus Christ.*Gal 1:3* Peace to you from God our Father and the Lord Jesus Christ.*Php 1:2* Peace to you from God our Father and the Lord Jesus Christ.*1Co 1:3* Peace to you from God our Father and the Lord Jesus Christ.*2Co 1:2* Peace to you from God our Father and the Lord Jesus Christ.*Ro 1:7* Peace to those in God the Father and the Lord Jesus Christ.*1Th 1:1* Peace from God the Father and the Lord Jesus Christ.*2Th 1:1-2* Peace is from God the Father and Christ Jesus our Lord.*2Ti 1:2* God the Father and Christ Jesus our Lord bring peace.*1Ti 1:2* Peace is the Spirit's fruit.*Gal 5:22-23* The Lord of peace may give you peace at all times and in every way when with you.*2Th 3:16* May the God of hope fill you with all peace as you trust in him.*Ro 15:13* The God of peace be with you.*Ro 15:33* Jesus taught that God blesses peacemakers, whom God calls his children.*Matt 5:9* The growing church experienced a time of peace and strengthening, living in the Lord's fear and with the Holy Spirit's encouragement.*Acts 9:31* When so many people crowded around Jesus and the disciples that they did not even have a chance to eat, he told them to come away with him to a quiet place to get some rest, and so they sought a solitary place.*Mk 6:30-32* Jesus said that when the disciples visited a house that they should say peace to the house and remain, eating and drinking whatever given, if anyone who promotes peace, on whom their own peace rests, is there.*Lk 10:5-6* When Jesus first appeared to the eleven disciples after his resurrection, Jesus stood among them, saying peace to them.*Lk 24:36, Jn 20:19* Jesus repeated that peace be with them.*Jn 20:21* The God who raised Jesus from the dead is the God of peace.*Heb 13:20* God makes peace through the Son's blood.*Col 1:20* Christ's purpose on the cross was to reconcile in him one new peaceful humanity out of the divided two sides, putting to death their hostility.*Eph 2:15-16* Our common faith as a family of believers is in peace from God the Father and Christ Jesus our Savior.*Tit 1:4* Our peace is Christ, who has destroyed the barrier, the dividing wall of hostility.*Eph 2:14-15* Christ came preaching peace.*Eph 2:17* Peace to all of you who are in Christ.*1Pe 5:14* Peace with faith from God the Father and the Lord Jesus Christ, to the brothers and sisters.*Eph 6:23* Apostles of Christ Jesus bring a message of peace from God our Father and the Lord Jesus Christ.*Eph 1:1-2* Faith's justification gave us peace with God through our Lord Jesus Christ.*Ro 5:2* With prayer, God's peace, transcending all understanding, will guard your heart and mind in Christ Jesus.*Php 4:7* We will receive peace in abundance knowing God, our Lord Jesus.*2Pe 1:1-2* Jesus says that his peace will not be an outward but an inward peace, and his peace will thus look initially more like a sword turning family members against one another when they do not all believe, because one must love Jesus more than one's closest family member.*Matt 10:34-37, Lk 12:51-53, Lk 14:25-26* Peace to you from him who is, was, and is to come, and from Jesus Christ, the faithful witness, firstborn from the dead, and ruler of earth's kings.*Rev 1:4-5*

Rest. God rested from all his works on the seventh day of creation.*Heb 4:4* God has a Sabbath rest for his people.*Heb 4:9* Be careful not to fall short of God's standing promise of entering his rest.*Heb 4:1* We enter God's rest by believing.*Heb 4:3* Anyone entering God's rest also rests from their work, just as God did from his.*Heb 4:10* Make every effort to enter God's rest, so that no one will perish in disobedience.*Heb 4:11* Jesus said to come to him when weary and burdened so that he can give you rest.*Matt 11:28* Jesus said to submit to him and learn from him because he is gentle and humble, and he will give your soul rest.*Matt 11:29* Jesus added that his yoke is easy and his burden light.*Matt 11:30* Those who disobey in unbelief will never enter God's rest.*Heb 3:17-19* Some are yet to enter God's rest, while others who heard the good news rejected God's rest out of disobedience.*Heb 4:6* We belong to the truth and set our condemning hearts at rest when we acknowledge that God is greater than our hearts and knows everything.*1Jn 3:19-20* When you visit a deserving home, let your peace rest on it, but let your peace return to you if the home is not deserving.*Matt 10:13* When a sinful woman wet Jesus's feet with her tears, wiped them with her hair, and anointed them with perfume, Jesus forgave her sins, said her faith had saved her, and told her to go in peace.*Lk 7:36-50*

Seeking. Make every effort to do what leads to peace and mutual edification.*Ro 14:19* Make every effort to be at peace with the patient God as you await the end of all things.*2Pe 3:14-16* Everyone who does good may expect peace.*Ro 2:10* Those who have no fear of God will not know peace.*Ro 2:17-18* Keep the Spirit's unity through the bond of peace.*Eph 4:3* Let the peace of Christ rule in your hearts because as members of one body God called you to peace.*Col 3:15* Make every effort to live in peace with everyone.*Heb 12:14* Live peacefully with each other.*1Th 3:13* Wish to one another peace from God our Father and the Lord Jesus Christ.*Phm 1-3* Teach the people to be peaceable.*Tit 3:1-2* If you want to enjoy life with good days, then seek peace.*1Pe 3:10-11* Practice what you learn so that the God of peace is with you.*Php 4:9* Stand firm with your feet fitted with the readiness that comes from the gospel of peace.*Eph 6:14-15* Pray for all people including those in authority that you may live peaceful lives.*1Ti 2:1-2* Live in peace, and the God of love and peace will be with you.*2Co 13:11*

Glory. The Word became flesh, dwelling among us, so that we saw the glory of the one and only Son from the Father, full of grace and truth.*Jn 1:14* God exalted Jesus over everyone for his glory as the Father.*Php 2:11* That God will redeem those of us whom he possesses is to his glory's praise.*Eph 1:13-14* Be overjoyed at seeing his glory.*1Pe 4:13* To God be the power forever.*1Pe 5:11* God chose you with the purpose that you declare his praises.*1Pe 2:9-10* We praise our Lord and Father.*Jas 3:9* God adopted us through Jesus Christ for the praise of his glorious grace.*Eph 1:5-6* Your righteousness is to God's glory and praise.*Php 1:11* To our God and Father be glory forever.*Php 4:20* Now to God, who can do immeasurably more than all we ask or imagine by his power at work within us, be glory in the church and in Christ Jesus forever.*Eph 3:20-21* The gospel concerns the blessed God's glory.*1Ti 1:11* The King eternal, immortal, invisible, the only God, has honor and glory forever.*1Ti 1:17* To the Lord be glory forever.*2Ti 4:18* Praise the Lord, everyone, with everyone extolling him.*Ro 15:11* Give God the glory forever.*Ro 11:36* Glorify God for his mercy.*Ro 15:8-9* Glory forever through Jesus Christ to the only wise God.*Ro 16:27* Glory to God forever.*Heb 13:21* Jesus said that true worshipers worship the Father in the Spirit and in truth because God is spirit and his worshipers must worship in the Spirit and in truth.*Jn 4:23-24* Jesus said that bearing much fruit, showing yourself to be his disciple, is to his Father's glory.*Jn 15:8*

Jesus. When the apostle John turned around in the Spirit toward the loud voice like a trumpet, he saw standing among seven golden lampstands someone like a son of man, dressed in a robe with a golden sash, his hair white as wool or snow, eyes blazing like fire, feet glowing like bronze in a furnace, voice sounding like rushing waters, and face shining like a brilliant sun, holding seven stars in his right hand and with a sharp doubled-edged sword coming from his mouth.*Rev 1:11-16* John fell at his feet as though dead, but putting his right hand on John, he said not to fear, that he was the First, Last, and Living One, dead but now alive forever, and holding the keys of death and Hades.*Rev 1:17-18* The prophet Isaiah saw Jesus's glory and spoke about Jesus.*Jn 12:41* Jesus said that he did not seek glory but one who is the judge seeks it.*Jn 8:50* Jesus repeated that if he glorified himself, then his glory meant nothing but that his Father glorifies him.*Jn 8:54* When Jesus said that he would not ask the Father to save him from the approaching hour of his crucifixion because he had come for that hour to glorify the Father's name, a voice from heaven replied that he had glorified it and would do so again.*Jn 12:27-29* Some in the crowd thought that an angel had spoken while others that the sky had thundered, but Jesus said that the voice was to benefit them, not him.*Jn 12:29-30* After Judas left the Last Supper to betray Jesus, Jesus told the remaining disciples that now God glorified the Son of Man in himself at once and also received glory in him.*Jn 13:31-32* At Jesus's baptism, God the Father gave Jesus glory from heaven.*2Pe 1:17* Jesus revealed his glory and caused his disciples to believe, when he gave his first sign by turning water into wine.*Jn 2:11* Jesus said that whoever does not honor the Son does not honor the Father.*Jn 5:23* When God glorified Jesus, believers received the Spirit.*Jn 7:37-39* Only after God glorified Jesus, did the disciples understand all that had happened leading up to his crucifixion.*Jn 12:16* When some Greeks who accompanied those who went up to worship at the Passover festival asked to see Jesus, Jesus said that his hour had come for God to glorify him.*Jn 12:20-22* Jesus Christ our Lord is the one before all ages to whom God gave glory, majesty, power, and authority, to present you before his glorious presence.*Jude 24-25* The prophets searched for salvation, the grace that was to come to us, to discover through Christ's Spirit when and how the Messiah would come, suffer, and receive his glory.*1Pe 1:10-11* Rulers crucified the Lord of glory.*1Co 2:8* To Jesus Christ be glory forever.*Gal 1:5* The Lord's holy people who believed in Jesus, including you, will glorify Jesus on his return.*2Th 1:10-11* We who hope in Christ as we hear the true message of gospel salvation should praise his glory.*Eph 1:11-13* Everyone should praise

God through Jesus Christ, who has glory and power forever.*1Pe 4:11* God took up Christ in glory.*1Ti 3:16* After his hometown rejected him, Jesus said that a prophet has no honor in his own town and home.*Matt 13:57-58* Jesus said that the Son of Man is going to come in his Father's glory with his angels to reward each person according to what they have done.*Matt 16:27* When the Son of Man comes in his glory, with all the angels, he will sit on his glorious throne.*Matt 25:31* The Son of Man will return in his Father's glory with the holy angels.*Mk 8:38* Jesus said that he does not accept glory from humans.*Jn 5:41* Jesus said that the Jewish leaders who rejected him accepted glory from one another without seeking God's glory.*Jn 5:44* Jesus said that a man whom he healed was born blind not because of sin but to display God's works in him.*Jn 9:2-3* When Jesus said to take the stone away from Lazarus's tomb, when he was about to bring Lazarus back to life, Jesus added that those who believed would see God's glory.*Jn 11:38-40* Jesus said that the Spirit of truth glorifies Jesus because the Spirit receives from Jesus what he reveals to you.*Jn 16:14* Jesus looked toward heaven to pray that the Father, in his hour that had come, would glorify his Son and his Son glorify him.*Jn 17:1* Jesus prayed that he had brought the Father glory on earth by finishing his assigned work and that the Father now glorify Jesus in his presence with the glory that Jesus had with the Father before the world began.*Jn 17:4-5* Jesus prayed that he had given all believers the glory that the Father gave him, that all believers may be one as the Father and Jesus are one, Jesus in believers, the Father in Jesus, for complete unity.*Jn 17:22-24* Glory forever for him who loves us, freed us from our sins by his blood, and made us a kingdom and priests to serve his God and Father.*Rev 1:5-6*

Shared. God called us to share in our Lord Jesus Christ's glory.*2Th 2:14* The Spirit testifies with our spirit that we are God's children who, if we suffer with Christ, inherit Christ's glory with him.*Ro 8:16-17* Our suffering does not compare with the glory that God will reveal in us.*Ro 8:18* Those whom God justified, he also glorified.*Ro 8:30* God showed his wrath and power to us, while patiently bearing those who rejected him to their destruction, to let those of us whom he prepared in advance for glory know the riches of his glory.*Ro 9:22-23* Praise God the Father of our Lord Jesus Christ, who brings us every spiritual blessing in Christ.*Eph 1:3* The gospel of Christ in you is the hope of glory.*Col 1:27* When Christ appears, you will appear with him in glory.*Col 3:4* God calls you into his glory.*1Th 2:12* Fellow believers are your glory when our Lord Jesus comes.*1Th 2:19-20* May we glorify the name of our Lord Jesus and receive his glory, by the grace of God and the Lord Jesus Christ.₂Th 1:12 The elect obtaining salvation in Christ Jesus receive eternal glory.₂Ti 2:10

Pursuit. God gives eternal life to those who seek glory by persistent good works.Ro 2:7 Do everything for God's glory.1Co 10:31 Everyone who does good may expect glory and honor.Ro 2:10 We boast in the hope of the glory of God even while we glory in our sufferings.Ro 5:3 Glory in Christ Jesus in your service to God.Ro 15:17 Thanksgiving overflows to God's glory, as grace reaches ever more people.2Co 4:15 Our eternal glory far outweighs our troubles that achieve that glory for us.2Co 4:17 When Jesus returns, God will shut out from the glory of the Lord's might those who do not know God.2Th 1:8-10 All sin, falling short of God's glory.Ro 2:23 The ministry that brought death, engraved in letters on tablets, came with so much glory that the Israelites could not look at Moses, transitory though it was.2Co 3:7 The Spirit's ministry bringing righteousness is even more glorious than the ministry that brought condemnation.2Co 3:8-9 What was glorious has no glory compared to the surpassing glory.2Co 3:10 If the transitory had glory, then the eternal has much greater glory.2Co 3:11 Those with dulled minds still read the old covenant with veiled faces because only in Christ does the veil fall away.2Co 3:14 A veil covers their hearts as they read Moses.2Co 3:15 You have no need to cover your face like Moses so that others cannot see the old glory pass away.2Co 3:13 Whenever anyone turns to the Lord, he takes the veil away.2Co 3:16 The Lord transforms into his image with growing glory, all who with unveiled faces contemplate the Lord's glory, which comes from the Lord who is the Spirit.2Co 3:18

Power. We see and understand God's eternal power and divine nature from what he made.Ro 1:20 God showed his wrath and power to us, to let those of us whom he prepared in advance for glory know the riches of his glory.Ro 9:22-23 By his power, God raised the Lord from the dead and will also raise us.1Co 6:14 Rest your faith not on human wisdom but on God's power.1Co 2:5 God's power shields us in our faith until the salvation comes that he will reveal in the last time.1Pe 1:5 God's power for believers is the same as the mighty strength he exerted when he raised Christ from the dead and seated him at his right hand in the heavenly realms, over all rule, authority, power, and dominion.Eph 1:19-21 Suffering is for the gospel, by the power of God.2Ti 1:8 Have no shame over the gospel because its power of God brings salvation to everyone who believes.Ro 1:16 The gospel came not simply with words but also power, the Holy Spirit, and deep conviction.1Th 1:5 We preach Christ crucified, a stumbling block to Jews and foolishness to other non-believers but God's power and wisdom to those whom God called.*1Co 1:22-24* God hardens whom he wants to harden, to display his power and see his name proclaimed in all the earth.*Ro 9:17-18* God's kingdom is not a matter of talk but of power.*1Co 4:20* Now to God, who can do immeasurably more than all we ask or imagine by his power at work within us, be glory in the church and in Christ Jesus forever.*Eph 3:20-21* To God be the power forever.*1Pe 5:11* We become the gospel's servants by the gift of God's grace given us through his power.*Eph 3:7* Pray that the Spirit may enlighten our heart that we may know God's hope, his glorious inheritance in us, and his incomparably great power for us who believe.*Eph 1:18-19* We have the gospel treasure in jars of clay to show that all-surpassing power is from God and not us.*2Co 4:7* Jesus prayed that while he left the world to come to the Father, the Father would protect the disciples who remained in the world, by the power of the Father's name, the name the Father gave Jesus.*Jn 17:11* The Lord's word spread widely and grew in power, as many Ephesians believed and confessed.*Acts 19:18-20*

Christ. John baptized with water representing repentance, but the more-powerful Jesus, whose sandals John was not worthy to carry, baptizes with the Holy Spirit and fire.*Matt 3:11, Lk 3:16* As Jesus ministered, people tried to touch Jesus for the power that was coming from him for their healing.*Lk 6:19* When a woman with bleeding touched Jesus's cloak for healing, Jesus knew that power had gone out of him.*Lk 8:43-46* After his baptism and tempting, Jesus returned to Galilee in the Spirit's power to teach in the synagogues.*Lk 4:14-15* People would try to touch Jesus for the power that was coming from him for their healing.*Lk 6:19* God gave Jesus Christ our Lord glory, majesty, power, and authority.*Jude 24-25* God will reveal the Lord Jesus from heaven in blazing fire with his powerful angels.*2Th 1:7* Christ is the head over every power and authority.*Col 2:10* Jesus Christ our Lord is the one before all ages to whom God gave glory, majesty, power, and authority.*Jude 24-25* Praise God through Jesus Christ, who has glory and power forever.*1Pe 4:11* Assemble with the Lord Jesus's power present, to hand wrongdoers among you over to Satan to destroy the flesh, so that God may save the disobedient one's spirit on the Lord's day.*1Co 5:4-5* Jesus Christ sustains all things by his powerful word.*Heb 1:3* The cross is God's power to us whom God saves.*1Co 1:18-19* Men crucified Christ in weakness, but Christ lives by God's power.*2Co 13:4* Christ triumphed over evil powers and authorities by the cross.*Col 2:15* Wise and eloquent preaching must not empty Christ's cross of its power.*1Co 1:17* Desire to know the power of Christ's resurrection and participation in his sufferings, becoming like him in his death and so attaining to resurrection from death.*Php 3:10-11* Our Savior the Lord Jesus Christ will by his complete power transform our lowly bodies to be like his glorious body.*Php 3:20-21* Christ is not weak but powerful in dealing with you.*2Co 13:1-3* Power for him who loves us, freed us from our sins by his blood, and made us a kingdom and priests to serve his God and Father.*Rev 1:5-6*

Evil. When the governor told Jesus that he had the power to crucify him, Jesus said that his only power was what came from above.*Jn 19:10-11* Lawlessness's secret power already works, even though the Lord Jesus will overthrow and destroy the lawless one.*2Th 2:7-8* All are under sin's power.*Ro 2:8-11* Jesus shared in our humanity because we are human, so that by his death he would break the devil's power of death.*Heb 2:14* The lawless one comes in the wicked way that Satan works, using all sorts of powerfully deceiving displays.*2Th 2:9* God permits those who reject the truth and instead delight in wickedness, to suffer the powerful delusion that condemns them as they believe the lie.*2Th 2:11-12* We struggle not against flesh and blood but against rulers, authorities, and powers of this dark world and spiritual forces of evil in the heavenly realms.*Eph 6:12* Death has no victory or sting, when death's sting is sin and sin's power is the law.*1Co 15:55-56* The law had no power to free us from sin, but God sent his own Son to meet the law's righteous requirement in those of us who live by the Spirit rather than the flesh.*Ro 8:3-4* Neither death nor life, angels nor demons, nor any powers, nor anything else in all creation, can separate us from God's love in Christ Jesus our Lord.*Ro 8:38-39* Christ disarmed and triumphed over evil powers and authorities, making a public spectacle of them.*Col 2:15* When a viper bit and held onto the apostle Paul's hand at a fire after their shipwreck, the islanders thought Paul would die, but after he shook the viper off into the fire and showed no ill effects, the islanders called him a god.*Acts 28:1-6*

You. After his resurrection, Jesus told the eleven disciples that he was going send them what his Father had promised and to stay in Jerusalem until power clothed them from on high.*Lk 24:49* Jesus said that the disciples would receive the Holy Spirit's power to be Jesus's witnesses to the ends of the earth.*Acts 1:8* Jesus said that he gave his disciples authority to overcome all the enemy's power.*Lk 10:19* Be strong in the Lord in his mighty power.*Eph 6:10* Although men crucified Christ, Christ lives by God's power, just as you are weak in him but live by

God's power in dealing with the sin of one another.*2Co 13:4* The Lord's grace is sufficient for you because he makes his power perfect in your weakness.*2Co 12:8* Boast all the more gladly about weaknesses, so that Christ's power rests on you.*2Co 12:9* God, though all-powerful, still leaves you to your own will.*Ro 9:19-20* Christ died for us when we were powerless sinners, demonstrating his extraordinary love for us because no one dies for sinners even if for the good.*Ro 5:6-8* The Spirit God gave you does not leave you timid but gives you power, love, and self-discipline.*2Ti 1:7* When leading others to obey God, you act through the Spirit of God's power.*Ro 15:18-19* May you overflow with hope by the Holy Spirit's power.*Ro 15:13* God makes us worthy of his calling, by his power granting our every desire for goodness and every deed prompted by faith.*2Th 1:11* Because we know his glory and goodness, God by his great and precious promises and power gives us everything for a godly life, to participate in his divine nature and escape the world's corruption that evil desires cause.*2Pe 1:3-4* Conduct yourselves appropriately in purity, understanding, patience, and kindness, in God's power and with weapons of righteousness in both hands.*2Co 6:6-7* Speak of no service other than what Christ accomplished through you, through the Spirit of God's power.*Ro 15:18-19* We proclaim Christ with all wisdom and all the energy Christ so powerfully works in us.*Col 1:28* In prayer, receive God's strength with all power according to his glorious might so that you endure with great patience.*Col 1:10-11* Constantly pray for one another that our God make us worthy of his calling and by his power grant our every desire for goodness and every deed prompted by faith.*2Th 1:11*

Others. God gives some miraculous powers.*1Co 12:8-10* God's grace and power filled Stephen, who performed great signs and wonders, and against whom opposition could not stand.*Acts 6:8-10* Saul grew more and more powerful after he believed and received the Holy Spirit.*Acts 9:17-22* After a female slave's owners had Paul and Silas severely flogged and thrown into prison for rebuking a spirit out of the slave, Paul and Silas were praying and singing hymns to God when an earthquake shook the prison, the doors flew open, and their chains fell off.*Acts 16:19-26* When the jailer told Paul that the magistrates had given Paul and Silas their release, Paul told the jailer to tell the magistrates to escort them out for beating Roman citizens without a trial.*Acts 16:35-40* God did extraordinary miracles through Paul, so that handkerchiefs and aprons that touched him cured the sick.*Acts 19:11-12* Fight with weapons not of the world but having divine power to demolish strongholds.*2Co 10:4* Angels are stronger and more powerful than the arrogant non-believers who heap abuse on them, but angels still let the Lord judge them.$_{1Pe\ 2:10-11}$ Abraham believed God's power and promise, and so became the father of many nations.$_{Ro\ 4:18-21}$ Heroes' faith conquered kingdoms, routed armies, and escaped the sword by making those heroes powerful in battle.$_{Heb\ 11:32-34}$ Jesus Christ's resurrection saves you because he is in heaven at God's right hand with angels, authorities, and powers submitting to him.$_{1Pe\ 3:21-22}$ God sows the body in dishonor but raises it in glory, sows it in weakness but raises it in power.$_{1Co\ 15:43}$ Jesus Christ is in heaven at God's right hand with angels, authorities, and powers submitting to him.$_{1Pe\ 3:21-22}$ The end will come when Christ hands God's kingdom to the Father after destroying all dominion, authority, and power.$_{1Co\ 15:24}$ The prayer of a righteous person is powerful and effective.$_{Jas\ 5:16-18}$ We pray that out of God's glorious riches he strengthens you in your inner being with power through his Spirit, so that Christ dwells in your heart through faith.$_{Eph\ 3:16-17}$

Obedience

The New Testament gives clear direction that we should obey. We should discern what God's word requires and then do as it commands, just as Christ kept his Father's word. We should do likewise in our conduct, respecting the authority of others. Our goal should be to run the race to get the prize at the end. See how the New Testament addresses obedience. Do you listen for God and read his word to obey?

Obedience. Jesus said that if you love him, then keep his commands.*Jn 14:15* Jesus added that whoever has and keeps his commands is the one who loves him.*Jn 14:21* Jesus repeated that anyone who loves him obeys his teaching, and his Father will then love them, and Jesus and his Father will make their home with them.*Jn 14:23* Anyone who does not love Jesus does not obey his teaching.*Jn 14:24* Jesus said that we are his friends if we do what he commands.*Jn 15:14* You may have the right to do anything, but not everything benefits you or is constructive.*1Co 10:23* Obeying God's word makes our love for God complete in us.*1Jn 2:5* Do not be fickle in intent or make worldly plans so that in the same breath you say both yes and no.*2Co 1:17* As God is faithful, let your message be consistent rather than contradictory.*2Co 1:18* Guard what others entrust to your care.*1Ti 6:20* Keep your head in all situations, discharging all the duties of your ministry.*2Ti 4:5* We must put to death the body's misdeeds to live, rather than live for the flesh in which case we die.*Ro 8:12-13* Do not be overcome by evil, but overcome evil with good.*Ro 12:21* You do well when you bear unjust suffering because conscious of God.*1Pe 2:19* Suffering for wrongdoing is nothing, but suffering for good commends you to God because Christ suffered for you as example.*1Pe 2:20-21* After Pentecost, God's word spread, and many priests obeyed the faith.*Acts 6:7*

God. Jesus said that we remain in his love when we keep his commands, just as he has kept his Father's commands and remains in his Father's love._{Jn 15:10} Even though Jesus was God's Son, Jesus learned obedience from what he suffered._{Heb 5:8} When the disciples told Jesus to eat something, Jesus replied that his food was to do the will of the one who sent him and to finish his work._{Jn 3:31-34} Those with faith obey the good news proclaimed to us, while those who do not share the faith do not obey._{Heb 4:2} Keeping Jesus's commands proves we know him, while failing to keep his commands proves that we don't know him and don't have the truth._{1Jn 2:3-4} As Christ's soldier, do not entangle yourself in other affairs, but instead please your commanding officer._{2Ti 2:4} When we live as Jesus lived, we know we are in him._{1Jn 2:6} We belong to the truth and set our condemning hearts at rest when we acknowledge that God is greater than our hearts and knows everything._{1Jn 3:19-20} When we keep God's commands by doing what pleases him, our hearts do not condemn us, and we receive from God anything we ask._{1Jn 3:21-22} God's command is to believe in his Son Jesus Christ and then to love one another._{1Jn 3:22} When we keep God's commands, we live in him and he in us, as the Spirit he gave us tells us._{1Jn 3:24} Obeying the law, not just hearing the law, makes one righteous in God's sight._{Ro 2:13}

Others. Be careful to do right in everyone's eyes._{Ro 12:17} Obey human authority whom God sends to punish those who do wrong and commend those who do right._{1Pe 2:13-14} Respect everyone, love the family of believers, fear God, and honor the ruler._{1Pe 2:17} Fearing God, obey your employer, not only when your employer is good and considerate but also when harsh._{1Pe 2:18} Workers should fully respect their supervisors so that no one slanders God's name and our teaching._{1Ti 6:} Those who work for believing supervisors should not show disrespect just because they are fellow believers but should instead serve them even better, as dear fellow believers devoted to the worker's welfare._{1Ti 6:2} Let your affection for one another be all the greater when you remember others' obedience._{2Co 7:15} Charity belongs to older, faithful widows, well known for good deeds like raising children, showing hospitality, and washing the feet of the Lord's people, helping those in trouble._{1Ti 5:9-10} Note and avoid anyone who does not obey instruction, that they may feel shame, while warning them rather than treating them as an enemy._{2Th 3:14-15} Christ appointed leaders to call non-believers to the obedience that comes from faith._{Ro 1:5} Be ready to punish every act of disobedience, once you complete your own obedience._{2Co 10:6}

Strive. Watch carefully that you keep your full reward and do not lose that for which you worked.₂Jn 8 Compete by the rules so that you win.₂Ti 2:5 When you feel poured out like a drink offering with the time for your departure near, be sure to have fought the good fight, finished the race, and kept the faith.₂Ti 4:6-7 Everyone who hears about your obedience rejoices because of you.Ro 16:19 Run to get the prize because all racers run the race, but only one gets the prize.1Co 9:24 Everyone in competition does strict training to get a temporary crown, but you train to get a crown that lasts forever.1Co 9:25 Don't run aimlessly like others or fight like a boxer beating the air.1Co 9:26 Instead, strike a blow to your body to make it your slave so that after you preach to others, God will not disqualify you for the prize.1Co 9:27 Stand the test, obedient in everything.2Co 2:9 Celebrate when followers testify about one another's faithfulness to the truth.3Jn 3-4 Live a life worthy of the Lord, pleasing him in every way, bearing fruit in every good work, and growing in the knowledge of God.Col 1:10-11

Authority. Jesus said that God had given him all authority in heaven and on earth.Matt 28:18-20 Jesus said that the Father had given him authority to judge because he is the Son of Man.Jn 5:27 Jesus said that the reason the Father loves him is because he laid down his life of his own accord, only to take it up again, as Jesus had authority and as his Father commanded.Jn 10:17-18 Jesus said that he did not speak on his own authority but instead the Father in him was doing his work.Jn 14:10 Jesus's teaching amazed the people because unlike the law teachers, Jesus taught with authority.Mk 1:21-22 Jesus amazed the people with his teaching and that impure spirits obeyed his authority.Mk 1:27 Jesus said that the Son of Man has authority to forgive sins on earth and then showed so by healing the paralyzed man.Mk 2:5-12, Lk 5:17-25 When Jesus turned over the money changers' tables in the temple courts, and the Jews asked his authority, Jesus replied that he would raise the temple again if they destroyed it, referring to his body, not the building.Jn 2:18-21 Jesus said that he did nothing by himself but only what he saw his Father do because the Father loves the Son and shows the Son all that the Father does.Jn 5:19-20 Jesus prayed that the Father had granted him authority over all people so that he could give eternal life to all those whom the Father had given him.Jn 17:2 God's power for believers is the same as the mighty strength he exerted when he raised Christ from the dead and seated him at his right hand in the heavenly realms, over all rule, authority, power, and dominion, and every name not only now but in the future.Eph 1:19-21 God gave Jesus Christ our

Lord glory, majesty, power, and authority.*Jude 24-25* Christ is the head over every power and authority.*Col 2:10* The law has authority over someone only as long as that person lives.*Ro 7:1* The Lord who delivers also destroys in eternal fire those who do not believe, even binding for judgment day angels who refuse his authority.*Jude 5-7* The end will come when Christ hands God's kingdom to the Father after destroying all dominion, authority, and power.*1Co 15:24* The chief priests and elders asked Jesus when he taught in the temple courts who gave him such authority.*Matt 21:23, Mk 11:27-28* Jesus replied that he would tell them only if they told him the source of John's baptism.*Matt 21:24-25, Mk 11:29-30* They refused to answer Jesus, and so Jesus refused to answer them.*Matt 21:25-27, Mk 11:31-33* Jesus said to fear the one who has authority to throw you into hell.*Lk 12:5*

Instituted. A centurion knew that Jesus could by just saying the word heal the centurion's servant from a distance because the centurion said that he himself was a man under authority with soldiers under his authority.*Lk 7:6-8* Jesus gave authority to his disciples to drive out demons.*Lk 9:1* Jesus gave his disciples authority to trample on snakes and scorpions and overcome all the enemy's power so that nothing harmed them.*Lk 10:19* Those in authority are God's servants for your good, wrath's agents to punish wrongdoers, and so if you do wrong, then you should fear the ruler's sword for good reason.*Ro 13:4* The Lord gives some authority to build you up rather than tear you down.*2Co 10:8* Anyone rebelling against the authority rebels against what God instituted, bringing judgment on themselves.*Ro 13:2* Instruct one another by the Lord Jesus's authority how to live to please God, urging one another more and more to live as you are living in the Lord Jesus.*1Th 4:1-2* Write to correct others when absent so as not, when present, to be harsh with the authority the Lord gave you for building up others, not for tearing them down.*2Co 13:10* Pay your taxes because the authorities, who are God's servants, give their time to governing.*Ro 13:6* Dreams and animal instincts lead ungodly people to reject authority, when even the archangel Michael did not dare condemn the devil's slander but said instead that the Lord would rebuke him.*Jude 8-10* Obey human authority, whom God sends to punish those who do wrong and commend those who do right.*1Pe 2:13-14*

Rulers. Submit to the authorities not just to avoid punishment but also out of conscience.*Ro 13:5* Subject yourself to governing authorities because God established them.*Ro 13:1* Anyone rebelling against authority rebels against what God instituted, bringing judgment on themselves.*Ro*

13:2 Rulers hold no terror for those who do right, only those who do wrong, and so do what is right to be free from fear and instead receive commendation.*Ro 13:3* Those in authority are God's servants for your good, wrath's agents to punish wrongdoers, and so if you do wrong, then you should fear the ruler's sword for good reason.*Ro 13:4* Pay your taxes because the authorities, who are God's servants, give their time to governing.*Ro 13:6* Jesus had Peter go to the lake, catch a fish, and take a coin from its mouth with which to pay the temple tax for both of them.*Matt 17:24-27* The Pharisees tried to trap Jesus into saying not to pay Caesar's imperial tax, but Jesus showed them Caesar's picture on the coin and said to give to Caeasar what is Caesar's and to God what is God's, amazing the Pharisees.*Matt 22:18-22, Mk 12:13-17, Lk 20:20-26* Give to everyone what you owe them, including taxes if you owe taxes, revenue if you owe revenue, respect when respect is due, and honor when honor is due.*Ro 13:7* Pay every debt, and let no debt remain outstanding except the continuing debt to love one another, out of which you fulfill the law.*Ro 13:8* Paul said that the scriptures say not to speak evil of the ruler of your people.*Acts 23:5*

Others. Pray for all people including those in authority, that you may live peaceful lives.*1Ti 2:1-2* Women should learn in submission, quietly, without assuming authority over those who teach or giving in to deception.*1Ti 2:11-13* God did not create man for woman but woman for man, so that women should, for the angels, have authority over their own head.*1Co 11:9-10* Share intimacy with your spouse, yielding to one another as the other wishes, giving your spouse authority over your own body.*1Co 7:3-4* Make petitions, prayers, and intercession for all people, including for those in authority, that you may live peaceful and quiet lives in all godliness and holiness.*1Ti 2:1-2* Encourage others with all authority.*Tit 2:15* The law teacher Gamaliel told the Sanhedrin to consider carefully before killing the apostles because if their purpose is of human origin, then it will fail, while if they are from God, then no one can stop them.*Acts 5:35-39*

Repentance. Godly sorrow brings repentance, leading to salvation without regret, while worldly sorrow brings only death.*2Co 7:10* Godly sorrow produces earnestness, eagerness to clear oneself, indignation, alarm, longing, concern, readiness to see justice done, and effort to establish innocence.*2Co 7:11* John the Baptist, who preached a baptism of repentance for forgiveness of sins, urged the crowds who came to him for baptism to produce repentance's fruit rather than rely on their heritage as Abraham's children because the ax was ready to cut down every tree that did not produce good fruit.$_{Lk\ 3:1,\ 8-9}$ Do not show contempt for the riches of God's kindness, forbearance, and patience, because he intends his kindness to lead you to repentance.$_{Ro\ 2:4}$ Those who confess the Lord's name must turn away from wickedness.$_{2Ti\ 2:19}$ Confess your sins to each other.$_{Jas\ 5:16-18}$ Stubborn and unrepentant hearts store up God's wrath for judgment day.$_{Ro\ 2:5}$ Purify the heart, stop sinning, and stop the double-mindedness, while ruing your former sin.$_{Jas\ 4:8-9}$ Repent of impurity, sexual sin, and debauchery in which others indulge.$_{2Co\ 12:21}$ As obedient children of God, reject the evil desires you had when you didn't know God, and instead be holy in all you do like God is holy.$_{1Pe\ 1:14-16}$ Regret hurting one another, but don't regret causing sorrow with the truth.$_{2Co\ 7:8}$ Be happy not for bringing sorrow to others or harming others but when that sorrow leads others to repent as God intends.$_{2Co\ 7:9}$ Gently instruct opponents in the hope that God will grant them repentance, leading them to a knowledge of the truth, and that they come to their senses.$_{2Ti\ 2:25-26}$ No one repents again whom the Holy Spirit has already enlightened and has tasted the heavenly gift, goodness of God's word, and coming age's power, but has nonetheless fallen away.$_{Heb\ 6:4-6}$ After Pentecost, Peter told the crowd to repent and turn to God, who would wipe out their sins.$_{Acts\ 3:19}$ Peter said that God raised up his servant to bless the people by turning them from their wicked ways.$_{Acts\ 3:26}$ Paul declared to both Jews and Greeks that they must turn to God in repentance with faith in our Lord Jesus.$_{Acts\ 20:21}$

Christ. After his baptism and tempting, Jesus began to preach repentance because the kingdom of heaven had come near.$_{Matt\ 4:17}$ Jesus said that if a brother or sister sins against you, then rebuke them, but if they repent, then forgive them, even if they sin and repent again seven times in a day.$_{Lk\ 17:3-4}$ Jesus pronounced woes on towns where he did most of his miracles, when they did not repent, saying that even Sodom would have it better on judgment day.$_{Matt\ 11:20-24}$ Jesus sent the twelve disciples out to preach that people should repent.$_{Mk\ 6:7-12}$ Jesus told the parable of the two sons, one who said he wouldn't do his father's work but changed his mind and did it, and the other who said he would but didn't.$_{Matt\ 21:28-30}$ Doing is what counts, Jesus added, like the prostitutes and tax collectors who repented and entered the kingdom, and not like the chief priests and elders who refused to repent.$_{Matt\ 21:31-32}$ When some told Jesus how Pilate had killed some Galileans, Jesus said that those Galileans were no worse sinners than any others, just because they had died, when all needed to repent or they, too, would perish.$_{Lk\ 13:1-3}$ Jesus said that the same was true for those who died when the tower of Siloam fell on them, that they were no worse than all others in Jerusalem, all of whom needed to repent or perish.*Lk 13:4-5* Jesus then told the parable of the fruitless fig tree whose owner wanted to cut it down, but the vineyard manager pleaded with the owner to leave it for one more year while he tended it and only then to cut it down if it bore no fruit.*Lk 13:6-9* Jesus also told the parable of the woman who lost one of ten coins but searched diligently until she found the lost one, as God's angels rejoice over one sinner who repents.*Lk 15:8-10* Jesus also told the parable of the lost son who squandered his inheritance in dissolute living before repenting to return destitute to his father, the father killing the fattened calf in celebration for the lost son's return.*Lk 15:11-24* The father told the other son who had remained righteous that all the father had was still that son's but that they should celebrate the recovery of the lost son.*Lk 15:25-32* Foundational teaching in Christ includes repenting from acts leading to death.*Heb 6:1-2* The Lord waits patiently to return, wanting everyone to repent rather than any to perish.*2Pe 3:9*

Humility. The disciples argued among them who was the greatest.*Mk 9:34, Lk 9:46, Lk 22:24* Jesus said whoever wants to be first must be last, the servant of all.*Mk 9:34-35* Jesus also said that the greatest is the one who is least among them.*Lk 9:48* Jesus said that while other kings lord it over subjects, the greatest in his kingdom is like the youngest and the one who rules like the one who serves.*Lk 22:25-26* Jesus said that the greatest among you must be a servant because those who exalt themselves God humbles while those who humble themselves God exalts.*Matt 23:11-12* Some of you have become arrogant, as if a teacher were not on the way soon to correct you, Lord willing.*1Co 4:18-19* Don't be arrogant, or the teacher will bring a rod of discipline, rather than come in love and with a gentle spirit.*1Co 4:21* Those who are rich materially should not be arrogant.*1Ti 6:17* Give others opportunity to take pride in you, so that they can answer those who take pride in the seen rather than in the unseen heart.*2Co 5:12* Show the humility and gentleness of Christ in your appeals to one another, especially face to face.*2Co 10:1* Don't compare yourself with others who commend themselves, because they unwisely measure themselves by themselves and compare themselves with themselves.*2Co 10:12* Some with great revelations will suffer a thorn in their flesh from Satan, to torment them and keep them from conceit.*2Co 12:7* Jesus taught that God blesses the poor in spirit, who receive the kingdom of heaven, and the meek, who inherit the earth.*Matt 5:3,5* Jesus said that the greatest in heaven's kingdom is the one who takes the lowly position of a child.*Matt 18:1-4* Jesus said that even as to heaven's kingdom, many who are first here will be last there, and many last here first there.*Matt 19:30* When Jesus noticed how guests took places of honor, he said instead to take the lowest place so that your host doesn't humiliate you by moving you to a lower place but instead calls you to an honored place.*Lk 14:7-10* While many Jews even among the leaders believed in Jesus, they would not profess their faith because they feared being put out of the synagogue where they would lose human praise for God's praise.*Jn 12:39-43* All who exalt themselves will see humbling, while all who are humble will see exalting.*Lk 14:11*

Boasting. Rid yourself of boasting that, like leavened yeast, works its way through everything, so that you may be without sin, as you really are in Christ, our sacrificed Passover lamb.*1Co 5:6-7* God chose the world's foolish things to shame the wise and weak things to shame the strong.*1Co 1:27* God chose the world's lowly things, despised things, and even things that are not, to nullify the things that are, so that no one may boast before him.*1Co 1:28-29* Do not boast beyond proper limits, but confine your boasting to the service that God assigns to you.*2Co 10:13* One doesn't boast too far when boasting in those who accept from you Christ's gospel.*2Co 10:14* One doesn't boast too far about work others do, while the faith of those others continues to grow, expanding your own preaching sphere into other regions.*2Co 10:15-16* When boasting, boast in the Lord.*1Co 1:31* Let our only boast be in the cross of our Lord Jesus Christ that crucified the world to us, and us to the world.*Gal 6:14* Boast in the Lord.*2Co 10:17* Many boast in the way the world does.*2Co 11:18* If you must boast, then boast of things showing your weakness.*2Co 11:30* Boast only about your weaknesses.*2Co 12:5* Refrain from boasting, so that no one thinks more of you than what you do and say warrants.*2Co 12:6* Boast all the more gladly about weaknesses, so that Christ's power rests on you.*2Co 12:9*

Clearheadedness. Do not think too highly of yourself, but instead use sober judgment with the faith God gave you.*Ro 12:3* Do not deceive yourself by thinking you are something you are not, but instead test your own actions, taking pride in doing the best you can, without comparing yourself to someone else.*Gal 6:3-4* Do not claim that you have all you want, are already rich, and have begun to reign, when you have not.*1Co 4:8* Know the truth so that you remain humble.*Ro 11:25-26* Do not be proud or conceited, but instead be willing to associate with people of low position.*Ro 12:16* Humble yourselves under God, that he may lift you up in due time.*1Pe 5:6* Be completely humble, gentle, and patient, bearing with one another in love.*Eph 4:2* God saved us out of his own purpose and grace, not because of anything we have done.*2Ti 1:9* Remember what you were like when God first called you, neither wise nor influential, and not many of noble birth.*1Co 1:26* When a crowd in Lystra saw Paul heal a man lame from birth, and the crowd called Paul and Barnabas gods and prepared to offer them sacrifices, Paul and Barnabas tore their clothes and rushed into the crowd shouting that they were only human.*Acts 14:11-18* Paul said that he served the Lord with great humility and with tears in the midst of severe testing by his Jewish opponents.*Acts 20:19*

Ambition. The mother of Zebedee's sons James and John came to Jesus asking that her sons sit at his right and left hands in his kingdom.*Matt 20:20-21* James and John asked if Jesus would grant them what they asked, and when Jesus asked what they wanted, they said to sit at his right and left in his glory.*Mk 10:35-37* After asking James and John whether they could drink the cup that he would drink, Jesus answered that his Father, not he, would grant who sat to his right or left.*Matt 20:22-23* The other disciples were indignant at the request of James and John, but Jesus told them that although the world's rulers lord it over their subjects, whoever wishes to be great should instead become a servant or slave, like the Son of Man came to serve and give his life to ransom many.*Matt 20:24-28, Mk 10:41-45* Your ambition should indeed be to lead a quiet life, minding your own business while working with your hands, as instructed, to win outsiders' respect and not to depend on anyone.*1Th 4:11* Take pride when humbling and humiliation instead lift you up, because all things pass away quickly even as we go about our business.*Jas 1:9-11* You may not be inferior to esteemed others, and may deserve commending, even though you are nothing.*2Co 12:11* The Lord's commending approves, rather than commending that comes from oneself.*2Co 10:18* Show no selfish ambition or vain conceit but instead humbly value others above yourselves, looking to the interests of others over your own interest.*Php 2:3-4* Women who profess God should dress modestly, adorned not with elaborate hairstyles or jewelry, or expensive clothes, but with good deeds.*1Ti 2:9-10* Women should learn in submission, quietly, without assuming authority over those who teach and without giving in to deception.*1Ti 2:11-13* Do not puff yourself up as a follower of one teacher over another.*1Co 4:6* You are no different from anyone else in having only what you received, so that you cannot boast.*1Co 4:7* Jesus said to submit to him and learn from him because he is gentle and humble, and he will give your soul rest.*Matt 11:29*

Forgiveness. The apostle Peter said that all the prophets testify that everyone who believes in Jesus receives forgiveness of sins through his name.*Acts 10:43* God forgives our wickedness and remembers our sins no more.*Heb 8:12* Our redemption and forgiveness of sins is in Jesus Christ.*Col 1:14* Jesus said that the Son of Man has authority on earth to forgive sins.*Matt 9:6* Jesus showed that he has authority to forgive sins on earth by healing the paralyzed man whom he forgave.*Mk 2:5-12, Lk 5:17-25* If we say we are without sin, then we lie and deceive, while suggesting Christ lies, and while rejecting his word, but if we admit sin, the faithful and just Christ forgives and purifies us.*1Jn 1:8-10* In forgiving our sins, God canceled the indebtedness that stood against us and condemned us.*Col 2:14* Christ redeems us through his blood, the forgiveness of sins, as God lavished his grace's riches on us.*Eph 1:7-8* God forgives our sins and blesses us with righteousness apart from our works.*Ro 4:6-7* The law required that nearly everything be cleansed with blood, without which God would not forgive.*Heb 9:22* Sacrifice for sin is no longer necessary, where God has forgiven.*Heb 10:18* Jesus said that God can forgive every kind of sin and slander but does not forgive blasphemy against his own Holy Spirit.*Matt 12:31, Mk 3:28-29* Blaspheming the Holy Spirit is an eternal sin.*Mk 3:29* Jesus said that anyone speaking against the Son of Man, God will forgive, but not anyone speaking against the Holy Spirit, now or later.*Matt 12:32, Lk 12:10* When a sinful woman wet Jesus's feet with her tears, wiped them with her hair, and anointed them with expensive perfume, Jesus said that he had forgiven her many sins because she loved much, while the one like his Pharisee host who sought little forgiveness loved little.*Lk 7:36-48*

Others. After his resurrection, Jesus told the disciples that they could now forgive or not forgive anyone's sins.*Jn 20:23* Jesus said to forgive a brother or sister who sins against you not just seven times but seventy-seven times.*Matt 18:21-22* Jesus told the parable of the unmerciful servant whose king forgave his debt but who refused to forgive a debt owed him and instead threw the debtor in prison.*Matt 18:23-30* The other servants complained to the king who handed him over to the jailer for torture until he repaid all he owed.*Matt 18:31-34* Jesus said that his heavenly Father will treat us the same way unless we forgive brothers and sisters from our hearts.*Matt 18:35* Jesus said that if a brother or sister sins against you but then repents, to forgive them, even if they sin and repent again seven times in a day.*Lk 17:3-4* Jesus said that if you forgive others when they sin against you, then your heavenly Father forgives you, but if you don't forgive others who sin against you, then your Father does not forgive your sins._{Matt 6:14-15} Be kind and compassionate to one another, forgiving each other, just as God forgave you in Christ._{Eph 4:32} Put up with one another, forgiving any against whom you have a grievance, just like the Lord forgave you._{Col 3:13} If you forgive, then others will also forgive, all in Christ's sight for your sake, so that Satan, of whose schemes we know, does not outwit us._{2Co 2:10-11} Forgive those who fail to come to your defense and instead desert you._{2Ti 4:16} The majority may punish the one causing grief, but then forgive, comfort, and reaffirm your love so that excessive sorrow does not overcome that one._{2Co 2:6-8} Pray for the sinner so that through faithful prayer God will forgive the sinner._{Jas 5:13-15} Have nothing to do with people who are unforgiving._{2Ti 3:2-5}

Service. Jesus said that he came down from heaven to do his Father's will, not his own will._{Jn 6:38} Jesus said that as long as day is here, we must do the works of him who sent Jesus._{Jn 9:4} Jesus said that just calling out his name doesn't get you into heaven when you do nothing of his heavenly Father's will._{Matt 7:21-22} Jesus knows those who do his Father's will rather than the evildoers._{Matt 7:23} Putting Jesus's words into practice makes you the wise one who builds on the rock foundation against the storms._{Matt 7:24-25, Lk 6:46-48} The fool who hears but ignores Jesus's words builds a house on sand that crashes down in the storm._{Matt 7:26-27, Lk 6:49} Jesus said that deeds prove wisdom right._{Matt 11:19} Jesus told the parable of the two sons, one who said he wouldn't do his father's work but changed his mind and did it, and the other who said he would but didn't._{Matt 21:28-30} Doing is what counts, Jesus added, like the prostitutes and tax collectors who repented and entered the kingdom, and not like the chief priests and elders who refused to repent._{Matt 21:31-32} Don't just listen to God's word, while deceiving yourself; instead do what the word says. _{Jas 1:22} If you only listen but don't act, then you forget what you look like in not acting as the word says._{Jas 1:23-24} Instead, when you look deeply into God's perfect word that gives freedom and then do what the word says, God will bless you in what you do._{Jas 1:25} You do no good when you wish well someone without clothes and daily food but do nothing to help them._{Jas 2:15-16} We sin when we know the good that we ought to do but don't do it._{Jas 4:17} We must love with truthful actions rather than just words._{1Jn 3:17-18} Be an example in conduct for believers._{1Ti 4:11} Good deeds are obvious, while even those that are not obvious cannot remain hidden forever._{1Ti 5:25} Simply believing in God is not enough because even shuddering demons do that._{Jas 2:19} You avoid harm when eager to do good, but God blesses you even if you suffer for doing right, so that you need not fear threats.*1Pe 3:13-14*

Faith. Claiming faith when that faith produces no deeds won't save you.*Jas 2:14* Better, if God wills, to suffer for doing good than for doing evil, just like the righteous Christ, killed in body while raised in Spirit, suffered to take our sin away and bring us to God.*1Pe 3:17-18* Your good deeds should prove your faith.*Jas 2:18* It works both ways that while the body dies without the spirit, so, too, faith dies without deeds.*Jas 2:26* When you merely wish someone well who has needs, you only show your faith without action to be dead.*Jas 2:17* If you still need evidence that faith without deeds is useless, then look at the reward that God gave to Abraham for offering his son, his faith making complete what he did.*Jas 2:20-22* The good life of deeds done in humility will prove the wise and understanding among you.*Jas 3:13* God wills that you do good to silence foolish people's ignorant talk.*1Pe 2:15* Never lack zeal, instead keeping your spiritual fervor while serving the Lord.*Ro 12:11* Do not receive God's grace in vain.*2Co 6:1* Jesus said that followers must preach the gospel to all nations.*Mk13:10* Jesus said to go making disciples of all nations, baptizing in the name of the Father, Son, and Holy Spirit, teaching obedience in all that Jesus said.*Matt 28:18-20*

Charity. Remember the poor, being eager to help.*Gal 2:10* Help orphans and widows when they need it, while refusing to let the world pollute you, and God our Father will judge your religion pure and faultless.*Jas 1:27* Recognize widows who are really in need.*1Ti 5:3* Children and grandchildren should put their religion into practice by caring for their family, especially a widow.*1Ti 5:4* Anyone who does not provide for their relatives, especially their own household, denies the faith and is worse than an unbeliever.*1Ti 5:8* Followers must learn to devote themselves to doing good, to provide for urgent needs and live productive lives.*Tit 3:14* Do something useful with your own hands, that you may share with those in need.*Eph 4:28* Spur one another on toward good deeds.*Heb 10:24* The King on his return will say that he was hungry and the righteous gave him food, thirsty and they gave him drink, a stranger and they invited him in, without clothes and they clothed him, sick and they cared for him, and a prisoner and they visited him.*Matt 25:35-36* The righteous will ask when they did these things for him, and the King will answer that they did these things for him every time that they did them for his least brothers and sisters.*Matt 25:37-40* Jesus said that when you hold a banquet, invite the poor, crippled, lame, and blind who cannot repay you by inviting you back, so that at the righteous's resurrection you receive your payment.*Lk 14:12-14* The apostles chose persons filled with faith and the Holy Spirit to distribute food to widows.*Acts 6:1-6* When a prophet through the Spirit predicted widespread famine, the disciples provided help to the brothers and sisters in Judea, sending gifts through Barnabas and Saul.*Acts 11:27-30*

Others. Jesus told the parable of the good Samaritan who, after a priest and a Levite passed a beaten man on the road, stopped to bandage and rescue him.*Lk 10:30-35* Jesus told the law expert who had tried to justify himself over who was his neighbor, to go and do as the good Samaritan had done.*Lk 10:36-37* Risk your life to help others whom others cannot help.*Php 2:30* Supply what others fail to supply, refreshing others' spirit, while also recognizing those who do.*1Co 16:17-18* Though free and belonging to no one, make yourself a slave to everyone to win as many as possible.*1Co 9:19* To those under the law become as if under the law to win those under the law.*1Co 9:20* To those not having the law become like one not having the law, even though under Christ's law, to win those not having the law.*1Co 9:21* To the weak become weak to win the weak, just as you should become all things to all people so as by all possible means to save some.*1Co 9:22* Workers, obey your earthly supervisors in everything, not only when they watch you and to curry favor but with sincere heart, out of reverence for the Lord.*Col 3:22* Supervisors should treat workers the same way, without threats, because God in heaven is over both supervisor and worker, favoring neither over the other.*Eph 6:9* Provide your workers with what is right and fair because you, too, have a Master in heaven.*Col 4:1*

Gifts. Jesus said that whoever believes in him will do even greater works than he did because was going to the Father.*Jn 14:12* If your gift is telling the future, then do so faithfully.*Ro 12:6* If your gift is serving, then serve faithfully.*Ro 12:7* If your gift is teaching, then teach faithfully.*Ro 12:7* If your gift is to encourage, then encourage faithfully.*Ro 12:8* If your gift is giving, then give generously.*Ro 12:8* If your gift is to lead, then lead diligently.*Ro 12:8* If your gift is to show mercy, then do so cheerfully.*Ro 12:8* The same Lord accepts different kinds of service.*1Co 12:5* The same God works in everyone and in different kinds of work.*1Co 12:6* Use your gifts to serve others, stewarding God's manifold graces.*1Pe 4:10* Serve with the strength God provides, so that everyone praises God.*1Pe 4:11* When in need, do not desire another's gifts, but desire that God credit more to the giver's account.*Php 4:17* Treat gifts of support as fragrant offerings and acceptable sacrifices pleasing to God.*Php 4:18*

God. You serve God.*2Ti 1:3* Cleanse yourself from articles of common use in favor of articles for special purposes so that you are your Master's holy instrument for good work.*2Ti 2:20-21* God breathed all Scripture for training so that God's servant is ready for every good work.*2Ti 3:16-17* God is just to remember your work and loves you to reveal him as you help his people.*Heb 6:10* Help others in their ministry.*2Ti 4:11* Do not seek your own good but the good of others.*1Co 10:24* Try to please everyone in every way, seeking the good of many rather than your own good, that God may save them.*1Co 10:33* Stay on where great doors for effective work open to you, even though many oppose you.*1Co 16:9* See that those who do the Lord's work have nothing to fear while with you.*1Co 16:10* No one should treat the Lord's workers with contempt but send them on their way in peace to return to their mentors.*1Co 16:11* Devote yourselves to the service of the Lord's people.*1Co 16:15* Submit yourselves to the Lord's people and everyone who joins in and labors at the work.*1Co 16:16*

Christ. Jesus said that whoever serves him must follow him because wherever he is, his servant will also be.*Jn 12:26* Jesus also said that his Father honors those who serve Jesus.*Jn 12:26* Jesus said that he was always at work, even on the Sabbath, because his Father was always at work.*Jn 5:16-18* Jesus said not to work for food that spoils but for food that endures to eternal life, which the Son of Man, on whom God the Father placed his seal of approval, gives you.*Jn 6:26-27* When asked what works God required, Jesus said God's work is to believe in the one whom God sent.*Jn 6:28-29* Jesus said that he was among us as one who serves.*Lk 22:27* While the Last Supper was still in progress, after Judas had left to betray Jesus, Jesus got up, took off his outer clothing, wrapped a towel around his waist, and washed the disciples' feet, to show them that they should do so for one another.*Jn 13:2-17* At the Last Supper, Jesus also said that he is the true vine and his Father the gardener, cutting off branches that bear no fruit but pruning branches that do bear fruit, for more fruit.*Jn 15:1-2* Jesus added to remain in him, as he remains in you, because no branch bears fruit by itself, but as branches, we must remain in Jesus, the vine, to bear much fruit.*Jn 15:4-5* Anyone who serves Christ pleases God and receives human approval.*Ro 14:18* Glory in Christ Jesus in your service to God.*Ro 15:17* Speak of no service other than what Christ accomplished through you in leading others to obey God by what you said and did through the Spirit of God's power.$_{Ro\ 15:18-19}$ We are God's handiwork, created in Christ Jesus to do good works that God prepared in advance for us to do.$_{Eph\ 2:10}$ Show Jesus Christ's genuine concern for one another's welfare rather than just looking out for your own interest.$_{Php\ 2:20-21}$ Christ himself gave the apostles, the prophets, the evangelists, the pastors and teachers to equip his people for works of service, so that they may build up the body of Christ.$_{Eph\ 4:11-12}$ Workers should obey earthly supervisors sincerely just as they would obey Christ, not to win favor only when watched but instead wholeheartedly as if working for Christ, doing God's will for God's reward.$_{Eph\ 6:5-8}$ Our Lord Jesus Christ and God our Father strengthen us in every good deed and word.$_{2Th\ 2:16-17}$ God equips you with everything good for doing his will, while working in you to please him, through Jesus Christ.$_{Heb\ 13:21}$

Gospel. Do everything for the gospel's sake to share in its blessings.$_{1Co\ 9:23}$ We become the gospel's servants by the gift of God's grace given us through his power.$_{Eph\ 3:7}$ We should count ourselves less than the least of all the Lord's people, serving him by grace.$_{Eph\ 3:8}$ Work with all your heart as working for the Lord, not for others.$_{Col\ 3:23}$ Prove yourself serving with others in gospel work.$_{Php\ 2:22}$ Send co-workers and fellow soldiers to care for one another's needs.$_{Php\ 2:25}$ Help those who contend as co-workers in the gospel's cause.$_{Php\ 4:3}$ Churches may praise one for service to the gospel.$_{2Co\ 8:18}$ Let co-workers in God's service of spreading Christ's gospel strengthen and encourage you in your faith.$_{1Th\ 3:2}$

Share. Share in giving and receiving, sending aid whenever you see a believer in need.$_{Php\ 4:15-16}$ Do good and share with others, pleasing God with your sacrifices.$_{Heb\ 13:16}$ Share in one another's struggles.$_{Php\ 4:14}$ Share every word and deed in the Lord Jesus's name.$_{Col\ 3:17}$ We serve the gospel.$_{Col\ 1:23}$ Work hard for one another.$_{Col\ 4:13}$ Acknowledge those who work hard among you, who care for you in the Lord and who admonish you, holding them in highest regard because of their work.$_{1Th\ 5:12-13}$ Help the weak.$_{1Th\ 5:14}$ Share with the Lord's people who are in need, practicing hospitality.$_{Ro\ 12:13}$

Strive. Strive to do what is good for each other and everyone else.$_{1Th\ 5:15}$ You know how to follow a good example, working hard not to burden anyone, so that you, too, are a model for others to imitate.$_{2Th\ 3:7-10}$ Be busy rather than an idle and disruptive busybody who needs to settle down and earn the food they eat.$_{2Th\ 3:11}$ Never tire of doing good.$_{2Th\ 3:13}$

Each should show the same diligence to the very end, so that you realize that for which you hope.$_{Heb\ 6:11}$ Do not be lazy, but instead imitate those who through faith and patience inherit the promised reward.$_{Heb\ 6:12}$ Those who do not work will not eat.$_{2Th\ 3:10}$ Jesus said that when a servant is done with one job, the servant does not sit down to eat, looking for thanks for doing his duty, but the servant instead does the next job, admitting that they are unworthy and only doing their duty.$_{Lk\ 17:7-10}$

Sowing. Jesus said that the fields were ripe for harvest, the reaper drawing a wage and harvesting a crop for eternal life with the sower.$_{Jn\ 4:35-36}$ Jesus said that while one sows and another reaps, he sent the disciples to reap the benefit of others' hard labor.$_{Jn\ 4:37-38}$ Jesus said that judgment will pull up by the roots every plant that his heavenly Father has not planted.$_{Matt\ 15:13}$ One reaps holiness and eternal life as a slave to God because God's gift is eternal life in Christ Jesus our Lord.$_{Ro\ 6:21-22}$ The Lord assigns each teacher to his task, some planting, some watering, but God making it grow.$_{1Co\ 3:5-6}$ Teachers are co-workers in God's service, while you are God's field.$_{1Co\ 3:9}$ Neither the planter nor the waterer is anything, but only God, who makes things grow.$_{1Co\ 3:7}$ The planter and waterer have one purpose, each rewarded for their own labor.$_{1Co\ 3:8}$ The plant must die to sow the seed that comes to life.$_{1Co\ 15:36}$ When we sow to please the Spirit, we reap from the Spirit eternal life.$_{Gal\ 6:8}$ Having godly qualities in increasing measure keep us from being ineffective and unproductive in knowing our Lord Jesus Christ.$_{2Pe\ 1:8}$ Stress trustworthy doctrine so that those trusting God excel in doing good, profiting everyone.$_{Tit\ 3:8}$ Sowing is not planting what will be but instead planting only the seed of what will be.$_{1Co\ 15:37}$ God gives the seed a body as he determines, giving each seed its own body.$_{1Co\ 15:38}$ God who supplies seed to the sower and bread for food also supplies and increases your store of seed to enlarge your righteousness harvest.$_{2Co\ 9:10}$

Good. The thing is to persevere in doing good because the harvest is indeed coming for those of us who do not give up.$_{Gal\ 6:9}$ Do good wherever the opportunity arises but especially among the family of believers.$_{Gal\ 6:10}$ Support and work together with followers who go out sharing Christ's name because they'll get no help from those who don't follow Christ.$_{3Jn\ 7-8}$ Be pleased to make a contribution for the poor among the Lord's people because you may owe them material blessings to repay spiritual blessings.$_{Ro\ 15:26-27}$ Keep doing good in the faithful Creator's name even as you suffer for it.$_{1Pe\ 4:19}$ Plan visits to have a harvest among others.$_{Ro\ 1:13}$ Whoever sows generously reaps generously.*2Co 9:6* God won't let us get away with it: we reap what we sow.*Gal 6:7* When we sow pursuing desires, we reap destruction.*Gal 6:8* One reaps no benefit from sin, only shame and death, because sin's wage is death.*Ro 6:21-22* Call to account and put out of the church those who spread malicious nonsense, who refuse to welcome other followers, and who stop other followers who want to help.*3Jn 9-10* Repay evil with blessing rather than evil, so that you inherit blessing.*1Pe 3:9* Whoever sows sparingly reaps sparingly.*2Co 9:6*

Church

The New Testament addresses at length the nature and role of God's church to make his gospel wisdom known. The church is Christ's body, over which Christ is the head. We are his household, supporting one another in faith. God gives church members different gifts, which we should exercise in order and unity. Above all, we should not give up meeting together as the church. See how the New Testament addresses the church. Do you support the church consistent with the role and significance that the Bible treats it?

Role. God's intent was that the church make known God's manifold wisdom to the rulers and authorities in the heavenly realms, as is God's eternal purpose already accomplished in Christ Jesus our Lord._{Eph 3:10-11} God's church is those whom he sanctifies in Christ Jesus and calls as his holy people, those everywhere who call on the name of our Lord Jesus Christ._{1Co 1:2} God the Father and the Lord Jesus Christ bring grace and peace to the church in God our Father and the Lord Jesus Christ._{2Th 1:1-2} God gives grace to the churches._{2Co 8:1} God's household, the church of the living God, is the pillar and foundation of the truth._{1Ti 3:15} The church helps widows with real need._{1Ti 5:16} Churches may praise one for service to the gospel._{2Co 8:18} Be church representatives honoring Christ._{2Co 8:23} Christ loved the church so much that he gave himself up for her, making her holy by cleansing her with his word so that he could present her to himself as radiant, without stain, wrinkle, or other blemish, but instead blameless._{Eph 5:25-27} Christ and the church are a profound mystery._{Eph 5:32} Imitate God's churches in Christ Jesus, even when suffering from your own people the same things those churches suffer._{1Th 2:14} Paul said that God bought his church with his blood._{Acts 20:28}

Body. The Son is the head of the body, the church._{Col 1:18} Christ heads his body the church, of which he is the Savior._{Eph 5:22-23} Christ is the head from whom the whole body grows as God causes it to grow.*Col 2:19* From Christ the whole body, held together by everyone, grows in love, as each part does its work.*Eph 4:16* God placed all things under Christ's feet and appointed him head over everything for the church, which is his body, the fullness of him who fills everything in every way.*Eph 1:22-23* Speaking the truth in love, we will grow to become in every way the mature body, with Christ as the head.*Eph 4:15* Christ feeds and cares for the church as his own body, of which we are members.*Eph 5:29-30* We are members of one body, sharing the promise in Christ Jesus.*Eph 3:6* Christ created in him one body, reconciled to God through the cross.*Eph 2:15-16* We are all members of one body.*Eph 4:25* God's people serve to build up the body of Christ.*Eph 4:11-12* God calls us to get along as members of one body.*Col 3:15* In Christ, you are no longer foreigners and strangers but fellow citizens with God's people, members of his household built on the foundation of those who went before you, with Christ Jesus as the chief cornerstone.*Eph 2:19-20* In Christ, the whole building joins and rises to become a holy temple in the Lord.*Eph 2:21* In Christ, we join to become a dwelling in which God lives by his Spirit.*Eph 2:22* A church may meet in your house.*1Co 16:19-20* Just like a natural body has parts, in Christ we form one body belonging to one another, but with different gifts, as God gave each of us grace.*Ro 12:5-6* We must build up the body of Christ until we all reach unity in the faith, knowing the Son of God, becoming mature, and attaining to the whole measure of Christ's fullness.*Eph 4:12-13* Put off falsehood and speak truthfully to your neighbor, for we are all members of one body.*Eph 4:25* You have only one body and one Spirit, just as God called you to one hope.*Eph 4:4* Let the peace of Christ rule in your hearts because as members of one body God called you to peace.*Col 3:15*

Unity. Let teaching on the good way of life agree in every church.*1Co 4:17* While you should not associate with sexually immoral people, you must inevitably associate with the world's immoral and greedy people, swindlers, and idolaters, because otherwise you would have to leave this world.*1Co 5:10* But still don't associate and eat with any immoral or greedy person or idolaters, slanderers, drunkards, or swindlers, when they claim to be a believer.*1Co 5:11* In other words, don't judge those who are outside the church, whom God will instead judge, but do judge and expel the wicked person inside the church among you.*1Co 5:12-13* Don't come together as a church with divisions among you.*1Co 11:17-18* You are not eating the Lord's Supper together because some of you have your own private suppers, leaving one hungry while another gets drunk.*1Co 11:20-21* Eat and drink in your own homes if you must, but don't despise God's church by humiliating those who have nothing.*1Co 11:22* Do not assume your church inferior to other churches or that your teachers think your church so.*2Co 12:13* God's churches persevere in faith through persecutions and trials.*2Th 1:4* The growing church experienced a time of peace and strengthening, living in the Lord's fear and with the Holy Spirit's encouragement.*Acts 9:31* When the high priest Caiaphas said that better one man Jesus die for the people than the whole nation perish, he prophesied that Jesus would die to bring together the scattered children of God, making them one.*Jn 11:49-52* Live in harmony with one another.*Ro 12:16* As much as possible, live at peace with everyone.*Ro 12:18* Let your actions show and reputation be that you stand firm in the one Spirit, striving together as one for gospel faith.*Php 1:27* All followers should be like-minded, sympathetic, compassionate, and humble, while loving one another.*1Pe 3:8* Make every effort to keep the Spirit's unity through the bond of peace.*Eph 4:3* You have only one Lord, one faith, and one baptism.*Eph 4:5* And you have only one God and Father of all, who is over, through, and in all.*Eph 4:4-6* Plead with one another to be of the same mind in the Lord.*Php 4:2* Live peacefully with each other.*1Th 3:13* To unite with the Lord is to be one with him in spirit.*1Co 6:17* Avoid discord, jealousy, fits of rage, selfish ambition, slander, gossip, arrogance, and disorder.*2Co 12:20* Warn the disruptive, and be patient with everyone.*1Th 5:14* Let no bitter root grow up to cause trouble and defile many.*Heb 12:15* Men should pray and lift holy hands without disputing.*1Ti 2:8* Be of one mind, and God will be with you.*2Co 13:11* We are all together in Christ Jesus, not the insider or outsider, slave or free, or male or female.*Gal 3:28* In uniting with Christ, comforted by his love, have the same minds, spirit, tenderness, compassion, and love, while sharing with one another in the Spirit.*Php 2:2* Live such good lives among those who do not follow Christ that even as they condemn you, they see your good deeds and glorify God.*1Pe 2:12* Accept one another just as Christ accepted you, to bring praise to God.*Ro 15:7* In our Lord Jesus Christ's name, you should all agree with one another in what you say so that no divisions exist among you and you are in perfect unity in mind and thought.*1Co 1:10* May the God who gives endurance and encouragement give you the same attitude of mind toward each other that Christ Jesus had, so that with one mind and voice you glorify the God and Father of our Lord Jesus Christ.*Ro 15:6-7* Peace and love with faith from God the Father and the Lord Jesus Christ, to the brothers and sisters.*Eph 6:23*

Meeting. Keep meeting together, rather than giving up, so that you encourage one another, and all the more as the last day approaches.*Heb 10:25* Your meetings do more harm than good when you come together as a church, with divisions among you.*1Co 11:17-18* Your disputes cheat and do wrong to yourself and your brothers and sisters.*1Co 6:8* Your differences will show which of you have God's approval.*1Co 11:19* You are not eating the Lord's Supper together because some of you have your own private suppers, leaving one hungry while another gets drunk.*1Co 11:20-21* Eat and drink in your own homes if you must, but don't despise God's church by humiliating those who have nothing.*1Co 11:22* When you gather to eat, you should all eat together.*1Co 11:33* Anyone who is hungry should eat at home so as to avoid judgment when you gather.*1Co 11:34* From one elder to another, I say shepherd God's flock eagerly as the example that God wants you to be, not because you must or for pride or dishonest gain, but so that the Chief Shepherd can give you an eternal crown of glory.*1Pe 5:4* The younger should submit to their elders, all clothing themselves with humility toward one another, because God opposes the proud while favoring the humble.*1Pe 5:5*

Communion. At the Last Supper, on the night of his betrayal, Jesus took bread, gave thanks, broke it, gave it to the disciples, and told them to take and eat the bread as his body.*Matt 26:26, Mk 14:22, Lk 22:19* He then took a cup, gave thanks, passed it to them, and told them to drink from it as his blood of the covenant, poured out for many for forgiveness of sins.*Matt 26:27-28, Mk 14:23-24, Lk 22:17-20* Jesus called it the new covenant in his blood.*Lk 22:20* Jesus said that he would not drink again with them until in his Father's kingdom.*Matt 26:29, Mk 14:25, Lk 22:18* The letters repeat that on the night a disciple betrayed him, the Lord Jesus took bread, gave thanks, and broke it, saying that the bread was his body for you and that you should do as he did in his remembrance.*1Co 11:23-24* Likewise, after supper he said the cup is the new covenant in his blood to drink in remembrance of him.*1Co 11:25* The bread we break participates in Christ's body.*1Co 10:16* The thanksgiving cup for which we give thanks participates in Christ's blood, while the bread we break participates in Christ's body, just as eating the sacrifices participates in the altar.*1Co 10:16,18* Whenever you eat the bread and drink the cup, you proclaim the Lord's death until he comes.*1Co 11:26* Our ancestors all ate the same spiritual food and drank the same spiritual drink from the spiritual rock Christ who accompanied them.*1Co 10:3-4* Whoever eats Jesus's flesh and drinks his blood has eternal life, Jesus raising them up at the last day, because his flesh and blood are real food and drink.*Jn 6:52-55* Eating his flesh and drinking his blood keeps one in Jesus, so that the one who feeds on Jesus lives because of him.*Jn 6:56-57* Although a fellowship of believers takes communion together, some are not eating the Lord's Supper together, instead having their own private suppers, leaving one hungry while another gets drunk.*1Co 11:20-21* Eat and drink in your own homes if you must, but don't despise God's church by humiliating those who have nothing.*1Co 11:22* When you gather to eat, you should all eat together.*1Co 11:33* Anyone who is hungry should eat at home so as to avoid judgment when you gather.*1Co 11:34* Examine yourself before eating the bread and drinking from the cup.*1Co 11:28* You cannot drink the Lord's cup and the demons' cup, too, taking part in both the Lord's table and demons' table.*1Co 10:21* Those who unworthily eat the Lord's bread or drink the Lord's cup sin against the Lord's body and blood.*1Co 11:27* Those who eat and drink without discerning Christ's body judge themselves.*1Co 11:29* Many among you are weak and sick, and a number of you have fallen asleep, for this reason.*1Co 11:30*

Order. God is not over disorder but peace, as in all congregations of the Lord's people.*1Co 14:33* No more than three at most should speak in an unknown language, while someone must interpret.*1Co 14:27* Without an interpreter, the speaker should keep quiet in church, speaking only to himself and God.*1Co 14:28* Two or three may foretell the future, while others weigh carefully their words.*1Co 14:29* If someone sitting down has a revelation, then the first speaker should stop.*1Co 14:30* Speak in turn so that everyone receives instruction and encouragement.*1Co 14:31* You control your spirit as to when to speak.*1Co 14:32* Women should remain silent in the churches, in submission.*1Co 14:34* They should ask questions of their own husband at home, for speaking in church disgraces a woman.*1Co 14:35* Do everything in fit and orderly way.*1Co 14:40* Elders face daily pressing concerns for the churches.*2Co 11:28* Paul and Barnabas appointed elders in each church, with fasting and prayer committing the elders to the Lord.*Acts 14:23* Paul and Timothy traveled from town to town strengthening the churches in the faith, so that they daily grew in number, and delivering to the churches the decisions that the Jerusalem apostles and elders made for the people to obey.*Acts 16:1-5*

Leaders. Join together in following good models, keeping your eyes on those who live right.*Php 3:17* As God's witnesses, see how holy, righteous, and blameless your leaders are among you as they deal with you like their own children.*1Th 2:10-11* God sets apart leaders for the gospel.*Ro 1:1* God chose apostles of Christ Jesus to address the faithful in

Christ Jesus, bringing messages of grace and peace from God our Father and the Lord Jesus Christ.$_{Eph\ 1:1-2}$ An apostle of Christ Jesus is by the will of God.$_{2Ti\ 1:1}$ Gospel heralds, apostles, and teachers suffer without shame, believing and trusting Jesus.$_{2Ti\ 1:11-12}$ An apostle's true marks include signs, wonders, and miracles.$_{2Co\ 12:12}$ Those who serve well gain excellent standing and great assurance in their faith in Christ Jesus.$_{1Ti\ 3:13}$ No boasting about human leaders.$_{1Co\ 3:21}$ Follow the life and adopt the faith of your leaders who spoke God's word to you.$_{Heb\ 13:7}$ Everything is yours, whether that of one teacher or another.$_{1Co\ 3:21-23}$ Leaders who are away physically may still be with you in spirit, passing judgment in the Lord Jesus's name on those among you who practice a sexual immorality that not even non-believers practice.$_{1Co\ 5:1-4}$

Servants. Commend servants of the church to one another, receiving them in the Lord in a way worthy of the Lord's people and giving them any help they may need from you, when they have benefited many people, including you.$_{Ro\ 16:2}$ Greet co-workers in Christ Jesus who risk their lives for you, for whom the churches are grateful.$_{Ro\ 16:3-4}$ Greet members of house churches, and greet the first in their area to convert to Christ.$_{Ro\ 16:5}$ Greet one another with a holy kiss, sending greetings from all the churches of Christ.$_{Ro\ 16:16}$ Greet one another warmly in the Lord, with a holy kiss.$_{1Co\ 16:20}$ Accept and enjoy with the whole church the hospitality of a generous believer among you.$_{Ro\ 16:23}$ Let the churches see your love for one another.$_{2Co\ 8:24}$ Paul and Barnabas gathered the church together to report all that God had done through them in opening a door of faith to the Gentiles.$_{Acts\ 14:27}$ The church sent Paul and Barnabas to Jerusalem to see the apostles and elders about the question of circumcision.$_{Acts\ 15:2}$ The Jerusalem church to which Paul and Barnabas reported everything welcomed them, just as their news of how Gentiles were believing made all the believers along the way glad.$_{Acts\ 15:3-4}$ Paul greeted the church at Caesarea.$_{Acts\ 18:22}$

Elders. Paul and Barnabas appointed elders in each church, with fasting and prayer committing the elders to the Lord.$_{Acts\ 14:23}$ Paul and Timothy traveled from town to town strengthening the churches in the faith, so that they daily grew in number, and delivering to the churches the decisions that the Jerusalem apostles and elders made for the people to obey.$_{Acts\ 16:1-5}$ Establish order by appointing elders who are blameless and faithful, and who have believing children who are not wild and disobedient.$_{Tit\ 1:6}$ Elders managing God's household must not be overbearing, quick-tempered, given to drunkenness, or violent, or pursue dishonest gain.$_{Tit\ 1:7}$ Rather, an elder must be hospitable, one who loves what is good, who is self-controlled, upright, holy, and disciplined.$_{Tit\ 1:8}$ While our leaders in Christ could be bold, ordering us to do what we should, yet they should prefer to appeal to us on based on love.$_{Phm\ 8-9}$ An elder must hold firmly to the gospel's trustworthy message just as they learned it, so that the elder can encourage others with sound doctrine and refute those who oppose the message.$_{Tit\ 1:9}$ Elders face daily pressing concerns for the churches.$_{2Co\ 11:28}$ Elders feel weak for the weak, and burn inwardly for those led into sin.$_{2Co\ 11:29}$ Deacons are also to be worthy of respect, sincere, not indulging in much wine, and not pursuing dishonest gain.$_{1Ti\ 3:8}$ First test deacons, letting them serve only if having nothing against them.$_{1Ti\ 3:10}$ Deacons must hold onto the deep truths of the faith with a clear conscience.$_{1Ti\ 3:9}$ A deacon must be faithful to his wife and manage his children and household well.$_{1Ti\ 3:12}$ Be faithful ministers in the Lord.$_{Col\ 4:7}$ Complete the ministry you have received in the Lord.$_{Col\ 4:17}$

Administrators. Administrators of God's grace are willing prisoners of Christ Jesus for the sake of the rest of us.$_{Eph\ 3:1-2}$ Paul said to keep watch over the flock of which the Holy Spirit has made you an overseer, as a shepherd of God's church, which he bought with his blood.$_{Acts\ 20:28}$ Overseers are to be above reproach, faithful to one's wife, temperate, self-controlled, respectable, hospitable, able to teach, not given to drunkenness, not violent but gentle, not quarrelsome, and not a lover of money.$_{1Ti\ 3:2-3}$ An overseer must manage his own family well and see that his children obey him, and must do so worthy of respect.$_{1Ti\ 3:4}$ He who can't manage his own family can't manage God's church.$_{1Ti\ 3:5}$ An overseer must not be a recent convert, or he may become conceited and fall under the same judgment as the devil.$_{1Ti\ 3:6}$ An overseer must also have a good reputation with outsiders, so that he will not fall into disgrace and into the devil's trap.$_{1Ti\ 3:7}$ Trust that aspiring to oversee a church is to desire a noble task.$_{1Ti\ 3:1}$ Only those who can manage their own family can manage God's church.$_{1Ti\ 3:5}$

Gifts. God placed in the church first apostles, second prophets, third teachers, then miracles, and then gifts of healing, helping, guidance, and different tongues.$_{1Co\ 12:28}$ Not all are apostles, prophets, or teachers, nor do all work miracles.$_{1Co\ 12:29}$ Not all have gifts of healing, speak in tongues, or interpret.$_{1Co\ 12:30}$ Eagerly desire greater gifts.$_{1Co\ 12:31}$ Unknown languages are a sign for non-believers, not for believers, while foretelling the future is for believers, not non-believers.$_{1Co\ 14:22}$ If everyone in church speaks in unknown languages, then inquirers and non-believers will think you are out of your mind._{1Co 14:23} But everyone foretelling the future convicts a non-believer or inquirer of sin and brings them under judgment, laying bare their secrets so they fall down to worship God among you._{1Co 14:-2425} In church, each of you should share a hymn, word of instruction, revelation, language, or interpretation to build up the church._{1Co 14:26}

Support. Help leaders on their journeys wherever they go._{1Co 16:6} Share with one another how your leaders are and what they are doing, for encouragement._{Eph 6:21-22} Pray that God restores your leaders to you soon._{Heb 13:19} You benefit from supporting and submitting to your leaders, making their work a joy rather than burden, because while they lead, they also must account._{Heb 13:17} Greet your leaders._{Heb 13:24} Give double honor to elders who direct the church's affairs, especially those who preach and teach, because they deserve their wages._{1Ti 5:17-18} Do not entertain accusations against elders unless by two or three witnesses._{1Ti 5:19} Reprove sinning elders before everyone, so that others get the warning._{1Ti 5:20} Do not be hasty in laying on hands._{1Ti 5:22} Paul reported to the elders in detail what God had done among the Gentiles through his ministry, at which the elders praised God._{Acts 21:19-20} Collect in the churches for the Lord's people._{1Co 16:1} The first day of every week, set aside and save money based on your income, for the collection._{1Co 16:2} Designate approved persons to collect and distribute your collection gifts._{1Co 16:3} Churches choose individuals to carry the offering, administered to honor the Lord and show eagerness to help._{2Co 8:19} Avoid any criticism of the way you administer giving._{2Co 8:20} Take pains to do right with giving, not only in the Lord's eyes but also in human eyes._{2Co 8:21}

Jesus. Jesus said that who has ears should hear what the Spirit says to the churches._{Rev 2:7, 11, 17, 29} To the church in Ephesus, Jesus said that he knows its deeds, hard work, and perseverance, that it could not tolerate the wicked and had tested and disproved those who claimed to be apostles but were not, had persevered and endured hardships for his name without wearying, and had rejected Nicolaitan practices that Jesus also hates, but that it had forsaken its first love and fallen far, needing to repent and do what it first did._{Rev 2:2-6} To the church in Smyrna, Jesus said that he knows its afflictions and poverty, and the slander of Satan's synagogue, but that it was rich, not to fear, and to be faithful to the point of death when the devil puts some of them in prison and persecutes them.*Rev 2:9-10* To the church in Pergamum, Jesus said that he knows that it lives where Satan has his throne but that it remains true to his name and did not renounce its faith in him, but that some hold to Balaam's teaching enticing the Israelites to sin and others to the Nicolaitans' teaching, and so to repent or he would come fight against them soon with his mouth's sword.*Rev 2:13-16* To the church in Thyatira, Jesus said that he knows its deeds, love, faith, service, and perseverance, and that it is doing more than it first did, but that it tolerates Jezebel who misleads his servants into sexual immorality and toward idols, and some have learned Satan's so-called deep secrets, but that it should repent, or he would repay each of them according to their deeds.*Rev 2:19-24* To the church in Sardis, Jesus said that it has the reputation of being alive but is dead and so should wake up to strengthen what remains because its deeds are unfinished, and should recall what it received and repent.*Rev 3:1-3* To the church in Philadelphia, Jesus said that he knows its deeds, that he has placed it before an open door that no one can shut, it has little strength, but it has kept his word and not denied his name, and that he will make those who are of Satan's synagogue fall at their feet to acknowledge that Jesus loves them, while keeping them from the coming hour of trial because they endured patiently.*Rev 3:7-10* To the church in Laodicea, Jesus said that he knows their deeds, that they are neither cold nor hot, when he wished they were one or the other, and so he is going to spit them out for having said they were rich when they are instead wretched, pitiful, poor, blind, and naked, and should buy from Jesus fire-refined gold, white clothes for their nakedness, and eye salve to see.*Rev 3:15-18* Jesus, the Root and Offspring of David, the bright Morning Star, sent his angel with this testimony for the churches, so that the Spirit and bride may say for him to come.*Rev 22:16-17*

Fellowship. In fellowship with one another, keep Christ Jesus's humble and obedient servant mindset.*Php 2:5-8* We appeal for those who join us as children in the family of faith, who were formerly useless to us but have become useful to all.*Phm 9-11* We do not withhold others, even those who are our very heart, from one another in the family of faith but share their fellowship, even when we are in special need.*Phm 12-13* When we do separate from one another for a little while, we do so that we may have one another back forever, no longer as slaves but as dear brothers and sisters in the Lord.*Phm 15-16* If one in the family of faith does another any wrong or owes another anything, then let the charge be to you and you pay it back, even if the person you pay owes you.*Phm 18-19* Pray to restore one another to the family of faith, while you prepare a guest room for the one for whom you pray.$_{Phm\ 22}$ Be like young children in humble innocence among other believers.$_{1Th\ 2:7}$ We are apostles, disciples, and followers of Christ Jesus by God's will, faithful brothers and sisters in Christ, a holy people.$_{Col\ 1:1-2}$ Give your right hand in fellowship to those in whom you recognize God's grace.$_{Gal\ 2:9}$

Greeting. Jesus said that whoever welcomes a child in his name welcomes him.$_{Matt\ 18:5,\ Mk\ 9:36-37,\ Lk\ 9:48}$ Welcome and comfort co-workers for God's kingdom when they visit.$_{Col\ 4:10-11}$ Greet and encourage those who love one another in the faith.$_{Tit\ 3:15}$ Greet all God's people in Christ Jesus, carrying the greetings of other brothers and sisters.$_{Php\ 4:21-22}$ Greet all God's people with a holy kiss.$_{1Th\ 5:26}$ Greet those who work very hard for you.$_{Ro\ 16:6}$ Greet fellow believers who suffer with you and were outstanding apostles in Christ before you were.$_{Ro\ 16:7}$ Greet dear friends in the Lord.$_{Ro\ 16:8}$ Greet co-workers and dear friends in Christ.$_{Ro\ 16:9}$ Greet those whose fidelity to Christ stands the test, and greet believing households.$_{Ro\ 16:10}$ Greet those in households who are in the Lord.$_{Ro\ 16:11}$ Greet women friends who work very hard in the Lord.$_{Ro\ 16:12}$ Greet those chosen in the Lord and those mothers who have been a mother to you, too.$_{Ro\ 16:13}$ Greet brothers and sisters and all the Lord's people who are with them.$_{Ro\ 16:15}$ Greet one another warmly in the Lord, with a holy kiss.$_{1Co\ 16:19-20}$ Greet one another with a holy kiss.$_{2Co\ 13:12}$ Send greetings to one another.$_{2Co\ 13:13}$ Greet the Lord's people.$_{Heb\ 13:24}$

Kindness. Be kind and compassionate to one another, forgiving each other, just as God forgave you in Christ.$_{Eph\ 4:32}$ Be hospitable to one another without complaint.$_{1Pe\ 4:9}$ As God's people, clothe yourselves with compassion, kindness, humility, gentleness, and patience.$_{Col\ 3:12}$ Conduct yourselves in the world, and especially with other believers, with integrity and godly sincerity, not relying on worldly wisdom but on God's grace.$_{2Co\ 1:12}$ Speak freely to one another, opening wide your hearts.$_{2Co\ 6:11}$ Don't withhold affection from one another.$_{2Co\ 6:12}$ As a fair exchange, open wide your hearts.$_{2Co\ 6:13}$ Make room for one another in your hearts, especially those who wrong, corrupt, and exploit no one.$_{2Co\ 7:2}$ Have such a place in your hearts for one another that you would live and die with them.$_{2Co\ 7:3}$ Take great pride in one another.$_{2Co\ 7:4}$ Tell one another about your longing for one another, your deep sorrow and ardent concern for one another, so that your joy may be greater than ever.$_{2Co\ 7:7}$ Prove your love to one another and reason for your pride in one another.$_{2Co\ 8:24}$ When visiting another, try to be as they wish you to be and find them as you want them to be, without discord, jealousy, fits of rage, selfish ambition, slander, gossip, arrogance, or disorder.*2Co 12:20*

Benefit. Benefit one another in the Lord by refreshing one another's heart in Christ.*Phm 20* Do even more than another in the family of faith asks.*Phm 21* Don't desire the possessions of another but desire their benefit, as parents save up for their children rather than children for parents.*2Co 12:14* Do not burden another, especially if it helps you capture them.*2Co 12:16* Don't exploit anyone through others whom you send.*2Co 12:17-18* We resist doing anything without one another's consent, so that we do not force any favor one does for another but ensure that every favor is voluntary.*Phm 14* Hesitate to grieve one another, lest you have no one to make you glad.*2Co 2:2* Strive to make one another rejoice rather than distressed, having confidence that you will share one another's joy.*2Co 2:3* Your deep love for one another should lead you to great distress, anguish of heart, and many tears, when one grieves another.*2Co 2:4* The one caused grief grieves all together more so than just one.*2Co 2:5* The majority may punish the one causing grief, but then forgive, comfort, and reaffirm your love so that excessive sorrow does not overcome that one.*2Co 2:6-8* Don't intercede just for wrongdoers or injured parties but instead that they see their own devotion before God.*2Co 7:12*

Christ. God called you into fellowship with his Son, Jesus Christ our Lord.*1Co 1:9* Submit to one another out of reverence for Christ.*Eph 5:21* We thank our God every time we remember one another as brothers and sisters in Christ.*Php 1:3* Our hearts rejoice in Christ Jesus's affection for one another and in our common salvation in God's grace, no matter our own preaching or persecution.*Php 1:7-8* While we prefer to die to join Christ, we live instead to help one another progress in faith and joy until our boasting in Christ Jesus abounds.*Php 1:24-26* When away from your fellow believers, be present with them in spirit, delighting at how firm in faith in Christ they are.*Col 2:5* Among believers we see no insider or outside, sinner or saint, slave or free, but Christ is everything and in everyone.*Col 3:11* Fellow believers are your hope, joy, and crown, in which you will glory when our Lord Jesus comes.*1Th 2:19-20* Walk with fellow believers in the same footsteps by the same Spirit.*2Co 12:18* Avoid defending yourself to others, and instead speak in God's sight as those in Christ, doing everything to strengthen the other.*2Co 12:19* May the fellowship of the Holy Spirit be with you.*2Co 13:14*

Sharing. Church leaders sent a letter and prophets to guide and encourage the church and strengthen believers.*Acts 15:22-32* Paul and Silas traveled together, strengthening the churches.*Acts 15:40-41* Exhort one another, those believers whom you love, for whom you long, and who are your joy and crown, to stand firm in the Lord as dear friends.*Php 4:1* Renew your concern for fellow believers, looking for opportunities to show it.*Php 4:10* Be dear fellow servants in the Lord, sharing news of one another and events to encourage your hearts.*Col 4:7-9* Others long to know that you remain strong in your faith, that their labors for you have not been in vain.*1Th 3:5* Bring good news about others' faith and love, recalling pleasant memories of one another whom you long to see.*1Th 3:6* Impart spiritual gifts to one another to encourage each other's faith and make you strong.*Ro 1:11-12* Make every effort, out of intense longing, to see again fellow believers from whom you separate for a short time, in person rather than thought, even when Satan blocks your way.*1Th 2:17* Long to see other believers, so that joy may fill you.*2Ti 1:4* Pray that God's will is that you rejoin one another.*Ro 1:9-10*

Comfort. Look to Jesus, who endured such opposition from sinners, for encouragement when you are weary and losing heart.*Heb 12:3* Jesus told his disciples what would happen to him so that they would not fall away.*Jn 16:1* Jesus told the disciples so that they would remember his warning when their time came.*Jn 16:4* With God for us, no one can be against us.*Ro 8:31* Let co-workers in God's service strengthen and encourage you in your faith.*1Th 3:2* Take comfort and encouragement from witnessing your holy, righteous, and blameless leaders.*1Th 2:10-11* The Lord gives some authority to build you up rather than tear you down.*2Co 10:8* The strong should bear the weak's failings not to please themselves but to please their neighbors for their good, to build them up.*Ro 15:1-2* Even Christ did not please himself but instead bore insults directed toward others.*Ro 15:3* Our Lord Jesus Christ and God our Father encourage our hearts.*2Th 2:16-17* We draw hope from the encouragement the Scriptures provide.*Ro 15:4* God gives encouragement.*Ro 15:6-7* God comforts the downcast, sending others whom God has comforted, to comfort you.*2Co 7:6-7* Jesus says that God blesses those who weep now but who will later laugh.*Lk 6:21*

Care. Encourage one another daily, so that sin's deceitfulness hardens none of you.*Heb 3:13* Encourage one another with how God treats believers on Christ's return.*1Th 4:18* Encourage those who love one another in the faith.*Tit 3:15* Be dear fellow servants in the Lord, sharing news of one another to encourage your hearts.*Col 4:7-9* Encourage one another, building each other up just as you are doing.*1Th 5:11* Encourage the disheartened.*1Th 5:14* An elder should encourage others with sound doctrine.*Tit 1:9* Share with one another how your leaders are and what they are doing, for encouragement.*Eph 6:21-22* The love of believers for one another gives us great encouragement, refreshing the hearts of the Lord's people.*Phm 7* Encourage with all authority.*Tit 2:15* Take as your goal that you encourage believers' hearts.*Col 2:2* Encourage with great patience and careful instruction.*2Ti 4:2* Encourage each other's faith, making one another strong.*Ro 1:11-12* Take great encouragement from one another.*2Co 7:4* Be encouraged for yourself but especially delighted to see how happy others are for spirits others have refreshed.*2Co 7:13* Encourage one another.*2Co 13:11* Jesus said that anyone who welcomes a professing believer welcomes Jesus and his Father.*Matt 10:40* Those who welcome prophets gain prophet rewards, while those who welcome the righteous gain righteous rewards.*Matt 10:41* Give so little as a cup of cold water to Jesus's disciple, and you will certainly receive a reward.*Matt 10:42* The growing church experienced a time of peace and strengthening, living in the Lord's fear and with the Holy Spirit's encouragement.*Acts 9:31* Paul and Silas met with the brothers and sisters to encourage them.*Acts 16:40* Paul traveled throughout the region of Galatia and Phrygia, strengthening all the disciples.*Acts 18:23* Paul traveled through Macedonia, encouraging the people with many words.*Acts 20:1-2* When Priscilla and Aquila heard a Jew Apollos teach with great fervor and accurately about Jesus, but only knowing John's baptism, they explained to him God's way more adequately, encouraging him on his way to refute his Jewish opponents in public debate, proving from scriptures that Jesus is the Messiah.*Acts 18:24-28* The brothers and sisters in Rome came out to meet Paul and his companions, encouraging Paul who thanked God.*Acts 28:14-15*

Workers. After Pentecost, the apostles devoted themselves to teaching, fellowship, breaking bread, and prayer.*Acts 2:42* All the believers were together and had everything in common, selling property and possessions to give to anyone in need.*Acts 2:44* They continued to meet together in the temple courts, broke bread in their homes, and ate together with glad and sincere hearts, praising God and enjoying the favor of all people.*Acts 2:46-47* Paul was by God's grace what he was, and God's grace had good effect, making him work harder than the other apostles.*1Co 15:10* We are together prisoners of Christ Jesus, brothers and sisters, dear friends, fellow workers, and fellow soldiers, meeting in church and home, as we wish to one another grace and peace from God our Father and the Lord Jesus Christ.*Phm 1-3* Greet one another as fellow workers and prisoners in Christ Jesus, that the grace of the Lord Jesus Christ is with one another's spirit.*Phm 23-25* Regard one another as servants of Christ, entrusted with the mysteries that God has revealed.*1Co 4:1* Be partners and co-workers, an honor to Christ.*2Co 8:23* Welcome the friend of a partner in faith as you would welcome the partner.*Phm 17* Let your affection for one another be all the greater when you remember others' obedience.*2Co 7:15* Be glad when you can have complete confidence in another.*2Co 7:16* Prove your zeal to one another in many ways, while having great confidence in one another.*2Co 8:22* Jesus said that fire will salt everyone, salt is good, have salt among one another, and be at peace with one another.*Mk 9:49-50*

Love. Jesus told his disciples at the Last Supper the new command to love one another as Jesus had loved them.*Jn 13:34* Jesus said that his command was to love each other.*Jn 15:17* Everyone recognizes a Jesus disciple in that they love one another.*Jn 13:35* Jesus prayed that he had made the Father known to believers and would continue to do so, so that the love the Father has for Jesus will be in them and Jesus himself will be in them.*Jn 17:25-26* Summing up the law and prophets, Jesus said that in everything, do for others what you would have them do for you.*Matt 7:12* Jesus told religious leaders who asked him the greatest commandment, to love the Lord your God with all your heart, soul, and mind.*Matt 22:34-38, Mk 12:28-30* He then added that the second greatest is to love your neighbor as yourself, adding that all the law and prophets rest on these two commandments.*Matt 22:39-40, Mk 12:31-32* Jesus told a law teacher who wisely confirmed Jesus's answers, that the teacher was not far from God's kingdom, when saying that the greatest commands were to love God and neighbor.*Mk 12:34* Jesus said that if you love him, then keep his commands.*Jn 14:15* Jesus added that whoever has and keeps his commands is the one who loves him.*Jn 14:21* Anyone who does not love Jesus does not obey his teaching.*Jn 14:24* Jesus's command is to love one another as he loved us.*Jn 15:12* Do everything in love.*1Co 16:14* Spur one another on toward love.*Heb 10:24* Love one another as brothers and sisters.*Heb 13:1* You've heard from the start: love one another, and you will go from death to life.*1Jn 3:11-14* Wear love as a breastplate.*1Th 3:8* Love comes from a pure heart, good conscience, and sincere faith.*1Ti 1:5* Be an example in love for believers.*1Ti 4:11* Thank God for brothers and sisters whose love for one another increases.*2Th 1:3* Pursue love with those who call on the Lord out of a pure heart.*2Ti 2:22*

Expression. Jesus said that no one has greater love than to lay down one's life for one's friends.*Jn 15:13* Devote yourselves to one another in love, honoring one another above yourselves.*Ro 12:10* Put on love over all other virtues because love binds all virtues together in perfect unity.*Col 3:14* Love each other deeply to cover many sins.*1Pe 4:8* Care for one another like a nursing mother cares for her children, out of love, delighted to share your lives.*1Th 2:7-8* Be sincere with your love, hating evil while clinging to good.*Ro 12:9* Love does no harm to a neighbor and thus fulfills the law.*Ro 13:10* Show hospitality to strangers because some have unknowingly shown hospitality to angels.*Heb 13:2* Remember those in prison as if you were with them, and remember the mistreated as if you suffered, too.*Heb 13:3* Be faithful in helping followers even when they are strangers to you, so that they may tell the church about your love.*3Jn 5-6* Now that your obedience to the truth has purified you so that you love one another, love deeply, from the heart.*1Pe 1:22* Show your gentleness to all because the Lord is near.*Php 4:5* Although we all have knowledge, knowledge only puffs up while love instead builds up.*1Co 8:1* Love those to whom you preach.*2Co 11:11*

God. Because God is love, whoever lives in love lives in God, and God in them.*1Jn 4:16* Whoever loves God, God knows.*1Co 8:3* We love because he loved us.*1Jn 4:19* To love God is to keep his commands.*1Jn 5:3* God sums up the commandments not to commit adultery, not to murder, not to steal, and not to covet, and any other command, by commanding to love your neighbor as yourself.*Ro 13:9* We have had from the beginning the command to love one another, when love is itself obedience to God's commands. *2Jn 5-6* God loves his holy people.*Ro 1:7* One only has the love of God in one if one shares one's possessions with brothers and sisters in need.*1Jn 3:17* We should love one another because love comes from God and loving shows we know our Father.*1Jn 4:7* Those who do not love do not know God who is love.*1Jn 4:8* We should love one another because God loved us.*1Jn 4:11* Even though no one has seen God, if we love one another, then God who lives in us makes his love complete in us.*1Jn 4:12* Anyone claiming to love God but who nonetheless hates a brother or sister lies because anyone who does not love one whom they have seen cannot love God whom they have not seen, which is why God commands us to love brother and sister.*1Jn 4:20-21* God taught you to love each other, as you do love God's family, as you should more and more.*1Th 4:9-10* The

Lord directs the heart into God's love.₂Th 3:5 Believers in God should pursue love.₁Ti 6:11 God poured his love into our hearts through the Holy Spirit.Ro 5:5 God's Spirit gives us love.₂Ti 1:7 Love is the Spirit's fruit.Gal 5:22 May the love of God be with you.₂Co 13:14 Jesus said that his Father loves whoever loves Jesus, who will love and show himself to them.Jn 14:21 Jesus told the disciples that the Father loves them because they loved Jesus and believed that Jesus came from God.Jn 16:27

Christ. To love God, we must love his Son Jesus Christ and those who follow his Son, too.₁Jn 5:1-2 When God did not spare his own Son but gave him up for us, he showed that he graciously gives us everything.Ro 8:32 No one and nothing separates us from the love of Christ, even though we face death all day long.Ro 8:35-36 In everything, we are more than conquerors through him who loved us.Ro 8:37 Neither death nor life, angels nor demons, present nor future, nor any powers, neither height nor depth, nor anything else in all creation, can separate us from God's love in Christ Jesus our Lord.Ro 8:38-39 Follow God's example as dearly loved children by walking in love's way, like Christ loved and gave himself up for us as a fragrant offering and sacrifice to God.Eph 5:1 Carry each other's burdens, fulfilling Christ's law.Gal 6:2 By laying down his life for us, Jesus Christ showed us that we should lay down our lives for our brothers and sisters.₁Jn 3:16 God showed his love among us by sending his only Son to us that we might live through him.₁Jn 4:9 Our loving him matters little next to his loving us by sending his Son as a sacrifice to atone for our sins.₁Jn 4:10 Love one another in Christ Jesus.₁Co 16:24 Let Christ's love compel you, convinced that one died for all and thus all died.₂Co 5:14 Jesus said that the Jewish leaders who rejected him but who would accept others did not have God's love in their hearts.Jn 5:42-43 Jesus loved Mary, Martha, and Lazarus.Jn 11:5 John was the disciple reclining next to Jesus at the table, whom Jesus loved.Jn 13:23 The Jews believed that Jesus loved Lazarus so much that he wept at Lazarus's tomb before bringing him back to life.Jn 11:34-36 Jesus loved his own who were in the world, so that when Jesus knew that his hour had come to leave the world to go to the Father, he loved his own to the end.Jn 13:1 Jesus said that as his Father loved him, so he has loved us, and that we should remain in his love.Jn 15:9 Jesus said that we remain in his love when we keep his commands, just as he has kept his Father's commands and remains in his Father's love.Jn 15:10

Enemies. Jesus said to love your enemies, doing good to those who hate you, blessing those who curse you, and praying for those who mistreat you.*Lk 6:27-28* Jesus said that rather than exchange injury for injury, do not even resist an evil person, instead letting them slap you on one cheek just as on the other.*Matt 5:38-39, Lk 6:29* To the one who sues you to take your shirt, give them your coat, too.*Matt 5:40, Lk 6:29* With the one who forces you to go one mile, go two miles.*Matt 5:41* Jesus said that rather than love your neighbor and hate your enemy, you should love your enemies, too, even praying for those who persecute you, so that you may be your Father's children in heaven.*Matt 5:43-45* Jesus said that God causes his sun to rise on both the evil and good, and sends rain on both the righteous and unrighteous.*Matt 5:45* You get no special reward for loving those who love you because even non-believers do that.*Matt 5:46* Same thing if you greet only your own acquaintances, when again you are doing nothing more than non-believers, who also do the same.*Matt 5:47* Jesus said instead to be perfect, as your heavenly Father is perfect.*Matt 5:48* Jesus said that even sinners do good to those who do good to them.*Lk 6:33* Even sinners lend to those whom they expect to repay.*Lk 6:34* We should love enemies, do good to them, and lend to them without expecting repayment, so that our reward will be great in heaven and we will be the Most High's children, because he is kind to the ungrateful and wicked.*Lk 6:35* Jesus also said that the love of most will grow cold because of wickedness's increase toward the age's end.*Matt 24:12*

Cautions. If you speak in other languages, even of angels, but without love, then you only make an instrument's loud noise.*1Co 13:1* If you foretell the future and fathom every mystery, and your faith moves mountains, but without love, then you are nothing.*1Co 13:2* If you give everything to the poor and your body to hardship just to boast, but without love, you gain nothing.*1Co 13:3* Love is patient and kind, does not envy or boast, and is not proud.*1Co 13:4* Love does not dishonor others, seek itself, easily anger, or keep record of wrongs.*1Co 13:5* Love does not delight in evil but instead rejoices in truth.*1Co 13:6* Love always protects, trusts, hopes, and perseveres.*1Co 13:7* Love never fails, even though prophecies cease, speaking stops, and knowledge disappears.*1Co 13:8* We know and we prophesy only in part, but when things are finally complete, parts disappear.*1Co 13:9-10* We were once children, talking, thinking, and reasoning like children, but when we grew up, we stopped acting childishly.*1Co 13:11* We now see only a rough reflection but then will see face to face, just as we now know only a little but then will know everything, even as others will know us fully.*1Co 13:12* Only faith, hope, and love remain, with love the greatest.*1Co 13:13*

Joy. Jesus told us about his love and his Father's love so that his joy could be in us, completing our joy.*Jn 15:11* Jesus told the disciples that they would rejoice when he returned again, like a woman giving birth forgets her anguish out of joy for the child, and no one would take away the disciples' joy.*Jn 16:21-22* Jesus prayed that he was coming to the Father but telling the disciples about it so that they could have the full measure of Jesus's joy within them.*Jn 17:13* The disciples were overjoyed when Jesus appeared to them after his resurrection.*Jn 20:20* Your faith rewards you with inexpressible and glorious joy in salvation.*1Pe 1:9* Give joyful thanks to the Father for sharing in the kingdom of light.*Col 1:12* Joy is the Spirit's fruit.*Gal 5:22* We take great joy in Jesus Christ our Lord presenting us before his glorious presence.*Jude 24-25* Rejoice in the Lord always, rejoice!*Php 4:4* Show the Holy Spirit's joy when suffering for the gospel message.*1Th 1:6* When the disciples returned rejoicing at their authority, the Holy Spirit filled Jesus with joy, and he praised his Father in heaven for hiding things from the wise while revealing things to his little children.*Lk 10:21* Jesus Rejoice always.*1Th 5:16* Be joyful in hope.*Ro 12:12* May the God of hope fill you with all joy as you trust in him.*Ro 15:13* Everyone who hears about your obedience rejoices because of you.*Ro 16:19* Rejoice as you strive for full restoration.*2Co 13:11* God set the Son above, anointing him with the oil of joy.*Heb 1:9* Brothers and sisters, rejoice in the Lord!*Php 3:1* Sing and make music from your heart to the Lord.*Eph 5:19-20* Jesus says to rejoice and be glad for persecution because of him, because your reward in heaven will be great.*Matt 5:12* Jesus says that God blesses those who weep now but who will later laugh.*Lk 6:21*

Others. Our greatest joy is when followers testify about one another's faithfulness to the truth.*3Jn 3-4* Unity in Christ makes one another's joy complete.*Php 2:2* Even when suffering in faithful sacrifice and service, be glad and rejoice with other believers.*Php 2:17-18* The love of believers for one another gives us great joy and encouragement, refreshing the hearts of the Lord's people.*Phm 7* We take heartfelt joy in our common salvation in God's grace.*Php 1:7-8* We take great joy when our children walk in the truth. *2Jn 4* We pray with joy for other believers.*Php 1:4-5* Let news of one another cheer you.*Php 2:19* Welcome a fellow believer in the Lord with great joy and honor, especially when they almost die for Christ's work.*Php 2:29-30* Rejoice greatly in the Lord when renewing your concern for a fellow believer.*Php 4:10* Rejoice in suffering for others as Christ suffered.*Col 1:24* Fellow believers are your joy.*1Th 2:19-20* Take joy in others' faith.*1Th 3:9* Long to see other believers, so that joy may fill you.*2Ti 1:4* Pray that the Lord's people favorably receive contributions that you share, so that you have joy and refreshing company.*Ro 15:31-32* Enjoy the hospitality of a generous believer among you.*Ro 16:23* Take such great pride in one another that in all your trouble, your joy knows no bounds.*2Co 7:4* Tell one another about your longing, sorrow, and concern for one another, so that your joy may be greater than ever.*2Co 7:7* Rejoice with those who rejoice, while mourning with those who mourn.*Ro 12:15*

Demonstrations. When appearing to the eleven disciples after his resurrection, Jesus led them out near Bethany, lifted his hands, blessed them, and went up into heaven, after which the disciples returned to Jerusalem with great joy, praising God continually at the temple.*Lk 24:50-53* After the Sanhedrin had the apostles flogged for proclaiming Christ's resurrection against their orders, the apostles rejoiced for God counting them worthy of suffering for Jesus's name.*Acts 5:41* Joy filled a jailer who believed in God and accepted baptism with his whole household, after Paul and Silas prayed and sang hymns, the earth shook, the prison doors flew open, and their chains fell off.*Acts 16:34*

Teaching

The New Testament makes plain that teaching is critically important, as Jesus's Great Commission itself said. The New Testament is, in effect, a teaching manual, calling us to preach with courage. God calls preachers and teachers to share the power of Christ's cross. The purpose of teaching is to share Christ's gospel and only the true gospel, not false doctrine, to save the lost while strengthening believers. Preachers and teachers deserve a wage, yet volunteers earn their own reward. See how the New Testament addresses teaching. Are you prepared in season and out to teach the gospel accurately?

Teachers. Jesus said that teachers who are kingdom disciples are like homeowners who bring out both old and new stored treasures.*Matt 13:52* The apostle Peter said that neglecting the ministry of the word of God to wait on tables is not right, and so the apostles appointed others to distribute food so that they could attend to prayer and the ministry of the word.*Acts 6:1-5* Hesitate to teach because God judges teachers more strictly.*Jas 3:1* Share all good things with the one who instructs you in God's word.*Gal 6:6* Sound teachers back up their writings with actions.*2Co 10:11* Training as a speaker does not matter next to knowledge.*2Co 11:6* Follow a teacher's example, as the teacher follows Christ's example.*1Co 11:1* You may imitate those believers whose gospel message you welcome, even as you imitate the Lord, even when suffering severely.*1Th 1:6* You may also become a model to other believers who learn of your faith in God.*1Th 1:7-8* Do not take into your house or welcome anyone who teaches incorrectly, or you will share in their wicked work. *2Jn 10-11* Speak to sensible people, letting them judge for themselves what you say.*1Co 10:15* The Lord's servant must be kind to everyone and able to teach.*2Ti 2:24* Jesus said that students should aspire to be like their teachers, not above their teachers.*Matt 10:24-25, Lk 6:40* When Priscilla and Aquila heard a Jew

Apollos teach with great fervor and accurately about Jesus, but only knowing John's baptism, they explained to him God's way more adequately, encouraging him on his way to refute his Jewish opponents in public debate, proving from scriptures that Jesus is the Messiah._{Acts 18:24-28}

Preaching. Jesus said that followers must first preach the gospel to all nations before the age's end._{Mk13:10} Jesus said to teach obedience in all that Jesus said._{Matt 28:18-20} Paul and Barnabas preached the gospel from city to city, winning a large number of disciples, strengthening the disciples, and encouraging them to remain faithful._{Acts 14:21-22} The Holy Spirit prevented Paul and his companions from entering one region to preach, and Jesus's Spirit would not allow them to enter another region, but a vision led Paul into Macedonia to preach the gospel there._{Acts 16:6-10} Paul reasoned with the Jews in the synagogue at Ephesus._{Acts 18:19-21} Preach the word, prepared in season and out of season, correcting and rebuking with great patience and careful instruction._{2Ti 4:2} Preach your message not with wise and persuasive words but demonstrating the Spirit's power._{1Co 2:4} Jesus said to speak at day what he tells you at night, and proclaim from rooftops what he whispers in your ear._{Matt 10:27} No one preaches unless sent to bring the good news._{Ro 10:15} The commanded preaching of a godly servant leader who follows Jesus Christ must further the faith of God's elect in the truth, fostering godliness leading to the promised eternal life._{Tit 1:1-3} Some preach Christ out of envy, rivalry, and selfish ambition to make trouble for those who preach Christ out of goodwill and love, in the gospel's defense._{Php 1:15-16} But whether one preaches from false or true motives, what matters is that we preach Christ and rejoice._{Php 1:18} Read scripture publicly, preaching and teaching diligently with your whole self and showing progress, rather than neglect your gift given to you through prophecy in elders' laid-on hands._{1Ti 4:13-15} A preacher serves God in the preacher's spirit when preaching the gospel of God's Son._{Ro 1:9}

Courage. The courage of the apostles Peter and John, whom the religious leaders knew were unschooled, ordinary men, astonished the leaders, who knew they had been with Jesus._{Acts 4:13} A crowd in Lystra, stirred up by some Jews from Antioch and Iconium, stoned Paul and dragged him outside the city, thinking he was dead, but Paul got up and returned to the city before leaving the next day._{Acts 14:19-20} Paul said that he did not hesitate to preach publicly and from house to house anything that would help._{Acts 20:20} Paul spent two years in Rome proclaiming God's kingdom and teaching about the Lord Jesus Christ with all boldness and no hindrance.*Acts 28:30-31* God may give Christ Jesus's ministers grace to boldly remind others of important points.*Ro 15:15* Teach and rebuke with all authority, not letting anyone despise you.*Tit 2:15* Do not let the sufferings of a teacher discourage you because they are your glory.*Eph 3:13* Repeat your admonitions as safeguards for one another.*Php 3:1* We proclaim Christ, admonishing and teaching everyone with all wisdom and all the energy Christ so powerfully works in us, strenuously contending so that we may present everyone fully mature in Christ.*Col 1:28* Contend hard not only for those whom you know but even those whom you have not met.*Col 2:1* Look for results when courageously preaching the gospel with God's help to fellow believers, even when facing strong opposition.*1Th 2:1-2* Remember the toil and hardship of fellow believers who work day and night not to be a burden to anyone while preaching God's gospel.*1Th 2:9* Be confident in the Lord that others will do as commanded.*2Th 3:4* Have confidence through Christ before God.*2Co 3:4* Pray that God keeps preachers safe from persecuting non-believers.*Ro 15:31-32* Join in one another's struggles to proclaim the gospel by praying for one another.*Ro 15:30* Death works against our teachers so that life works in us. *2Co 4:12*

God. God commissions gospel servants to present his word in its fullness.*Col 1:25* God appoints true and faithful teachers.*1Ti 2:7* No prophecy is by the prophet's own interpretation because prophecy never originated in human will, but prophets instead spoke from God as the Holy Spirit carried them along.*2Pe 1:20-21* Speak as approved by God and entrusted with the gospel, to please God rather than people.*1Th 2:4* Urge one another to live worthy of God.*1Th 2:10-12* Instruct one another by the Lord Jesus's authority how to live to please God, urging one another more and more to live as you are living in the Lord Jesus.*1Th 4:1-2* Do not claim competence in yourself but instead competence from God.*2Co 3:5* God makes us competent ministers of a new covenant not of the letter but of the Spirit, for the letter kills while the Spirit gives life.*2Co 3:6* State the truth plainly, and so commend yourself to everyone's conscience in God's sight.*2Co 4:2* Because God's mercy grants us this teaching ministry, we do not lose heart.*2Co 4:1* Persuade others out of your own fear of the Lord, because you are plain to God, and thus keep your conscience clear.*2Co 5:11* Be out of your mind for God but in your right mind for others.*2Co 5:13* We are Christ's ambassadors, God as if appealing through us, imploring on Christ's behalf to reconcile to God.*2Co 5:20*

Christ. Jesus amazed the crowds whom he taught because, unlike the law teachers, he had authority.*Matt 7:28-29* Jesus said that if they obey his teaching, then they will obey your teaching, too.*Jn 15:20* We do not preach ourselves but Jesus Christ as Lord, with ourselves as your servants for Jesus.*2Co 4:5* Wise and eloquent preaching must not empty Christ's cross of its power.*1Co 1:17* Proclaim God's testimony not with eloquence or human wisdom but instead knowing only Jesus Christ crucified, and that in weakness with great fear and trembling.*1Co 2:1-3* Our grace is to preach to Christ's boundless riches, making plain to everyone the mystery that our creator God hid in himself for ages past.*Eph 3:8-9* Persist in Christ's teaching, rather than running ahead without it, that you may retain both Father and Son.*2Jn 9* Be ready at all times to gently and respectfully tell others that Jesus is the reason for your hope, even as your good behavior contradicts and shames those who slander you.*1Pe 3:15-16* Take as your goal that you encourage hearts and unite in love, for the full riches of knowing God's mystery, namely, Christ.*Col 2:2* Let Christ's message dwell among you richly as you teach and admonish one another with all wisdom through psalms, hymns, and songs from the Spirit.*Col 3:16* Teachers should thank Christ Jesus our Lord, who strengthens them, that he considers them trustworthy, appointing them to his service.*1Ti 1:12*

Doctrine. Sound doctrine conforms to the gospel concerning the blessed God's glory.*1Ti 1:11* Stand firm and hold fast to sound teachings by word of mouth or writing.*2Th 2:15* Everything in the Scriptures is to teach us.*Ro 15:4* Speak God's words.*1Pe 4:11* Speak the truth in Christ, conscience confirming through the Holy Spirit.*Ro 9:1* Command and teach right things, without letting anyone look down on you because you are young.*1Ti 4:11* Teach only sound doctrine.*Tit 2:1* Demolish arguments and pretensions against knowing God, to capture every thought for obedience to Christ.*2Co 10:5* If the Spirit so encourages, then meet privately with esteemed leaders to ensure that you preach the true gospel rather than run your race in vain.*Gal 2:2* Do your best to present yourself to God for approval as a worker who correctly handles the word of truth.*2Ti 2:15* Teach using everyday examples.*Ro 6:19* My believing brothers and sisters are filled with knowledge and competent to instruct one another.*Ro 15:14* Send to one another faithful sons in the Lord that they may remind you of the good way of life in Christ Jesus, agreeing with the teaching in every church.*1Co 4:17* Who preaches doesn't matter because what gets preached matters, and what we believe matters.*1Co 15:11*

Evangelism. After the Sanhedrin stoned Stephen, and a great persecution broke out against the church, those whom the persecution scattered preached the word wherever they went.*Acts 8:1-4* Philip proclaimed the Messiah in Samaria, where crowds paid close attention after he performed signs, impure spirits came out of many, and many paralyzed and lame were healed, bringing great joy.*Acts 8:5-8* Paul said that his only aim was to testify to the good news of God's grace, preaching the kingdom, and that he did not hesitate to proclaim God's whole will, so that he was innocent of anyone's blood.*Acts 20:24-27* When large numbers of Rome's Jews came to hear Paul, Paul witnessed to them from morning until evening, explaining about God's kingdom, and trying from the law and prophets to persuade them about Jesus.*Acts 28:22-23* Do the work of an evangelist.*2Ti 4:5* Fully proclaim Christ's gospel.*Ro 15:19* To call on the Lord one must believe in him, while to believe in him one must hear of him, and to hear of him someone must preach.*Ro 10:14* Preach Christ's gospel where the Lord opens a door for you.*2Co 2:12* Make your ambition to preach Christ's gospel where not known, so that you do not build on someone else's foundation, and those whom no one told about Christ may see, hear, and understand.*Ro 15:20-21* Thank God, who always leads us as captives in Christ's triumphal procession, using us to spread the aroma of the knowledge of him everywhere.*2Co 2:14* To God, we are Christ's pleasing aroma among those whom he is saving and those who perish.*2Co 2:15* To one we are an aroma bringing death, while to the other an aroma bringing life, but who is equal to such a task?*2Co 2:16*

Sinners. Turning a sinner from the error of their way saves them from death while covering over many sins.*Jas 5:19-20* We preach the gospel even to those who are still dead in sin, so that while they live according to human standards as to the body, they might come to live by God as to the spirit.*1Pe 4:6* Put no stumbling block in anyone's path, to discredit your ministry.*2Co 6:3* Some must preach to the non-believer, while others to the believer, the same Spirit at work in each.*Gal 2:7-8* A preacher's obligation is both to the wise and foolish, which is reason to be eager to preach.*Ro 1:14-15* Gently instruct opponents in the hope that God will grant them repentance leading them to a knowledge of the truth and that they come to their senses.*2Ti 2:25-26* One may take pride in ministry to outsiders in the hope that insiders will envy enough to turn to salvation.*Ro 11:13-14*

Others. Help older men to be temperate, worthy of respect, self-controlled, and sound in faith, loving, and enduring, and older women to be reverent, not to slander or to drink much wine, and to teach the good.~Tit 2:1-3~ Older women should urge younger women to love their husbands and children and be self-controlled, pure, busy at home, kind, and subject to their husband, so that no one maligns God's word.~Tit 2:4-5~ Older men should set a good example for young men to be self-controlled.~Tit 2:6-7~ Teaching should have integrity, seriousness, and soundness that no one can condemn, shaming opponents who thus have nothing bad to say.~Tit 2:7-8~ Teach workers to obey their supervisors in everything, to please them, not to talk back to them, and not to steal from them, instead showing their trustworthiness, to make attractive teaching about God our Savior.~Tit 2:9-10~ Teach the people to submit to rulers and authorities, obey, do good, slander no one, be peaceable and considerate, and be gentle toward everyone.~Tit 3:1-2~ Instruct how people should conduct themselves in the church.~1Ti 3:15~ Instruct the people so that no one may be open to blame.~1Ti 5:7~ Instruct without partiality or favoritism, as in the sight of God and Christ Jesus and the elect angels.~1Ti 5:21~ Write to correct others when absent, so as not when present to be harsh with the authority the Lord gave you for building up others, not for tearing down.~2Co 13:10~ Jesus cautioned not to give dogs what is sacred or throw your pearls to pigs, because they'll just trample them while tearing you to pieces.~Matt 7:6~

Wages. Jesus said to his disciples not to take money while traveling to teach because the worker is worth the keep.~Matt 10:9-10, Mk 6:8, Lk 9:3, 10:7~ Just search for a worthy person in whose home to stay.~Matt 10:11~ If a town welcomes you, then heal the sick while eating what they offer and telling them that God's kingdom is near.~Lk 10:8~ If no one welcomes and supports you, then still tell them that God's kingdom is near, but leave, knowing that judgment day will be very bad for that town.~Matt 10:14-15, Mk 6:10-11, Lk 10:10-12~ Leave that town, shaking the dust off your feet.~Lk 9:4-5, Lk 10:10-11~ Those who preach and teach deserve their wages.~1Ti 5:17-18~ Teachers could reasonably claim food, drink, and other support from you so that they need not work, and could take along with them a believing wife, just as soldiers do not serve at their own expense, vineyard planters get to eat their own grapes, and those tending flocks get to drink the flock's milk.~1Co 9:4-7~ Human authority and the Law say the same thing, not to muzzle an ox while treading the grain, when we're not talking about oxen here.~1Co 9:8-9~ God says so for human teachers that whoever plows and threshes should share the harvest.~1Co 9:10~ Those who sow spiritual seed should reap a material harvest.~1Co 9:11~ If others get your support, then teachers of the word should also, even if they choose to decline it and instead accept anything rather than hinder Christ's gospel.*1Co 9:12* Those who serve in the temple get their food from the temple, and those who serve at the altar share in the offering.*1Co 9:13*

Volunteers. The Lord commands that those who preach the gospel should receive their living from the gospel, even if some choose not to use these rights and prefer to die for the ability to so boast.*1Co 9:14-15* The Lord compels some to preach.*1Co 9:16* Those who preach voluntarily have a reward, but those whom the Lord compels to preach simply discharge their trust.*1Co 9:17* Preaching the gospel for free rather than claiming a gospel preacher's rights creates a reward.*1Co 9:18* Unlike so many, some do not peddle God's word for profit but in Christ speak before God with sincerity, as sent from God.*2Co 2:17* Appreciate rather than condemn those who preach God's gospel to you free of charge.*2Co 11:7* Other churches pay when preachers serve some, perhaps you, for free.*2Co 11:8* Teachers remove an obstacle when they keep from burdening those to whom they preach.*2Co 11:9* Respect the teaching of the free apostle who saw Jesus our Lord and wrote you letters, making you the result of his work and seal of his apostleship in the Lord.*1Co 9:1-3*

Building. Look forward to the city with foundations, whose architect and builder is God.*Heb 11:10* You are God's building, on which, by God's grace, another laid a foundation as a wise builder, after which someone else builds on it but should build with care.*1Co 3:9-10* No one can lay any foundation other than the one already laid, which is Jesus Christ.*1Co 3:11* If anyone builds on this foundation using gold, silver, costly stones, wood, hay, or straw, then judgment day's fire will test and show their work for what it is.*1Co 3:12-13* Make your ambition to preach Christ's gospel where not known, so that you do not build on someone else's foundation, and those whom no one told about Christ may see, hear, and understand.*Ro 15:20-21* As you approach the living stone Jesus whom God chose as precious but humans rejected, God is building you like living stones into a spiritual house and ministry offering sacrifices God accepts through Jesus.*1Pe 2:4-5*

Builder. Don't say anything unwholesome but only what builds others up as they need, benefitting those who listen.*Eph 4:29* Build each other up just as you are doing.*1Th 5:11* The strong should bear the weak's failings not to please themselves but to please their neighbors for their good, to build them up.*Ro 15:1-2* When you build yourself up in your most holy faith and pray in the Holy Spirit, you keep yourself in God's love.~Jude 20-21~ When the building survives, then the builder receives a reward.~1Co 3:14~ If the building burns, then the builder loses but God still saves, even while the builder escapes through the flames.~1Co 3:15~

Temple. When Jesus turned over the money changers' tables in the temple courts, and the Jews asked his authority, Jesus replied that he would raise the temple again if they destroyed it, referring to his body, not the building.~Jn 2:18-21~ When the disciples called Jesus's attention to the temple and its buildings, Jesus replied that every stone would fall.~Matt 24:1-2, Mk 13:1-2, Lk 21:5-6~ You are God's temple, with God's Spirit dwelling in your midst.~1Co 3:16~ If anyone destroys God's temple, then God will destroy that person, because God's temple is sacred, and you together are that temple.~1Co 3:17~ We are the living God's temple, God living with us and walking among us, he our God, and we his people.~2Co 6:16~ The Lord gives some persons authority to build you up rather than tear you down.~2Co 10:8~ Jesus was faithful to God who appointed him, just as Moses was faithful in God's house.~Heb 3:2~ Jesus gets greater honor than Moses, just as a house's builder has greater honor than the house.~Heb 3:3~ Someone builds every house, but God builds everything.~Heb 3:4~ Moses was a faithful servant in God's house, witnessing what God would say in the future.~Heb 3:5~ Christ is the faithful Son over God's house, where we are God's house, if we hold firmly to our confidence and the hope in which we glory.~Heb 3:6~ Jesus told the disciples at the Last Supper not to let things trouble their hearts because his Father's house with many rooms has a place that Jesus was preparing for them and that he would come back to take them there so that they could be where he is.~Jn 14:1-3~

Discerning. Entrust to reliable and qualified teachers the sound teaching that you learn.~2Ti 2:2~ Hold, with faith and love in Christ Jesus, to the sound teaching that you learned, guarding the good deposit entrusted you, with the help of the Holy Spirit living in you.~2Ti 1:13-14~ Praise to you for remembering your teacher in everything and for holding to the teaching just as taught.~1Co 11:2~ Remember the lessons you learned from teachers who were with you.~2Th 2:5~ Don't make a teacher have to be bold toward you in person by living under the standards of this world.~2Co 10:2~ Don't let hard teaching frighten you unduly, even when weighty and forceful.~2Co 10:9-10~ Some receive visions and revelations from the Lord.~2Co 12:1~ Some God catches up to paradise to hear inexpressible things that no one may tell.~2Co 12:4~ Believers cannot do anything against the truth but only for the truth.~2Co 13:8~ Jesus said to submit to him and learn from him because he is gentle and humble, and he will give your soul rest.~Matt 11:29~

Obedient. Thank God that you now obey the teaching from your heart.*Ro 6:17* You should rely completely on the gospel prophecy, paying attention to it as to a light shining in a dark place, until the day dawns in your heart.*2Pe 1:19* Do not be foolish, but know the Lord's will.*Eph 5:17* Others taught you to put off your former way of life and old self corrupted by its deceitful desires.*Eph 4:22* Teachers taught you to be made new in the attitude of your minds while putting on the new self, created to be like God in true righteousness and holiness.*Eph 4:23-24* Even while you obey God, whether your teachers are present or absent, continue to work out your salvation with fear and trembling, so that God may work in you to fulfill his good purpose.*Php 2:12-13* Anyone who rejects instruction rejects not just a person but God.*1Th 4:8* Keep away from idle believers who do not live as taught.*2Th 3:6* Do not refuse God who warned you from heaven because those who refused his earthly warning did not escape, and how much less you will escape.*Heb 12:25* Then, his voice shook the earth, but now he promises that his voice will shake earth and heaven, leaving only what does not shake.*Heb 12:26-27* The angels' message bound those who heard it, so that every violation and disobedience received just punishment.*Heb 2:2*

Mature. Move beyond elementary teachings about Christ, to maturity, not just to foundations like repenting from acts leading to death, having faith in God, cleansing rites, laying on of hands, resurrection of the dead, and eternal judgment.*Heb 6:1-2* God will permit you to reach maturity.*Heb 6:3* Stop thinking like children, except as to evil, but otherwise think like adults.*1Co 14:20* Like babies, crave pure spiritual milk, growing up in your salvation while knowing that the Lord is good.*1Pe 2:2-3* Be a good minister of Christ Jesus, nourished on the faith's truths and good teaching.*1Ti 4:6* Get ready for solid spiritual food, not just milk.*1Co 3:2* If you must live on milk, as still a spiritual infant, then you will not learn about righteousness.*Heb 5:13* Desire solid food for the mature, constantly training yourself to distinguish good from evil.*Heb 5:14* Aspire to teach rather than to need someone to teach you again elementary truths of God's word.*Heb 5:12* Jesus said to Nicodemus of the Jewish ruling council that even though Nicodemus was Israel's teacher, Nicodemus did not even believe of earthly things, no less the heavenly things of which Jesus spoke.*Jn 3:10-12*

Listening. Jesus said that the reason he was born and came into the world was to testify to the truth and that everyone on truth's side listens to him.*Jn 18:37* Jesus said that whoever has ears to hear, let them hear.*Mk 4:9,*

Mk 4:23, Lk 8:8 Jesus also said to consider carefully what you hear because with the measure you use, God will measure to you and even more, giving more to those who have and taking the little from those who do not have.*Mk 4:24-25* Jesus also said that whoever listens to his disciples listens to him, but whoever rejects them rejects him.*Lk 10:16* Jesus added that blessed are the eyes that see what the disciples saw because many prophets and kings wanted to see and hear it but did not.*Lk 10:23-24* Jesus said that whoever belongs to God hears what God says and that if you do not hear God, then you do not belong to God.*Jn 8:47* Mary sat at Jesus's feet listening to Jesus while preparations distracted Martha, worrying and upsetting Martha that Mary wasn't helping.*Lk 10:38-40* Jesus said that one needs only one thing, and Mary had chosen the better thing, which no one would take away.*Lk 10:41-42* Jesus also said that God blesses those who hear and obey his word.*Lk 11:28* After Pentecost, Peter told the crowd that Moses had said that the Lord your God would raise up a prophet from among them to whom they must listen or be completely cut off.*Acts 3:22-23* The apostle Paul warned the sailors who took him to Rome that if they sailed in the dangerous conditions, then their voyage would be a disaster, but they didn't listen to him and so lost everything including the ship in a storm, although they listened to Paul at the shipwreck and so all lived, after Paul told them to eat, thanked God, and broke bread for them.*Acts 27:10-44* Pay the most careful attention to what you have heard so as not to drift away.*Heb 2:1* Some people do not listen even when the Lord speaks to them in other languages and through foreigners.*1Co 14:21* Listen first before speaking.*Jas 1:19* Unless you who believe yourself religious hold your tongue, your religion is worthless.*Jas 1:26* All of us fail in many ways, but if you speak only without fault, then you do better keeping yourself from failing.*Jas 3:2* Just as a bit turns a horse, a rudder turns a ship, and a small spark sets a forest on fire, so, too, does the tongue turn and enflame us in evil with its great boasts.*Jas 3:3-6* We tame many animals but cannot tame our own tongue, the restless evil from which spreads deadly poison.*Jas 3:7-8* Even though we praise our Lord and Father, we immediately curse others whom God made in his likeness, proving our praise corrupt because one spring cannot produce two different waters or one tree two different fruit.*Jas 3:9-12* Jesus said that the evil person with an evil heart speaks evil, just as the bad tree bears bad fruit, whereas a good person speaks good from stored-up good.*Matt 12:33-35* Jesus also said that on judgment day, everyone must account for every empty word they've spoken because words either acquit or condemn.*Matt 12:36-37* You did not harden your heart when you heard about Christ and learned from others the truth that is in Jesus.*Eph 4:20-21* Listen to what benefits you and builds you up.*Eph 4:29*

Christ. When the disciples returned rejoicing at their authority, the Holy Spirit filled Jesus with joy, and he praised his Father in heaven for hiding things from the wise while revealing things to his little children.*Lk 10:21* You must accept the preaching that God raised Christ from the dead, rather than say resurrection doesn't happen.*1Co 15:12* Only those who are perishing do not see the gospel.*2Co 4:3* This age's god has blinded the minds of non-believers, so that they cannot see the gospel's light displaying the glory of Christ, who is the image of God.*2Co 4:4* Regard no one from a worldly perspective, as you once regarded Christ but no longer do.*2Co 5:16* Do not ignore the Lord's greater salvation message, confirmed by those who heard him.*Heb 2:3* God testified to the salvation message by signs, wonders, miracles, and the Holy Spirit's gifts distributed at his will.*Heb 2:4* Holy brothers and sisters, share in your heavenly calling by fixing your thoughts on Jesus, our apostle and high priest.*Heb 3:1* Your teachers need not commend themselves or have letters of recommendation because you are written on their hearts, a letter that everyone knows and reads.*2Co 3:1-2* You are a letter from Christ, the result of another's ministry, written not with ink but with the Spirit of the living God, not on stone tablets but on tablets of human hearts.*2Co 3:3*

Striving. Train yourself to be godly, for while physical training is of some value, godliness has value for all things in the present life and life to come.*1Ti 4:7-9* Labor and strive, having put your hope in the living God.*1Ti 4:10* Watch your life and doctrine closely, persevering in them to save both yourself and your hearers.*1Ti 4:16* The teaching and way of life you should know involves purpose, faith, patience, love, and endurance.*2Ti 3:10-11* Continue in what you learned and are convinced because you know those from whom you learned it and its source in the Holy Scriptures.*2Ti 3:14-15* Apply these things to yourself to benefit others, so that they may learn from you not to go beyond the writing.*1Co 4:6* God said that if you hear his voice, then not to harden your heart.*Heb 4:7* You will be hard to teach if you no longer try to understand.*Heb 5:11* Jesus said that Pharisees and Sadducees can read the sky for the weather but can't discern the signs of the times.*Matt 16:1-4* Jesus challenged the crowd that they could tell when it would rain or be hot but that they were hypocrites for not interpreting the times.*Lk 12:54-56* They needed to judge for themselves what was right.*Lk 12:57* When someone asked Jesus if God would save only a few, Jesus repeated to enter through the narrow door because many will try to enter, but the house's owner will close the door, leaving many knocking and pleading outside, to whom the owner will say that he doesn't know those evildoers.*Lk 13:22-27*

Wisdom. If you want wisdom, then ask God who will give you lots of it whether you have faults or not.*Jas 1:6* As long as you live, think of these words rather than just know them, and help others do likewise, so that you remain firmly established in the truth you now have.*2Pe 1:12 -14* Think about true, noble, right, pure, lovely, admirable, excellent and praiseworthy things.*Php 4:8* Practice whatever you learn, receive, or hear from the wise, or see in them, so that the God of peace is with you.*Php 4:9* You are in Christ Jesus, who is our wisdom from God, our righteousness, holiness, and redemption, because of God.*1Co 1:30* The Lord gives insight.*2Ti 2:7* The Holy Scriptures make you wise for salvation through faith in Christ Jesus.*2Ti 3:14-15* Remember what you were like when God first called you, neither wise nor influential, and not many of noble birth.*1Co 1:26*

Speaking. Jesus said not to worry beforehand what to say when brought before your persecutors because he will give you words and wisdom to say, that your adversaries will not be able to resist or contradict.*Lk 21:14-15* Speak wisdom among the mature, but not the wisdom of this age or of the rulers of this age, who are coming to nothing.*1Co 2:6* Declare God's wisdom, a hidden mystery that God destined for our glory before time began.*1Co 2:7* Rulers did not understand it, or they would not have crucified the Lord of glory.*1Co 2:8* Stimulate one another to wholesome thinking so that you recall the prophets' words and our Lord and Savior's commands shared through the apostles.*2Pe 3:1-2* Be wise in the way you interact with outsiders, making the most of every opportunity to season with salt your graceful conversation, knowing how to answer everyone.*Col 4:5-6*

Distinguishing. Jesus said that wisdom's children prove wisdom right.*Lk 7:35* Bitter envy and selfish ambition that somehow pass for wisdom are not God's wisdom but are instead earthly and demonic, sowing disorder and evil.*Jas 3:14-16* God's wisdom is pure, peace-loving, considerate, submissive, full of mercy and good fruit, and impartial and sincere, helping you sow in peace and reap righteousness.*Jas 3:17-18* Do not treat prophecies with contempt but test them all.*1Th 5:19-22* Be wise about what is good and innocent about what is evil.*Ro 16:19* Jesus said to be as shrewd as snakes while as innocent as doves.*Matt 10:16* Although we all have knowledge, knowledge only puffs up while love instead builds up.*1Co 8:1* Those who think they know don't know as they should know.*1Co 8:2* Jews demand signs and Greeks look for wisdom, but we preach Christ crucified, a stumbling block to Jews and foolishness to other non-believers but God's power and wisdom to those whom God called.*1Co 1:22-24* Jesus said that deeds prove wisdom right.*Matt 11:19*

World. Jesus praised his Father, Lord of heaven, for hiding the gospel from the wise and learned while revealing it to little children.*Matt 11:25-26* God makes foolish the world's wisdom.*1Co 1:20* God's wisdom is that the world not know him through its own wisdom, but instead, seemingly foolish gospel preaching pleased God to save those who believe.*1Co 1:21* God's foolishness is wiser than human wisdom, and God's weakness is stronger than human strength.*1Co 1:25* God chose the world's foolish things to shame the wise and weak things to shame the strong.*1Co 1:27* Rest your faith not on human wisdom but on God's power.*1Co 2:5* The message we speak is not human wisdom but as the Spirit taught us, explaining spiritual realities with Spirit-taught words.*1Co 2:13* The world's wisdom is foolishness in God's sight because he catches the wise in their craftiness.*1Co 3:19* The Lord knows that thoughts of the wise are futile.*1Co 3:20*

Families

The New Testament addresses families at length. Marriage is right, but unmarried devotion to the Lord is better. Those who marry should remain married, although the believing spouse may let the non-believing spouse go. A husband should give himself up for his wife, like Christ has for the church. A wife should likewise love her husband, women being the glory of men. Intimacy is for marriage. Children should obey and care for their family, while fathers should not discourage or exasperate their children. And within families, we should practice the disciplines that keep us spiritually fit. See how the New Testament addresses families. Are you conducting yourself within your family as you should?

Unmarried. When the disciples asked Jesus if not marrying was better than marrying, Jesus said that whether one cannot engage in sexual intimacy or chooses not to do so, one should accept it if one can.*Matt 19:10-12* When Jesus spoke with the Samaritan woman at the well, he told her that she'd had five husbands and that the man she was with then was not her husband.*Jn 4:16-18* The unmarried and widows should find remaining unmarried good, unless they cannot control themselves, in which case they should marry so as not to burn with passion.*1Co 7:9* Outside of any command, and instead as a trustworthy judgment, the unmarried should find remaining unmarried good.*1Co 7:25-26* Those who are already engaged to marry should not seek release, but if you are not yet engaged, then don't look for a spouse.*1Co 7:27* If you can, then avoid marriage concerns and needing to please one's spouse, thus avoiding the world's affairs, and focus instead on pleasing the Lord, involved in the Lord's affairs.*1Co 7:32-34* This advice is not to restrict you but for your own good, to live right in undivided devotion to the Lord.*1Co 7:35* Marrying is right, but not marrying is better.*1Co 7:38* The widow is probably happier if she stays unmarried.$_{1Co\ 7:40}$ Those who care for widows should not let them burden the church, so that the church can help widows with real need.$_{1Ti\ 5:16}$

Marriage. If you do marry, then you have not sinned, although those who marry face many troubles in this life that they could avoid.$_{1Co\ 7:28}$ You do not sin by marrying one toward whom you might not be acting honorably while engaged, because of strong passions, if you want to marry and feel you should.$_{1Co\ 7:36}$ But nothing compels you to do so if you make up your mind and control your will.$_{1Co\ 7:37}$ The Lord's command to the married is that wife must not separate from husband, and if separated must stay unmarried or reconcile, and husband must not divorce wife.$_{1Co\ 7:10}$ Outside of any command, if you marry a non-believer with whom you are willing to live, then don't divorce.$_{1Co\ 7:12-13}$ A believing spouse sanctifies a non-believing spouse, making the children holy.$_{1Co\ 7:14}$ But if the unbelieving spouse leaves, let that spouse go, because nothing binds the believing spouse then, God having called believers to live in peace.$_{1Co\ 7:15}$ A believing spouse doesn't know if their faith will save the other.$_{1Co\ 7:16}$ When religious leaders asked Jesus whose wife a woman would be at the resurrection if she married seven times with each marriage ending in her husband's death, Jesus answered that people at the resurrection will not be married because they will be like angels in heaven.$_{Matt\ 22:23-30,\ Mk\ 12:18-24}$

Divorce. Jesus said that anyone who divorces, except for sexual immorality, makes the divorced spouse the victim of adultery, and anyone who marries a divorced person commits adultery.$_{Matt\ 5:31-32}$ When the Pharisees asked Jesus about divorce, Jesus said that God created men and women for a man to leave parents to unite with his wife, the two becoming one flesh.$_{Matt\ 19:3-5,\ Mk\ 10:6-8}$ Jesus then said that no one should separate the one flesh that God has joined together.$_{Matt\ 19:6,\ Mk\ 10:9}$ When the Pharisees pointed out that Moses permitted divorce, Jesus replied that Moses did so because their hearts were hard, when it had not been so from the beginning.$_{Matt\ 19:8,\ Mk\ 10:3-5}$ Jesus then said that any man who divorces his wife, except for sexual immorality, to marry another woman, commits adultery.$_{Matt\ 19:9}$ Jesus repeated that a man divorcing to marry another woman or woman divorcing to marry another man commits adultery.$_{Lk\ 16:18}$ Privately to the disciples, Jesus said that whether man or woman divorces, if they remarry, they commit adultery.$_{Mk\ 10:10-12}$ A woman must remain married to her husband while he lives, but if her husband dies, then she may marry whomever she wishes if he belongs to the Lord.$_{1Co\ 7:39}$

Husbands. Husband, love your wife rather than be harsh with her._{Col 3:19} A husband should treat his gentler wife with respect, as fellow heir of God's gracious gift of life, so that nothing hinders the husband's prayers._{1Pe 3:7} Like Christ loved and gave himself up for the church, a husband must love and give himself up for his wife so that she is holy, cleansed by God's word, and pure, radiant, and blameless toward her husband._{Eph 5:25-27} A husband should love his wife as his own body and self because no one hates their own body._{Eph 5:28-29} A husband must leave father and mother, uniting to his wife to become one flesh._{Eph 5:31} A husband must love his wife as he loves himself, while the wife must respect her husband._{Eph 5:33} The head of every man is Christ, of woman is man, and of Christ is God._{1Co 11:3} Man did not come from woman, but woman from man._{1Co 11:8} Men who pray or prophesy with covered head dishonor the head._{1Co 11:4} Men should not cover the head because they are the image and glory of God._{1Co 11:7} The nature of things teaches you that long hair disgraces a man, while long hair is woman's covering glory._{1Co 11:14-15} No one need contend because God's churches have no other practice._{1Co 11:16}

Wives. Wife, submit yourself to your husband, as befits the Lord._{Col 3:18} A wife should win her husband to the word by her pure, reverent, and submissive behavior._{1Pe 3:1-2} A wife's beauty should not come from fancy hair and clothes, gold jewelry, and other outward adornment but from the inner unfading beauty of a gentle and quiet spirit in which God sees great worth, like holy women in the past._{1Pe 3:3-6} A wife should submit to her husband in everything as we all submit to the Lord, with the husband wife's head as Christ heads his body, the church submitting to Christ._{Eph 5:22-24} Women who pray or prophesy with uncovered head dishonor the head as if shaved._{1Co 11:5-6} God did not create man for woman but woman for man, so that women should for the angels have authority over their own head._{1Co 11:9-10} Still, in the Lord, women and men depend on one another because as woman came from man, so woman bears man, with everything coming from God._{1Co 11:11} Judge for yourselves whether women should pray to God with head uncovered._{1Co 11:13} Women should be worthy of respect, not malicious talkers but temperate and trustworthy in everything._{1Ti 3:11} Women are the glory of men._{1Co 11:7}

Intimacy. Having no sexual relations is good, but to avoid sexual immorality, have sexual relations only with one's own spouse._{1Co 7:1-2} Share intimacy with your spouse, yielding to one another as the other wishes, giving your spouse authority over your own body.*1Co 7:3-4* Avoid depriving one another when agreeing to devote yourselves to prayer for a time, but then come together again so that Satan does not tempt your lack of self-control.*1Co 7:5* Having spousal relations is a concession, not a command, because having no spouse or relations may be better, although each has one's own gift from God.*1Co 7:6-7* Honor marriage, and keep the marriage bed pure, because God judges adulterers and the sexually immoral.*Heb 13:4* A younger widow whom sensual desire tempts should remarry, have children, manage the home, and give the enemy no opportunity for slander, rather than turning away to follow Satan.*1Ti 5:14-15* Mourn and put out of your fellowship those among you who practice sexual immorality that not even non-believers practice, like a man sleeping with his father's wife.*1Co 5:1-2* Treat younger men as brothers, older women as mothers, and younger women as sisters, with absolute purity.*1Ti 5:1-2*

Children. Jesus said not to despise a little child because their heavenly angels always see his Father's face in heaven.*Matt 18:10* When the disciples tried sending away parents who brought their little children to Jesus for him to touch them and pray for them, Jesus said to let the little children come to him because heaven's kingdom belongs to such as them.*Matt 19:13-15, Mk 10:13-15* Jesus then took the little children in his arms, placed his hands on them, and blessed them.*Mk 10:16* Children should obey their parents in the Lord, honoring father and mother, as the first commandment with a promise says, that they may enjoy a long and good earthly life.*Eph 6:1-3* Children, obey your parents in everything to please the Lord.*Col 3:20* Fathers should not exasperate their children but instead teach and train them in the Lord.*Eph 6:4* Fathers, don't make your children bitter, discouraging them.*Col 3:21* While many may guard you in Christ, few will be fathers to you in Christ Jesus, although one may through the gospel.*1Co 4:15* Imitate one who becomes like a father to you in Christ.*1Co 4:16* Do not rebuke an older man harshly, but exhort him as if your father.*1Ti 5:1* We celebrate that our children walk in the truth, just as the Father commanded.*2Jn 4* Children and grandchildren should put their religion into practice by caring for their family and so repaying parents and grandparents, because doing so pleases God.*1Ti 5:4*

Body. When Jesus turned over the money changers' tables in the temple courts, and the Jews asked his authority, Jesus replied that he would raise the temple again if they destroyed it, referring to his body, not the building.*Jn 2:18-21* When Christ came into the world, he said that

God did not desire sacrifice and offering, which did not please God, but instead God had prepared a body for Christ.*Heb 10:5-6* And by God's will and Jesus Christ's sacrifice of his body once for all, God has made us holy.*Heb 10:10* Be confident entering the Most Holy Place by Jesus's blood, the new and living way he opened for us, that is, his body.*Heb 10:19-20* God's revealed mystery is that through the gospel we are heirs together with his chosen people, members of one body, sharing the promise in Christ Jesus.*Eph 3:6*

Church. The Son is the head of the body, the church.*Col 1:18* God placed all things under Christ's feet, appointed him head over everything for the church, which is his body, the fullness of him who fills everything in every way.*Eph 1:22-23* Let the peace of Christ rule in your hearts because as members of one body, God called you to peace.*Col 3:15* You have only one body and one Spirit, just as God called you to one hope.*Eph 4:4* The bread we break participates in Christ's body.*1Co 10:16* We who are many are one body because we share one loaf.*1Co 10:17* Just as one body has many parts, so it is with Christ.*1Co 12:12* One Spirit baptized all, whether insider or outsider, slave or free, to form one body, giving each the same Spirit to drink.*1Co 12:13*

Parts. Even so the body has many parts, not just one.*1Co 12:14* Just like a natural body has parts, in Christ we form one body belonging to one another but with different gifts as God gave each of us grace.*Ro 12:5-6* No body part stops being part of the body, without the body losing sense.*1Co 12:15-17* God placed each part in the body, just as he wanted them to be.*1Co 12:18* The body would be nowhere if all parts were the same.*1Co 12:19* The one body has many parts.*1Co 12:20* No part can reject another part.*1Co 12:21* On the contrary, the weaker body parts are indispensable.*1Co 12:22* The less-honorable parts we treat with special honor, while unpresentable parts we treat with special modesty.*1Co 12:23* Ordinary parts need no special treatment, but God assembles the body, giving greater honor to parts lacking honor.*1Co 12:24* The body should have no division, its parts instead having equal concern for each other.*1Co 12:25* If one part suffers, then every part suffers with it, while if one part receives honor, every part rejoices.*1Co 12:26* You are Christ's body, and each one of you is a part.*1Co 12:27*

You. Strike a blow to your body to make it your slave so that after you preach to others, God will not disqualify you for the prize.*1Co 9:27* Your body is a temple of the Holy Spirit, who is in you and whom you received from God._1Co 6:19_ Honor God with your body because you are not your own, and God instead bought you at a price._1Co 6:20_ Our old self's crucifixion with him killed the sinful body, setting us free from sin and making us no longer slaves to sin._Ro 6:6-7_ Because God is merciful, offer your body as a living sacrifice, holy and pleasing to God, as your true and proper worship._Ro 12:1_ Do not let sin reign in your body, obeying its evil desires._Ro 6:12_ Do not offer any part of yourself as an instrument of wickedness._Ro 6:13_ God's will is that you control your own body to be holy and honorable._1Th 4:3-6_ We must put to death the body's misdeeds to live, rather than live for the flesh in which case we die._Ro 8:12-13_

Rules. Useless rules like those not to handle, taste, or touch certain things are merely human commands and teachings having only a false appearance of wisdom based on the body's harsh treatment._Col 2:21-23_ We preach the gospel even to those who are still dead in sin, so that while they live according to human standards as to the body, they might come to live by God as to the spirit._1Pe 4:6_ Yet God did not mean the body for sexual immorality but for the Lord, and the Lord for the body._1Co 6:13_ Never unite with a prostitute your body, which is a member of Christ, because the two bodies then become one flesh._1Co 6:15-16_ Flee sexual immorality because while all other sins are outside the body, sexual sin is against one's own body._1Co 6:18_ God did not mean the body for sexual immorality but for the Lord, and the Lord for the body._1Co 6:13_ A husband should love his wife as his own body and self because no one hates their own body._Eph 5:28-29_ A husband must leave father and mother, uniting to his wife to become one flesh._Eph 5:31_

Heaven. If the earthly tent in which we live suffers destruction, God gives us an eternal house in heaven, not built by human hands._2Co 5:1_ If Christ is in you, then even though your body dies because of sin, the Spirit gives life because of righteousness._Ro 8:10_ May your whole spirit, soul, and body be blameless at our Lord Jesus Christ's return._1Th 5:23_ We long to be in our heavenly dwelling, which will not leave us exposed._2Co 5:2-3_ In our earthly tent, we groan with burden, fearing deadly exposure while wanting heaven's protection from death._2Co 5:4_ Know with confidence that to be at home in the body is to be away from the Lord._2Co 5:6_ Prefer to be away from the body and at home with the Lord._2Co 5:8_ Make your goal to please him, whether at home in the body or away from it._2Co 5:9_ We must all appear before Christ's judgment seat to receive our due for things we did in the body, whether good or bad._2Co 5:10_

Giving. The Father in heaven, who does not change, gives the good and perfect gifts from above.*Jas 1:17* When Christ ascended, he took many captives while giving gifts to his people.*Eph 4:8* God's gifts are irrevocable.*Ro 11:29* Know the Spirit's gifts.*1Co 12:1* The same Spirit distributes different gifts.*1Co 12:4* God gives to each one the Spirit's manifestation for the common good.*1Co 12:7* The same Spirit distributes each gift to each one, just as he determines.*1Co 12:11* To one person, God gives wisdom through the Spirit, to another person knowledge by the same Spirit, to another faith by the same Spirit, to another gifts of healing by that one Spirit, and to others miraculous powers, prophecy, distinguishing between spirits, speaking in different tongues, or interpretation of tongues.*1Co 12:8-10* Just like a natural body has parts, in Christ we form one body belonging to one another but with different gifts as God gave each of us grace.*Ro 12:5-6* Because you eagerly desire the Spirit's gifts, choose and excel in those that build up the church.*1Co 14:12* If you think the Spirit has gifted you, then acknowledge the Lord's command because if you ignore the command, then others will ignore you.*1Co 14:37-38* Jesus said that from those to whom God gives much, God demands much, while he asks much more of those whom he entrusts with much.*Lk 12:48*

Generosity. Even in very severe trial, let your overflowing joy and extreme poverty well up in rich generosity.*2Co 8:2* Our Lord Jesus Christ's grace was that although he was rich, he became poor for your sake, so that his poverty would make you rich.*2Co 8:9* Give as much as able, even beyond your ability, entirely on your own.*2Co 8:3* Urgently plead for the privilege of sharing in service to the Lord's people.*2Co 8:4* Exceed expectations, giving first to the Lord and then by God's will to others.*2Co 8:5* When you excel in everything, whether faith, speech, knowledge, earnestness, or love, excel also in the grace of giving.*2Co 8:7* Jesus said not to store up destructible treasure on earth but instead indestructible treasures in heaven.*Matt 6:19-20, Lk 12:33* Your heart is wherever you keep your treasure.*Matt 6:21, Lk 12:34* Jesus said you can only serve one master, not two masters, because with two masters, you would hate one while loving the other, and thus you must serve only God, not money.*Matt 6:24* Whoever sows sparingly reaps sparingly, and whoever sows generously reaps generously.*2Co 9:6* God can bless you abundantly, so that you always have all you need while abounding in good works.*2Co 9:8* As you scatter freely your gifts to the poor, your righteousness endures forever.*2Co 9:9* God, who supplies seed to the sower and bread for food, also supplies and increases your store of seed to enlarge your righteousness harvest.*2Co 9:10* God enriches you in every way so that you can always be generous, resulting in thanksgiving to God.*2Co 9:11*

Measure. When Jesus watched rich people throw large amounts into the temple treasury, while a poor widow gave two small copper coins, he told the disciples that the widow had given more out of her poverty, everything on which she had to live, than the rich gave out of their riches.*Mk 12:41-43, Lk 20:41-44, 21:1-4* Each give what your heart decides, not reluctantly or under compulsion, for God loves cheerful givers.*2Co 9:7* If you are willing to give, then your gift is good based on what you have, not what you do not have.*2Co 8:12* The point is not to relieve others while pressing you hard but that equality exists.*2Co 8:13* Let your present plenty supply others' need, so that their plenty can later supply your need, equally.*2Co 8:14* Then, the one who gathers much will not have too much, and the one who gathers little will not have too little.*2Co 8:15* Be eager to help, so that others can boast about your readiness to give and so your enthusiasm stirs others to action.*2Co 9:2* Be ready, though, to meet the expectation of those who boast about you.*2Co 9:3* Otherwise, you may make them ashamed for having had such confidence in you.*2Co 9:4* Finish arrangements for the generous gifts you promise, being ready to give rather than giving grudgingly.*2Co 9:5* Finish the charitable acts of grace that you start for others.*2Co 8:6* When you are first to give and to have the desire to do so, still finish your giving, so that you match your eager willingness by completing it as you are able.*2Co 8:11*

Others. Jesus said to give to the one who asks you, and don't turn away from the one who wants to borrow from you.*Matt 5:42* Jesus said to give, and you will receive a good measure poured into your lap, your measure measured back to you.*Lk 6:37-38* Jesus said that when you give to the needy, not to announce it to everyone, as hypocrites do for honor from others that then becomes their only reward.*Matt 6:2* Instead, when you give to the needy, give in secret so that your Father, who sees your secrets, rewards you.*Matt 6:3* God puts into the heart concern for one another.*2Co 8:16* Welcome appeals for one another, participating with enthusiasm and your own initiative.*2Co 8:17* Your gifts not only supply the Lord's people's needs but also overflow expressions of thanks to God.*2Co 9:12* The gifts by which you prove yourself lead others to praise God for your obedience in confessing Christ's gospel and generosity in sharing with them and everyone else.*2Co 9:13* Without commanding giving, test your love's sincerity with the earnestness of others.*2Co 8:8* Their hearts go out in prayers for you because of the surpassing grace God has given you.*2Co 9:14* Gladly spend everything for another believer, and receive for yourself as well, showing that you love them and letting them love you.*2Co 12:15* When the disciples said that the woman who anointed Jesus with an expensive perfume should instead have sold the perfume to give money to the poor, Jesus said that the poor will always be with us and that she had instead done a beautiful thing about which people would hear throughout the world.*Matt 26:6-13, Mk 14:3-9*

    Types. Love by eagerly desiring the Spirit's gifts, especially foretelling the future.*1Co 14:1* Foretelling the future strengthens, encourages, and comforts others.*1Co 14:3* Foretelling the future edifies the church.*1Co 14:4* Every one of you does well to speak in an unknown language, but the one who foretells the future is greater, unless someone interprets the unknown language to edify the church.*1Co 14:5* Be eager to foretell the future, but do not forbid speaking in unknown languages.*1Co 14:39* Use your gifts to serve others, stewarding God's manifold graces.*1Pe 4:10* Anyone who speaks in an unknown language speaks only to God, not people, and so no one understands them as they utter mysteries by the Spirit.*1Co 14:3* Speaking in an unknown language edifies only yourself.*1Co 14:4* What good is speaking in an unknown language unless some revelation, knowledge, prediction, or word of instruction results?*1Co 14:6* No one knows the instrument's tune unless the musician distinguishes the notes.*1Co 14:7* The trumpet must sound a clear call to get soldiers ready for battle.*1Co 14:8* The world has many languages, each with meaning.*1Co 14:10* Speaking in a foreign language does not convey meaning.*1Co 14:11* Thus, unless you speak intelligibly, no one knows what you say, and you just speak into the air.*1Co 14:9* If you speak in an unknown language, then pray for interpretation.*1Co 14:13* Indeed, your spirit praying in an unknown language leaves your mind unfruitful.*1Co 14:14* Pray with your spirit while also praying with understanding, even as you sing with your spirit while also singing with understanding.*1Co 14:15* Praise God in ways that others can agree rather than so they don't know what you are saying, because otherwise, you may give thanks well enough but edify no one.*1Co 14:16-17* Be glad to speak unknown languages, but in the church prefer to speak five intelligible words that instruct others than ten thousand unknown words.*1Co 14:18-19*

    Apostles. After Pentecost, all the believers were together and had everything in common, selling property and possessions to give to anyone in need.*Acts 2:44* All the believers were one in heart and mind, no one claiming any possessions but instead sharing everything that they had, leaving no needy persons among them.*Acts 4:34* Believers sold land and houses, putting the money at the apostles' feet to distribute to anyone who had need.*Acts 4:34-37* But when a man sold a piece of property and with his wife's knowledge kept back some of the money for himself before putting the rest at the apostles' feet, Peter told him that Satan had caused him to lie not just to humans but to the Holy Spirit and God, so that the man promptly died.*Acts 5:1-6* When the man's wife repeated the lie, she, too, immediately fell down dead after Peter told her that she had conspired to test the Lord's Spirit.*Acts 5:7-11* Paul said that his hands supplied his needs and those of his companions, by that kind of hard work helping the weak, while remembering the Lord's words that better to give than to receive.*Acts 20:34-35*

Prayer. Pray in the Spirit on all occasions with all kinds of prayers and requests, remaining alert to pray continually for all the Lord's people.*Eph 6:18* Present your prayers, petitions, and requests to God with thanksgiving.*Php 4:6* We have not stopped praying that God fill you with knowledge of his will.*Col 1:9* Devote yourself to watchful and thankful prayer.*Col 4:2* Continually mention fellow believers in prayer, remembering before God our Father their faithful work, loving labor, and endurance inspired by hope in our Lord Jesus Christ.*1Th 1:2-3* Pray earnestly night and day that you may supply what others lack in faith.*1Th 3:10* Pray continually.*1Th 5:17* Brothers and sisters, pray for one another.*1Th 5:25* Constantly pray for one another that our God makes us worthy of his calling and by his power grants our every desire for goodness and every deed prompted by faith.*2Th 1:11* The widow alone and in need hopes in God, praying day and night for help.*1Ti 5:5* Night and day, constantly remember others in your prayers.*2Ti 1:3* Constantly remember one another in prayer while praying that God's will is that you rejoin one another.*Ro 1:9-10* Be faithful in prayer.*Ro 12:12*

Confident. Jesus said that if you believe, then you will receive whatever you ask in prayer.*Matt 21:22* Jesus said that if you remain in him and he remains in you, then ask whatever you wish, and he will do it for you.*Jn 15:7* Jesus told his disciples that the time was coming when they would not ask him anything but instead the Father would give them anything that they asked in Jesus's name, making their joy complete.*Jn 16:23-24* The prayer of a righteous person is powerful and effective, like Elijah praying first for no rain and then for rain, both prayers that God answered.*Jas 5:16-18* We are rightly confident that if we ask anything according to God's will, then he hears us and we have whatever we ask of him.*1Jn 5:14-15* Jesus said that about whatever two believers agree to pray, his heavenly Father will do for them, because where two or three gather in his name, Jesus is there with them.*Matt 18:19-20* Jesus said not to pray as hypocrites pray, to be seen by others, thus receiving their only reward.*Matt 6:5* Instead, close the door to your room so as to pray secretly to your unseen Father, who will then reward you.*Matt 6:6* Jesus said not to pray babbling like non-believers pray, thinking more words means better hearing.*Matt 6:7* Your Father knows what you need before you ask him.*Matt 6:8* Jesus says to ask because God gives it, seek because you will find, and knock knowing God opens the door to you.*Matt 7:7* Everyone who asks receives, seeks finds, and by knocking gets in.*Matt 7:8* Fathers give sons bread when asked, not stones, and fish when asked, not snakes, and eggs when asked, not scorpions.*Matt 7:9-10, Lk 11:11-12* Your Father in heaven will give much better gifts than you would give for your children.*Matt 7:11* Indeed, your heavenly Father will give the Holy Spirit to those who ask.*Lk 11:13*

Intercessory. Jesus said to ask anything in his name, and he would do it for you to glorify his Father in the Son.*Jn 14:13-14* Jesus said to pray for those who mistreat you.*Lk 6:28* Make petitions, prayers, and intercession for all people, including for those in authority, that you may live peaceful and quiet lives in all godliness and holiness.*1Ti 2:1-2* Men everywhere should pray, lifting up holy hands.*1Ti 2:8* Receive anything consecrated by God's word and prayer.*1Ti 4:5* Pray for the sick so that faithful prayer will heal the sick.*Jas 5:13-15* Pray for each other for healing.*Jas 5:16* Our prayer for one another is to enjoy good health and that all go well, especially in the soul.*3Jn 2* Ask that our God and Father and the Lord Jesus help you gather with other believers.*1Th 3:11* Pray that the Lord make others' love increase and overflow for one another and everyone else, like your love increases and overflows.*1Th 3:12* Pray that the Lord's people favorably receive contributions that you share, so that you have joy and refreshing company.*Ro 15:31-32* Wrestle in prayer for one another, so that you may stand firm in all God's will, mature and fully assured.*Col 4:12* An angel of God told the devout centurion Cornelius that his prayers and gifts to the poor had come up as a memorial offering before God.*Acts 10:4*

Sin. Jesus said to pray that God forgive your debts just as you forgive others' debts to you.*Matt 6:12* Pray that God not lead you into temptation but instead deliver you from the evil one.*Matt 6:13* Jesus told the parable of the Pharisee who thanked God in prayer that he was not like other evildoers such as the tax collector, while the tax collector prayed for God to have mercy on him, a sinner.*Lk 18:9-13* Only the tax collector went home justified because those who exalt themselves God will humble, while those who humble themselves God exalts.*Lk 18:14* Pray for the sinner so that through faithful prayer God will forgive the sinner.*Jas 5:13-15* Pray for any brother or sister who sins, other than for sin that leads to death, because God will give them life.*1Jn 5:16-17* Pray that God strengthen hearts, so that others will be blameless and holy in the presence of our God and Father when our Lord Jesus comes.*1Th 3:13* Pray for one another that others have a clear conscience and desire to live honorably in every way.*Heb 13:18* Pray that God delivers us from evil people.*2Th 3:2* Pray that God keep preachers safe from persecuting unbelievers.*Ro 15:31-32* Pray for one another to help defeat persecution, in gracious favor.*2Co 1:11* Pray that God fully restores you.*2Co 13:9* Pray especially that God restores your leaders to you soon.*Heb 13:19*

Faith. Jesus said to pray to your Father in heaven, first hallowing his name, then asking that his kingdom come and his will occur on earth as in heaven.*Matt 6:9-10* Pray for daily provision.*Matt 6:11* Jesus taught the disciples that whatever they asked for in prayer, they should believe that they have received, so that it would be theirs.*Mk 11:24* He also taught that when they prayed, they should first forgive anyone of anything that they held against them, so that their Father in heaven would forgive their own sins.*Mk 11:25* We pray that our partnership in faith is effective in deepening our understanding of every good thing we share for the sake of Christ.*Phm 6* Your faith in the Lord Jesus and your love for all God's people makes us remember you in our prayers.*Eph 1:15-16* We thank our God as we remember one another in our prayers because we hear about one another's love for the holy people and faith in the Lord Jesus.*Phm 4-5* Pray that the God of our Lord Jesus Christ, the glorious Father, may give one another the Spirit of wisdom and revelation, so that we may know him better.*Eph 1:17* Pray that the Spirit may enlighten our heart that we may know God's hope, his glorious inheritance in us, and his incomparably great power for us who believe.*Eph 1:18-19* We pray that out of God's glorious riches he strengthens you in your inner being with power through his Spirit, so that Christ dwells in your heart through faith.*Eph 3:16-17*

Christ. One day when Jesus finished praying, a disciple asked him to teach them to pray as John had taught his disciples.*Lk 11:1* Jesus said to hallow the Father, invite his kingdom, ask for daily bread and forgiveness of sins, as we forgive others for sinning, and not to lead us to temptation.*Lk 11:2-4* Jesus then told a parable of a friend who went to another friend at midnight to ask for bread, which he would get not out of friendship but because of shameless audacity.*Lk 11:5-8* Jesus said to ask, seek, and knock, and you will receive.*Lk 11:9-10* Jesus also told a parable about a persistent widow to show the disciples that they should always pray while not giving up.*Lk 18:1* Her town had an unjust judge whom she kept entreating against her adversary until the judge finally relented and rewarded her as she asked.*Lk 18:2-6* God gives justice to his chosen ones who cry out for it day and night.*Lk 18:7-8* Pray that we may glorify the name of our Lord Jesus and receive his glory, by the grace of God and the Lord Jesus Christ.*2Th 1:12* When living on earth, Jesus prayed and petitioned fervently to God who could save him from death, and God heard Jesus because of his reverent submission.*Heb 5:7* Pray that you and all the Lord's holy people, rooted and established in love, can grasp how wide, long, high, and deep Christ's love is, and know his love surpasses knowledge, that God may fill you to his fullness.*Eph 3:17-19* Pray that the message of the Lord spreads rapidly.*2Th 3:1* Desire and pray to God that those who know of Jesus will turn to him for salvation.*Ro 10:1* Pray also for your teachers so that whenever they speak, the Spirit gives them fearless words making known the gospel's mystery. *Eph 6:19-20* In all prayers for believers, we always pray with joy for our partnership in the gospel.*Php 1:4-5* Join in one another's struggles to proclaim the gospel by praying for one another.*Ro 15:30* Always thank God, our Lord Jesus Christ's Father, when praying for those about whose faith in Christ Jesus and love for God's people you have heard.*Col 1:3-4* Pray that God opens doors for others to proclaim Christ's mystery clearly, as they should.*Col 4:3-4*

Apostles. After the religious leaders jailed and released Peter and John, Peter and John went back to the believers to pray that the Lord enable his servants to speak with great boldness, after which the place shook, the Holy Spirit filled them, and they spoke God's word boldly.*Acts 4:22-31* The apostle Peter told the other apostles that they should attend to prayer and the ministry of God's word rather than wait on tables.*Acts 6:1-4* The apostles prayed for the ones whom they designated to distribute food, laying hands on them.*Acts 6:5-6* After Philip proclaimed Jesus to Samaria and many believed and were baptized, Peter and John visited Samaria, praying that the believers would receive the Holy Spirit, which they did when Peter and John laid hands on them.*Acts 8:14-17* When Peter went up to a roof to pray, the Lord gave him a vision that he could kill and eat things that he previously thought unclean.*Acts 10:8-16* King Herod arrested Peter and put him in prison, but with the church earnestly praying to God for Peter, an angel of the Lord rescued him from his chains, led him out of the prison, and then disappeared, leaving Peter to go to the house where believers prayed for him.*Acts 12:3-17* After appointing elders in each church, Paul and Barnabas fasted and prayed to commit the elders to the Lord.*Acts 14:23* The apostles came upon a group of women when looking for a place to pray.*Acts 16:13* Another time, the apostles were heading to a place to pray when they met a female slave with a spirit.*Acts 16:16* While giving his farewell, Paul knelt down with all the believers and prayed, everyone weeping as they embraced and kissed Paul, over his statement that they would never see him again.*Acts 20:36-38* At their farewell, Paul and his companions knelt on the beach with all the believers, including wives and children, to pray.*Acts 21:5* Paul prayed that the Jew King Agrippa before whom Paul stood trial and all others who listened to Paul that day would become the believer that Paul was.*Acts 26:28-29* Paul thanked God, broke bread for everyone, and said that they would all survive, when a storm shipwrecked them on Paul's way to Rome.*Acts 27:33-35* Paul prayed before healing the island chief official Publius's father.*Acts 28:8*

Fasting. Jesus said that when you fast, don't show others your somber fasting look as hypocrites do to get only an earthly reward.*Matt 6:16* Instead, look fresh, as if you were not fasting, so that others don't notice and only your unseen Father notices, so that he rewards what you do in secret.*Matt 6:17-18* John's disciples and Pharisees fasted.*Mk 2:18* When John the Baptist's followers, and the Pharisees and law teachers, asked Jesus why John's disciples and the Pharisees fast often while Jesus's disciples do not fast, Jesus replied by parable that his disciples would fast only when Jesus was gone, not when he was with them.*Matt 9:14-16, Mk 2:18-19, Lk 5:33-34* He added by parables about unshrunk cloth and new wineskins that a trying religious practice like fasting would not then aid the disciples in persevering toward the new holiness that his salvation would bring.*Matt 9:16-17, Lk 5:36-39* Jesus also told the parable about the Pharisee who tried to justify himself to God in prayer by pointing to his fasting twice a week, while the tax collector who beat his breast and admitted that he was a sinner was the one whom God justified.*Lk 18:9-14* The Holy Spirit spoke to prophets and teachers who worshiped and fasted in Antioch's church, to set apart Barnabas and Saul for further work, and so they fasted, prayed, laid on hands, and sent them off.*Acts 13:1-3* After appointing elders in each church, Paul and Barnabas fasted and prayed to commit the elders to the Lord.*Acts 14:23*

Gratitude. Thank God for his indescribable gift.*2Co 9:15* Thank God that you receive his kingdom.*Heb 12:28-29* Thank God for the joy that the faith of others brings you.*1Th 3:9* Thank God with a clear conscience.*2Ti 1:3* Thank God for those whom God gives grace in Christ Jesus.*1Co 1:4* Thank God through Jesus Christ for believers whose faith others report all over the world.*Ro 1:8* Thank God continually when you receive the word of God from one another.*1Th 2:13* Always give thanks to God the Father for everything, in the name of our Lord Jesus Christ.*Eph 5:19-20* Give thanks in all circumstances, as God's will for you in Christ Jesus.*1Th 5:18* Give thanks to God the Father through Jesus Christ.*Col 3:17* Give joyful thanks to the Father for sharing the kingdom with his holy people.*Col 1:12* Present requests to God with thanksgiving.*Php 4:6* Sing to God with gratitude in your hearts.*Col 3:16* Jesus healed ten lepers, but only one came back praising God to thank Jesus, who told him that his faith had healed him.*Lk 17:11-19*

Others. Always thank God for fellow believers.*1Th 1:2* Always thank God for brothers and sisters loved by the Lord.*2Th 2:13* Always thank God for brothers and sisters whose faith grows more and more, and whose love for one another increases.*2Th 1:3* Always thank God for others' faith in Christ Jesus and love for God's people, about which you hear.*Col 1:3-4* Your faith in the Lord Jesus and your love for all God's people makes us give thanks for you.*Eph 1:15-16* Make your prayer thankful.*Col 4:2* Teachers should thank Christ Jesus our Lord that he considers them trustworthy.*1Ti 1:12* Give thanks for all people.*1Ti 2:1-2* Share thanksgiving in place of coarse talk.*Eph 5:4* Everything God created is good, not to reject but to receive with thanksgiving.*1Ti 4:4* The thanksgiving cup for which we give thanks participates in Christ's blood.*1Co 10:16* Give thanks for answered prayers defeating persecution.*2Co 1:11* Thanksgiving overflows to God's glory, as grace reaches ever more people.*2Co 4:15*

Healing. Jesus traveled throughout Galilee, healing the people's every disease and sickness.*Matt 4:23* Jesus instantly healed a man with leprosy who asked if Jesus was willing, to which Jesus said, indignantly, that he was willing.*Matt 8:2-3, Mk 1:40-42, Lk 5:12-13* Jesus healed a centurion's servant from a distance, amazed at the faith of the centurion's request.*Matt*

8:5-13, Lk 7:1-10 Jesus also healed a royal official's son from a distance when the official begged him, the son healed at the exact time that Jesus had said the son would live.*Jn 4:46-54* Telling him to pick up his mat and walk, Jesus healed an invalid at a pool near Jerusalem's Sheep Gate after asking the invalid if he wanted to get well.*Jn 5:1-9* Jesus healed Simon Peter's mother-in-law lying in bed with a fever, by touching her hand, after which she got up to wait on him.*Matt 8:14-15, Mk 1:29-31, Lk 4:38-39* People brought to Jesus many demon-possessed persons, for him to drive out the spirits with a word and heal all the sick, fulfilling Isaiah's prophecy that Jesus took up our infirmities and bore our diseases.*Matt 8:16-17* Jesus's healing of the paralyzed man on the mat so awed the crowd that they praised God for giving him such authority.*Matt 9:8, Lk 5:26* Jesus healed a woman who said to herself that a touch to Jesus's cloak would heal her.*Matt 9:20-22, Mk 5:25-34, Lk 8:40-48* Jesus restored sight to two blind men after they confirmed that they believed that he could do so.*Matt 9:27-31* Jesus traveled through all the towns and villages, healing every disease and sickness.*Matt 9:35* Jesus healed a man with a shriveled hand.*Mk 3:1-6* Jesus told a man with a shriveled hand to stretch it out, and Jesus had healed it as good as the other hand.*Matt 12:13, Lk 6:6-10* Jesus healed a blind, mute, demon-possessed man so that the man could talk and see.*Matt 12:22* Jesus healed the demon-possessed daughter of a Canaanite woman who showed Jesus that the woman had great faith.*Matt 15:21-28* Jesus healed a Greek woman's daughter after she showed Jesus that she had great faith.*Mk 7:24-30* Jesus healed a deaf and mute man by putting his fingers in the man's ears, touching the man's tongue, looking to heaven, and saying to open.*Mk 7:31-35* Jesus healed a blind man by spitting on the man's eyes, putting his hands on him, and when the man could only see what looked like trees walking around, putting his hands on the man's eyes again.*Mk 7:22-26, Jn 9:1-12* Jesus restored the sight of two blind men sitting by the Jericho roadside, calling to the Lord, Son of David, to have mercy on them.*Matt 20:29-34* A blind beggar shouted to Jesus, Son of David, to have mercy on him, and when the crowd told him that Jesus was calling for him, he got up and ran to Jesus who told him that his faith had restored his sight, and he indeed could then see.*Mk 10:46-52, Lk 18:35-43* Jesus healed the blind and lame who came to him at the temple.*Matt 21:14*

Raising. Jesus said that with his coming, the blind were seeing, lame walking, lepers cleansed, deaf hearing, and dead raised.*Matt 11:4-5* When Jesus saw a procession carrying a widow's dead son on a bier, his heart went out to the widow, and he touched the bier, raising the widow's son to life.*Lk 7:11-15* The people, filled with awe, said that God had come to help his people, and news spread throughout Judea.*Lk 7:16-17* Jesus raised from the dead a synagogue leader's daughter, after the leader told Jesus that Jesus's putting his hand on her would make her live again.*Matt 9:18-26, Mk 5:21-43, Lk 8:40-56* Jesus raised from the dead Lazarus, whose sister Mary poured perfume on Jesus's feet and wiped his feet with her hair, after Lazarus had been dead four days, so that those who saw it would believe.*Jn 11:1-44* Disciples sent for the apostle Peter when a disciple Tabitha, also known as Dorcas, who was always doing good and helping the poor, became sick and died.*Acts 9:36-38* When Peter arrived, he sent everyone out of the room, prayed on his knees, and told her to get up, which she promptly did, Peter helping her to her feet.*Acts 9:39-41* Paul raised a young man from the dead after the young man fell asleep listening to Paul preach, and fell from a third-story window.*Acts 20:7-12*

Apostles. After Pentecost, a man lame from birth begged Peter and John for money as they were going up to the temple.*Acts 3:1-3* Peter told the man that he had no silver or gold but would give him what he had, in Jesus's name telling him to walk, which when Peter helped him up, instantly healing the man's legs, he could walk and jump praising God to the crowd's amazement.*Acts 3:4-10* Peter told the onlookers that although they had disowned and killed the Holy and Righteous One, the author of life, faith in Jesus's name had completely healed the man.*Acts 3:11-16* The apostles performed many signs and wonders among the people so that, as more and more believed, they brought their sick into the streets so that Peter's shadow would fall on them, and crowds brought the sick and tormented, with all healed.*Acts 5:12-16* Philip proclaimed the Messiah in Samaria, where many paralyzed and lame were healed, bringing great joy.*Acts 8:5-8* Peter in his travels about the country met a paralyzed and bedridden man Aeneas to whom Peter said that Jesus Christ heals him and to get up and roll up his mat, which Aeneas promptly did, causing all those who saw the healing to turn to the Lord.*Acts 9:32-35* In Lystra, Paul looked straight at a man lame from birth and, seeing his faith for healing, told him to stand on his feet, at which the man jumped up to walk.*Acts 14:8-9* God did extraordinary miracles through Paul, so that handkerchiefs and aprons that touched him cured the sick.*Acts 19:11-12* Paul healed the sick father of the island chief official Publius, after praying and placing his hands on him, and then cured the rest of the sick on the island when they came to him.*Acts 28:7-9*

Conclusion

Extraordinary, isn't it, what the New Testament has to say to us? The New Testament has the most concise and critical core message one finds anywhere, that God sent his Son to die and rise for us, giving us life while bringing us back to him. Yet the New Testament also has unending other things to say to us, big and important things, small and comforting things, and everything in between. The follower who walks with Christ cannot imagine a world without him, which is simply more evidence that no such world exists. In revealing and confirming Christ's coming, the New Testament endorses what our hearts, minds, souls, and spirits know, which is that we have limitless and continual need of him, and that he more than fills that need, indeed leads us to glorious places of which we see only the slightest glimmer. I hope that the above reorganization of the New Testament helps in some small way to keep you in perfect tune with the Spirit who keeps us firmly on that path to his glory. God's peace and God's speed be with you.

Appendices

Abbreviations

Matthew	*Matt*	1 Timothy	*1Ti*
Mark	*Mk*	2 Timothy	*2Ti*
Luke	*Lk*	Titus	*Tit*
John	*Jn*	Philemon	*Phm*
Acts	*Acts*	Hebrews	*Heb*
Romans	*Ro*	James	*Jas*
1 Corinthians	*1Co*	1 Peter	*1Pe*
2 Corinthians	*2Co*	2 Peter	*2Pe*
Galatians	*Gal*	1 John	*1Jn*
Ephesians	*Eph*	2 John	*2Jn*
Philippians	*Php*	3 John	*3Jn*
Colossians	*Col*	Jude	*Jude*
1 Thessalonians	*1Th*	Revelation	*Rev*
2 Thessalonians	*2Th*		

Authors

While each New Testament author wrote under the Spirit, minimizing the significance of author identity, some readers are nonetheless naturally curious about the authors, the study of whom can lend additional insight into their writings. Bible scholars do with reasonable confidence share such insight into the Gospels authors Matthew, Mark, Luke, and John. The Gospel author Luke also wrote the book of Acts, while the Gospel author John also likely wrote Revelation. Sections below share a little of the scholarly insight into those authors and their glorious writings.

Scholars show less confidence in lending insight into the authorship and authors of some of the New Testament letters. The New Testament organizes the twenty-one letters by their authors. The first thirteen letters claim Paul's authorship, with a fourteenth letter Hebrews having no identified author but placed next in order after the thirteen letters attributed to Paul. These fourteen examples traditionally comprise the Pauline letters, notwithstanding substantial question over the authorship of some of the fourteen letters. The next letter identifies itself as having James as its author, followed by two letters claiming Peter's authorship, three letters claiming John's authorship, and a final letter claiming Jude's authorship. Questions also exist over the authorship of some of these last seven letters. Questions over authorship, as to letters claiming specific authors, in no sense imply that any anonymous authors meant to mislead readers as to attribution. To the contrary, devoted students, in the role of the attributed author's trusted scribe or memoirist, may have been the anonymous authors, in honorific attribution following a convention common to ancient schools. Thus, even if Paul, for instance, did not write several of the letters claiming his authorship, then the attribution still bears authority in tracing to Paul the experience that formed the thought, all under the Holy Spirit's inspiration. Keep that reassurance in mind when considering the following discussion of individual authors.

Matthew

While the Gospel Matthew does not name its own author, tradition attributes the Gospel to one of Jesus's twelve disciples by that name, also known as Levi and further identified as the son of Alphaeus. The Gospels identify Matthew as a tax collector whom Jesus called out of a tax collector's booth, likely along a trade route around the Galilean city of Capernaum. King Herod Antipas would have collected tolls or taxes from the commercial traffic on such trade routes. The Gospel author exhibits an intimate Old Testament knowledge and knowledge of Jewish customs, and records some financial and transactional details not included in the other Gospels, of the type that a Jewish tax collector might note and record in a tax collector's customary shorthand. Church leaders Origen and Iraneus, and church historian Eusebius, all of the second and third century, accept Matthew's authorship.

An early outside historical account confirms the Gospel's attribution to Matthew, although that account also introduces some question over the language in which Matthew wrote, whether Hebrew (as the account records), Aramaic (as the account may have intended), or Greek (as often assumed from the Gospel's similarity to Mark's Gospel written in Greek). Because Matthew's Gospel reproduces ninety percent of Mark's Gospel, and Mark's Gospel dates to between 50 and 55 A.D., scholars tend to date Matthew's Gospel to between 55 and 60 A.D., just predating the temple's destruction, which Matthew does not mention and may have done so had the event already occurred. Modern scholars may be less likely to attribute the Gospel to a disciple, whether Matthew or another, and more likely to attribute the Gospel to a later date. The author, a Jew writing to Jews, may have written the Gospel of Matthew in Judea or perhaps Antioch in Syria, given that the earliest reference to the Gospel was by Bishop Ignatius of Antioch.

Mark

While the Gospel Mark does not identify its author, tradition ascribes authorship of the Gospel to John Mark, the son of a widow Mary in whose home the book of Acts records the disciples meeting. The letter Colossians also identifies John Mark as the cousin of Barnabas, Mark and Barnabas traveling with the apostle Paul until Mark left for a time, as the book of Acts records, with Mark rejoining Paul and proving himself useful, again recorded in Colossians. John Mark, not himself a disciple of Jesus, is instead said to have followed the apostle Peter, transcribing Peter's teachings. Indeed, the Gospel focuses on Simon Peter's actions, reactions, and words. The author employs a fast-paced, emotional style with frequent use of Latin terms and frequent explanation of Jewish customs, suggesting that the author, who also showed some familiarity with members of the Roman church (in particular, Simon of Cyrene's sons Alexander and Rufus), wrote for a Roman audience. Speculation includes that John Mark may have been the follower in the Garden of Gethsemane who fled naked, a detail that only this Gospel includes. Early church sources without dissent confirm John Mark as the Gospel's author. While the Gospel could have a later or even a slightly earlier date, circumstances suggest attribution to around 50 to 55 A.D. John Mark, the only clear author candidate, very likely wrote the Gospel from Rome, where he supported and was a good friend to Peter, who called John Mark his son.

Luke

The Gospel Luke differs from the other synotpic Gospels Matthew and Mark (*synoptic* simply meaning summarizing) in that Luke begins with a prologue common to other Greek writings. Unfortunately, the prologue does not identify the Gospel's author. Scholars deduce the Gospel's authorship from the Gospel's common author with the book of Acts and from cross-referencing Acts with the apostle Paul's letters. The New Testament mentions the person Luke only three times, but the common Luke-Acts authorship, first-person accounts of events in Acts identifying Luke's probable presence, and references to Luke in Paul's letters, give scholars reasonable confidence in identifying Luke as the Gospel's author and the author of Acts. Early church leaders attributed the Gospel to the physician Luke and no other. The attribution of both the Gospel and Acts makes Luke the New Testament's most prolific author, having written about sixty percent of the New Testament, a fact not generally appreciated in light of the attention given to John for that Gospel and Revelation and Paul for the travels that Acts documents and for Paul's many letters. The voluminous writings do, though, show Luke to be a physician, companion to Paul, and Gentile rather than Jew, although not necessarily a Greek, as some suppose. Despite his Gentile status, Luke shows substantial familiarity with Judaism including the Old Testament. The Gospel was the latest of the three synoptic Gospels Matthew, Mark, and Luke but written before the book of Acts, dating it to approximately 55 to 64 A.D. The book of Acts has a date of as late as 64 A.D. but likely not later, given its abrupt ending with the apostle Paul still living. Most scholars believe that Luke wrote his Gospel while outside of Judea, possibly but not necessarily while in Rome, with Caesarea, Achaia, the Decapolis, and Asia Minor as other possible locations.

John

While the Gospel John does not identify its author, authority supports that the disciple John wrote the Gospel, in which he identifies himself as the disciple whom Jesus loved, leaning on Jesus's breast at the Last Supper the night of Jesus's betrayal. Tradition also attributes to Jesus's beloved disciple John the three letters 1 John, 2 John, and 3 John, on substantial internal and external evidence, and the book of Revelation. The book of Revelation four times identifies its author as John, which early church leaders and historians accepted as referring to the disciple of Jesus. Other, later historians suggested a different ancient figure John the Presbyter, but substantial scholarship continues to support the traditional view that Revelation's author was the beloved disciple.

John and his brother James, also a disciple of Jesus, were sons of Zebedee, the three of them working as unschooled and ordinary fishermen on the Sea of Galilee, when Jesus called John and James to discipleship. John, his brother James (not Jesus's brother James), and Peter were Jesus's inner circle of disciples who witnessed Jesus's Mt. Hermon transfiguration, saw Jesus raise Jairus's dead daughter, and accompanied Jesus (but slept) while Jesus prayed in the Garden of

Gethsemane. Some inference exists that John's mother was Salome, who could have been a sister of Jesus's mother Mary, which if so would have made John a cousin to Jesus. John wrote his Gospel as an eyewitness to key events of Jesus's life, including in great detail the Last Supper. John was especially close to Jesus in other ways beyond his unique position at Jesus's breast at the Lord's betrayal. Mark's Gospel records that Jesus nicknamed John and his brother James the Sons of Thunder for their outspoken quick tempers. On the cross, Jesus appointed John to care for Jesus's mother Mary. John was the one to recognize the resurrected Jesus the moment of the miraculous catch of fish. Because John in his Gospel referred to himself in the third person, John may also have been the disciple who knew the high priest and thus accompanied Jesus into the high priest's courtyard for Jesus's trial, and who ran with Peter to the empty tomb. The book of Acts records that John was with Peter for the lame man's healing at the temple, to preach before the Sanhedrin about Jesus's crucifixion and resurrection, and for arrest, release by an angel, and flogging. In Galatians, Paul identifies John with Peter and Jesus's brother James (not John's brother James, whom King Herod Agrippa I beheaded around a decade after Jesus's resurrection) as a pillar of the early church in Jerusalem.

External evidence suggests that John left Jerusalem to serve Asia Minor's churches in his later years. The book of Revelation and external sources record John's exile to the island of Patmos in the Aegean Sea between Asia Minor (modern-day Turkey) and Greece, assuming, as many accept, that John indeed wrote the book of Revelation. John's exile likely took place around 95 A.D. near the end of the Christian persecutor Dominian's reign. Dominian's assassination a year later likely enabled John to return to Asia Minor to die there, probably near Ephesus, around 98 A.D., with his reputed tomb in the ruins of St. John's Church at Selcuk. If that history is correct, then John may well have been the only one of the twelve disciples to die of natural causes, as the end of his Gospel suggests and tradition holds.

Traditionally, historians and scholars have dated John's Gospel to around 85 A.D., although some now suggest an earlier date of around 70 A.D., or even as early as 50 A.D. The later 85 A.D. date appears to remain the most reliable. The book of Revelation also gets various dates coinciding with Christian persecutions, from as early as 54 to 68 A.D., or as late as 81 to 96 A.D., with many selecting 95 A.D. as a reasonable single date. The book of Revelation contains several warnings of growing and coming persecution, concealing in representative imagery the identity of the persecutors justifying those warnings. John, like Paul and James, was plainly an extraordinary witness to author his Gospel and letters, and Revelation, under the Holy Spirit.

Paul

As just indicated, tradition recognizes the apostle Paul as the primary human author of the Bible's New Testament letters, acknowledging that the Holy Spirit is the divine author of each letter and all the Bible. Thirteen of the Bible's twenty-one letters attribute themselves by name to Paul, including Romans, 1 Corinthians, 2 Corinthians, Galatians, Ephesians, Philippians, Colossians, 1 Thessalonians, 2 Thessalonians, 1 Timothy, 2 Timothy, Titus, and Philemon. Some readers attribute a fourteenth letter Hebrews to Paul, although unlike the other thirteen letters, Hebrews does not claim Paul's authorship. Scholars show strong consensus that Paul wrote at least seven of the thirteen letters that claim his authorship, including Romans, 1 Corinthians, 2 Corinthians, Galatians, Philippians, 1 Thessalonians, and Philemon. Paul may have dictated the other six letters claiming his authorship, or other authors who sought Paul's mentoring and learned from Paul may have credited Paul with those other letters.

Paul had exquisite credit to author so many of the letters. Scholars generally attribute the apostle Paul's birth to Jewish parents in A.D. 6 in Tarsus. Tarsus would have been in the east of modern-day Turkey, also known as Asia Minor as the westernmost extension of the Asian continent. Paul, then known as Saul, was a Roman citizen from birth but spent his formative years in Jerusalem, studying the Jewish Torah under the prominent rabbinical scholar and Sanhedrin member Gamaliel. Paul was thus by his own claim or admission a Pharisee's Pharisee, so strict of a Jewish religious adherent that he persecuted the new Christians in Jerusalem and throughout Judea. Indeed, poignantly, Paul was present and approving at the first recorded Christian martyr Stephen's stoning, as the book of Acts documents.

Paul came to Christ around 33 A.D. in his dramatic encounter with the risen Lord on Paul's way to Damascus to persecute believers. The book of Acts records that Paul completed that trip blind, receiving his sight and the Holy Spirit when meeting the visiting convert Ananias. Paul then spent three years in Arabia before returning to Damascus briefly to preach Jesus, until persecution caused him to flee to Jerusalem. Paul met with the apostles in Jerusalem before returning home to Tarsus and the surrounding region, including Antioch, to preach for approximately the next decade from 36 A.D. to 46 A.D. Paul then spent another decade on three missionary journeys throughout the Eastern Mediterranean, from about 37 A.D. to 47 A.D., when he may have written about half of his letters. Paul spent much of his last seven years under arrest and imprisoned in Caesarea and Rome, guiding the churches and defending the faith even as he defended himself. He may have written the other half of his letters during this period, before his death by execution in Rome in A.D. 64.

James

Tradition holds that Jesus's brother James wrote the letter bearing that name, even though the letter itself refers to James only as a servant of God and the Lord Jesus Christ, not expressly Jesus's brother. Some readers prefer to call James a *half* brother of Jesus, holding that Jesus and James would have shared only Mary as their mother (Mary having other children, too). The Holy Spirit came on Mary when she conceived Jesus, while Mary's husband Joseph would have been James's father and the father of Mary's other children. Others prefer to treat James and his other siblings as Joseph's children from a prior marriage ending in his wife's death, and thus Mary's adopted children, or simply as cousins to Mary's Son Jesus, Mary thus maintaining her virginity. In any case, biologically related to Jesus or not, James until his death around 62 A.D. was a prominent leader in Jerusalem of the community of believers that the apostles formed and influenced. In dozens of places, the letter's text shows that its author was familiar with Jesus's sayings, before repetition spread and tradition fixed those sayings. Jesus's brother James could well have been the letter's author.

Yet others named James could instead have authored the letter. Interestingly, Jesus's two apostles James the son of Zebedee and James the son of Alphaeus were less likely the letters' author, Zebedee's son because of his early martyrdom as the book of Acts records, and

Alphaeus's son because of his lack of prominence in the biblical record. The letter implies that the James who wrote the letter was prominent, as Jesus's brother James surely was. Paul's letters described James, the brother of the Lord, as one of three church pillars. Jude, the author of another letter by that name, referred to himself not only as a slave of Jesus Christ, as James likewise did in his letter, but also as a brother of James, again taken by some as further evidence that Jesus's brother wrote the letter.

If indeed, Jesus's brother James, the early Jerusalem church's leader, wrote the letter by his name, then we do have an extraordinary witness to the Holy Spirit's testimony. John's Gospel records that Jesus's brothers did not believe in Jesus, and so James' conversion likely followed the resurrection. Paul in 1 Corinthians records that the resurrected Lord appeared to his brother James. Confirming James's prominence, some historians identify Jesus's brother James as James the Just, James of Jerusalem, and the Bishop of Jerusalem. James, Peter, and Paul each played leading roles in the early church. The authority one attributes to each depends to some degree on one's perspective, whether Catholic, Reformed, liberal, or otherwise. All three would likely dismiss any special authoritative claim, in humility making themselves the least among the apostles, as Paul acknowledged in his own letters. The Jewish historian Josephus records outside the biblical record that James, Jesus's brother, had the Pharisees' respect for his pious observance of the law, despite that enemies had James put to death in A.D. 62 in a brief period between local Roman governors.

The three great witnesses James, Peter, and Paul certainly knew and supported one another, if at times also contesting in the faith, as the book of Acts records Paul doing openly in Peter's presence. Acts also records Paul receiving in Antioch a messenger from James carrying an instruction to local believers that Paul rejected. Yet Acts also records Peter leaving a message for James and the other apostles when Peter was preparing to leave Jerusalem, much as Acts mentions Paul's visiting James on Paul's last time in Jerusalem. James clearly supported both Paul and Peter. In Galatians, Paul notes his visit to Peter and James in Jerusalem after Paul's conversion and a second visit to Peter, James, and John, whom Galatians records Paul regarding as the church's pillars. So again, in Jesus's brother James, the letter would have an extraordinary author. Yet whoever wrote the letter James, we know from its inclusion in the Bible and the profound quality of its text that we have the most-extraordinary witness to the Holy Spirit.

Peter

Some hold that the prominent disciple Peter wrote the letters 1 Peter and 2 Peter. Others, noting substantial differences in the letters' styles, and the similarities of 2 Peter to the following letter Jude, attribute 2 Peter to another author who may have accompanied and learned from Peter. Some hold that a single author wrote both 2 Peter and Jude. Among those who believe that a single author wrote both 2 Peter and Jude, one theory holds that the author's reference in Jude to desiring to write another letter when needing instead to urgently write the letter Jude, was a reference to 2 Peter, a theory that would both answer and put a neat bow on the question of both letters' authorship. That theory would then make the reference in 2 Peter to an earlier letter already sent, a reference to the letter Jude rather than, as many assume, a reference to 1 Peter. In any case, if Peter did not write 2 Peter, then readers can still have confidence that 2 Peter's author knew Peter, his experiences, and his teaching well.

We do in any case know a great deal about Peter's life from the four Gospels and the book of Acts, and from external accounts, amplified by tradition, a little bit about his imprisonment and death. Peter's original name was Simon, according to Luke's Gospel a Galilean fisherman brother of another disciple Andrew. Luke suggests that Simon and Andrew were the first two disciples whom Jesus called, both promptly walking away from their boats and nets on Jesus's invitation to be fishers instead of men. The Gospels portray Simon as an outspoken and often-erring leader of the disciples in their communication and interaction with Jesus. For example, at the Last Supper, he initially refused Jesus's offer to wash his feet but then impulsively asked Jesus to wash his entire body. Simon, though, was the first to call Jesus the Son of the living God, the Messiah. Jesus on that occasion renamed Simon as Peter, meaning *the rock*, implying the confession of Christ on which all else stands. As indicated above, Peter witnessed Jesus's Mt. Hermon transfiguration and various miracles, and was with Jesus as Jesus prayed in the Garden of Gethsemane, along with John and his brother James, the three comprising an inner circle of disciples.

While at the Last Supper, Peter professed willingness to die with Jesus, Peter then promptly denied Jesus three times outside the high priest's courtyard at Jesus's trial, as Jesus had predicted. Peter was nonetheless one of the two disciples who ran to the empty tomb immediately after Jesus's reported resurrection. Peter thereafter remained a leader among the disciples, especially after Jesus restored Peter along the Sea of Galilee's shores, three times telling Peter to feed Jesus's sheep. Peter preached boldly in Jerusalem at Pentecost, when the Spirit descended and thousands confessed Christ. As indicated above, Peter and John also preached boldly when brought before the Sanhedrin, for having healed another at the temple gate, and later suffered imprisonment before release by an angel, and flogging. As also indicated above, Peter was one of the three pillars of the early church in Jerusalem, along with John and Jesus's brother James. A vision brought Peter to eat with the gentile Cornelius, the event, with Paul's intercession, helping to enlarge Christianity's reach beyond Jewish converts to gentiles.

Many credit Peter with substantial contributions to Mark's Gospel. Mark, also known as John Mark, was not a disciple of Jesus but did travel extensively with Peter as Peter carried out Jesus's Great Commission. Mark's Gospel treats in detail events that only Peter and the other inner-circle members John and his brother James would have witnessed. No matter whether Peter dictated the Gospel to Mark, Peter may well have contributed to the Gospels' record over the course of the three-plus decades that Peter served as a witness after Christ's resurrection. Peter left Jerusalem carrying the gospel to other regions including likely Rome, where external accounts and tradition hold, consistent with Jesus's apparent prophecy at Peter's restoration, that Peter suffered death by crucifixion. Indeed, tradition holds that Emperor Nero granted Peter's wish to die crucified upside down, in humility to Jesus's glorious cross-borne victory. Tradition and external accounts further hold that Peter converted his jailers and dozens of others to Christ in the months before his death around A.D. 67, despite enduring horrible torture. Peter, like Paul, James, and John, was an extraordinary witness to author his letters, under the Holy Spirit.

Jude

As mentioned above in the treatment of the author James, the author of the letter Jude states that he is a brother of James, possibly intending the James who wrote the epistle by that name and thus indicating that Jude may be another of the Lord Jesus's half-brothers or step brothers, son of Joseph and possibly also of Mary. If that is so, that Jude was, like James, a member of Jesus's natural family, then Jude, like James, would not have been a follower of Jesus until after Jesus's resurrection, for the same reasons and based on the same accounts mentioned above as to James. The biblical record and other accounts give little more information about Jude, the brother of James and half-brother or step brother of Jesus, other than a reference in 1 Corinthians that the Lord's brothers and their wives made missionary trips. The author Jude, if the Lord's brother, thus served and traveled as a missionary like Paul, Peter, and James, and would, like those others, have been an extraordinary gospel witness.

Alternatively, the author Jude may, when writing that he is a brother of James, have meant that he was a spiritual rather than biological brother of James. The author Jude may also have referred to a different James entirely, rather than the Lord's brother. If so, then the biblical record includes several other Jude-brother candidates named James, although the record suggests no one candidate over another. Some believe that Jude could have been Jesus's disciple Judas, Jude being an equivalent name commonly substituted for Judas after the betrayal, understanding that two disciples went by that name and that the letter's author would have been the faithful Judas rather than the betrayer Judas who died shortly after the betrayal. The latter possibility raises another opportunity to believe Jude to be an extraordinary gospel witness. Given the questions over authorship and the little information that we have about any candidate author, the letter Jude is hard to date but probably followed Peter's writing 1 Peter around A.D. 65 and could have been between A.D. 67 and 80.

Anonymous

Again, you can see from the above uncertainties over the letters' authorship that a substantial chance exists that one or more of the letters had an author who remains anonymous to us. Hebrews may be the letter most likely to have had an anonymous author. Anonymity does not mean lack of prominence or credibility. For example, in addition to Paul, scholars speculate that Hebrews' author could have been Luke, Barnabas, Apollos, or Priscilla, among prominent others. While we should all appreciate the extraordinary experiences that the known authors had, we should also appreciate that the anonymity of any author makes no difference to writings that the Holy Spirit inspired. If God can talk through a donkey, as he did to the diviner Balaam, then God can talk to us through anonymous authors of exquisitely crafted letters, each of which clearly implies that the author, even if anonymous, had profound experiences, knew and interacted with historical figures, and above all heard and obeyed God's Holy Spirit. Thus, once again, have no concern over authorship, even as you take a healthy interest in the authors, their identities, and their experiences. The Bible, including each of its letters, is the inspired word of God.

Audiences

The New Testament's four Gospels Matthew, Mark, Luke, and John differ sufficiently to strongly suggest different audiences. Although the synoptic Gospels Matthew, Mark, and Luke share substantial content, they nonetheless point clearly toward different audiences having different needs, suggesting the authors' different purposes for writing. While the Gospels are not explicit about who those audiences were, each Gospel's different dominant theme, together with some scholarly insight, lend credence to opinions on the probable audiences, as the sections below indicate. Consideration of the audience for each Gospel can help the reader draw greater insight from each Gospel. The books Acts and Revelation also had probable audiences and purposes, as the sections below indicate.

Because the New Testament's twenty-one letters generally take the form of correspondence, they, even more so than the Gospels, presume certain audiences, from which we can learn more about the letters and their intended meaning. Appropriate to the prevailing conventions for correspondence, the letters typically begin with a greeting that identifies the letter's author and recipients. A thanksgiving prayer typically follows. The letters then devote their main content to practical instruction in tenets of Christian faith, often addressing specific challenges that the letter's recipients face. The letters tend to include relatively specific counsel and direction on conduct, drawn from the more-general doctrinal presentation. The letters typically conclude with personal information about the author and acquaintances, greetings, and pleas.

One can group the letters according to audience and attributes, beyond grouping the letters according to their stated or presumed authors, as shown in the foregoing appendix. For instance, four of the Pauline letters, including Ephesians, Philippians, Colossians, and Philemon, bear the mark of *captivity* letters, Paul having written from prison. Three other Pauline letters, including 1 Timothy, 2 Timothy, and Titus, we know as the *pastoral* letters because addressed to protégé pastors and carrying advice on how to guide the congregation. Aside from Hebrews, the other Pauline letters outside of the pastoral letters all had specific church communities as their audience. The last seven letters outside of the Pauline corpus, including James, 1 and 2 Peter, 1, 2, and 3 John, and Jude, we know as *catholic* or *universal* letters because not addressed to a specific church community. The universal letters have general application. The letters addressed to church communities facing specific challenges also have universal value and appeal for the warnings that they hold. Consider the following summaries of each New Testament book, in the order that they appear in the Bible.

Matthew

The Gospel Matthew had a Jewish audience, given that it focuses on the Old Testament's fulfillment in Jesus. Matthew quotes the Old Testament sixty-two times, more than any other Gospel. Unlike the other Gospels, Matthew does not explain Jewish traditions, its Jewish audience not needing any such explanations. Matthew is also the only Gospel to use the phrase *kingdom of heaven* rather than *kingdom of God*, likely out of a Jewish author's reverence for the kingdom and to respect the Jewish audience's equal reverence. The genealogy with which Matthew begins is further evidence of the Jewish author's intent to impress upon a Jewish audience that Jesus Christ was the Jews' long-anticipated Messiah. Indeed, Jesus's messianic character is the Gospel's dominant theme, with related sub-themes of the coming kingdom of heaven, conflict between Jesus and the Jewish religious leaders, and Jesus's return. The Gospel has a distinct literary structure of five discourses with parallels between the first and fifth discourses and second and fourth discourses, leaving a central focus on the parables constituting the third discourse.

Mark

The Gospel Mark had a Roman audience, clear from its use of several Roman terms and its explanation of Aramaic terms and Jewish customs. Indeed, the author, likely John Mark, may have written the letter from Rome to the church in Rome, as early outside sources and church leaders suggest. Given the Gospel's focus on Peter's experiences, witness, and words, the author may have written the Gospel to help Peter instruct and encourage the church in Rome and to preserve Peter's witness after his execution. Nero and later rulers were persecuting Christians in Rome, making useful, indeed critical, such instruction and encouragement. Adding chaotic context to the Gospel's short, action-packed style, the Gospel treats the disciples as often confused and inadequate, subject to Jesus's frequent admonishment. Adding emotional tension, the Gospel treats Jesus's messianic character as a secret until Peter's confession of Christ as the Messiah, after which the Gospel continues to portray the confession as a secret held by the disciples, the healed, and some demons, until the centurion's climactic Son-of-God declaration at the Messiah's death on the cross.

Luke

Luke's Gospel makes its purpose clear in its prologue, to write an investigated and organized account of Jesus's messianic fulfillment, following many prior accounts, for the Gospel's patron Theophilus. The prologue leaves the strong inference that the author was not an original eyewitness to Jesus's life and acts but instead a cautious chronologer. Theophilus could have been a genuine sponsor of Luke's writing or could have been a literary device presuming a patron sponsor. Theophilus means friend or lover of God, and so Luke was writing to a believer or one disposed to become a believer. Luke's references to Theophilus as *most excellent* suggests nobility status, meaning that if the patron was real, then he may have been a government official or influential citizen. The Gospel's content and tenor suggests broader purposes either to make a gentler, less-threatening case for Christianity, or to reassure followers that Christ would indeed return despite what some perceived to be unexpected delay. Speculation includes that Luke wrote the Gospel for Paul's defense to charges in Rome.

In any case, the Gospel Luke has clear value in supporting the church, confirming and clarifying the record, and encouraging followers. The Gospel's structure is one of redemption history, the first part focusing on the law and prophets, the second on the gospel of God's kingdom, and third as the church period anticipating Jesus's triumphant return. Salvation, including sympathy toward the outsider Gentiles, is another dominant theme. Several other themes, including a focus on the individual, compassion for women, children, and the poor or disreputable, and prayer, passion, and praise, further enrich the Gospel, giving it a broader-seeming scope and more-timeless character than the first two Gospels. Scholars note the author's high level of education from the high Greek language the Gospel used and also the author's interest in medical matters, consistent with the identification of Luke as a physician. Importantly, the Gospel Luke has a sequel in the book of Acts, addressed below after treatment of John's Gospel.

John

John's Gospel differs substantially from the three synoptic Gospels Matthew, Mark, and Luke, which share so much material. The record is not even clear that John was familiar with the other three Gospels when writing his Gospel. John takes a different approach, emphasizing the signs of Jesus's divinity and mission, and their theological import. The Gospel declares its own purpose that readers believe that Jesus is God's Son and the Christ, in whose name we receive life forever. The Gospel develops that theme in multiple discourses, none longer or more intimate than that of the Last Supper. The Gospel's account of Jesus's night-time instruction of the Jewish council member Nicodemus, that God so loved the world as to give his only Son, encapsulates the complete gospel message. The Gospel also serves to supplement the other Gospels with unique accounts of teaching, healing, and other miracles, to anticipate and correct potential heresies with its persistent and consistent theological development, and to oppose that anyone follow John the Baptist or others. The Gospel will forever remain a favorite New Testament book, paralleled and reinforced by John's exquisite book of Revelation.

Acts

As the title itself indicates, Luke wrote the book of Acts to chronicle the experiences, words, and deeds of the apostles. Acts thus begins with Peter as the central figure, documents the death of the first martyr Stephen and the actions of others such as Philip, and concludes with a singular focus on the great apostle Paul. The author in the book's latter half lapses into first-person-plural usage, indicating that Luke accompanied Paul on several of his key travels. Acts gives the extraordinary account of the Holy Spirit equipping a tiny, terrorized group of disciples to become courageous apostles spreading the brilliant new-but-ancient faith around the Eastern Mediterranean all the way to the most-powerful government leader in Rome, in three swift decades. The transition that Acts documents is not only geographic but also cultural, in that the book documents the faith's emergence from its Jewish chrysalis to reach Gentiles of all cultures, from the Ethiopian to the Syrian, Asian, Greek, Macedonian, and Roman.

Romans

Romans presents the gospel as clearly and forthrightly as any other letter, and with greater detail and comprehensiveness than most. For those reasons, many favor Romans as a first read for new Bible readers. Some evangelists use the so-called Roman Road to Salvation through the letter to lead explorers to Christ. Consensus is that in Romans, the author Paul wrote between A.D. 56 and A.D. 58 to a church in Rome that none of the apostles had yet visited. Jewish converts at Pentecost may have migrated to Rome ahead of any apostle, witnessing to new local Gentile converts, while establishing the church there. The letter appears to address both Jewish and Gentile believers. Despite that Paul expresses his deep love for the church's members, Paul was likely writing to believers whom he did not know, intending instead to introduce himself while also confirming with passion their remarkable and growing faith. Paul planned to visit the church but wanted in advance to confirm the gospel message that he would bring. Paul may have written Romans from Corinth while preparing to visit Jerusalem to deliver a collection, before heading to Rome and then on to Spain, having finished his work in the Eastern Mediterranean.

Although Romans includes greetings appropriate for a letter, the heart of Romans is a long and bold statement of faith and argument for the faith, much more so than correspondence addressed to a specific audience. Romans first declares the gospel's facts before confirming our desperate need to receive its salvation. Romans then presents the gospel as available to all, God having extended his grace to all, and anyone by faith alone able to accept God's grace. Romans next describes the freedom that salvation brings, before confirming God's plan for Christ's body to unite Jews with Gentiles. Romans then describes the service that follows submission to Christ, each believer having one's own spiritual gifts, exercised in unity to build one another up in faith. Romans ends with Paul describing his personal plans and extending greetings. The clear truths that Romans boldly expresses hold endless encouragement for readers at any point in their growing faith.

1 Corinthians

Paul wrote 1 Corinthians to the church in Corinth, a large and rich port city on the southern coastline of the western part of Greece, not far from Athens. Paul had founded the church in Corinth on his second missionary journey. Paul wrote 1 Corinthians around A.D. 55, on his third and last missionary journey, near the end of the three years that Paul was serving the church in Ephesus, a prominent city located on Asia Minor's westernmost coast across the Aegean Sea from Greece. The church in Corinth to whom Paul addressed 1 Corinthians was navigating an especially idolatrous and sexually corrupt culture. Rampant immorality threatened to undermine the spiritually immature church. Paul sought to fortify the church's faith with specific answers to the church members' immediate and quite-practical questions about how to conduct themselves in the face of such temptation, confusion, and opposition.

First Corinthians begins by stressing that the believers should remain unified around the faith's gospel tenets. Church leaders have specific roles that they should undertake with maturity. First Corinthians then addresses how the church should treat immoral members, the letter denouncing in the strongest terms the sexual sin that beset the church. The letter next addresses how to preserve and strengthen the weakened marriages typical in the corrupt culture. First Corinthians' spectacular love chapter breaks through other sections answering specific questions of conduct on worship, women, communion, and spiritual gifts. The long and rich letter next discusses death and the resurrection body, followed by parting thoughts, greetings, and benediction. First Corinthians remains a weighty and highly practical tool for preserving unity within a body of believers and instructing believers in how to relate to one another while resisting surrounding corruption. It also reveals priceless inspiration and comfort on death and the resurrected body.

2 Corinthians

Paul wrote 2 Corinthians to the same church in Corinth, largely in response to how the church had received his letter we know as 1 Corinthians. Paul wrote two other letters to the same church in Corinth, both of which are lost. In 2 Corinthians, Paul commends those who had taken to heart his 1 Corinthians counsel, thus maturing in their still-developing faith. But in 2 Corinthians, Paul felt compelled to defend himself against slanderous attacks of others, a small but dangerous number of false teachers, who had rejected his 1 Corinthians counsel. The letter is thus more personal than 1 Corinthians and plainly more painful for Paul to write. Paul had in effect to brag to establish his authority, which worked against Paul's godly humility. Paul not only defends himself in 2 Corinthians but also attacks false teachers. The letter also supplies additional practical counsel like that Paul wrote in 1 Corinthians, here though on how to collect money for the poor. The letter shows how intensely one ought to love the church and its members, and struggle for the truth. No doubt, 2 Corinthians will forever remain an inspired witness to that truth.

Galatians

Paul wrote the letter Galatians to the churches that Paul had founded on his first missionary journey through Galatia, the region in south-central Asia Minor. Because Paul did not address the letter to any specific church, he plainly intended that the Galatian churches circulate the letter among them. Paul wrote Galatians while in Antioch in central Asia Minor, just before Paul returned to Jerusalem in A.D. 50 for the council that settled an issue that Paul addressed in Galatians and elsewhere. As an early letter, Galatians addressed an issue that divided the early church, having to do with the relationship between Jewish and Gentile converts. Jewish leaders known as the Judaizers were advocating that Gentile converts to the new Christian faith must keep Jewish laws and traditions. To the Judaizers, faith in Christ was not enough. New Gentile converts must also comply with burdensome laws including those for circumcision. In Galatians, Paul rejected that position, opposing the apostle Peter, and advocating vigorously that faith in Christ was sufficient. The new faith-based covenant was one of life and liberty, whereas the old law-based covenant was one of demand and death. Galatians is a spectacular testimony that the gospel is authentic, superior, and sufficient.

Ephesians

Ephesians addresses itself both to the churches at Ephesus, on the western coast of Asia Minor across the Aegean Sea from Athens on the Greek peninsula, and to believers everywhere. Ephesus was a strategic, regional port city on the high order of Syria's Antioch and Egypt's Alexandria, while also on the main route between Rome and the East including Jerusalem. Paul, whom the letter credits as author, resided in Ephesus for three years, serving the local churches, supporting that the letter addressed close family and friends in the faith. The trusted Tychicus carried the letter to the Ephesians from Rome in about A.D. 60, where Paul was in prison. The letter does not address specific issues but instead supplies general encouragement, instructing believers in the church's nature and role. Its main message is that Christ unites believers in his life-giving body, which is the church, in one Spirit, under one God and Father over all. That broader perspective makes Ephesians one of the universal letters, a bright jewel in the King's crown and treasure to believers everywhere.

Philippians

Paul founded the church at Philippi on his second missionary journey. With Philippi located on the Aegean Sea's northern coast, outside of Asia Minor, the church was the first on the European continent. The church plainly held Paul in the highest regard because it had sent a gift for Paul whom Rome held in prison. Paul wrote Philippians around A.D. 61 to thank the church for the gift and encourage the church's members, and believers everywhere, in deepening their faith. Paul's one passion was to know Christ more for that opportunity's surpassing greatness, against which everything else, including all earthly riches, was loss, and any hardship meant nothing. Philippians is thus a letter of love, joy, and celebration, overflowing with the glorious Holy Spirit, a favorite of many believers, made even more encouraging by the fact that Paul was enduring such prison hardship while writing it.

Colossians

Colossians addresses itself to a church in Colosse, located inland in the southwestern part of Asia Minor. Paul, the letter's credited author, did not found or visit Colosse's church, which Epaphras, and others whom Paul's missionary preaching converted, seem instead to have founded. Paul was in prison in Rome in A.D. 60, the letter's approximate date. The letter indicates that misguided believers in Colosse's church were mixing their precious Christian faith with pagan and secular beliefs in a sort of religious relativism, the contemporary equivalent of which may be *cultural Christianity*. The letter thus directs its instruction to the sufficiency of faith in Christ alone. Given Christ's fullness and lordship, Christ *and* anything else is less than Christ and thus a loss and dangerous heresy. Colossians confronts that heresy with the truth that Christ is God and the head of the church, we are in Christ, and therefore we have no need for the world's legalism, philosophy's asceticism, or another world's mysticism. Christ has all power and authority. Colossians offers a timeless and precious grounding in the deepest reaches of our faith.

1 Thessalonians

Paul wrote 1 Thessalonians around A.D. 51 to the church in Thessalonica, an important land trade route and seaport located at the northern head of the Aegean Sea. Paul had founded the church on his second missionary journey. The letter came shortly later, to encourage the new believers in their growing faith. Indeed, Paul sent Timothy to encourage the church and confirm the members in their new faith. 1 Thessalonians thus carries ardent messages of assurance and reassurance, exhortation in the faith, and comfort in coming resurrection. Only toward the letter's end does Paul challenge the church to avoid sexual immorality while living righteously in a sinful world. Paul concludes the letter with specific counsel on preparing for Jesus's return, helping one another remain strong, and testing all teaching against the true gospel message, followed by benedictions and requests for prayer. First Thessalonians remains solid reassurance, especially to new believers needing encouragement in faith.

2 Thessalonians

The 2 Thessalonians letter from Paul in Corinth to the church in Thessalonica around A.D. 51 followed 1 Thessalonians by as little as a few months. Its brevity and content make clear that Paul wrote 2 Thessalonians to address confusion about the timing of Christ's return that 1 Thessalonians, and the church's continuing persecution, had raised. Some in the church had evidently misconstrued 1 Thessalonians' statement that Christ could come at any moment as an excuse for idleness. Those and others had also misconstrued their persecution as evidence that the Lord's day was indeed quite near, another excuse, those felt, for not pursuing more of the Lord's good work. Paul in 2 Thessalonians corrected the church, indicating that while Christ's return could be quite near, an expectation that is fully appropriate, his imminent return was no excuse for idleness. The Lord indeed desires patient and expectant waiting but also desires that the Lord's ministers, which includes all believers, should work as he desires. Evil will increase in the last days, bringing with it the believers' increased persecution, but those signs are simply greater reason to spread the gospel message, doing the Lord's commissioned work.

1 Timothy

In 1 Timothy, Paul addresses his young protégé, the son and grandson of godly Jewish women who had accepted Christ, raising Timothy in the faith as among the first second-generation Christians. Paul wrote the letter later in his ministry, around 64 A.D., just before his final Rome imprisonment. Timothy, though young, had substantial responsibility as the pastor of the church that Paul had served at Ephesus. Timothy thus faced considerable challenges both within the body of believers, to maintain the body's morality and unity, and from without, to resist the surrounding culture's pressure and help the members endure popular persecution. Paul begins 1 Timothy with fatherly counsel confirming Timothy in the faith while warning him about the peril of false teachers, a warning that Paul amplifies later in the letter. Paul next gives instructions for public worship in order and unity, followed by counsel on the qualifications of church elders or overseers, and deacons, thus coaching Timothy in how to build and maintain character and order in the church body. The letter includes substantial advice on pastoral care before concluding with exhortations to encourage the young pastor in his own motives, character, ministry, and faith. The letter remains core counsel for church leaders, surely as important of a witness to the Holy Spirit today as it was for the young Timothy.

2 Timothy

Paul wrote 2 Timothy just a couple of years later, around A.D. 66 or 67, during his second, short Rome imprisonment before execution. The letter is Paul's last. It thus constitutes a figurative passing of the torch from the apostolic generation, who met and knew the Lord, to those who would carry the church forward based instead on witness and faith. In 2 Timothy, Paul expresses the deep love the apostles had for their faith children on whose commission the gospel message would now depend. Paul urges Timothy to remember his calling and hold fast to the truth as he exercises his gifts to prepare the next generation's leaders. The letter warns again of deceivers and the word's power to expose and stand against them. Paul concludes with a final commission for Timothy to preach to the end, closing with a poignant request for some personal items and information. The letter stands as timeless testament to the strength of character and depth of love with which the Holy Spirit blesses enduring faith leaders.

Titus

Paul wrote the letter Titus around A.D. 64, between his two Rome imprisonments and about the time of 1 Timothy, to his special representative Titus who oversaw the churches on the island of Crete. Titus was a Greek protege whose faith Paul had long nurtured. Galatians records Titus meeting with the leaders of the Jerusalem church as evidence of the Holy Spirit's work among Gentile believers. Indeed, Titus served as Paul's ambassador in other work. The letter Titus is another, and likely last, step in Paul's careful development of another outstanding servant of the faith. In the letter, Paul counsels Titus on church affairs, much like Paul had counseled Timothy in 1 Timothy. Paul's counsel on how to treat different age groups of believers is a touching example. While the letter Titus includes precious counsel, its greater witness may be to the care that established faith leaders should take in identifying and developing the next generation of leaders. It would then have taken not much more than just one missed generation for the church to have disappeared. The same remains true today, confirming the Holy Spirit's enduring power and purpose in the letter Titus.

Philemon

Paul wrote the letter Philemon in about A.D. 60 to a wealthy slaveowner of that name, who may have been a member of the church at Colosse. The letter would have been extraordinary for the time, in calling Philemon's slave Onesimus, then in Paul's service but a thief runaway from Philemon, Philemon's brother in Christ. In the letter, Paul makes a plea that the slaveowner take the runaway slave back free, as a brother, because as Paul so tactfully puts it in the letter, the slaveowner owes his own life to Paul. All are dead apart from Christ, while all are free together in Christ. The short and spare letter's profound implications for the equality of all in Christ thus go far beyond the letter's simple plea that Philemon take Onesimus back as a faith brother. The letter Philemon testifies that Christ removes all legal, economic, social, and other barriers among believers, uniting all in freedom as members of the one body of Christ.

Hebrews

The letter to the Hebrews addressed Jews who were examining Christianity or had converted to Christianity but questioned how the new faith related to the previously all-important Jewish law and traditions. This important but precarious Jewish-Christian audience faced double challenges, opposition and persecution from both Jews who rejected Christ while demanding adherence to the religious laws and from Romans who perceived threats to their rule from the new faith. Hebrews thus addresses at length the supreme authority and complete sufficiency of Christ, and freedom from religious laws and traditions that Christian faith brings, while respecting that the same God instituted both the old and new covenants, for related reasons. Hebrews resolves in Christianity's favor critical theological issues, while still respecting the essential role of the old-covenant laws in preparing the ground for Christian faith. The letter, possibly written around A.D. 70 just before the Temple's destruction or perhaps as late as A.D. 90, must have been enormously heartening to Jewish converts who wondered at the seeming delay in Christ's return and who endured terrible persecution.

Hebrews first affirms at great length Jesus's superiority to angels, leaders, and priests, his new covenant's superiority to the old covenant, his body's superiority to the old Temple, and his sacrifice a better sacrifice than that of the priests. The Son radiates God's glory, as God's exact representation, the Son's word sustaining all things. The letter then examines the faith's practical implications including to hold onto one's confession and encourage one another in faith, while waiting patiently for Christ's return. Hebrews confirms the contrasting consequences, whether punishment or reward, of rejecting or persevering in the faith. The letter includes a rousing review of faith heroes that, again, must have deeply encouraged the letter's Jewish-Christian readers and hearers. The letter's high tone and sermon-like construction make it a unique read among the letters, a priceless message guaranteed to confirm and inspire Christian believers in every age and everywhere.

James

James wrote his letter from Jerusalem around A.D. 49 just before the Jerusalem council the next year, to Jewish Christians who had migrated outward from the Jerusalem church into surrounding Gentile areas. His Christian audience faced persecution, although the letter's content suggests that their greater threat may have been from their own hypocritical tendencies and poor behavior. James thus writes as their stern and authoritative former senior pastor, free to give frank counsel because of their close relationship and strong bond. James begins by telling them how Christians should live and act among others, next suggesting how faith moves into action. Faith, to be worthwhile, must make a difference in a believer's life. Behavior matters. James next cautions about holding one's tongue and warns against false earthly wisdom. James wants his former church members to avoid temptation in favor of godly living. He concludes the letter with encouragement to respect, support, and pray for one another. The letter James remains today an extraordinarily practical and direct manual for sound Christian living, invaluable to anyone earnestly practicing the faith.

1 Peter

The disciple Peter wrote his first letter around A.D. 62 to A.D. 64, possibly from Rome, just before Nero's awful persecution of Christians that included Peter's execution. Like James, Peter was writing to Jewish Christians whom persecution had driven from Jerusalem. Roman torture and execution of Christians throughout the empire was driving the Christian faith outward rather than extinguishing it. Peter's Jewish-Christian audience for his first letter had dispersed north into Asia Minor. The letter's purpose, then, was to bolster the fleeing Christians' faith against horrible persecution. The widely read letter opens with the revelation that persecution simply proves faith genuine, bringing not shame but rather, on Christ's return, glory and honor. God's blessings are what Christians seek, not human praise and honor. Peter's letter instructed the suffering believers in how to conduct themselves under terrible trial and how to guide other suffering believers. The comforting themes of 1 Peter include salvation as precious gift, persecution proving victory, the family of believers, and God's ultimate judgment. The letter continues to reveal to believers today the great weight of their coming glory.

2 Peter

If Peter was the author of his purported second letter, dated to around A.D. 67, rather than another author attributing Peter, then he wrote it shortly after his first letter and at the very end of his life just before his execution. The second letter's audience was the larger church, believers everywhere, rather than those of a certain ancestry or region. The assurances of 1 Peter are largely absent, replaced in 2 Peter with warnings against false teachers, a call to diligent action, a challenge to grow in faith, and an assurance of Christ's return in judgment against non-believers. The challenges that 2 Peter addresses are not external, such as Roman persecution, but internal, against heresy and spiritual malaise. Believers need comfort from suffering, but they also need reminders that faith involves moving forward confidently and responsibly, as 2 Peter continues to admonish.

1 John

The disciple John wrote the letter 1 John from Ephesus on the western coast of Asia Minor, likely between A.D. 85 and A.D. 90. The late date of John's letters would mean that Rome had already destroyed Jerusalem's Temple, Nero had already sought to rid Rome of its Christians, the other disciples had probably already been executed leaving John as the sole survivor, and Christians had followed the Jewish diaspora out of Jerusalem in all directions. John was thus writing not to any specific church or region but to believers everywhere, carrying the faith into the future. The letter opens without addressing itself to any audience, beginning instead with John's claim to have seen the Lord's incarnation. John portrays God as light and urges believers to walk in that light, obeying Christ and embracing the faith family while resisting antichrists opposing the gospel's truth. The letter next portrays God as love, irresistible and familial, God making us his children, while we reveal our family relationship with God through good deeds. Again, we must reject deceivers. The letter concludes with John portraying God as life, that life found in our relationship with his Son. The letter's clarity and succinctness beautifully reflect John's gospel, making the letter a pearl of incalculable value.

2 John

John wrote his very short second letter near the date of his first letter, probably around A.D. 90, still while in Ephesus and before his exile on the island of Patmos. John's second letter differs from his first in that he directs it to a *chosen lady* and her children, which might mean a member of a local church but could just as well mean a certain church and its members, or the broader church and believers everywhere. The letter, also different from his first letter in its instructional more so than inspirational emphasis, confirms that faith means following Christ, obeying his words. The letter both challenges and lifts readers. We must walk in obedience to Christ's commands, the primary one of which is to love one another. Christ is truth carried out in sacrificial love, set against false teachers and opposing popular culture's self-centeredness. John's second letter, like the first, lifts the face and opens the heart toward the glory of Christ.

3 John

John addresses his very short third letter, written from Ephesus around the A.D. 90 date of his second letter, to a dear friend Gaius to thank him for his hospitality. John and other traveling church leaders depended on believers like Gaius for food and shelter as they visited to preach and instruct the local congregation. In his third letter, John praises Gaius and another hospitable believer for their service and support, while disparaging another believer who had refused any hospitality and instead tried to commandeer and control the local church for his own benefit. John's letter thus serves as a brief reminder to care for leaders who serve the church faithfully, while the letter warns against false leaders who would instead have the church serve them. True to John's teacher's heart, though, the brief letter slips in a few short instructions to avoid evil, do good, and thus see God. John lets God's light shine even in a brief thank-you letter and reminder to support church leaders.

Jude

The short letter Jude, written around A.D. 65, addresses itself simply to those whom God called and Jesus kept, thus to believers everywhere. The whole of the letter urges that believers contend for the faith. The letter's first section documents the mendacious methods and corrupt characteristics of false teachers whom believers must identify, oppose, and reject. The letter's second section urges believers to fight for truth, persevere through trials, and stand firm in the faith. The letter ends with a stirring doxology to the God and Savior who keeps us and purifies us to present us to himself as witness to his glory. Jude's brevity, simplicity, and urgency make it a more-than-fitting conclusion to the letters, in anticipation of the Bible's concluding masterpiece Revelation.

Revelation

John wrote the book of Revelation to encourage believers everywhere to resist the growing persecution of Christians, especially by Roman caesars demanding emperor worship. Tyrants need weak enemies to increase and retain their power, and the church's growth gave Roman caesars a convenient new enemy. The threat to which Revelation responded was not extinction, though, but compromise. The book anticipates that many believers will die, just as many did in fact do so then and many continue to do so today, but communicates that death bears no threat to believers, like the threat of compromise. Jesus, the rider on the great white horse, prevails, and with him all those who remain steadfast, whether martyred or not. Scholars and other readers read Revelation in several different ways, each of them valuable and for different times appropriate. Revelation represents the spiritual battle symbolically in a distinctly apocalyptic form, presenting both an extraordinarily fitting last book to the New Testament and Bible, and a wondrously inspiring divine mystery.

Other Faith Books by Nelson Miller

Biblespeak: The Epistles

Following Jesus

Looking to Jesus

Answered Prayers

Secret Devotion

The Faithful Lawyer

Facing Death

Gospelspeak

Gospelspeak

www.ingramcontent.com/pod-product-compliance
Lightning Source LLC
Chambersburg PA
CBHW052013070526
44584CB00016B/1732